The Teachings of
Emanuel Swedenborg Vol. II

The Teachings of
Emanuel Swedenborg Vol. II
by Emanuel Swedenborg
translated by John Whitehead

White Horse
Brief Exposition
De Verbo
God the Savior
Interaction of the Soul and Body
The New Jerusalem and its Heavenly Doctrine

White Horse

THE WHITE HORSE mentioned in THE APOCALYPSE CHAPTER 19 In the Apocalypse of John the Word is thus described as to its spiritual or internal sense: I saw heaven opened, and behold a white horse, and He that sat upon him was called faithful and true, and in justice He doth judge and make war. His eyes were as a flame of fire; and upon His head were many diadems; and He hath a name written that no one knew but He Himself. And He was clothed with a vesture dipped in blood; and His name is called the Word of God. And the armies which were in the heavens followed Him upon white horses, clothed in fine linen white and clean. And He hath upon His vesture and upon His thigh a name written, King of kings and Lord of lords (19:11-14, 16). No one can know what each of these expressions involves, except from the internal sense. It is manifest that every expression is in some respect representative and significative: as when it is said, that "heaven was opened;" that there was "a white horse;" that "there was One sitting upon him;" that "in justice He doth judge and make war;" that "His eyes were as a flame of fire;" that "on His head were many diadems;" that "He had a name that no man knew but He Himself;" that "He was clothed with a vesture dipped in blood;" that "the armies which were in heaven followed Him upon white horses;" that "they were clothed in fine linen white and clean;" and that "on vesture and on His thigh He had a name written." It is expressly said, that it is "the Word" which is here described, and the Lord who is the Word; for it is said, "His name is called the Word of God;" and afterwards, "He hath on His vesture and on His thigh a name written, King of kings and Lord of lords." From the interpretation of each, expression it evidently appears, that the Word is here described as to its spiritual or internal sense. By "heaven being opened" is represented and signified, that the internal sense of the Word is seen in heaven, and thence by those in the world to whom heaven is opened. "The horse," which was white, represents and signifies the understanding of the Word as to its interiors; that this is the signification of "a white horse," will be shown presently. That "He that sat upon him" is the Lord as to the Word, thus the Word, is manifest, for it is said, "His name is called the Word of God;" who, from good, is called "faithful and judging in justice;" and from truth, is called "true, and who maketh war in justice;" for the Lord Himself is justice. "His eyes, as a flame of fire," signify the Divine truth, from the Divine good of His Divine love. "The many diadems upon His head," signify all the goods and truths of faith. "Having a name written that no one knew but He Himself," signifies that the quality of the Word in the internal sense is seen by no one but Himself, and those to whom He reveals it. "Clothed in a vesture dipped in blood," signifies the Word in the letter, to which violence has been offered. "The armies in the heavens which followed Him upon white horses," signify those who are in the understanding of the Word as to its interiors. "Clothed in fine linen, white and clean," signify the same persons in truth from good. "Upon His vesture and upon his thigh a name written" signifies truth and good, and their quality. From these particulars, and from those which precede and follow in that chapter, it is evident, that therein is predicted, that about the last time of the church the spiritual or internal sense of the Word would be opened; but what would come to pass at that time, is also described there (verses 17-21). That this is the signification of the words mentioned, it is unnecessary to prove in this place, as they are particularly explained in The Arcana Coelestia; where it is shown, That the Lord is the Word, because He is the Divine truth (n. 2533, 2803, 2884, 5272, 7835). That the Word is the Divine truth (n. 4692, 5075, 9987). That because the Lord is justice, therefore it is said, that "He who sat upon the horse in justice doth judge and make war;" and that the Lord is called "justice" for this reason, because of His own power He has saved the human race (n. 1813, 2025-2027, 9715, 9809, 10019, 10152). And that "justice" is the merit which belongs to the Lord alone (n. 9715, 9979). That "His eyes, as a flame of fire," signify the Divine truth from the Divine good of the Divine love, is, because "the eyes" signify the understanding and the truth of faith (n. 2701, 4403-4421, 4523-4534, 6923, 9051, 10569); and "a flame of fire" signifies the good of love (n. 934, 4906, 5215, 6314, 6832). That "the diadems which were upon His head" signify all the goods and truths of faith (n. 114, 3858, 6335, 6640, 9863, 9865, 9868, 9873, 9905). That "He hath a name written which no one knew but He Himself," signifies that the quality of the Word in the internal sense is seen by no one but Himself, and those to whom He reveals it, is because "a name" signifies the quality of a thing (n. 144, 145, 1754, 1896, 2009, 2724, 3006, 3237, 3421, 6674, 9310). That "clothed in a vesture dipped in blood," signifies the Word in the letter, to which violence has been offered, is because "a vesture" signifies truth because it clothes good (n. 1073, 2576, 5248, 5319, 5954, 9212, 9216, 9952, 10536); especially truth in the ultimates, thus the Word in the letter (n. 5248, 6918, 9158, 9212); and because "blood" signifies violence offered to truth by falsity (n. 374, 1005, 4735, 5476, 9127). That "the armies in heaven followed Him upon white horses," signify those who are in the understanding of the Word as to its interiors, is because "armies" signify those who are in the truths and goods of heaven and the church (n. 3448, 7236, 7988, 8019). And "a horse" signifies the understanding (n. 3217, 5321, 6125, 6400, 6531, 6534, 7024, 8146, 8318). And "white" signifies truth which is in the light of heaven, consequently interior truth (n. 3301, 3993, 4007, 5319). That "clothed in fine linen white and clean," signifies the same persons in truth from good, is because "fine linen," or "linen," signifies truth from a celestial origin, which is truth from good (n. 5319, 9469). That "a name written upon the vesture and upon the thigh," signifies truth and good, and their quality, is because "a vesture" signifies truth, and "a name" quality, as observed above, and "the thigh" signifies the good of love (n. 3021, 4277, 4280, 9961, 10485). "King of kings, and Lord of lords," is the Lord as to the Divine truth and as to the Divine good; the Lord is called "King" from the Divine truth (n. 3009, 5068, 6148). And He is called "Lord" from the Divine good (n. 4973, 9167, 9194). Hence it appears what is the quality of the Word in its spiritual or internal sense, and that there is no expression therein which does not signify something spiritual, that is, something of heaven and the church.

In the prophetical parts of the Word mention is very often made of the horse, but heretofore no one has known that "a horse" signifies the understanding, and his "rider" one who is intelligent; and this possibly, because it seems strange and wonderful, that by "a horse" such a thing should be meant in the spiritual sense, and thence in the Word. But nevertheless that it is so, may evidently appear from many passages therein; some of which only I will here adduce. In the prophecy of Israel, it is said of Dan: Dan is a serpent upon the way, an arrow-snake upon the highway, that biteth the horse's heels, so that his rider shall fall backward (Gen. 49:17, 18). No one can understand what this prophecy concerning one of the tribes of Israel signifies unless he knows what is signified by "a serpent," and what by "a horse" and his "rider;" everyone, however, knows that there is something spiritual involved therein; what therefore each expression signifies, may be seen in The Arcana Coelestia (n. 6398-6401), where this prophecy is explained. In Habakkuk: O God, Thou didst ride upon Thy horses. Thy chariots are salvation. Thou didst tread in the sea with Thy horses (Hab. 3:8, 16). That "horses" here signify what is spiritual, is evident, for they are said concerning God; in any other sense, what could be meant by saying, that "God rides upon His horses, and that He treads upon the sea with horses?" In like manner in Zechariah: In that day, there shall be upon the bells of the horses, holiness unto Jehovah (Zech. 14:20). In the same: In that day, saith Jehovah, I will smite every horse with astonishment, and his rider with madness; and I will open Mine eyes upon the house of Judah, and will smite every horse of the people with blindness (Zech. 12:4). It treats there of the vastation of the church, which takes place when there no longer remains the understanding of any truth; and which is described thus by "the horse and his rider;" what else could be the meaning of "smiting every horse with astonishment," and of "smiting the horse of the people with blindness"? What has this to do with the church? In Job: God hath caused her to forget wisdom, neither hath He imparted to her intelligence: what time she lifteth up herself on high, she scorneth the horse and his rider (39:17-19 seq.). That "the horse" here signifies the understanding, is manifestly evident. In like manner in David, where it is said: He rideth upon the word of truth (Ps. 45:4). And in many other passages. Moreover, who can know the reason why Elijah and Elisha were called "the chariot of Israel and the horsemen thereof;" and why "the boy of Elisha saw the mountain full of horses and chariots of fire;" except it be known what is signified by "chariots," and what was represented by "Elijah and Elisha"? For Elisha said to Elijah: My father, my father, the chariot and horsemen 2-1 of Israel and the horsemen thereof (2 Kings 2:11, 12). And Joash the king said to Elisha: My father, my father, the chariot of Israel and the horsemen thereof (2 Kings 13:14). And, speaking of the boy of Elisha, it is said: Jehovah opened the eyes of the boy of Elisha, and he saw and behold the mountain was full of horses and chariots of fire round about Elisha (2 Kings 6:17). The reason why Elijah and Elisha were called "the chariot of Israel and the horsemen thereof," is because they both represented the Lord as to the Word, and "a chariot" signifies doctrine from the Word, and "horsemen" intelligence. That "Elijah" and "Elisha" represented the Lord as to the Word, may be seen in The Arcana Coelestia (n. 5247, 7643, 8029, 9327). And that "chariots" signify doctrine drawn from the Word (n. 5321, 8215).

That a horse signifies the understanding, is from no other source than from the representatives in the spiritual world. In that world horses are frequently seen, and persons sitting upon horses, and also chariots; and there everyone knows that they signify intellectual and doctrinal things. I have often observed, when any were thinking from their understanding, that at such times they appeared as if riding on horses; their meditation was thus represented before

others, they themselves not knowing it. There is also a place there, where many
assemble who think and speak from the understanding concerning the truths
of doctrine; and when others approach, they see, the whole plain full of chariots
and horses; and novitiate spirits, who wonder whence this is, are instructed that
it is an appearance resulting from their intellectual thought. That place is called
the assembly of the intelligent and the wise. I have likewise seen bright horses
and chariots of fire, when some were taken up into heaven, which was a sign
that they were then instructed in the truths of heavenly doctrine, and became
intelligent, and thus were taken up; on seeing which, it occurred to my mind,
what is signified by "the chariot of fire and the horses of fire by which Elijah
was taken up into heaven;" and what is signified by "the horses and chariots of
fire" that were seen by the young man of Elisha, when his eyes were opened.

   That such is the signification of "chariots" and "horses" was well known in
the ancient churches; for those churches were representative churches, and
with those who were in them, the science of correspondences and
representations was the chief of all sciences. The signification of the horse, as
being understanding, was derived by the wise round about, even to Greece,
from those churches. Hence it was, when they would describe the sun, in which
they placed their God of wisdom and intelligence, that they attributed to it a
chariot and four horses of fire. And when they would describe the God of the
sea, since by the sea were signified sciences derived from the understanding,
that they also attributed horses to him. And when they would describe the
origin of the sciences from the understanding, they represented it by a winged
horse, which with its hoof broke open a fountain, at which sat nine virgins
called the sciences. For from the ancient churches they received the knowledge
that "the horse" signifies the understanding; "wings," spiritual truth; "the hoof,"
what is scientific from the understanding; and "a fountain," doctrine from which
sciences are derived. Nor is anything else signified by "the Trojan horse," than
an artificial contrivance devised by their understanding for the purpose of
destroying the walls. Even at this day, when the understanding is described
after the manner received from those ancients, it is usual to figure it by a flying
horse or Pegasus; so, likewise, doctrine is described by a fountain, and the
sciences by virgins; but scarcely anyone knows that "the horse," in the mystic
sense, signifies the understanding; still less that those significatives were
derived by the Gentiles from the ancient representative churches.

   Since "the White Horse" signifies the understanding of the Word as to its
spiritual or internal sense, those particulars concerning the Word and that
sense, which are shown in The Arcana Coelestia, are here subjoined: for in that
work the whole contents of Genesis and Exodus are explained according to the
spiritual or internal sense of the Word.

   THE WORD, AND ITS SPIRITUAL OR INTERNAL SENSE, FROM THE
ARCANA COELESTIA. The necessity and excellence of the Word. From the
light of nature nothing is known concerning the Lord, concerning heaven and
hell, concerning the life of man after death, nor concerning the Divine truths by
which man acquires spiritual and eternal life (n. 8944, 10318, 10319, 10320).
This may appear manifest from the consideration, that many, and among them
men of learning, do not believe those things, although they are born where the
Word is, and are thereby instructed concerning them (n. 10319). Therefore it

was necessary that there should be some revelation from heaven because man was born for heaven (n. 1775). Therefore in every age of the world there has been a revelation (n. 2895). Of the various kinds of revelation which have successively been made on this earth (n. 10355, 10632). To the most ancient men, who lived before the flood, whose time was called the golden age, there was an immediate revelation, and thence Divine truth was inscribed on their hearts (n. 2896). The ancient churches, which existed after the flood, had a historical and prophetical Word (n. 2686, 2897): concerning which churches see The New Jerusalem and its Heavenly Doctrine (n. 247). Its historical parts were called The Wars of Jehovah, and its prophetical parts, Enunciations (n. 2897). That Word, as to inspiration was like our Word, but accommodated to those churches (n. 2897). It is mentioned by Moses (n. 2686, 2897). But that Word is lost (n. 2897). Prophetical revelations were also made to others, as appears from the prophecies of Balaam (n. 2898). The Word is Divine in all and every particular part (n. 639, 680, 10321, 10637). The Word is Divine and holy as to every point and iota, from experience (n. 1349). How it is explained at this day, that the Word is inspired as to every iota (n. 1886). The church is especially where the Word is, and where the Lord is thereby known, and Divine truths are revealed (n. 3857, 10761). But it does not follow from thence, that they are of the church, who are born where the Word is, and where the Lord is thereby known; but they who, by means of truths from the Word, are regenerated by the Lord, who are they who live according to the truths therein, consequently, who lead a life of love and faith (n. 6637, 10143, 10153, 10578, 10645, 10829).

The Word is not understood, except by those who are enlightened. The human rational faculty cannot comprehend Divine, nor even spiritual things, unless it be enlightened by the Lord (n. 2196, 2203, 2209, 2654). Thus they only who are enlightened comprehend the Word (n. 10323). The Lord enables those who are enlightened to understand truths, and to discern those things which appear to contradict each other (n. 9382, 10659). The Word in its literal sense appears inconsistent, and in some places seems to contradict itself (n. 9025). And therefore by those who are not enlightened, it may be so explained and applied, as to confirm any opinion or heresy, and to defend any worldly and corporeal love (n. 4738, 10339, 10401). They are enlightened from the Word, who read it from the love of truth and good, but not they who read it from the love of fame, of gain, or of honor, thus from the love of self (n. 9382, 10548, 10549, 10550) They are enlightened who are in the good of life, and thereby in the affection of truth (n. 8694). They are enlightened whose internal is open, thus who as to their internal man are capable of elevation into the light of heaven (n. 10401, 10402, 10691, 10694). Enlightenment is an actual opening of the interiors of the mind, and also an elevation into the light of heaven (n. 10330). There is an influx of holiness from the internal, that is, from the Lord through the internal, with those who regard the Word as holy, though they themselves are ignorant of it (n. 6789). They are enlightened, and see truths in the Word, who are led by the Lord, but not they who are led by themselves (n. 10638). They are led by the Lord, who love truth because it is truth, who also are they that love to live according to Divine truths (n. 10578, 10645, 10829). The Word is vivified with man according to the life of his love and faith (n. 1776). The things derived from one's own intelligence have no life in themselves, because from man's proprium there is nothing good (n. 8941, 8944). They cannot be enlightened who have much confirmed themselves in false doctrine (n. 10640). It is the understanding which is enlightened (n. 6608, 9300). The understanding is the recipient of truth (n. 6242, 6608, 10659). In regard to every doctrine of the church, there are ideas of the understanding and of the thought thence, according to which the doctrine is perceived (n. 3310, 3825). The ideas of man during his life in the world are natural, because man then thinks in the natural; but still spiritual ideas are concealed therein, with those who are in the affection of truth for the sake of truth, and man comes into these ideas after death (n. 3310, 5510, 6201, 10236, 10240, 10550). Without ideas of the understanding, and of the thought thence, on any subject, there can be no perception (n. 3825). Ideas concerning the things of faith are laid open in the other life, and their quality is seen by the angels, and man is then conjoined with others according to those ideas, so far as they proceed from the affection which is of love (n. 1869, 3320, 5510, 6201, 8885). Therefore the Word is not understood except by a rational man; for to believe anything without an idea thereof, and without a rational view of the subject, is only to retain in the memory words destitute of all the life of perception and affection, which is not believing (n. 2533). It is the literal sense of the Word which admits of enlightenment (n. 3619, 9824, 9905, 10548).

The Word cannot be understood except by means of doctrine from the Word. The doctrine of the church must be from the Word (n. 3464, 5402, 6832, 10763, 10765). The Word without doctrine is not understood (n. 9025, 9409, 9424, 9430, 10324, 10431, 10582). True doctrine is a lamp to those who read the Word (n. 10401). Genuine doctrine must be from those who are in enlightenment from the Lord (n. 2510, 2516, 2519, 2524, 10105). The Word is understood by means of doctrine formed by one enlightened (n. 10324). They who are in enlightenment form for themselves doctrine from the Word (n. 9382, 10659). What is the difference between those who teach and learn from the doctrine of the church, and those who teach and learn from the sense of the letter of the Word alone (n. 9025). They who are in the sense of the letter of the Word without doctrine, do not come into any understanding concerning Divine truths (n. 9409, 9410, 10582). They may fall into many errors (n. 10431). They who are in the affection of truth for the sake of truth, when they become adults, and can see from their own understanding, do not simply abide in the doctrinals of their churches, but examine from the Word whether they be true or not (n. 5402, 5432, 6047). Otherwise everyone would have truth from another, and from his native soil, whether he were born a Jew or a Greek (n. 6047). Nevertheless such things as are become matters of faith from the literal sense of the Word, are not to be extinguished till after a full view (n. 9039). The true doctrine of the church is the doctrine of charity and faith (n. 2417, 4766, 10763, 10765). The doctrine of faith does not constitute the church, but the life of faith, which is charity (n. 809, 1798, 1799, 1834, 4468, 4677, 4766, 5826, 6637). Doctrinals are of no account, unless one lives according to them; and everyone may see they are for the sake of life, and not merely for the memory and thought thence derived (n. 1515, 2049, 2116). In the churches at this day the doctrine of faith is taught, and not the doctrine of charity, the latter being rejected to a science, which is called moral Theology 8-1 (n. 2417). The church would be one, if they should be acknowledged as men of the church from the life, thus from charity (n. 1285, 1316, 2982, 3267, 3445, 3451, 3452). How much superior the doctrine of charity is to that of faith separate from charity (n. 4844). They who know nothing concerning charity, are in ignorance with respect to heavenly things (n. 2435). They who only hold the doctrine of faith, and not that of charity, fall into errors; which errors are also described (n. 2383, 2417, 3146, 3325, 3412, 3413, 3416, 3773, 4672, 4730, 4783, 4925, 5351, 7623-7677, 7752-7762, 7790, 8094, 8313, 8530, 8765, 9186, 9224, 10555). They who are only in the doctrine of faith, and not in the life of faith, which is charity, were formerly called the uncircumcised, or Philistines (n. 3412, 3413, 3463, 8093, 8313, 9340). The ancients held the doctrine of love to the Lord and of charity towards the neighbor, and made the doctrine of faith subservient thereto (n. 2417, 3419, 4844, 4955). Doctrine formed by one enlightened may afterwards be confirmed by things rational and scientific; and that thus it is more fully understood, and is corroborated (n. 2553, 2719, 2720, 3052, 3310, 6047). See more on this subject in The New Jerusalem and its Heavenly Doctrine (n. 51). They who are in faith separate from charity, would have the doctrinal of the church simply believed, without any rational intuition (n. 3394). It is not the mark of a wise man to confirm a dogma, but to see whether it be true before it is confirmed; and that this is the case with those who are in enlightenment (n. 1017, 4741, 7012, 7680, 7950). The light of confirmation is a natural light, and not spiritual, and may exist even with the evil (n. 8780). All things, even falsities, may be so far confirmed, as to appear like truths (n. 2482, 2490, 5033, 6865, 8521).

In the Word there is a spiritual sense, which is called the internal sense. No one can know what the spiritual or internal sense of the Word is, unless he knows what correspondence is (n. 2895, 4322). Each and all things, even the most minute, which are in the natural world, correspond to spiritual things, and thence signify them (n. 2890-2893, 2897-3003, 3213-3227). The spiritual things to which natural things correspond, as assume another appearance in the natural, so that they are not recognized (n. 1887, 2396, 8920). Scarcely anyone knows wherein resides the Divine of the Word, when nevertheless it is in its internal and spiritual sense, which at this day is not known even to exist (n. 2980, 4989). The mystical contents of the Word are no other than those of its internal or spiritual sense, which treats of the Lord, of the glorification of His Human, of His kingdom, and of the church, and not of the natural things which are in the world (n. 4923). The prophetic writings are in many places unintelligible, and therefore of no use, without the internal sense, illustrated by examples (n. 2608, 8020, 8398). As for instance, with respect to what is signified by "the white horse" in Revelation (n. 2760 seq.). What by "the keys of the kingdom of the heavens," that were given to Peter, see the preface to Genesis 22, and n. 9410. What by "flesh," "blood," "bread," and "wine," in the Holy Supper (n. 8682). What by the prophecies of Jacob concerning his sons (Gen. 49; n. 6306, 6333-6465). What by many prophecies concerning Judah and Israel, which by no means tally with that nation, nor in the sense of the letter have any coincidence with their history (n. 6331, 6361, 6415, 6438, 6444). Besides many other instances (n. 2608). More may be seen of the nature of correspondence in the work on Heaven and Hell (n. 87-115 and 303-310). Of the internal or spiritual sense of the Word in a summary (n. 1767-1777, 1869-1879). In each and all things of the Word there is an internal sense (n. 1143, 1984, 2135, 2333, 2395, 2495, 2619). Such things do not appear in the sense of the letter, but nevertheless they are within it (n. 4442).

The internal sense of the Word is especially for the angels, and it is also for men. In order that it may be known what the internal sense is, the quality thereof, and whence it is, it may here be observed in general, that thought and speech in heaven are different from thought and speech in the world; for in heaven they are spiritual, but in the world natural; when, therefore, man reads the Word, the angels who are with him perceive it spiritually, whilst men perceive it naturally; hence it follows, that angels are in the internal sense, whilst men are in the external sense; but that nevertheless these two senses make a one by correspondence. That angels not only think spiritually, but also speak spiritually; that they are likewise present with man; and that they have conjunction with man by means of the Word, may be seen in the work on Heaven and Hell, where it treats of The Wisdom of the Angels of Heaven (n. 265-275). Of their Speech (n. 234-245). Of their Conjunction with Man (n. 291-302). And of their Conjunction by the Word (n. 303-310). The Word is understood differently by angels in the heavens, and by men on earth; the former perceiving the internal or spiritual sense, whilst the latter see only the external or natural sense (n. 1887, 2396). The angels perceive the Word in its internal sense, and not in its external sense, proved from the experience of those who have conversed with me from heaven, when I was reading the Word (n. 1769-1772). The ideas of the thought and also the speech of angels are spiritual, but the ideas and speech of men natural; that therefore there is an internal sense, which is spiritual, for the use of angels, illustrated from experience (n. 2333). Nevertheless the sense of the letter of the Word serves the spiritual ideas of angels as a means of conveyance, comparatively as the words of speech do with men to convey the sense of a subject (n. 2143). The things relating to the internal sense of the Word fall into such things as are of the light of heaven, thus into angelic perception (n. 2618, 2619, 2629, 3086). Therefore those things which the angels perceive from the Word, are precious to them (n. 2540, 2541, 2545, 2551). Angels do not understand a single expression of the Word in its literal sense (n. 64, 65, 1434, 1929). They do not know the names of persons and places recorded in the Word (n. 1434, 1888, 4442, 4480). Names cannot enter into heaven, nor be pronounced there (n. 1876, 1888). All the names in the Word signify things, and in heaven they are changed into ideas of the things (n. 768, 1888, 4310, 4442, 5225, 5287, 10329). Angels also think abstractly from persons (n. 6613, 8343, 8985, 9007). How elegant the internal sense of the Word is, even where nothing but mere names occur, shown by examples from the Word (n. 1224, 1888, 2395). Many names also in series express one thing in the internal sense (n. 5905). Likewise all numbers in the Word signify things (n. 482, 487, 647, 648, 755, 813, 1963, 1988, 2075, 2252, 3152, 4264, 6175, 9488, 9659, 10217, 10253). Spirits also perceive the Word in its internal sense in proportion as their interiors are open into heaven (n. 1771). The sense of the letter of the Word, which is the natural sense, is instantly changed into the spiritual sense with the angels, because there is a correspondence (n. 5648). And this without their hearing or knowing what is in the literal or external sense (n. 10215). Thus the sense of the letter or the external sense is only with man, and proceeds no further (n. 2015). There is an internal sense in the Word, and likewise an inmost or supreme sense, concerning which (n. 9407, 10604, 10614, 10627). The spiritual angels, or those who are in the spiritual kingdom of the Lord, perceive the Word in its internal sense; and the celestial angels, or those who are in the celestial kingdom of the Lord, perceive the Word in its inmost sense (n. 2157, 2275). The Word is for men, and also for angels, being accommodated to each (n. 7381, 8862, 10322). The Word is the means of uniting heaven and earth (n. 2310, 2493, 9212, 9216, 9357). The conjunction of heaven with man is through the Word (n. 9396, 9400, 9401, 10452). Therefore the Word is called a covenant (n. 9396). Because a covenant signifies conjunction (n. 665, 666, 1023, 1038, 1864, 1996, 2003, 2021, 6804, 8767, 8778, 9396, 10632). There is an internal sense in the Word, because the Word is from the Lord, it descended through the three heavens even to man 10-1 (n. 2310, 6397). And thereby it is accommodated to the angels of the three heavens and also to men (n. 7381, 8862). Hence it is that the Word is Divine (n. 2980, 4989). And it is holy (n. 10276). And it is spiritual (n. 4480). And it is Divinely inspired (n. 9094). This is inspiration (n. 9094). The regenerate man is actually in the internal sense of the Word, although he does not know it, since his internal man, which has spiritual perception, is open (n. 10401). But with him the spiritual of the Word flows into natural ideas, and thus is represented naturally, because while he lives in the world this spiritual thinks in the natural man, so far as it comes to the perception (n. 5614). Hence the light of truth, with those who are enlightened, is from their internal, thus through the internal, from the Lord (n. 10691, 10694). Also by the same way there is an influx of holiness with those who esteem the Word holy (n. 6789). Since the regenerate man is actually in the internal sense of the Word, and in the sanctity thereof, although he does not know it, therefore after death he comes into it of himself, and is no longer in the sense of the letter (n. 3226, 3342, 3343). The ideas of the internal man are spiritual; but man during his life in the world does not attend thereto, inasmuch as they are within his natural thought, and give it its rational faculty (n. 10236, 10240, 10500). But man after death comes into those his spiritual ideas, because they are proper to his spirit, and then he not only thinks, but also speaks therefrom (n. 2470, 2478, 2479, 10568, 10604). Hence, as was said, the regenerate man knows not that he is in the spiritual sense of the Word, and that he receives enlightenment thence.

In the internal or spiritual sense of the Word there are innumerable arcana. The Word in the internal sense contains innumerable things which exceed human comprehension (n. 3085, 3086). It also contains things ineffable and inexplicable (n. 1965). Which are manifest only to angels, and are understood by them (n. 167). The internal sense of the Word contains arcana of heaven, which relate to the Lord and His kingdom in the heavens and on earth (n. 1-4, 937). Those arcana do not appear in the sense of the letter (n. 937, 1502, 2161). Many things in the writings of the prophets appear to be unconnected, which yet in the internal sense cohere without a break 11-1 in a beautiful series (n. 7153, 9022). Not a single word 11-2, nor even a single iota, in its original language, can be taken from the sense of the letter of the Word, without an interruption in the internal sense; and therefore, by the Divine Providence of the Lord, the Word is preserved so entire as to every point (n. 7933). There are

14   Emanuel Swedenborg

innumerable things in the particulars of the Word (n. 6637, 8920). And in every
word (n. 1689). There are innumerable things contained in the Lord's prayer
and in every particular part thereof (n. 6619). And in the precepts of the
Decalogue; in the external sense whereof, notwithstanding some things are
such as are known to every nation without revelation (n. 8867, 8900). In every
tittle of the letter of the Word, in the original language, there is holiness, shown
from heaven; see the work on Heaven and Hell (n. 260), where these words of
the Lord are explained: Not one jot or one tittle shall pass from the law (Matt.
5:18). In the Word, particularly in the prophetical parts, there are two
expressions which seem to signify the same thing: but one has relation to good,
and the other to truth (n. 683, 707, 2516, 8339). In the Word goods and truths
are conjoined in a wonderful manner, and such conjunction appears to him only
who knows the internal sense (n. 10554). And thus in the Word, and in every
part thereof, there is a Divine marriage and a heavenly marriage (n. 683, 793,
801, 2173, 2516, 2712, 5138, 7022). The Divine marriage is the marriage of
Divine good and Divine truth, thus it is the Lord in heaven, in whom alone
there is that marriage (n. 3004, 3005, 3009, 4158, 5194, 5502, 6343, 7945, 8339,
9263, 9314). Jesus also signifies the Divine good, and Christ the Divine truth,
and thus both signify the Divine marriage in heaven (n. 3004, 3005, 3009). This
marriage is in every particular part of the Word in its internal sense, and thus
the Lord is therein as to the Divine good and the Divine truth (n. 5502). The
marriage of good and truth from the Lord in heaven and in the church is called
the heavenly marriage (n. 2508, 2618, 2803, 3004, 3211, 3952, 6179). Therefore
in this respect the Word is as it were heaven (n. 2173, 10126). Heaven is
compared in the Word to a marriage, on account of the marriage of good and
truth therein (n. 2758, 3132, 4434, 4834). The internal sense is itself the
genuine doctrine of the church (n. 9025, 9430, 10401.) They who understand the
Word according to the internal sense, know the true doctrine itself of the
church, because the internal sense contains it (n. 9025, 9430, 10401). The
internal of the Word is also the internal of the church, as it is likewise the
internal of worship (n. 10460). The Word is the doctrine of love to the Lord, and
of charity towards the neighbor (n. 3419, 3420). The Word in the literal sense
is as a cloud, and in the internal sense it is glory (see the preface to Gen. 18 and
n. 5922, 6343), where these words are explained: "The Lord shall come in the
clouds of heaven with glory." "Clouds" also in the Word signify the Word in the
sense of the letter, and glory the Word in its internal sense (see the preface of
Gen. 18 and n. 4060, 4391, 5922, 6343, 6752, 8106, 8781, 9430, 10551, 10574).
Things contained in the literal sense, respectively to those which are in the
internal sense, are like rude projections round a polished optical cylinder, from
which nevertheless is exhibited in the cylinder a beautiful image of a man (n.
1871). In the spiritual world they who desire and acknowledge only the sense
of the letter of the Word, are represented by a deformed old woman; but they
who desire and acknowledge the internal sense at the same time, are
represented by a virgin beautifully clothed (n. 1774). The Word in its whole
complex is an image of heaven; for the Word is the Divine truth, and the Divine
truth makes heaven, and heaven relates to one man, and therefore in this
respect the Word is as it were an image of man (n. 187). Heaven in one complex
resembles one man, may be seen in the work on Heaven and Hell (n. 59-67).

And the Divine truth proceeding 11-3 from the Lord makes heaven (n. 126-140, 200-212). The Word is represented before the angels under the most beautiful and agreeable forms (n. 1767, 1768). The sense of the letter is as the body, and the internal sense as the soul of that body (n. 8943). Hence the life of the Word is from the internal sense (n. 1405, 4857). The Word is pure in the internal sense, but it does not appear so in the sense of the letter (n. 2362, 2396). The things which are in the sense of the letter are holy from the internal contents (n. 10126, 10728). The historical parts of the Word also have an internal sense, but within them (n. 4989). Thus the historical as well as the prophetical parts of the Word contain arcana of heaven (n. 755, 1659, 1709, 2310, 2333). The angels do not perceive those parts historically, but dogmatically because spiritually (n. 6884). The interior arcana contained in the historical parts are less evident to man than those contained in the prophetical parts, by reason that the mind is engaged in viewing and considering the historical transactions (n. 2176, 6597). The nature of the internal sense of the Word is further shown (n. 1756, 1984, 2004, 2663, 3033, 7089, 10604, 10614). And illustrated by comparisons (n. 1873).

The Word is written by correspondences, and thus by representatives. The Word as to the sense of the letter is written by mere correspondences, that is, by such things as represent and signify the spiritual things of heaven and the church (n. 1404, 1408, 1409, 1540, 1619, 1659, 1709, 1783, 2179, 2763, 2899). This was done for the sake of the internal sense, which is there in every part (n. 2899). Consequently for the sake of heaven, since those who are in heaven do not understand the Word according to the sense of its letter, which is natural, but according to the internal sense, which is spiritual (n. 2899). The Lord spoke by correspondences, representatives, and significatives, because He spoke from the Divine (n. 9049, 9063, 9086, 10126, 10728). The Lord thus spoke before the world, and at the same time before heaven (n. 2533, 4807, 9049, 9063, 9086). The things spoken by the Lord went through the whole heaven (n. 4637). The historicals of the Word are representatives, and the words significative (n. 1540, 1659, 1709, 1783, 2687). The Word could not be written in any other style, so that through it there might be communication and conjunction with the heavens (n. 2899, 6943, 9481). They greatly err, who despise the Word on account of the apparent simplicity and rudeness of its style, and who think that they would receive the Word if it had been written in a different style (n. 8783). The method and style of writing which prevailed amongst the most ancient people, was by correspondences and representatives (n. 605, 1756, 9942). The ancient wise men were delighted with the Word, because of the representatives and significatives therein, from experience (n. 2592, 2593). If a man of the Most Ancient Church had read the Word, he would have seen clearly the things contained in the internal sense, and obscurely the things contained in the external sense (n. 449). The sons of Jacob were brought into the land of Canaan, because all the places in that land, from the most ancient times, were made representative (n. 1585, 3686, 4441, 5136, 6516). And thus the Word might be there written, wherein those places should be mentioned for the sake of the internal sense (n. 3686, 4447, 5136, 6416). But nevertheless the Word, as to the external sense was changed for the sake of that nation, but not as to the internal sense (n. 10453, 10461, 10603, 10604) Many passages adduced from the

Word concerning that nation, which must be understood according to the internal sense, and not according to the letter (n. 7051). Inasmuch as that nation represented the church, and the Word was written with them and concerning them, therefore Divine celestial things were signified by their names, as by Reuben, Simeon, Levi, Judah, Ephraim, Joseph, and the rest: and by "Judah" in the internal sense is signified the Lord as to celestial love, and His celestial kingdom (n. 3654, 3881, 3882, 5583, 5782, 6362-6381). That it may be known what correspondences are and their nature, and what is the nature of representatives in the Word, something shall be here said concerning them. All things which correspond likewise represent, and thereby signify, so that correspondences and representations are one (n. 2890, 2897, 2971, 2987, 2989, 2990, 3002, 3225). The nature of correspondences and representations shown from experience and examples (n. 2703, 2987, 3002, 3213-3226, 3337-3352, 3472-3485, 4218-4228, 9280). The science of correspondences and representations was the chief science with the ancients (n. 3021, 3419, 4280, 4749, 4844, 4964, 4965, 6004, 7729, 10252). Especially with the Orientals (n. 5702, 6692, 7097, 7779, 9391, 10252, 10407). And in Egypt more than in other countries (n. 5702, 6692, 7097, 7779, 9391, 10407). Also with the Gentiles, as in Greece, and in other places (n. 2762, 7729). But that at this day the science of correspondences and representations is lost, particularly in Europe (n. 2894, 2895, 2994, 3630, 3632, 3747-3749, 4581, 4966, 10252). Nevertheless this science is more excellent than all other sciences, inasmuch as without it the Word cannot be understood, nor the signification of the rites of the Jewish Church which are recorded in the Word, nor can it be known what the nature of heaven is, nor what the spiritual is, nor in what manner a spiritual influx takes place into what is natural, nor how the case is with respect to the influx of the soul into the body, with many other matters (n. 4180), and in the places above cited. All things which appear before spirits and angels, are representative according to correspondences (n. 1971, 3213-3226, 3457, 3475, 3485, 9481, 9574, 9576, 9577). The heavens are full of representatives (n. 1521, 1532, 1619). Representatives are more beautiful, and more perfect, in proportion as they are more interior in the heavens (n. 3475). Representatives there are real appearances, because they are from the light of heaven which is Divine truth, and which is the very essential of the existence of all things (n. 3485). The reason why each and all things in the spiritual world are represented in the natural world, is, because what is internal assumes to itself a suitable clothing in what is external, whereby it makes itself visible and apparent (n. 6275, 6284, 6299). Thus the end assumes a suitable clothing that it may exist as the cause in a lower sphere, and afterwards that it may exist as the effect in a sphere still lower; and when the end, by means of the cause, becomes the effect, it then becomes visible, or appears before the eyes (n. 5711). This may be illustrated by the influx of the soul into the body, whereby the soul assumes a clothing of such things in the body as enable it to express all its thoughts and affections in a visible form; wherefore thought, when it flows down into the body, is there represented by such gestures and actions as correspond to it (n. 2988). The affections of the mind are manifestly represented in the face, by the variations of the countenance, so as to be there seen (n. 4791-4805, 5695). Hence it is evident, that in each and all things in nature there lies hidden a cause and an end from the spiritual world (n. 3562, 5711). Since those things which are in nature are the ultimate effects, within which are the prior things (n. 4240, 4939, 5051, 6275, 6284, 6299, 9216). That internal things are the objects represented, and external things the objects representing (n. 4292). What is further meant by correspondences and representations may be seen in the work on Heaven and Hell, where it treats of the correspondence between all things of Heaven, and all things of Man (n. 87-102). Of the Correspondence of Heaven with all things on Earth (n. 103-115). And of Representatives and Appearances in Heaven (n. 170-176). Since all things in nature are representative of spiritual and celestial things, therefore in the churches which existed in ancient times, all the externals, which were rituals, were representative, and therefore those churches were called representative churches (n. 519, 521, 2896). The church instituted with the sons of Israel was a representative church (n. 1003, 2179, 10149). All the rituals therein were externals, which represented internals, which are of heaven and the church (n. 4288, 4874). The representatives of the church and of worship ceased when the Lord came into the world and manifested Himself, because the Lord opened the internals of the church, and because all things of that church in the highest sense regarded Him (n. 4832).

Of the sense of the letter, or the eternal sense of the Word. The sense of the letter of the Word is according to appearances in the world (n. 584, 926, 1719, 1720, 1832, 1874, 2242, 2520, 2533). And adapted to the conceptions of the simple (n. 2533, 9049, 9063, 9086). The Word, in the sense of the letter, is natural (n. 8783). Because what is natural is the ultimate, wherein spiritual and celestial things find their limits, and upon which they rest like a house upon its foundation; and that otherwise the internal sense of the Word, without the external, would be like a house without a foundation (n. 9360, 9430, 9433, 9824, 10044, 10436). The Word because it is such contains both a spiritual and celestial sense (n. 9407). And of consequence, that it is holy and Divine in the sense of the letter as to all and every part thereof, even to every iota (n. 639, 680, 1319, 1870, 9198, 10321, 10637). The laws enacted for the sons of Israel, although abrogated, are yet the holy Word, on account of the internal sense in them (n. 9210, 9259, 9349). Among the laws, judgments, and statutes, ordained in the Israelitish or Jewish Church, which was a representative church, there are some which are still in force both in their external and internal sense; which ought strictly to be observed in their external sense; some which may be of use, if one is so disposed; and some which are altogether abrogated (n. 9349). The Word is Divine even in those statutes which are abrogated, on account of the heavenly things which lie concealed in their internal sense (n. 10637). What the quality of the Word is in the sense of the letter, if not understood at the same time as to the internal sense, or, what is the same thing, according to true doctrine from the Word (n. 10402). An immense number of heresies spring up from the sense of the letter of the Word without the internal sense, or without genuine doctrine drawn from the Word (n. 10401). They who are in externals without internals, cannot bear the interior things of the Word (n. 10694). The Jews were of this description and they are such also at the present day (n. 301-303, 3479, 4429, 4433, 4680, 4844, 4847, 10396, 10401, 10407, 10695, 10701, 10707).

The Lord is the Word. The Word in its inmost sense treats solely of the Lord, describing all the states of the glorification of His Human, that is, of its union with the Divine itself, and likewise all the states of the subjugation of the hells, and the reducing to order of all things therein, and in the heavens (n. 2249, 7014). Thus the inmost sense describes the Lord's whole life in the world, and thereby the Lord is continually present with the angels (n. 2523). Therefore the Lord alone is in the inmost part of the Word, and the Divinity and the holiness of the Word is from thence (n. 1873, 9357). The Lord's saying, that the Scripture was fulfilled concerning Him, signifies, that all things were fulfilled which are contained in the inmost sense (n. 7933). The Word signifies the Divine truth (n. 4692, 5075, 9987). The Lord is the Word because He is the Divine truth (n. 2533). The Lord is the Word also because the Word is from Him, and treats of Him (n. 2859). And because it treats of the Lord alone in its inmost sense; thus the Lord Himself is therein (n. 1873, 9357). And because in each and all things of the Word there is a marriage of the Divine good and the Divine truth, which marriage is in the Lord alone (n. 3004, 3005, 3009, 4158, 5194, 5502, 6343, 7945, 8339, 9263, 9314). Divine truth is the only reality; and that in which it is, and which is from the Divine, is the only thing substantial (n. 5272, 6880, 7004, 8200). And because the Divine truth proceeding from the Lord as the sun in heaven is light there, and the Divine good is heat there; and inasmuch as all things in heaven derive their existence therefrom, as all things in the world derive their existence from light and heat, which are also in their own substances, and act by means thereof; and inasmuch as the natural world exists by means of heaven or the spiritual world; it is plain that all things which were created 14-1 were created from the Divine truth, thus from the Word, according to these words in John: In the beginning was the Word, and the Word was with God, and God was the Word, and by it all things were made that were made; and the Word was made flesh (John 1:1-3, 14; n. 2803, 2884, 5272, 7830). Further particulars concerning the creation of all things from the Divine truth, consequently by the Lord, may be seen in the work on Heaven and Hell (n. 137); and more fully in the article concerning the Sun in Heaven, where it is shown that the Lord is that Sun, and that it is His Divine love (n. 116-125). And that the Divine truth is Light, and the Divine good is Heat, proceeding from that sun in heaven (n. 126-140). The conjunction of the Lord with man is effected by the Word, by means of the internal sense (n. 10375). This conjunction is effected by each and all things of the Word, and herein the Word is more wonderful than all other writings (n. 10632-10634). Since the time of writing the Word, the Lord thereby speaks with men (n. 10290). For further particulars respecting the Conjunction of Heaven with man by means of the Word, see the work on Heaven and Hell (n. 303-310).

Of those who are against the Word. Of those who despise, blaspheme, and profane the Word (n. 1878). Their quality in the other life (n. 1761, 9222). They relate to the viscous parts of the blood (n. 5719). How great the danger is from profaning the Word (n. 571-582). How hurtful it is, if principles of falsity, particularly those which favor self-love and the love of the world, are confirmed by the Word (n. 589). They who are in no affection of truth for its own sake, utterly reject the things appertaining to the internal sense of the Word, and nauseate them, from experience of such in the world of spirits (n. 5702). Of some in the other life, who endeavored altogether to reject the interior things of the Word; such are deprived of rationality (n. 1879).

Which are the books of the Word. The books of the Word are all those which have the internal sense; but those which have not the internal sense are not the Word. The books of the Word in the Old Testament are, THE FIVE BOOKS OF MOSES; THE BOOK OF JOSHUA; THE BOOK OF JUDGES; THE TWO BOOKS OF SAMUEL; THE TWO BOOKS OF KINGS; THE PSALMS OF DAVID; THE PROPHETS ISAIAH, JEREMIAH, LAMENTATIONS, EZEKIEL, DANIEL, HOSEA, JOEL, AMOS, OBADIAH, JONAH, MICAH, NAHUM, HABAKKUK, ZEPHANIAH, HAGGAI, ZECHARIAH, MALACHI. In the New Testament, the four Evangelists, MATTHEW, MARK, LUKE, JOHN; and the APOCALYPSE. The rest have not the internal sense (n. 10325). The book of Job is an ancient book, which indeed contains an internal sense, but not in series (n. 3570, 9942).

Further particulars Concerning the Word. The term "Word," in the Hebrew language, signifies various things; as speech, thought of the mind, everything that really exists, and also something (n. 9987). The Word signifies the Divine truth and the Lord (n. 2533, 4692, 5075, 9987). Words signify truths (n. 4692, 5075). They signify doctrinals (n. 1288). The ten words signify all Divine truths (n. 10688). In the Word, particularly in the prophetic parts, there are two expressions that signify one thing, and the one has relation to good and the other to truth, which are thus conjoined (n. 683, 707, 5516, 8339). It can be known only from the internal sense of the Word, what expression refers to good and what to truth; for there are proper words by which things appertaining to good are expressed, and proper words by which things appertaining to truth are expressed (n. 793, 801). And this so determinately, that it may be known merely from the words made use of, whether the subject treated of is good, or whether it is truth (n. 2722). Sometimes also one expression involves a general, and the other expression implies a certain specific particular from that general (n. 2212). There is a species of reciprocation in the Word, concerning which see n. 2240. Most expressions in the Word have also an opposite sense (n. 4816). That the internal sense proceeds regularly according to the subject predicated (n. 4502). They who have been delighted with the Word, in the other life receive the heat of heaven, wherein is celestial love, according to the quality and degree of their delight from love (n. 1773). END OF THE WHITE HORSE. 1.THE WHITE HORSE mentioned in THE APOCALYPSE CHAPTER 19 In the Apocalypse of John the Word is thus described as to its spiritual or internal sense: I saw heaven opened, and behold a white horse, and He that sat upon him was called faithful and true, and in justice He doth judge and make war. His eyes were as a flame of fire; and upon His head were many diadems; and He hath a name written that no one knew but He Himself. And He was clothed with a vesture dipped in blood; and His name is called the Word of God. And the armies which were in the heavens followed Him upon white horses, clothed in fine linen white and clean. And He hath upon His vesture and upon His thigh a name written, King of kings and Lord of lords (19:11-14, 16). No one can know what each of these expressions involves, except from the internal sense. It is manifest that every expression is in some respect representative and significative: as when it is said, that "heaven was opened;" that there was "a

white horse;" that "there was One sitting upon him;" that "in justice He doth
judge and make war;" that "His eyes were as a flame of fire;" that "on His head
were many diadems;" that "He had a name that no man knew but He Himself;"
that "He was clothed with a vesture dipped in blood;" that "the armies which
were in heaven followed Him upon white horses;" that "they were clothed in
fine linen white and clean;" and that "on vesture and on His thigh He had a
name written." It is expressly said, that it is "the Word" which is here described,
and the Lord who is the Word; for it is said, "His name is called the Word of
God;" and afterwards, "He hath on His vesture and on His thigh a name
written, King of kings and Lord of lords." From the interpretation of each,
expression it evidently appears, that the Word is here described as to its
spiritual or internal sense. By "heaven being opened" is represented and
signified, that the internal sense of the Word is seen in heaven, and thence by
those in the world to whom heaven is opened. "The horse," which was white,
represents and signifies the understanding of the Word as to its interiors; that
this is the signification of "a white horse," will be shown presently. That "He
that sat upon him" is the Lord as to the Word, thus the Word, is manifest, for
it is said, "His name is called the Word of God;" who, from good, is called
"faithful and judging in justice;" and from truth, is called "true, and who maketh
war in justice;" for the Lord Himself is justice. "His eyes, as a flame of fire,"
signify the Divine truth, from the Divine good of His Divine love. "The many
diadems upon His head," signify all the goods and truths of faith. "Having a
name written that no one knew but He Himself," signifies that the quality of the
Word in the internal sense is seen by no one but Himself, and those to whom He
reveals it. "Clothed in a vesture dipped in blood," signifies the Word in the
letter, to which violence has been offered. "The armies in the heavens which
followed Him upon white horses," signify those who are in the understanding
of the Word as to its interiors. "Clothed in fine linen, white and clean," signify
the same persons in truth from good. "Upon His vesture and upon his thigh a
name written" signifies truth and good, and their quality. From these
particulars, and from those which precede and follow in that chapter, it is
evident, that therein is predicted, that about the last time of the church the
spiritual or internal sense of the Word would be opened; but what would come
to pass at that time, is also described there (verses 17-21). That this is the
signification of the words mentioned, it is unnecessary to prove in this place, as
they are particularly explained in The Arcana Coelestia; where it is shown,
That the Lord is the Word, because He is the Divine truth (n. 2533, 2803, 2884,
5272, 7835). That the Word is the Divine truth (n. 4692, 5075, 9987). That
because the Lord is justice, therefore it is said, that "He who sat upon the horse
in justice doth judge and make war;" and that the Lord is called "justice" for this
reason, because of His own power He has saved the human race (n. 1813,
2025-2027, 9715, 9809, 10019, 10152). And that "justice" is the merit which
belongs to the Lord alone (n. 9715, 9979). That "His eyes, as a flame of fire,"
signify the Divine truth from the Divine good of the Divine love, is, because "the
eyes" signify the understanding and the truth of faith (n. 2701, 4403-4421,
4523-4534, 6923, 9051, 10569); and "a flame of fire" signifies the good of love (n.
934, 4906, 5215, 6314, 6832). That "the diadems which were upon His head"
signify all the goods and truths of faith (n. 114, 3858, 6335, 6640, 9863, 9865,

9868, 9873, 9905). That "He hath a name written which no one knew but He Himself," signifies that the quality of the Word in the internal sense is seen by no one but Himself, and those to whom He reveals it, is because "a name" signifies the quality of a thing (n. 144, 145, 1754, 1896, 2009, 2724, 3006, 3237, 3421, 6674, 9310). That "clothed in a vesture dipped in blood," signifies the Word in the letter, to which violence has been offered, is because "a vesture" signifies truth because it clothes good (n. 1073, 2576, 5248, 5319, 5954, 9212, 9216, 9952, 10536); especially truth in the ultimates, thus the Word in the letter (n. 5248, 6918, 9158, 9212); and because "blood" signifies violence offered to truth by falsity (n. 374, 1005, 4735, 5476, 9127). That "the armies in heaven followed Him upon white horses," signify those who are in the understanding of the Word as to its interiors, is because "armies" signify those who are in the truths and goods of heaven and the church (n. 3448, 7236, 7988, 8019). And "a horse" signifies the understanding (n. 3217, 5321, 6125, 6400, 6531, 6534, 7024, 8146, 8318). And "white" signifies truth which is in the light of heaven, consequently interior truth (n. 3301, 3993, 4007, 5319). That "clothed in fine linen white and clean," signifies the same persons in truth from good, is because "fine linen," or "linen," signifies truth from a celestial origin, which is truth from good (n. 5319, 9469). That "a name written upon the vesture and upon the thigh," signifies truth and good, and their quality, is because "a vesture" signifies truth, and "a name" quality, as observed above, and "the thigh" signifies the good of love (n. 3021, 4277, 4280, 9961, 10485). "King of kings, and Lord of lords," is the Lord as to the Divine truth and as to the Divine good; the Lord is called "King" from the Divine truth (n. 3009, 5068, 6148). And He is called "Lord" from the Divine good (n. 4973, 9167, 9194). Hence it appears what is the quality of the Word in its spiritual or internal sense, and that there is no expression therein which does not signify something spiritual, that is, something of heaven and the church. 2.In the prophetical parts of the Word mention is very often made of the horse, but heretofore no one has known that "a horse" signifies the understanding, and his "rider" one who is intelligent; and this possibly, because it seems strange and wonderful, that by "a horse" such a thing should be meant in the spiritual sense, and thence in the Word. But nevertheless that it is so, may evidently appear from many passages therein; some of which only I will here adduce. In the prophecy of Israel, it is said of Dan: Dan is a serpent upon the way, an arrow-snake upon the highway, that biteth the horse's heels, so that his rider shall fall backward (Gen. 49:17, 18). No one can understand what this prophecy concerning one of the tribes of Israel signifies unless he knows what is signified by "a serpent," and what by "a horse" and his "rider;" everyone, however, knows that there is something spiritual involved therein; what therefore each expression signifies, may be seen in The Arcana Coelestia (n. 6398-6401), where this prophecy is explained. In Habakkuk: O God, Thou didst ride upon Thy horses. Thy chariots are salvation. Thou didst tread in the sea with Thy horses (Hab. 3:8, 16). That "horses" here signify what is spiritual, is evident, for they are said concerning God; in any other sense, what could be meant by saying, that "God rides upon His horses, and that He treads upon the sea with horses?" In like manner in Zechariah: In that day, there shall be upon the bells of the horses, holiness unto Jehovah (Zech. 14:20). In the same: In that day, saith Jehovah, I will smite

every horse with astonishment, and his rider with madness; and I will open
Mine eyes upon the house of Judah, and will smite every horse of the people
with blindness (Zech. 12:4). It treats there of the vastation of the church, which
takes place when there no longer remains the understanding of any truth; and
which is described thus by "the horse and his rider;" what else could be the
meaning of "smiting every horse with astonishment," and of "smiting the horse
of the people with blindness"? What has this to do with the church? In Job: God
hath caused her to forget wisdom, neither hath He imparted to her intelligence:
what time she lifteth up herself on high, she scorneth the horse and his rider
(39:17-19 seq.). That "the horse" here signifies the understanding, is manifestly
evident. In like manner in David, where it is said: He rideth upon the word of
truth (Ps. 45:4). And in many other passages. Moreover, who can know the
reason why Elijah and Elisha were called "the chariot of Israel and the
horsemen thereof;" and why "the boy of Elisha saw the mountain full of horses
and chariots of fire;" except it be known what is signified by "chariots," and
what was represented by "Elijah and Elisha"? For Elisha said to Elijah: My
father, my father, the chariot and horsemen 17-1 of Israel and the horsemen
thereof (2 Kings 2:11, 12). And Joash the king said to Elisha: My father, my
father, the chariot of Israel and the horsemen thereof (2 Kings 13:14). And,
speaking of the boy of Elisha, it is said: Jehovah opened the eyes of the boy of
Elisha, and he saw and behold the mountain was full of horses and chariots of
fire round about Elisha (2 Kings 6:17). The reason why Elijah and Elisha were
called "the chariot of Israel and the horsemen thereof," is because they both
represented the Lord as to the Word, and "a chariot" signifies doctrine from the
Word, and "horsemen" intelligence. That "Elijah" and "Elisha" represented the
Lord as to the Word, may be seen in The Arcana Coelestia (n. 5247, 7643, 8029,
9327). And that "chariots" signify doctrine drawn from the Word (n. 5321, 8215).
3.That a horse signifies the understanding, is from no other source than from
the representatives in the spiritual world. In that world horses are frequently
seen, and persons sitting upon horses, and also chariots; and there everyone
knows that they signify intellectual and doctrinal things. I have often observed,
when any were thinking from their understanding, that at such times they
appeared as if riding on horses; their meditation was thus represented before
others, they themselves not knowing it. There is also a place there, where many
assemble who think and speak from the understanding concerning the truths
of doctrine; and when others approach, they see, the whole plain full of chariots
and horses; and novitiate spirits, who wonder whence this is, are instructed that
it is an appearance resulting from their intellectual thought. That place is called
the assembly of the intelligent and the wise. I have likewise seen bright horses
and chariots of fire, when some were taken up into heaven, which was a sign
that they were then instructed in the truths of heavenly doctrine, and became
intelligent, and thus were taken up; on seeing which, it occurred to my mind,
what is signified by "the chariot of fire and the horses of fire by which Elijah
was taken up into heaven;" and what is signified by "the horses and chariots of
fire" that were seen by the young man of Elisha, when his eyes were opened.
4.That such is the signification of "chariots" and "horses" was well known in the
ancient churches; for those churches were representative churches, and with
those who were in them, the science of correspondences and representations

was the chief of all sciences. The signification of the horse, as being understanding, was derived by the wise round about, even to Greece, from those churches. Hence it was, when they would describe the sun, in which they placed their God of wisdom and intelligence, that they attributed to it a chariot and four horses of fire. And when they would describe the God of the sea, since by the sea were signified sciences derived from the understanding, that they also attributed horses to him. And when they would describe the origin of the sciences from the understanding, they represented it by a winged horse, which with its hoof broke open a fountain, at which sat nine virgins called the sciences. For from the ancient churches they received the knowledge that "the horse" signifies the understanding; "wings," spiritual truth; "the hoof," what is scientific from the understanding; and "a fountain," doctrine from which sciences are derived. Nor is anything else signified by "the Trojan horse," than an artificial contrivance devised by their understanding for the purpose of destroying the walls. Even at this day, when the understanding is described after the manner received from those ancients, it is usual to figure it by a flying horse or Pegasus; so, likewise, doctrine is described by a fountain, and the sciences by virgins; but scarcely anyone knows that "the horse," in the mystic sense, signifies the understanding; still less that those significatives were derived by the Gentiles from the ancient representative churches. 5.Since "the White Horse" signifies the understanding of the Word as to its spiritual or internal sense, those particulars concerning the Word and that sense, which are shown in The Arcana Coelestia, are here subjoined: for in that work the whole contents of Genesis and Exodus are explained according to the spiritual or internal sense of the Word. 6.THE WORD, AND ITS SPIRITUAL OR INTERNAL SENSE, FROM THE ARCANA COELESTIA. The necessity and excellence of the Word. From the light of nature nothing is known concerning the Lord, concerning heaven and hell, concerning the life of man after death, nor concerning the Divine truths by which man acquires spiritual and eternal life (n. 8944, 10318, 10319, 10320). This may appear manifest from the consideration, that many, and among them men of learning, do not believe those things, although they are born where the Word is, and are thereby instructed concerning them (n. 10319). Therefore it was necessary that there should be some revelation from heaven because man was born for heaven (n. 1775). Therefore in every age of the world there has been a revelation (n. 2895). Of the various kinds of revelation which have successively been made on this earth (n. 10355, 10632). To the most ancient men, who lived before the flood, whose time was called the golden age, there was an immediate revelation, and thence Divine truth was inscribed on their hearts (n. 2896). The ancient churches, which existed after the flood, had a historical and prophetical Word (n. 2686, 2897): concerning which churches see The New Jerusalem and its Heavenly Doctrine (n. 247). Its historical parts were called The Wars of Jehovah, and its prophetical parts, Enunciations (n. 2897). That Word, as to inspiration was like our Word, but accommodated to those churches (n. 2897). It is mentioned by Moses (n. 2686, 2897). But that Word is lost (n. 2897). Prophetical revelations were also made to others, as appears from the prophecies of Balaam (n. 2898). The Word is Divine in all and every particular part (n. 639, 680, 10321, 10637). The Word is Divine and holy as to every point and iota, from experience (n. 1349). How it is explained at this day, that the Word is inspired as to every iota (n. 1886). The church is especially where the Word is, and where the Lord is thereby known, and Divine truths are revealed (n. 3857, 10761). But it does not follow from thence, that they are of the church, who are born where the Word is, and where the Lord is thereby known; but they who, by means of truths from the Word, are regenerated by the Lord, who are they who live according to the truths therein, consequently, who lead a life of love and faith (n. 6637, 10143, 10153, 10578, 10645, 10829). 7. The Word is not understood, except by those who are enlightened. The human rational faculty cannot comprehend Divine, nor even spiritual things, unless it be enlightened by the Lord (n. 2196, 2203, 2209, 2654). Thus they only who are enlightened comprehend the Word (n. 10323). The Lord enables those who are enlightened to understand truths, and to discern those things which appear to contradict each other (n. 9382, 10659). The Word in its literal sense appears inconsistent, and in some places seems to contradict itself (n. 9025). And therefore by those who are not enlightened, it may be so explained and applied, as to confirm any opinion or heresy, and to defend any worldly and corporeal love (n. 4738, 10339, 10401). They are enlightened from the Word, who read it from the love of truth and good, but not they who read it from the love of fame, of gain, or of honor, thus from the love of self (n. 9382, 10548, 10549, 10550) They are enlightened who are in the good of life, and thereby in the affection of truth (n. 8694). They are enlightened whose internal is open, thus who as to their internal man are capable of elevation into the light of heaven (n. 10401, 10402, 10691, 10694). Enlightenment is an actual opening of the interiors of the mind, and also an elevation into the light of heaven (n. 10330). There is an influx of holiness from the internal, that is, from the Lord through the internal, with those who regard the Word as holy, though they themselves are ignorant of it (n. 6789). They are enlightened, and see truths in the Word, who are led by the Lord, but not they who are led by themselves (n. 10638). They are led by the Lord, who love truth because it is truth, who also are they that love to live according to Divine truths (n. 10578, 10645, 10829). The Word is vivified with man according to the life of his love and faith (n. 1776). The things derived from one's own intelligence have no life in themselves, because from man's proprium there is nothing good (n. 8941, 8944). They cannot be enlightened who have much confirmed themselves in false doctrine (n. 10640). It is the understanding which is enlightened (n. 6608, 9300). The understanding is the recipient of truth (n. 6242, 6608, 10659). In regard to every doctrine of the church, there are ideas of the understanding and of the thought thence, according to which the doctrine is perceived (n. 3310, 3825). The ideas of man during his life in the world are natural, because man then thinks in the natural; but still spiritual ideas are concealed therein, with those who are in the affection of truth for the sake of truth, and man comes into these ideas after death (n. 3310, 5510, 6201, 10236, 10240, 10550). Without ideas of the understanding, and of the thought thence, on any subject, there can be no perception (n. 3825). Ideas concerning the things of faith are laid open in the other life, and their quality is seen by the angels, and man is then conjoined with others according to those ideas, so far as they proceed from the affection which is of love (n. 1869, 3320, 5510, 6201, 8885). Therefore the Word is not understood except by a rational man; for to believe anything without an idea thereof, and without a rational view of the subject, is only to retain in the memory words destitute of all the life of perception and affection, which is not believing (n. 2533). It is the literal sense of the Word which admits of enlightenment (n. 3619, 9824, 9905, 10548). 8.The Word cannot be understood except by means of doctrine from the Word. The doctrine of the church must be from the Word (n. 3464, 5402, 6832, 10763, 10765). The Word without doctrine is not understood (n. 9025, 9409, 9424, 9430, 10324, 10431, 10582). True doctrine is a lamp to those who read the Word (n. 10401). Genuine doctrine must be from those who are in enlightenment from the Lord (n. 2510, 2516, 2519, 2524, 10105). The Word is understood by means of doctrine formed by one enlightened (n. 10324). They who are in enlightenment form for themselves doctrine from the Word (n. 9382, 10659). What is the difference between those who teach and learn from the doctrine of the church, and those who teach and learn from the sense of the letter of the Word alone (n. 9025). They who are in the sense of the letter of the Word without doctrine, do not come into any understanding concerning Divine truths (n. 9409, 9410, 10582). They may fall into many errors (n. 10431). They who are in the affection of truth for the sake of truth, when they become adults, and can see from their own understanding, do not simply abide in the doctrinals of their churches, but examine from the Word whether they be true or not (n. 5402, 5432, 6047). Otherwise everyone would have truth from another, and from his native soil, whether he were born a Jew or a Greek (n. 6047). Nevertheless such things as are become matters of faith from the literal sense of the Word, are not to be extinguished till after a full view (n. 9039). The true doctrine of the church is the doctrine of charity and faith (n. 2417, 4766, 10763, 10765). The doctrine of faith does not constitute the church, but the life of faith, which is charity (n. 809, 1798, 1799, 1834, 4468, 4677, 4766, 5826, 6637). Doctrinals are of no account, unless one lives according to them; and everyone may see they are for the sake of life, and not merely for the memory and thought thence derived (n. 1515, 2049, 2116). In the churches at this day the doctrine of faith is taught, and not the doctrine of charity, the latter being rejected to a science, which is called moral Theology 17-2 (n. 2417). The church would be one, if they should be acknowledged as men of the church from the life, thus from charity (n. 1285, 1316, 2982, 3267, 3445, 3451, 3452). How much superior the doctrine of charity is to that of faith separate from charity (n. 4844). They who know nothing concerning charity, are in ignorance with respect to heavenly things (n. 2435). They who only hold the doctrine of faith, and not that of charity, fall into errors; which errors are also described (n. 2383, 2417, 3146, 3325, 3412, 3413, 3416, 3773, 4672, 4730, 4783, 4925, 5351, 7623-7677, 7752-7762, 7790, 8094, 8313, 8530, 8765, 9186, 9224, 10555). They who are only in the doctrine of faith, and not in the life of faith, which is charity, were formerly called the uncircumcised, or Philistines (n. 3412, 3413, 3463, 8093, 8313, 9340). The ancients held the doctrine of love to the Lord and of charity towards the neighbor, and made the doctrine of faith subservient thereto (n. 2417, 3419, 4844, 4955). Doctrine formed by one enlightened may afterwards be confirmed by things rational and scientific; and that thus it is more fully understood, and is corroborated (n. 2553, 2719, 2720, 3052, 3310, 6047). See more on this subject in The New Jerusalem and its Heavenly Doctrine (n. 51). They who are in faith separate from charity, would have the doctrinal of the church simply believed, without any rational intuition (n. 3394). It is not the mark of a wise man to confirm a dogma, but to see whether it be true before it is confirmed; and that this is the case with those who are in enlightenment (n. 1017, 4741, 7012, 7680, 7950). The light of confirmation is a natural light, and not spiritual, and may exist even with the evil (n. 8780). All things, even falsities, may be so far confirmed, as to appear like truths (n. 2482, 2490, 5033, 6865, 8521). 9.In the Word there is a spiritual sense, which is called the internal sense. No one can know what the spiritual or internal sense of the Word is, unless he knows what correspondence is (n. 2895, 4322). Each and all things, even the most minute, which are in the natural world, correspond to spiritual things, and thence signify them (n. 2890-2893, 2897-3003, 3213-3227). The spiritual things to which natural things correspond, as assume another appearance in the natural, so that they are not recognized (n. 1887, 2396, 8920). Scarcely anyone knows wherein resides the Divine of the Word, when nevertheless it is in its internal and spiritual sense, which at this day is not known even to exist (n. 2980, 4989). The mystical contents of the Word are no other than those of its internal or spiritual sense, which treats of the Lord, of the glorification of His Human, of His kingdom, and of the church, and not of the natural things which are in the world (n. 4923). The prophetic writings are in many places unintelligible, and therefore of no use, without the internal sense, illustrated by examples (n. 2608, 8020, 8398). As for instance, with respect to what is signified by "the white horse" in Revelation (n. 2760 seq.). What by "the keys of the kingdom of the heavens," that were given to Peter, see the preface to Genesis 22, and n. 9410. What by "flesh," "blood," "bread," and "wine," in the Holy Supper (n. 8682). What by the prophecies of Jacob concerning his sons (Gen. 49; n. 6306, 6333-6465). What by many prophecies concerning Judah and Israel, which by no means tally with that nation, nor in the sense of the letter have any coincidence with their history (n. 6331, 6361, 6415, 6438, 6444). Besides many other instances (n. 2608). More may be seen of the nature of correspondence in the work on Heaven and Hell (n. 87-115 and 303-310). Of the internal or spiritual sense of the Word in a summary (n. 1767-1777, 1869-1879). In each and all things of the Word there is an internal sense (n. 1143, 1984, 2135, 2333, 2395, 2495, 2619). Such things do not appear in the sense of the letter, but nevertheless they are within it (n. 4442). 10.The internal sense of the Word is especially for the angels, and it is also for men. In order that it may be known what the internal sense is, the quality thereof, and whence it is, it may here be observed in general, that thought and speech in heaven are different from thought and speech in the world; for in heaven they are spiritual, but in the world natural; when, therefore, man reads the Word, the angels who are with him perceive it spiritually, whilst men perceive it naturally; hence it follows, that angels are in the internal sense, whilst men are in the external sense; but that nevertheless these two senses make a one by correspondence. That angels not only think spiritually, but also speak spiritually; that they are likewise present with man; and that they have conjunction with man by means of the Word, may be seen in the work on Heaven and Hell, where it treats of The Wisdom of the Angels of Heaven (n. 265-275). Of their Speech (n. 234-245). Of their Conjunction with Man (n. 291-302). And of their Conjunction by the Word (n. 303-310). The Word is understood differently by angels in the heavens, and by men on earth; the former perceiving the internal or spiritual sense, whilst the latter see only the external or natural sense (n. 1887, 2396). The angels perceive the Word in its internal sense, and not in its external sense, proved from the experience of those who have conversed with me from heaven, when I was reading the Word (n. 1769-1772). The ideas of the thought and also the speech of angels are spiritual, but the ideas and speech of men natural; that therefore there is an internal sense, which is spiritual, for the use of angels, illustrated from experience (n. 2333). Nevertheless the sense of the letter of the Word serves the spiritual ideas of angels as a means of conveyance, comparatively as the words of speech do with men to convey the sense of a subject (n. 2143). The things relating to the internal sense of the Word fall into such things as are of the light of heaven, thus into angelic perception (n. 2618, 2619, 2629, 3086). Therefore those things which the angels perceive from the Word, are precious to them (n. 2540, 2541, 2545, 2551). Angels do not understand a single expression of the Word in its literal sense (n. 64, 65, 1434, 1929). They do not know the names of persons and places recorded in the Word (n. 1434, 1888, 4442, 4480). Names cannot enter into heaven, nor be pronounced there (n. 1876, 1888). All the names in the Word signify things, and in heaven they are changed into ideas of the things (n. 768, 1888, 4310, 4442, 5225, 5287, 10329). Angels also think abstractly from persons (n. 6613, 8343, 8985, 9007). How elegant the internal sense of the Word is, even where nothing but mere names occur, shown by examples from the Word (n. 1224, 1888, 2395). Many names also in series express one thing in the internal sense (n. 5905). Likewise all numbers in the Word signify things (n. 482, 487, 647, 648, 755, 813, 1963, 1988, 2075, 2252, 3152, 4264, 6175, 9488, 9659, 10217, 10253). Spirits also perceive the Word in its internal sense in proportion as their interiors are open into heaven (n. 1771). The sense of the letter of the Word, which is the natural sense, is instantly changed into the spiritual sense with the angels, because there is a correspondence (n. 5648). And this without their hearing or knowing what is in the literal or external sense (n. 10215). Thus the sense of the letter or the external sense is only with man, and proceeds no further (n. 2015). There is an internal sense in the Word, and likewise an inmost or supreme sense, concerning which (n. 9407, 10604, 10614, 10627). The spiritual angels, or those who are in the spiritual kingdom of the Lord, perceive the Word in its internal sense; and the celestial angels, or those who are in the celestial kingdom of the Lord, perceive the Word in its inmost sense (n. 2157, 2275). The Word is for men, and also for angels, being accommodated to each (n. 7381, 8862, 10322). The Word is the means of uniting heaven and earth (n. 2310, 2493, 9212, 9216, 9357). The conjunction of heaven with man is through the Word (n. 9396, 9400, 9401, 10452). Therefore the Word is called a covenant (n. 9396). Because a covenant signifies conjunction (n. 665, 666, 1023, 1038, 1864, 1996, 2003, 2021, 6804, 8767, 8778, 9396, 10632). There is an internal sense in the Word, because the Word is from the Lord, it descended through the three heavens even to man 17-3 (n. 2310, 6397). And thereby it is accommodated to the angels of the three heavens and also to men (n. 7381, 8862). Hence it is that the Word is Divine (n. 2980, 4989). And it is holy (n. 10276). And it is spiritual (n. 4480). And it is Divinely inspired (n. 9094). This is inspiration (n. 9094). The regenerate man is actually in the internal sense of the Word, although he does not know it, since his internal man, which has spiritual perception, is open (n. 10401). But with him the spiritual of the Word flows into natural ideas, and thus is represented naturally, because while he lives in the world this spiritual thinks in the natural man, so far as it comes to the perception (n. 5614). Hence the light of truth, with those who are enlightened, is from their internal, thus through the internal, from the Lord (n. 10691, 10694). Also by the same way there is an influx of holiness with those who esteem the Word holy (n. 6789). Since the regenerate man is actually in the internal sense of the Word, and in the sanctity thereof, although he does not know it, therefore after death he comes into it of himself, and is no longer in the sense of the letter (n. 3226, 3342, 3343). The ideas of the internal man are spiritual; but man during his life in the world does not attend thereto, inasmuch as they are within his natural thought, and give it its rational faculty (n. 10236, 10240, 10500). But man after death comes into those his spiritual ideas, because they are proper to his spirit, and then he not only thinks, but also speaks therefrom (n. 2470, 2478, 2479, 10568, 10604). Hence, as was said, the regenerate man knows not that he is in the spiritual sense of the Word, and that he receives enlightenment thence. 11.In the internal or spiritual sense of the Word there are innumerable arcana. The Word in the internal sense contains innumerable things which exceed human comprehension (n. 3085, 3086). It also contains things ineffable and inexplicable (n. 1965). Which are manifest only to angels, and are understood by them (n. 167). The internal sense of the Word contains arcana of heaven, which relate to the Lord and His kingdom in the heavens and on earth (n. 1-4, 937). Those arcana do not appear in the sense of the letter (n. 937, 1502, 2161). Many things in the writings of the prophets appear to be unconnected, which yet in the internal sense cohere without a break 17-4 in a beautiful series (n. 7153, 9022). Not a single word 17-5, nor even a single iota, in its original language, can be taken from the sense of the letter of the Word, without an interruption in the internal sense; and therefore, by the Divine Providence of the Lord, the Word is preserved so entire as to every point (n. 7933). There are innumerable things in the particulars of the Word (n. 6637, 8920). And in every word (n. 1689). There are innumerable things contained in the Lord's prayer and in every particular part thereof (n. 6619). And in the precepts of the Decalogue; in the external sense whereof, notwithstanding some things are such as are known to every nation without revelation (n. 8867, 8900). In every tittle of the letter of the Word, in the original language, there is holiness, shown from heaven; see the work on Heaven and Hell (n. 260), where these words of the Lord are explained: Not one jot or one tittle shall pass from the law (Matt. 5:18). In the Word, particularly in the prophetical parts, there are two expressions which seem to signify the same thing: but one has relation to good, and the other to truth (n. 683, 707, 2516, 8339). In the Word goods and truths are conjoined in a wonderful manner, and such conjunction appears to him only who knows the internal sense (n. 10554). And thus in the Word, and in every part thereof, there is a Divine marriage and a heavenly marriage (n. 683, 793, 801, 2173, 2516, 2712, 5138, 7022). The Divine marriage is the marriage of Divine good and Divine truth, thus it is the Lord in heaven, in whom alone there is that marriage (n. 3004, 3005, 3009, 4158, 5194, 5502, 6343, 7945, 8339, 9263, 9314).

Jesus also signifies the Divine good, and Christ the Divine truth, and thus both signify the Divine marriage in heaven (n. 3004, 3005, 3009). This marriage is in every particular part of the Word in its internal sense, and thus the Lord is therein as to the Divine good and the Divine truth (n. 5502). The marriage of good and truth from the Lord in heaven and in the church is called the heavenly marriage (n. 2508, 2618, 2803, 3004, 3211, 3952, 6179). Therefore in this respect the Word is as it were heaven (n. 2173, 10126). Heaven is compared in the Word to a marriage, on account of the marriage of good and truth therein (n. 2758, 3132, 4434, 4834). The internal sense is itself the genuine doctrine of the church (n. 9025, 9430, 10401.) They who understand the Word according to the internal sense, know the true doctrine itself of the church, because the internal sense contains it (n. 9025, 9430, 10401). The internal of the Word is also the internal of the church, as it is likewise the internal of worship (n. 10460). The Word is the doctrine of love to the Lord, and of charity towards the neighbor (n. 3419, 3420). The Word in the literal sense is as a cloud, and in the internal sense it is glory (see the preface to Gen. 18 and n. 5922, 6343), where these words are explained: "The Lord shall come in the clouds of heaven with glory." "Clouds" also in the Word signify the Word in the sense of the letter, and glory the Word in its internal sense (see the preface of Gen. 18 and n. 4060, 4391, 5922, 6343, 6752, 8106, 8781, 9430, 10551, 10574). Things contained in the literal sense, respectively to those which are in the internal sense, are like rude projections round a polished optical cylinder, from which nevertheless is exhibited in the cylinder a beautiful image of a man (n. 1871). In the spiritual world they who desire and acknowledge only the sense of the letter of the Word, are represented by a deformed old woman; but they who desire and acknowledge the internal sense at the same time, are represented by a virgin beautifully clothed (n. 1774). The Word in its whole complex is an image of heaven; for the Word is the Divine truth, and the Divine truth makes heaven, and heaven relates to one man, and therefore in this respect the Word is as it were an image of man (n. 187). Heaven in one complex resembles one man, may be seen in the work on Heaven and Hell (n. 59-67). And the Divine truth proceeding 17-6 from the Lord makes heaven (n. 126-140, 200-212). The Word is represented before the angels under the most beautiful and agreeable forms (n. 1767, 1768). The sense of the letter is as the body, and the internal sense as the soul of that body (n. 8943). Hence the life of the Word is from the internal sense (n. 1405, 4857). The Word is pure in the internal sense, but it does not appear so in the sense of the letter (n. 2362, 2396). The things which are in the sense of the letter are holy from the internal contents (n. 10126, 10728). The historical parts of the Word also have an internal sense, but within them (n. 4989). Thus the historical as well as the prophetical parts of the Word contain arcana of heaven (n. 755, 1659, 1709, 2310, 2333). The angels do not perceive those parts historically, but dogmatically because spiritually (n. 6884). The interior arcana contained in the historical parts are less evident to man than those contained in the prophetical parts, by reason that the mind is engaged in viewing and considering the historical transactions (n. 2176, 6597). The nature of the internal sense of the Word is further shown (n. 1756, 1984, 2004, 2663, 3033, 7089, 10604, 10614). And illustrated by comparisons (n. 1873). 12.The Word is written by correspondences, and thus by representatives. The Word as to the sense of the

letter is written by mere correspondences, that is, by such things as represent
and signify the spiritual things of heaven and the church (n. 1404, 1408, 1409,
1540, 1619, 1659, 1709, 1783, 2179, 2763, 2899). This was done for the sake of
the internal sense, which is there in every part (n. 2899). Consequently for the
sake of heaven, since those who are in heaven do not understand the Word
according to the sense of its letter, which is natural, but according to the
internal sense, which is spiritual (n. 2899). The Lord spoke by correspondences,
representatives, and significatives, because He spoke from the Divine (n. 9049,
9063, 9086, 10126, 10728). The Lord thus spoke before the world, and at the
same time before heaven (n. 2533, 4807, 9049, 9063, 9086). The things spoken
by the Lord went through the whole heaven (n. 4637). The historicals of the
Word are representatives, and the words significative (n. 1540, 1659, 1709,
1783, 2687). The Word could not be written in any other style, so that through
it there might be communication and conjunction with the heavens (n. 2899,
6943, 9481). They greatly err, who despise the Word on account of the apparent
simplicity and rudeness of its style, and who think that they would receive the
Word if it had been written in a different style (n. 8783). The method and style
of writing which prevailed amongst the most ancient people, was by
correspondences and representatives (n. 605, 1756, 9942). The ancient wise men
were delighted with the Word, because of the representatives and significatives
therein, from experience (n. 2592, 2593). If a man of the Most Ancient Church
had read the Word, he would have seen clearly the things contained in the
internal sense, and obscurely the things contained in the external sense (n.
449). The sons of Jacob were brought into the land of Canaan, because all the
places in that land, from the most ancient times, were made representative (n.
1585, 3686, 4441, 5136, 6516). And thus the Word might be there written,
wherein those places should be mentioned for the sake of the internal sense (n.
3686, 4447, 5136, 6416). But nevertheless the Word, as to the external sense
was changed for the sake of that nation, but not as to the internal sense (n.
10453, 10461, 10603, 10604) Many passages adduced from the Word concerning
that nation, which must be understood according to the internal sense, and not
according to the letter (n. 7051). Inasmuch as that nation represented the
church, and the Word was written with them and concerning them, therefore
Divine celestial things were signified by their names, as by Reuben, Simeon,
Levi, Judah, Ephraim, Joseph, and the rest: and by "Judah" in the internal
sense is signified the Lord as to celestial love, and His celestial kingdom (n.
3654, 3881, 3882, 5583, 5782, 6362-6381). That it may be known what
correspondences are and their nature, and what is the nature of representatives
in the Word, something shall be here said concerning them. All things which
correspond likewise represent, and thereby signify, so that correspondences and
representations are one (n. 2890, 2897, 2971, 2987, 2989, 2990, 3002, 3225). The
nature of correspondences and representations shown from experience and
examples (n. 2703, 2987, 3002, 3213-3226, 3337-3352, 3472-3485, 4218-4228,
9280). The science of correspondences and representations was the chief science
with the ancients (n. 3021, 3419, 4280, 4749, 4844, 4964, 4965, 6004, 7729,
10252). Especially with the Orientals (n. 5702, 6692, 7097, 7779, 9391, 10252,
10407). And in Egypt more than in other countries (n. 5702, 6692, 7097, 7779,
9391, 10407). Also with the Gentiles, as in Greece, and in other places (n. 2762,

7729). But that at this day the science of correspondences and representations is lost, particularly in Europe (n. 2894, 2895, 2994, 3630, 3632, 3747-3749, 4581, 4966, 10252). Nevertheless this science is more excellent than all other sciences, inasmuch as without it the Word cannot be understood, nor the signification of the rites of the Jewish Church which are recorded in the Word, nor can it be known what the nature of heaven is, nor what the spiritual is, nor in what manner a spiritual influx takes place into what is natural, nor how the case is with respect to the influx of the soul into the body, with many other matters (n. 4180), and in the places above cited. All things which appear before spirits and angels, are representative according to correspondences (n. 1971, 3213-3226, 3457, 3475, 3485, 9481, 9574, 9576, 9577). The heavens are full of representatives (n. 1521, 1532, 1619). Representatives are more beautiful, and more perfect, in proportion as they are more interior in the heavens (n. 3475). Representatives there are real appearances, because they are from the light of heaven which is Divine truth, and which is the very essential of the existence of all things (n. 3485). The reason why each and all things in the spiritual world are represented in the natural world, is, because what is internal assumes to itself a suitable clothing in what is external, whereby it makes itself visible and apparent (n. 6275, 6284, 6299). Thus the end assumes a suitable clothing that it may exist as the cause in a lower sphere, and afterwards that it may exist as the effect in a sphere still lower; and when the end, by means of the cause, becomes the effect, it then becomes visible, or appears before the eyes (n. 5711). This may be illustrated by the influx of the soul into the body, whereby the soul assumes a clothing of such things in the body as enable it to express all its thoughts and affections in a visible form; wherefore thought, when it flows down into the body, is there represented by such gestures and actions as correspond to it (n. 2988). The affections of the mind are manifestly represented in the face, by the variations of the countenance, so as to be there seen (n. 4791-4805, 5695). Hence it is evident, that in each and all things in nature there lies hidden a cause and an end from the spiritual world (n. 3562, 5711). Since those things which are in nature are the ultimate effects, within which are the prior things (n. 4240, 4939, 5051, 6275, 6284, 6299, 9216). That internal things are the objects represented, and external things the objects representing (n. 4292). What is further meant by correspondences and representations may be seen in the work on Heaven and Hell, where it treats of the correspondence between all things of Heaven, and all things of Man (n. 87-102). Of the Correspondence of Heaven with all things on Earth (n. 103-115). And of Representatives and Appearances in Heaven (n. 170-176). Since all things in nature are representative of spiritual and celestial things, therefore in the churches which existed in ancient times, all the externals, which were rituals, were representative, and therefore those churches were called representative churches (n. 519, 521, 2896). The church instituted with the sons of Israel was a representative church (n. 1003, 2179, 10149). All the rituals therein were externals, which represented internals, which are of heaven and the church (n. 4288, 4874). The representatives of the church and of worship ceased when the Lord came into the world and manifested Himself, because the Lord opened the internals of the church, and because all things of that church in the highest sense regarded Him (n. 4832). 13. Of the sense of the letter, or the eternal sense of the Word. The sense of the letter of the Word is according to appearances in the world (n. 584, 926, 1719, 1720, 1832, 1874, 2242, 2520, 2533). And adapted to the conceptions of the simple (n. 2533, 9049, 9063, 9086). The Word, in the sense of the letter, is natural (n. 8783). Because what is natural is the ultimate, wherein spiritual and celestial things find their limits, and upon which they rest like a house upon its foundation; and that otherwise the internal sense of the Word, without the external, would be like a house without a foundation (n. 9360, 9430, 9433, 9824, 10044, 10436). The Word because it is such contains both a spiritual and celestial sense (n. 9407). And of consequence, that it is holy and Divine in the sense of the letter as to all and every part thereof, even to every iota (n. 639, 680, 1319, 1870, 9198, 10321, 10637). The laws enacted for the sons of Israel, although abrogated, are yet the holy Word, on account of the internal sense in them (n. 9210, 9259, 9349). Among the laws, judgments, and statutes, ordained in the Israelitish or Jewish Church, which was a representative church, there are some which are still in force both in their external and internal sense; which ought strictly to be observed in their external sense; some which may be of use, if one is so disposed; and some which are altogether abrogated (n. 9349). The Word is Divine even in those statutes which are abrogated, on account of the heavenly things which lie concealed in their internal sense (n. 10637). What the quality of the Word is in the sense of the letter, if not understood at the same time as to the internal sense, or, what is the same thing, according to true doctrine from the Word (n. 10402). An immense number of heresies spring up from the sense of the letter of the Word without the internal sense, or without genuine doctrine drawn from the Word (n. 10401). They who are in externals without internals, cannot bear the interior things of the Word (n. 10694). The Jews were of this description and they are such also at the present day (n. 301-303, 3479, 4429, 4433, 4680, 4844, 4847, 10396, 10401, 10407, 10695, 10701, 10707). 14.The Lord is the Word. The Word in its inmost sense treats solely of the Lord, describing all the states of the glorification of His Human, that is, of its union with the Divine itself, and likewise all the states of the subjugation of the hells, and the reducing to order of all things therein, and in the heavens (n. 2249, 7014). Thus the inmost sense describes the Lord's whole life in the world, and thereby the Lord is continually present with the angels (n. 2523). Therefore the Lord alone is in the inmost part of the Word, and the Divinity and the holiness of the Word is from thence (n. 1873, 9357). The Lord's saying, that the Scripture was fulfilled concerning Him, signifies, that all things were fulfilled which are contained in the inmost sense (n. 7933). The Word signifies the Divine truth (n. 4692, 5075, 9987). The Lord is the Word because He is the Divine truth (n. 2533). The Lord is the Word also because the Word is from Him, and treats of Him (n. 2859). And because it treats of the Lord alone in its inmost sense; thus the Lord Himself is therein (n. 1873, 9357). And because in each and all things of the Word there is a marriage of the Divine good and the Divine truth, which marriage is in the Lord alone (n. 3004, 3005, 3009, 4158, 5194, 5502, 6343, 7945, 8339, 9263, 9314). Divine truth is the only reality; and that in which it is, and which is from the Divine, is the only thing substantial (n. 5272, 6880, 7004, 8200). And because the Divine truth proceeding from the Lord as the sun in heaven is light there, and the Divine good is heat there; and inasmuch as all things in heaven derive their existence therefrom, as all things in the world derive their existence from light and heat, which are also in their own substances, and act by means thereof; and inasmuch as the natural world exists by means of heaven or the spiritual world; it is plain that all things which were created 17-7 were created from the Divine truth, thus from the Word, according to these words in John: In the beginning was the Word, and the Word was with God, and God was the Word, and by it all things were made that were made; and the Word was made flesh (John 1:1-3, 14; n. 2803, 2884, 5272, 7830). Further particulars concerning the creation of all things from the Divine truth, consequently by the Lord, may be seen in the work on Heaven and Hell (n. 137); and more fully in the article concerning the Sun in Heaven, where it is shown that the Lord is that Sun, and that it is His Divine love (n. 116-125). And that the Divine truth is Light, and the Divine good is Heat, proceeding from that sun in heaven (n. 126-140). The conjunction of the Lord with man is effected by the Word, by means of the internal sense (n. 10375). This conjunction is effected by each and all things of the Word, and herein the Word is more wonderful than all other writings (n. 10632-10634). Since the time of writing the Word, the Lord thereby speaks with men (n. 10290). For further particulars respecting the Conjunction of Heaven with man by means of the Word, see the work on Heaven and Hell (n. 303-310). 15.Of those who are against the Word. Of those who despise, blaspheme, and profane the Word (n. 1878). Their quality in the other life (n. 1761, 9222). They relate to the viscous parts of the blood (n. 5719). How great the danger is from profaning the Word (n. 571-582). How hurtful it is, if principles of falsity, particularly those which favor self-love and the love of the world, are confirmed by the Word (n. 589). They who are in no affection of truth for its own sake, utterly reject the things appertaining to the internal sense of the Word, and nauseate them, from experience of such in the world of spirits (n. 5702). Of some in the other life, who endeavored altogether to reject the interior things of the Word; such are deprived of rationality (n. 1879). 16.Which are the books of the Word. The books of the Word are all those which have the internal sense; but those which have not the internal sense are not the Word. The books of the Word in the Old Testament are, THE FIVE BOOKS OF MOSES; THE BOOK OF JOSHUA; THE BOOK OF JUDGES; THE TWO BOOKS OF SAMUEL; THE TWO BOOKS OF KINGS; THE PSALMS OF DAVID; THE PROPHETS ISAIAH, JEREMIAH, LAMENTATIONS, EZEKIEL, DANIEL, HOSEA, JOEL, AMOS, OBADIAH, JONAH, MICAH, NAHUM, HABAKKUK, ZEPHANIAH, HAGGAI, ZECHARIAH, MALACHI. In the New Testament, the four Evangelists, MATTHEW, MARK, LUKE, JOHN; and the APOCALYPSE. The rest have not the internal sense (n. 10325). The book of Job is an ancient book, which indeed contains an internal sense, but not in series (n. 3570, 9942).

Further particulars Concerning the Word. The term "Word," in the Hebrew language, signifies various things; as speech, thought of the mind, everything that really exists, and also something (n. 9987). The Word signifies the Divine truth and the Lord (n. 2533, 4692, 5075, 9987). Words signify truths (n. 4692, 5075). They signify doctrinals (n. 1288). The ten words signify all Divine truths (n. 10688). In the Word, particularly in the prophetic parts, there are two expressions that signify one thing, and the one has relation to good and the other to truth, which are thus conjoined (n. 683, 707, 5516, 8339). It can be known only from the internal sense of the Word, what expression refers to good and what to truth; for there are proper words by which things appertaining to good are expressed, and proper words by which things appertaining to truth are expressed (n. 793, 801). And this so determinately, that it may be known merely from the words made use of, whether the subject treated of is good, or whether it is truth (n. 2722). Sometimes also one expression involves a general, and the other expression implies a certain specific particular from that general (n. 2212). There is a species of reciprocation in the Word, concerning which see n. 2240. Most expressions in the Word have also an opposite sense (n. 4816). That the internal sense proceeds regularly according to the subject predicated (n. 4502). They who have been delighted with the Word, in the other life receive the heat of heaven, wherein is celestial love, according to the quality and degree of their delight from love (n. 1773).

Brief Exposition

Several works and tracts having been published by me, during some years past, concerning the New Jerusalem, by which is meant the New Church about to be established by the Lord; and the book of Revelation having been revealed, I have come to a determination to bring to light the entire doctrine of that church in its fullness. But, as this is a work of some years, I have thought it advisable to draw up some sketch thereof, in order that a general idea may first be formed of that church and its doctrine; because when general principles precede, each and every thing will afterwards appear extant in its breadth in light, for these enter into generals, as things homogenous into their receptacles. This compendium, however, is not designed for critical examination, but is only offered to the world by way of information, as its contents will be fully demonstrated in the work itself. But the doctrinals at present maintained concerning justification shall be prefixed, that the following contrast between the doctrines of the present church, and those of the New Church, may be clearly understood.

THE DOCTRINALS OF THE ROMAN CATHOLICS CONCERNING JUSTIFICATION, FROM THE COUNCIL OF TRENT. In the bull of Pope Pius IV., dated 13th November, 1564, are the following words: "I embrace and receive each and everything which the most holy council of Trent hath determined and declared concerning Original Sin and Justification."

From the Council of Trent, concerning Original Sin. (a) That Adam, by the offense of his transgression, experienced an entire change and depravation of nature, both in body and soul; and that the ill effects of Adam's transgression were not confined to himself, but also extended to his posterity; and that it not only transmitted death and corporal sufferings upon all mankind, but likewise sin, which is the death of the soul (Sess. v. 1, 2). (b) That this sin of Adam, which originally was a single transgression, and has been transmitted by propagation, and not by imitation, is so implanted in the proprium of every man, and cannot be taken away by any other means than by the merit of the only Saviour our Lord Jesus Christ, who has reconciled us to God by His blood, being made unto us justice, sanctification, and redemption (Sess. v. 3). (c) That by the transgression of Adam, all men lost their innocence, and became unclean, and by nature the sons of wrath (Sess. vi. chap. 1).

Concerning Justification. (a) That our heavenly Father, the Father of mercies, sent Christ Jesus His Son to men, in the blessed fulness of time, as well to the Jews who were under the law, as to the Gentiles who followed not justice, that they might all lay hold of justice, and all receive the adoption of sons. Him God offered to be a propitiation through faith in His blood, not only for our sins, but likewise for the sins of the whole world (Sess. vi. chap. 3). (b) Nevertheless all do not receive the benefit of His death, but only they to whom the merit of His passion is communicated; so that unless they are born again in Christ, they can never be justified (Sess. vi. chap. 3). (c) That the beginning of justification is to be derived from the preventing grace of God through Christ Jesus, that is, from His call (Sess. vi. chap. 5). (c) That men are disposed to justice, when being stirred up by Divine grace, and conceiving faith from hearing, they are freely moved towards God, believing those things to be true which are Divinely revealed and promised; and especially this, that the ungodly are justified by

God through His grace, through redemption, which is by Christ Jesus; and when, being convinced of sin from the fear of Divine justice, by which they are profitably disquieted, they are encouraged in hope, trusting that God, for Christ's sake, will be propitious to them (Sess. vi. chap. 6). (d) That the consequence of this disposition and preparation is actual justification, which is not only a remission of sins, but likewise a sanctification and renovation of the interior man by the reception of Divine grace and gifts, whereby man from being unjust, becomes just, and from being an enemy becomes a friend, so as to be an heir according to the hope of eternal life (Sess. vi. chap. 7). (e) The final cause of justification is the glory of God and of Christ, and life eternal. The efficient cause is God, who freely cleanses and sanctifies. The meritorious cause is the Dearly-Beloved and Only-Begotten of God, our Lord Jesus Christ, who when we were enemies, through the great charity wherewith He loved us, by His most holy passion upon the wood of the cross, merited for us justification, and made satisfaction for us to God the Father. The instrumental cause is the sacrament of baptism which is a sacrament of faith, without which no one can ever reach justification. The formal cause is the sole justice of God; not that whereby He is just Himself, but that whereby He makes us just, with which being gifted by Him, we are renewed in the spirit of our mind; and are not only reputed just, but are truly called and are just, each according to his own measure, which the Holy Spirit imparts to everyone as it pleases Him (Sess. vi. chap. 7, 2). (f) That justification is a translation from that state, wherein man is born a son of the first Adam, into a state of grace and adoption of the sons of God by the second Adam, our Saviour Jesus christ (Sess. vi. chap. 4).

Concerning Faith, Charity, Good Works and Merits. (a) When the apostle says, that man is justified by faith and freely, these words are to be understood in the sense wherein the Catholic church has uniformly held and expressed them; namely, that we are said to be justified by faith, because faith is the commencement of man's salvation, the foundation and root of all justification, without which it is impossible to please God, and attain to the fellowship of His sons. But we are said to be justified freely, because none of those things which precede justification, whether faith or works, merit the actual grace of justification; for if it be grace, it is not from works, otherwise grace would not be grace (Sess. vi. chap. 8). (b) Although no one can be just, but they to whom the merits of the passion of our Lord Jesus Christ are communicated, nevertheless that is effected in justification, when by the merit of the same most holy passion, the charity of God is infused by the Holy Spirit into the hearts of those who are justified, and abides in them. Hence in the act of justification, man receives, together with the remission of his sins, all these things infused into him at once by Jesus Christ, in whom he is ingrafted by faith, hope, and charity. For faith, unless charity be added to it, neither unites perfectly with Christ, nor constitutes a living member of His body (Sess. vi. chap. 7, 3). (c) That Christ is not only the Redeemer in whom they have faith, but also a Lawgiver, whom they obey (Sess. vi. chap. 16, Can. 21). (d) That faith without works is dead and vain, because in Christ Jesus neither circumcision availeth anything, nor uncircumcision, but faith which worketh through charity. For faith without hope and charity cannot avail unto eternal life; wherefore also they hearken to the word of Christ, "If thou wilt enter into life, keep the commandments." Thus they who are born again, receiving true Christian justice, are commanded to keep it white and unspotted, as their first robe, given them by Jesus Christ, instead of that which Adam lost both for himself and us by his disobedience, that they may present it before the tribunal of our Lord Jesus Christ, and obtain eternal life (Sess. vi. chap. 7). (e) That there is a continual influx of power from Jesus Christ Himself into those who are justified, as from a head into the members, and from a vine into the branches; which power always precedes, accompanies, and follows their good works, and without which they could not by any means be acceptable and meritorious in the sight of God; wherefore we are to believe, that nothing more is wanting to those who are justified, but they may be fully assured, that by those works which have been wrought in God, they have merited eternal life, which will be bestowed upon them in due time (Sess. vi. chap. 16). (f) We do not mean our own justice, as though it were our own from ourselves; for that which is termed our justice, is the justice of God, because it is infused into us by God through the merit of Christ. Far be it, therefore, from any Christian man either to trust or glory in himself, and not in the Lord, whose goodness towards us men is so great, that He vouchsafes to regard those things as our merits, which are His own gifts (Sess. vi. chap. 16). (g) For of ourselves, as of ourselves, we can do nothing; but by His cooperation, who strengthens us, we can do all things. Thus man has not whereof to glory, but all our glory is in Christ, in whom we live, in whom we merit, in whom we make satisfaction, bringing forth fruits worthy of repentance, which have their efficacy from Him, are offered unto the Father by Him, and are accepted by the Father through Him (Sess. xiv. chap. 8). (h) Whosoever shall say that man may be justified in the sight of God, by his own works, which are done either through the powers of human nature, or through the teaching of the law, without Divine grace through Christ Jesus, let him be accursed (Sess. vi. can. 1). (i) Whosoever shall say that man may believe, hope, and love (that is, have faith, hope, and charity), as is necessary in order that the grace of justification may be conferred upon him, without the preventing inspiration of the Holy Spirit, and its assistance, let him be accursed (Sess. vi. Can. 2). (k) Whosoever shall say that man is justified without the justice of christ, whereby He has merited for us, let him be accursed (Sess. vi. Can. 10). Not to mention many more passages, principally relating to the conjunction of faith with charity or good works, and the condemnation of their separation.

Concerning Free-will. (a) That free-will is by no means destroyed by Adam's sin, although it is debilitated and warped thereby (Sess. vi. chap. 1). (b) Whosoever shall say that the free-will of man, when moved and stirred up by God, cannot at all cooperate by concurring with God, who stirs it up and calls it, whereby man may dispose and prepare himself to receive the grace of justification; or that he cannot dissent if he will, but that, like a thing inanimate, he can do nothing at all, and is merely passive, let him be accursed (Sess. vi. Can. 4).

The Doctrinals of the Roman Catholics concerning Justification, collected from the Decrees of the Council of Trent may be summed up and arranged in a series thus. That the sin of Adam was transfused into the whole human race, whereby his state, and likewise the state of all men, became perverted, and alienated from God, and thus they were made enemies and sons of wrath; that therefore God the Father graciously sent His Son to reconcile, expiate, atone, satisfy, and thus redeem, and this by His being made justice. That Christ accomplished and fulfilled all this, by offering up Himself a sacrifice to God the Father upon the wood of the cross, thus by His passion and blood. That Christ alone has merited, and that this His merit is graciously imputed, attributed, applied, and transferred to the man who is recipient thereof, by God the Father through the Holy Spirit; and that thus the sin of Adam is removed from man; lust, however, still remaining in him as an incentive to sin. That justification is the remission of sins, and that from thence a renovation of the interior man takes place, whereby man from an enemy becomes a friend, and from being a son of wrath, a son of grace; and that thus union with Christ is effected, and being reborn he becomes a living member in His body.

That faith comes by hearing, when a man believes those things to be true which are Divinely revealed, and believes in the promises of God. That faith is the beginning of man's salvation, the foundation and root of all justification, without which it is impossible to please God, and enter into the fellowship of His children. That justification is effected by faith, hope, and charity; and that unless faith be accompanied by hope and charity, it is not living but dead, which cannot unite with Christ. That man ought to cooperate; that he has the power to approach and recede, otherwise nothing could be given unto him, for he would be like an inanimate body. That inasmuch as the reception of justification renews man, and as this is effected by the application of the merit of Christ, during man's cooperation, it follows that works are meritorious; but inasmuch as they are done from grace, and by the Holy Spirit, and as Christ alone has merited, therefore God considers His own gifts in man as meritorious; whence it follows, that no one ought to attribute anything of merit to himself.

THE DOCTRINALS OF THE PROTESTANTS CONCERNING JUSTIFICATION, FROM THE FORMULA CONCORDIAE. The book from which the following extracts are collected, is called the Formula Concordiae, and was composed by men attached to the Augsburg Confession; and as the pages will be cited where the quotations are to be met with, it is proper to observe, that I have made use of the edition printed at Leipzig in the year 1756.

From the Formula Concordiae, concerning original sin. (a) That since the fall of Adam, all men naturally descended from him are born with sin, which condemns, and brings eternal death upon those who are not born again, and that the merit of Christ is the only means whereby they are regenerated, consequently the only remedy whereby they are healed (pp. 9, 10, 52, 53, 55, 317, 641, 644, and Appendix, pp. 138, 139). (b) That original sin is such a total corruption of nature, that there is no spiritual soundness in the powers of man either as to his soul or body (p. 574). (c) That it is the source of all actual sins (pp. 317, 577, 639, 640, 942; Appendix, p. 139). (d) That it is a total absence or privation of the image of God (p. 640). (e) That we ought to distinguish between our nature, such as God created it, and original sin which dwells in our nature (p. 645). (f) Moreover, original sin is there called the work of the devil, spiritual poison, the root of all evils, an accident and a quality; whereas our nature is there called the work and creature of God, the personality of man, a substance, and an essence; and that the difference between them is the same as the difference between a man infected with a disease and the disease itself.

Concerning justification by faith. The general principles are these. (a) That by the Word and the sacraments the Holy Spirit is given, who effects faith when and where He pleases, in those who hear the Gospel. (b) That contrition, justification by faith, renovation, and good works, follow in order; that they are to be properly distinguished; and that contrition and good works contribute nothing to salvation, but faith alone. (c) That justification by faith alone, is remission of sins, deliverance from damnation, reconciliation with the Father, adoption as sons, and is effected by the imputation of the merit or justice of Christ. (d) That hence faith is that justice itself, whereby we are accounted just before God, and that it is a trust and confidence in grace. (e) That renovation, which follows, is vivification, regeneration, and sanctification. (f) That good works, which are the fruits of faith, being in themselves works of the Spirit, follow that renovation. (g) That this faith may be lost by grievous evils. The general principles concerning the Law and the Gospel are these. (h) That we must carefully distinguish between the Law and the Gospel, and between the works of the Law and the works of the Spirit, which are the truths of faith. (i) That the Law is doctrine which shows that man is in sins, and therefore in condemnation and the wrath of God, thus exciting terror; but that the Gospel is doctrine which teaches atonement for sins, and the deliverance from damnation by Christ, and thus of consolation. (k) That there are three uses of the Law, namely, to keep the wicked within bounds, to bring men to acknowledgment of their sins, and to teach the regenerate a rule of life. (l) That the regenerate are in the Law, but not under the Law, for they are under grace. (m) That it is the duty of the regenerate to exercise themselves in the Law, because, during their life in the world, they are prompted to sin by the flesh; but that they become pure and perfect after death. (n) That the regenerate are also reproved by the Holy Spirit, and endure various afflictions, but that nevertheless they do the Law spontaneously, and thus being the sons of God, they live in the Law. (o) That with those who are not regenerated, the veil of Moses still remains before their eyes, and the old Adam bears rule; but that with the regenerate the veil of Moses is taken away, and the old Adam is put to death.

Particulars from the Formula Concordiae, concerning justification by faith without the works of the Law. (a) That faith is imputed for justice without works, on account of the merit of Christ which is laid hold of by faith (pp. 78, 79, 80, 584, 689). (b) That charity follows justifying faith, but that faith does not justify as being formed by charity, as the Papists say (pp. 81, 89, 94, 117, 688, 691; Appendix, p. 169). (c) That neither the contrition which precedes faith, nor the renovation and sanctification which follow after it, nor the good works then performed, have anything to do with justification by faith (pp. 688, 689). (d) That it is folly to dream that the works of the second table of the Decalogue justify before God, for with that table we act with men, and not properly with God; and in justification we act with God and appease His wrath (p. 102). (e) If any one, therefore, believes he can obtain the remission of his sins, because he has charity, he brings a reproach on Christ; because he has an impious and vain confidence in his own justice (pp. 87, 89). (f) That good works are utterly to be excluded, in treating of justification and eternal life (p. 589). (g) That good works are not necessary as a meritorious cause of salvation, and that they do not enter into the act of justification (pp. 589, 590, 702, 704; Appendix, p. 173). (h) That the position, that good works are necessary to salvation, is to be rejected, because it takes away the consolation of the gospel, gives occasion to doubt of the grace of God, instills an opinion of one's own justice, and because they are accepted by the Papists to support a bad cause (p. 704). (i) The expression that good works are necessary to salvation, is rejected and condemned (p. 591). (k) That expressions implying that works are necessary unto salvation, ought not to be taught and defended, but rather exploded and rejected by the churches as false (p. 705). (l) That works which do not proceed from a true faith, are regarded as sins before God, that is, they are defiled with sin, because an evil tree cannot bring forth good fruit (p. 700). (m) That faith and salvation are neither preserved nor retained by good works, because these are only evidences that the Holy Spirit is present, and dwells in us (pp. 590, 705; Appendix, p. 174). (n) That the decree of the Council of Trent is deservedly to be rejected, which affirms that good works preserve salvation, or that justification by faith, or even faith itself, is maintained and preserved, either in the whole, or in the least part, by our works (p. 707).

Particulars from Formula Concordiae, Concerning the fruits of faith. (a) That a difference is to be observed between the works of the Law, and the works of the Spirit, and that the works which a regenerate person performs with a free and willing mind are not works of the Law, but works of the Spirit, which are the fruits of faith; because they who are born again are not under the Law, but under grace (pp. 589, 590, 721, 722). (b) That good works are the fruits of repentance (p. 12). (c) That the regenerate receive by faith a new life, new affections, and new works, and that these are from faith in repentance (p. 134). (d) That man after conversion and justification begins to be renewed in his mind, and at length in his understanding, and that then his will is not inactive in performing daily exercises of repentance (pp. 582, 673, 700). (e) That we ought to repent as well on account of original sin, as on account of actual sins (p. 321; Appendix, p. 159). (f) That repentance with Christians continues until death, because they have to wrestle with the remains of sin in the flesh throughout life (p. 327). (g) That we must enter upon, and advance more and more in the practice of the Law of the Decalogue (pp. 85, 86). (h) That the regenerate, although delivered from the curse of the Law, ought nevertheless still to exercise themselves in the Divine Law (p. 718). (i) That the regenerate are not without the Law, though not under the Law, for they live according to the Law of the Lord (p. 722). (k) That the Law ought to be considered by the regenerate as a rule of religion (pp. 596, 717; Appendix, p. 156). (l) That the regenerate do good works; not by compulsion, but spontaneously and freely, as though they had received no command, had heard of no threats, and expected no reward (pp. 596, 701). (m) That with them faith is always occupied in some good work, and he who does not thus perform good works, is destitute of true faith, for where there is faith, there are good works (p. 701). (n) That charity and good fruits follow faith and regeneration (pp. 121, 122, 171, 188, 692). (o) Faith and works agree well together, and are inseparably connected; but faith alone lays hold of the blessing without works, and yet it is not alone; hence it is that faith without works is dead (pp. 692, 693). (p) That after man is justified by faith, his faith being then true and alive is operative by charity, for good works always follow justifying faith, and are most certainly discovered with it; thus faith is never alone, but is always accompanied by hope and charity (p. 586). (y) We confess that where good works do not follow faith, in such case it is a false and not a true faith (p. 336). (r) That it is as impossible to separate good works from faith, as heat and light from fire (p. 701). (s) That as the old Adam is always inherent in our very nature, the regenerate have continual need of admonition, doctrine, threatenings, and even of chastisements of the Law, for they are reproved and corrected by the Holy Spirit through the Law (pp. 719, 720, 721). (t) That the regenerate must wrestle with the old Adam, and that the flesh must be kept under by exhortations, threatenings, and stripes, because renovation of life by faith is only begun in the present life (pp. 595, 596, 724). (u) That there remains a perpetual wrestling between the flesh and the spirit, in the elect and truly regenerate (pp. 675, 679). (z) That the reason why Christ promises remission of sins to good works, is, because they follow reconciliation, and also because good fruits must necessarily follow, and because they are the signs of the promise(pp. 116, 117). (y) That saving faith is not in those who have not charity, for charity is the fruit which certainly and necessarily follows true faith (p. 688). (z) That good works are necessary on many accounts, but not as a meritorious cause (pp. 11, 17, 64, 95, 133, 589, 590, 702; Appendix, p. 172). (aa) That a regenerate person ought to cooperate with the Holy Spirit, by the new powers and gifts which he has received, but in a certain way (pp. 582, 583, 674, 675; Appendix, p. 144). (bb) In the Confession of the Churches in the Low Countries, which was received in the Synod of Dort, we read as follows: "Holy faith cannot be inactive in man, for it is a faith working by charity; and works, which proceed from a good root of faith, are good and acceptable before God, like fruits of a good tree; for we are bound by God to good works, but not God to us, inasmuch as it is God that doeth them in us."

Concerning merits, from the Formula Concordiae. (a) That it is false that our works merit remission of sins; false, that men are accounted just by the justice of reason; and false, that reason of its own strength can love God above all things, and do the law of God (p. 64). (b) That faith does not justify because it is in itself so good a work, and so excellent a virtue, but because it lays hold of the merit of Christ in the promise of the gospel (pp. 76, 684). (c) That the promise of remission of sins, and justification for Christ's sake, does not involve any condition of merit, because it is freely offered (p. 67). (d) That a sinner is justified before God, or absolved from his sins, and from the most just sentence of damnation, and adopted into the number of the sons of God, without any merit of his own, and without any works of his own, whether past, present, or future, of mere grace, and only on account of the sole merit of Christ, which is imputed to him for justice (p. 684). (e) That good works follow faith, remission of sins, and regeneration; and whatever of pollution or imperfection is in them, is not accounted sinful or defective, and that for Christ's sake; and thus that the whole man, both as to his person and his works, is rendered and pronounced just and holy, out of mere grace and mercy in Christ, shed abroad, displayed, and magnified towards us; wherefore we cannot glory on account of merit (pp. 74, 92, 93, 336). (f) He who trusts in works, thinking he can merit anything thereby, despises the merit and grace of Christ, and seeks a way to heaven without Christ, by human strength (pp. 16, 17, 18, 19). (g) Whosoever desires to ascribe something to good works in the article of justification, and to merit the grace of God thereby, to such a man works are not only useless, but even pernicious (p. 708). (h) The works of the Decalogue are enumerated, and other necessary works, which God vouchsafes to reward (pp. 176, 198). (i) We teach that good works are meritorious, not indeed of remission of sins, grace, and justification, but of other temporal rewards, and even spiritual rewards in this life, and after this life, because Paul says, "Every one shall receive a reward according to his labor"; and Christ says, "Great will be your reward in the heavens"; and it is often said, that "it shall be rendered unto every one according to his works"; wherefore we acknowledge eternal life to be a reward, because it is our due according to promise, and because God crowns His own gifts, but not on account of our merits (pp. 96, 133, 134, 135, 136, 137, 138). (k) That the good works of believers, when they are performed on account of true causes, and directed to right ends, such as God requires from the regenerate, are signs of eternal salvation; and that God the Father accounts them acceptable and pleasing for Christ's sake, and promises to them excellent rewards of the present life, and of that which is to come (p. 708). (That although good works merit rewards, yet neither from their worthiness nor fitness do they merit the remission of sins, or the glory of eternal life (pp. 96, 135, 139, seq.; Appendix, p. 174). (m) That Christ at the Last Judgment will pass sentence on good and evil works, as the proper effects and evidences of men's faith (p. 134; Appendix, p. 187). (n) That God rewards good works, but that it is of grace that He crowns His own gifts, is asserted in the Confession of the Churches in the Low Countries.

Concerning free-will, from the Formula Concordiae. (a) That man has plenary impotence in spiritual things (pp. 15, 18, 219, 318, 579, 656, seq.; Appendix, p. 141). (b) That man by the fall of his first parents is become so totally corrupt, that he is by nature blind with respect to spiritual things which relate to conversion and salvation, and judges the Word of God to be a foolish thing; and that he is and continues to be an enemy to God, until by the power of the Holy Spirit, through preaching and hearing of the Word, he is of mere grace, without any the least cooperation on his part, converted, gifted with faith, regenerated and renewed (pp. 656, 657). (e) That man is altogether corrupt and dead to what is good, so that in the nature of man, since the fall, and before regeneration, there is not so much as a spark of spiritual strength subsisting or remaining, whereby he can prepare himself for the grace of God, or apprehend it when offered, or of and by himself be capable of receiving it, or understand, believe, embrace, think, will, begin, perfect, act, operate, cooperate in spiritual things, or apply or accommodate himself to grace, or contribute anything towards his conversion, either in the whole, the half, or the least part (pp. 656, 658). (d) That man in spiritual and Divine things, which regard salvation, is like the statue of salt into which Lot's wife was turned, and like a stock or a stone without life, which have neither the use of eyes, mouth, nor any of the senses (pp. 661, 662). (c) That still man has a locomotive power, by virtue whereof he can govern his outward members, attend public assemblies, and hear the Word and the Gospel; but that in his private thoughts he despises it as a foolish thing; and in this respect is worse than a stock, unless the Holy Spirit is efficacious in him (pp. 662, 671, 672, 673). (f) That still it is not with man in his conversion, as in the forming of a stone into a statue, or the stamping of an impression upon wax, which have neither knowledge, sense, nor will (pp. 662, 681). (g) That man in his conversion is a merely passive subject, and not an active one (pp. 662, 681). (h) That man in his conversion does not at all cooperate with the Holy Spirit (pp. 219, 579, 583, 672, 676; Appendix, pp. 143, 144). (i) That man since the fall retains and possesses the faculty of knowing natural things, as also free-will in some measure to choose natural and civil good (pp. 14, 218, 641, 664; Appendix, p. 142). (j) That the assertions of certain fathers, and modern doctors, that God draws man, but draws him in a manner consistent with his will, are not consonant with Holy Scripture (pp. 582-583). (k) That man, when he is born again by the power of the Holy Spirit, cooperates, though in much weakness, from the new powers and gifts, which the Holy Spirit has begun to operate in him at his conversion, not indeed forcibly, but spontaneously (pp. 582, seq., 673-675); Appendix, p. 144). (l) That in the regenerate, not only the gifts of God, but likewise Christ Himself dwells by faith, as in His temples (pp. 695, 697, 698; Appendix, p. 130). (m) There is an immense difference between baptized and not baptized men; for it is the doctrine of Paul, that all who have been baptized, have put on Christ, and are truly regenerate, having thereby acquired a freedom of will, that is to say, being again made free, as Christ testifies, whence they not only hear the Word of God, but are likewise enabled, though in much weakness, to assent to it and embrace it by faith (p. 675). It is proper to observe, that the foregoing extracts are taken from a book called Formula Concordiae, which was composed by men attached to the Augsburg Confession; but that nevertheless the like doctrines concerning justification by faith alone are maintained and taught by the Reformed in England and Holland; wherefore the following treatise is intended for all; see below (n. 17, 18).

A SKETCH OF THE DOCTRINALS OF THE NEW CHURCH. There now follows a brief Exposition of the Doctrine of the New Church, which is meant by the New Jerusalem in Revelation (chaps. 21 and 22). This doctrine, which is not only a doctrine of faith, but also of life, will be divided in the work itself into three parts. THE FIRST PART will treat: I. Of the Lord God the Saviour, and of the Divine Trinity in Him. II. Of the Sacred Scripture, and its Two Senses, the Natural and the Spiritual, and of its Holiness thence derived. III. Of Love to God, and Love towards our Neighbor, and of their Agreement. IV. Of Faith, and its Conjunction with those Two Loves. V. The Doctrine of Life from the Commandments of the Decalogue. VI. Of Reformation and Regeneration. VII. Of Free-Will, and Man's Co-operation with the Lord thereby. VIII. Of Baptism. IX. Of the Holy Supper. X. Of Heaven and Hell. XI. Of Man's Conjunction therewith, and of the State of Man's Life after Death according to that Conjunction. XII. Of Eternal Life. THE SECOND PART will treat: I. Of the Consummation of the Age, or End of the present Church. II. Of the Coming of the Lord. III. Of the Last Judgment. IV. Of the New Church, which is the New Jerusalem. THE THIRD PART will point out the Disagreements between the dogmas of the present church, and those of the New Church. But we will dwell a little upon these now, because it is believed both by the clergy and laity, that the present church is in the light itself of the Gospel and in its truths, which cannot possibly be disproved, overturned, or controverted, not even by an angel if one should descend from heaven: neither does the present church see any otherwise, because it has withdrawn the understanding from faith, and yet has confirmed its dogmas by a kind of sight beneath the understanding, for falsities may there be confirmed even so as to appear like truths; and falsities there confirmed acquire a fallacious light, before which the light of truth appears as thick darkness. For this reason we shall here dwell a little upon this subject, mentioning the disagreements, and illustrating them by brief remarks, that such as have not their understanding closed by a blind faith, may see them as at first in twilight, and afterwards as in morning light, and at length, in the work itself, as in the light of day. The disagreements in general are as follows.

I. The churches which by the Reformation separated themselves from the Roman Catholic Church, differ in various things; but they all agree in the articles concerning a Trinity of Persons in the Divinity, original sin from Adam, imputation of the merit of Christ, and justification by faith alone.

BRIEF ANALYSIS. The churches which by the Reformation separated themselves from the Roman Catholic Church, are from those who call themselves Evangelical and Reformed, likewise Protestants, or from the names of their leaders, Lutherans and Calvinists, among which the church of England holds the middle place. We shall say nothing here of the Greek church, which long ago separated from the Roman Catholic church. That the Protestant churches differ in various things, particularly concerning the Holy Supper, Baptism, election, and the Person of Christ, is known to many; but that they all agree in the articles of a Trinity of Persons in the Divinity, original sin, imputation of the merit of Christ, and justification by faith alone, is not universally known. The reason of this is, because few study into the differences of dogmas among the churches, and consequently the agreements. It is only the clergy that study the dogmas of their church, while the laity rarely enter deeply into them, and consequently into their differences. That nevertheless they agree in the four articles above mentioned, both in their general principles, and in most of the particulars, will appear evident to anyone if he will consult their books, or attend to their sermons. This, however, is premised and brought to the attention, on account of what follows.

II. The Roman Catholics, before the Reformation, taught exactly the same things as the Reformed did after it, concerning the four articles above mentioned, namely, a Trinity of Persons in the Divinity, original sin, the imputation of the merit of Christ, and justification by faith therein, only with this difference, that they conjoined that faith with charity or good works.

BRIEF ANALYSIS. That there is such a conformity between the Roman Catholics and the Protestants in these four articles, so that there is scarcely any important difference, except that the former conjoin faith and charity, while the latter divide between them, is scarcely known to anyone, and indeed is so unknown, that the learned themselves will wonder at the assertion. The reason of this ignorance is, because the Roman Catholics rarely approach God our Saviour, but instead of Him, the Pope as His vicar, and likewise the saints; hence they have deeply buried in oblivion their dogmas concerning the imputation of the merit of Christ, and justification by faith. Nevertheless that these dogmas are received and acknowledged by them, evidently appears from the decrees of the Council of Trent, quoted above (n. 3-8) and confirmed by Pope

Pius IV. (n. 2). If these be compared with the dogmas extracted from the Augsburg Confession, and from the Formula Concordiae thence derived (n. 9-12), the difference between them will be found to be more verbal than real. The doctors of the church, by reading and comparing the above passages together, may indeed see some conformity between them, but still rather obscurely; that these, therefore, as well as those who are less learned, and also the laity, may see this, the subject shall be more clearly illustrated in what follows.

III. The leading reformers, Luther, Melancthon, and Calvin, retained all the dogmas concerning a Trinity of Persons in the Divinity, original sin, imputation of the merit of Christ, and justification by faith, just as they were and had been with the Roman Catholics; but they separated charity or good works from that faith, and declared that they were not at the same time saving, with a view to be totally severed from the Roman Catholics as to the very essentials of the church, which are faith and charity.

BRIEF ANALYSIS. That the four articles above mentioned, as at present taught in the churches of the Reformed were not new, and first broached by those three leaders, but were handed down from the time of the Council of Nice, and taught by the writers after that period, and thus preserved in the Roman Catholic church, is evident from the books of ecclesiastical history. The reason why the Roman Catholics and the Reformed agree in the article of a Trinity of Persons in the Divinity, is, because they both acknowledge the three creeds, the Apostles', the Nicene, and the Athanasian, in which a Trinity is taught That they agree in the article of the imputation of the merit of Christ, is evident from the extracts from the Council of Trent (n. 3-8) compared with those from The Formula Concordiae (n. 10-15). Their agreement in the article of justification shall now be the subject of discussion.

The Council of Trent delivers this concerning justifying faith: "It has always been the consensus of the Catholic church, that faith is the beginning of man's salvation, the foundation and root of all justification, without which it is impossible to please God, and attain to the fellowship of His sons," see above (n. 5). (a) Also, "That faith comes by hearing the Word of God" (n. 4). (c) Moreover that Roman Catholic council joined faith and charity, or faith and good works, may clearly be seen from the quotations above (n. 4, 5, 7, 8). But that the Reformed churches, from their leaders, have separated them, declaring salvation to consist in faith, and not at the same time in charity or works, to the intent that they might be totally severed from the Roman Catholics, as to the very essentials of the church, which are faith and charity, I have frequently heard from the above mentioned leaders themselves. As also, that they established such separation by the following considerations, namely, "that no one can do good which confers salvation of himself, nor can he fulfil the law"; and moreover, lest thereby any merit in man should enter into faith. That from these principles, and with this view, they excluded the goods of charity from faith, and thereby also from salvation, is plain from the quotations from The Formula Concordiae above (n. 12); among which are these: "That faith does not justify, as being formed by charity, as the Papists allege (n. 12). (b) That the position, that good works are necessary to salvation, ought to be rejected for many reasons, and among others, because they are accepted by the Papists to support an evil cause (n. 12). (h) That the decree of the Council of Trent that good works preserve and retain salvation and faith, is deservedly to be rejected" [n. 12 (n)]; besides many other things there. That still, however, the Reformed conjoin faith and charity into one at the same time saving, and only differ from the Roman Catholics respecting the quality of the works, will be shown in the following article.

IV. Nevertheless the leading reformers adjoined good works, and also conjoined them, to their faith, but in man as a passive subject: whereas the Roman Catholics conjoin them in man as an active subject; and that notwithstanding this, there is actually a conformity between the one and the other as to faith, works, and merits.

BRIEF ANALYSIS. That the leading reformers, although they separated faith and charity, still adjoined and even conjoined them, but would not admit of their being united into one, so as to be both together saving, is evident from their books, sermons, and declarations; for after they have separated them, they conjoin them, and even express this conjunction in clear terms, and not in such as admit of two senses; as for instance in the following. That faith after justification is never alone, but is accompanied by charity or good works, and if not, that faith is not living but dead, see above [n. 13 (o) (p) (q) (r) (y) (bb)]. Yea that good works necessarily follow faith [n. 13 (x) (y) (z)]. Then that the regenerate person, by new powers and gifts, cooperates with the Holy Spirit [n. 13 (aa)]. That the Roman Catholics teach exactly the same is plain from the passages collected from the Council of Trent (n. 4-8).

That the reformers profess nearly the same things with the Roman Catholics concerning the merits of works, is evident from the following quotations from The Formula Concordiae That good works are rewarded by virtue of the promise and by grace, and that from thence they merit rewards both temporal and spiritual [n. 14 (i) (k) (l) (n)]. And that God crowns His own gifts with a reward [n. 14 (n)]. The like is asserted in the Council of Trent, namely, That God of His grace makes His own gifts to be merits [n. 5 (f)]. And moreover, that salvation is not of works, but of promise and grace, because God operates them by the Holy Spirit [n. 5 (e) (f) (g) (h) (i) (k)].

From comparing the one and the other, it appears at the first view, as though there was an entire conformity between them; but lest this should be the case, the reformers distinguished between the works of the law proceeding from man's purpose and will, and works of the spirit proceeding from faith as from a free and spontaneous source, which latter they called the fruits of faith, as may be seen above [n. 11. (h) (I)], and [n. 13 (a) (i) (I)], and [n. 15 (k)]. Hence, on an accurate examination and comparison, there does not appear to be any difference in the works themselves, but only in the quality of them, namely, that the latter sort proceed from man as from a passive subject, but the former as from an active subject; consequently they are spontaneous when they proceed from man's understanding, and not at the same time from his will. This is said, because man, while he does good works, cannot but be conscious that he is doing them, and consciousness is from the understanding. Nevertheless, as the Reformed likewise preach the exercise of repentance, and wrestlings with the flesh [n. 13 (d) (p) (f) (g) (h) (k)], and these cannot be done by man but from his purpose and will, and thus by him as from himself, it follows, that there is still an actual conformity.

As regards free-will in conversion, or in the act of justification, it appears as if their dogmas were entirely opposite to each other; but that they still agree, may be seen if we duly consider and compare the passages transcribed from the Council of Trent [n. 6 (a) (b)], with those from The Formula Concordiae [n. 15 (m)]; for in Christian countries all are baptized, and from thence are in a state of free-will, so as to be enabled not only to hear the Word of God, but likewise to assent to the same, and embrace it by faith; consequently no one in the Christian world is like a stock.

Hence then appears the truth of what is asserted (n. 19 and n. 21), namely, that the reformers derived their opinions concerning a Trinity of Persons in the Divinity, original sin, the imputation of the merit of Christ, and justification by faith, from the Roman Catholics. These things have been advanced, in order to point out the origin of their dogmas, especially the origin of the separation of faith from good works, or the doctrine of faith alone, and to show that it was with no other view than to be severed from the Roman Catholics, and that, after all, their disagreement is more in words than in reality. From the passages above adduced, it evidently appears upon what foundation the faith of the Reformed churches has been erected and from what inspiration it took its rise.

V. The whole system of Theology in the Christian world, at this day, is founded on an idea of Three Gods, arising from the doctrine of a Trinity of Persons.

BRIEF ANALYSIS. We will first say something concerning the origin or source from whence the idea of a Trinity of Persons in the Divinity, and thereby of three Gods, proceeded. There are three Creeds, which are called the Apostles', the Nicene, and the Athanasian, which specifically teach a Trinity: the Apostles' and the Nicene assert simply a Trinity, but the Athanasian a Trinity of Persons. These three Creeds are to be met with in many Psalters, the Apostles' Creed next the Psalm which is sung, the Nicene after the Decalogue, and the Athanasian apart by itself. 31-1 The Apostles' Creed was written after the times of the Apostles; the Nicene Creed at the Council of Nice, a city of Bithynia, to which all the bishops in Asia, Africa, and Europe, were summoned by the Emperor Constantine, in the year 325 31-2; but the Athanasian Creed was composed since that council by one or more persons, with an intent utterly to overthrow the Arians and was afterwards received by the churches as oecumenical. In the two former creeds the confession of a Trinity was evident, but from the third or Athanasian Creed the profession of a Trinity of Persons was spread abroad: that hence arose the idea of three Gods, shall now be shown.

That there is a Divine Trinity, is manifest from the Lord's words in Matthew: Jesus said, go make disciples of all nations, baptizing them in the name of the Father, of the Son, and of the Holy Spirit (chap. 28:19). And from these words in the same: When Jesus was baptized, lo, the heavens were opened unto Him, and He saw the Holy Spirit descending like a dove, and coming upon Him, and lo, a voice from heaven, this is My beloved Son, in whom I am well pleased (chap. 3:16, 17). The reason why the Lord sent His disciples to baptize in the name of the Father, Son and Holy Spirit, was, because in Him then glorified there was the Divine Trinity; for in the preceding verse 18, He says: All power is given unto Me in heaven and in earth. And in the 20th verse following: Lo, I am with you all the days, even unto the consummation of the age. Thus He spoke of Himself alone, and not of three. And in John: The Holy Spirit was not yet, because Jesus was not yet glorified (chap. 7:39). The former words He uttered after His glorification, and His glorification was His complete unition with His Father, Who was the Divine itself in Him from conception; and the Holy Spirit was the Divine proceeding from Him glorified (John 20:22).

The reason why the idea of three Gods has principally arisen from the Athanasian Creed, where a Trinity of Persons is taught, is, because the word Person begets such an idea, which is further implanted in the mind by the following words in the same Creed: "There is one Person of the Father, another of the Son, and another of the Holy Spirit"; and afterwards: The Father is God and Lord, the Son is God and Lord, and the Holy Spirit is God and Lord"; but more especially by these: "For like as we are compelled by the Christian verity to acknowledge every Person by Himself to be God and Lord, so are we forbidden by the Catholic religion to say there be three Gods or three Lords"; the result of which words is this, that by the Christian verity we are bound to confess and acknowledge three Gods and three Lords, but by the Catholic religion we are not allowed to say, or to name three Gods and Lords; consequently we may have an idea of three Gods and Lords, but not an oral confession of them. Nevertheless, that the doctrine of the Trinity in the Athanasian Creed is agreeable to the truth, if only instead of a Trinity of Persons there be substituted a Trinity of Person, which Trinity is in God the Saviour Jesus Christ, may be seen in The Doctrine of the New Jerusalem concerning the Lord, published at Amsterdam, in the year 1763 (n. 55-61.)

It is to be observed, that in the Apostles' Creed it is said, "I believe in God the Father, in Jesus Christ, and in the Holy Spirit"; in the Nicene Creed, "I believe in one God, the Father, in one Lord Jesus Christ, and in the Holy Spirit," thus only in one God; but in the Athanasian Creed it is, "In God the Father, God the Son, and God the Holy Spirit," thus in three Gods. But whereas the authors and favorers of this creed clearly saw that an idea of three Gods would unavoidably result from the expressions therein used, therefore, in order to remedy this, they asserted that one substance or essence belongs to the three; but still there arises from thence no other idea, than that there are three Gods unanimous and agreeing together: for when it is said of the three that their substance or essence is one and indivisible, it does not remove the idea of three, but confounds it, because the expression is a metaphysical one, and the science of metaphysics, with all its ingenuity, cannot of three Persons, each whereof is God, make one; it may indeed make of them one in the mouth, but never in the idea.

That the whole Christian theology at this day is founded on an idea of three Gods, is evident from the doctrine of justification, which is the head of the doctrines of the church with Christians, both among Roman Catholics and Protestants. That doctrine sets forth that God the Father sent His Son to redeem and save men, and give the Holy Spirit to operate the same; every man who hears, reads, or repeats this, cannot but in his thought, that is, in his idea, divide God into three, and perceive that one God sent another, and operates by a third. That the same thought of a Divine Trinity distinguished into three Persons, each whereof is God, is continued throughout the rest of the doctrinals of the present church, as from a head into its body, will be demonstrated in its proper place. In the meantime consult what has been premised concerning justification, consult theology in general and in particular, and at the same time, consult yourself, while listening to preachings in temples, or while praying at home, whether you have any other perception and thought thence resulting than of three Gods; and especially while you are praying or singing first to one, and then to the other two separately, as is often done. Hence is established the truth of the proposition, that the whole theology in the Christian world at this day, is founded on an idea of three Gods.

That a trinity of Gods is contrary to the Sacred Scripture, is known, for we read: Am not I Jehovah, and there is no God else beside Me, a just God and a Saviour, there is none beside Me (Isa. 45:21, 22). I Jehovah am thy God, and thou shalt acknowledge no God beside Me, and there is no Saviour beside Me (Hos. 13:4). Thus said Jehovah the King of Israel and his Redeemer, Jehovah of Hosts, I am the First and the Last, and beside Me there is no God (Isa. 46:6). Jehovah of Hosts is His name, and thy Redeemer the Holy One of Israel, the God of the whole earth shall He be called (Isa. 54:5). In that day Jehovah shall be King over the whole earth; in that day there shall be one Jehovah, and His name One (Zech. 14:9). Beside many more passages elsewhere.

That a trinity of Gods is contrary to enlightened reason, may appear from many considerations. What man of sound reason can bear to hear that three Gods created the world; or that creation and preservation, redemption and salvation, together with reformation and regeneration, are the work of three Gods, and not of one God? And on the other hand, what man of sound reason is not willing to hear that the same God who created us, redeemed us, and regenerates and saves us? As the latter sentiment, and not the former, enters into the reason, there is therefore no nation upon the face of the whole earth, possessed of religion and sound reason, but what acknowledges one God. That the Mohammedans, and certain nations in Asia and Africa, abhor Christianity, because they believe that it worships three Gods, is known; and the only answer of the Christians is, that the three have one essence, and thus are one God. I can affirm, that from the reason which has been given me, I can clearly see, that neither the world, nor the angelic heaven, nor the church, nor anything therein, could have existed, nor can subsist, but from one God.

Here I will add something from the Confession of the Dutch Churches received at the Synod of Dort, which is this: "I believe in one God, who is one essence, in which are three Persons, truly and really distinct, incommunicable properties from eternity, namely, the Father, the Son, and the Holy Spirit; the Father is of all things, both visible and invisible, the cause, origin, and beginning; the Son is the Word, wisdom, and image of the Father; the Holy Spirit is the eternal virtue and power proceeding from the Father and the Son. However, it must be confessed, that this doctrine far exceeds the comprehension of the human mind; we must therefore wait till we come to heaven for a perfect knowledge thereof."

VI. The dogmas of that theology appear to be erroneous, after the idea of a Trinity of Persons, and thence of three Gods, has been rejected, and the idea of One God, in whom is the Divine Trinity, is received in its stead.

BRIEF ANALYSIS. The reason why the dogmas of the present church, which are founded upon the idea of three Gods, derived from the doctrine of a Trinity of Persons literally understood, appear erroneous, after the idea of one God, in whom is the Divine Trinity, has been received in its stead, is, because, till this truth is received, we cannot see what is erroneous. The case herein is like a person, who in the night time, by the light of some stars only, sees various objects, especially images, and believes them to be living men; or like one, who in the twilight before sunrise, as he lies in his bed, fancies he sees specters in the air, and believes them to be angels; or like a person, who sees many things in the delusive light of fantasy, and believes them to be real; such things, it is known, do not appear according to their true qualities, until the person comes into the light of the day, that is, until he comes into the light of the understanding awake. The case is the same with the spiritual things of the church, which have been erroneously and falsely perceived, and also confirmed, when genuine truths also present themselves to be seen in their own light, which is the light of heaven. Who is there that cannot understand, that all dogmas founded on the idea of three Gods, must be interiorly erroneous and false? I say interiorly, because the idea of God enters into all things of the church, religion, and worship; and theological matters have their residence above all others in the human mind, and the idea of God is in the supreme place there; wherefore if this be false, all beneath it, in consequence of the principle from whence they flow, must likewise be false or falsified; for that which is supreme, being also the inmost, constitutes the very essence of all that is derived from it; and the essence, like a soul, forms them into a body, after its own image; and when in its descent it lights upon truths, it even infects them with its own blemish and error. The idea of three Gods in theology may be compared to a disease seated in the heart or lungs, in which the patient fancies himself to be in health, because his physician, not knowing his disease, persuades him that he is so; but if the physician knows it, and still persuades, he may justly be charged with deep malignity.

VII. Then truly saving faith, which is faith in one God, united, with good works, is acknowledged and received.

BRIEF ANALYSIS. The reason why this faith, which is a faith in one God, is acknowledged and received as truly saving, when the former faith, which is a faith in three gods, is rejected, is because till this is the case it cannot be seen in its own form; for the faith of the present day is set forth as the only saving faith, because it is a faith in one God, and a faith in the Savior; but still there are two faces of that faith, the one internal and the other external; its internal face is formed from the perception of three Gods, for who perceives or thinks otherwise? let every one consult himself; but its external face is formed from the confession of one God, for who confesses or speaks otherwise? let every one consult himself. These two faces are altogether discordant with each other; so that the external is not acknowledged by the internal, nor is the internal known by the external. From this disagreement, and the vanishing of the one out of sight of the other, a confused idea of things pertaining to salvation has been conceived and brought forth in the church. It is otherwise when the internal and external faces agree together, and mutually regard and acknowledge each other as one unanimous thing; that this is the case, when one God, in whom is the Divine Trinity, is not only perceived by the mind, but is likewise acknowledged by the mouth, is self-evident. That the dogma of the Father's being alienated from mankind, is then abolished, and thence also that of His reconciliation; and that an altogether different doctrine goes forth concerning imputation, remission of sins, regeneration, and salvation thence derived, will clearly be seen in the work itself, in the light of reason illustrated by Divine truths from the Sacred Scripture. This faith is called a faith united with good works, because faith in one God without union with good works is not given.

VIII. And this faith is in God the Savior Jesus Christ which in its simple form is as follows: I. That there is One God in Whom is the Divine Trinity, and He is the Lord Jesus Christ. II. Saving Faith is to believe in Him. III. Evils ought to be shunned, because they are of the devil, and from the devil. IV. Goods ought to be done, because they are of God, and from God. V. And they ought to be done by man as of himself, but it is to be believed that they are from the Lord, with him and through him.

BRIEF ANALYSIS. This is the faith of the New Church in its simple form, which will appear more fully in the Appendix, and in its full form in the work itself, in its First Part; where we shall treat of the Lord God the Saviour, and of the Trinity in Him; of love to God, and love towards the neighbor; of faith and its conjunction with those two loves; and also in the other parts, which will follow in order there. But it is necessary that this preliminary concerning that faith should here be briefly illustrated. Its first, namely, That there is one God, in whom there is the Divine Trinity, and He is the Lord Jesus Christ, is summarily illustrated in the following manner. It is a certain and established truth, that God is one, and His essence is indivisible, and that there is a Trinity; since, therefore, God is One, and His essence is indivisible, it follows, that God is one Person, and when He is one Person, that the Trinity is in that Person. That this is the Lord Jesus Christ, appears from this, that He was conceived from God the Father (Luke 1:34, 35); and thus as to His soul and life itself He is God; and therefore, as He Himself said, that: The Father and He are One (John 10:30). He is in the Father, and the Father in Him (John 14:10, 11). He who seeth Him and knoweth Him, seeth and knoweth the Father (John 14:7, 9). No one seeth and knoweth the Father, but He who is in the bosom of the Father (John 1:18). All things of the Father are His (John 3:35; 16:15). He is the Way, the Truth, and the Life, and no one cometh unto the Father but by Him (John 14:6); thus from Him, because He is in Him, and thus is He Himself; and according to Paul that: All the fulness of the Divinity dwells in Him bodily (Col. 2:9). And according to Isaiah: Unto us a Boy is born, unto us a Son is given, whose name is God, Father of Eternity (9:5). And again, that: He hath power over all flesh (John 17:2). And: He hath all power in heaven and on earth (Matt. 28:18). Thence it follows that He is the God of heaven and earth. Second, That saving faith is to believe in Him, is illustrated by these: Jesus said, he that believeth in Me, shall not die to eternity, but shall live (John 11:25, 26). This is the will of the Father, that everyone who believeth in the Son may have eternal life (John 6:40). God so loved the world, that He gave His Only-begotten Son, that whosoever believeth in Him, should not perish, but have eternal life (John 3:15, 16). He that believeth in the Son, hath eternal life, but he that believeth not the Son, shall not see life, but the wrath of God abideth on him (John 3:36). The three remaining propositions, namely, That evils ought to be shunned, because they are of the devil and from the devil; and that goods ought to be done, because they are of God and from God; but that it is to be believed that they are from the Lord, with him and through him. There is no need to illustrate and demonstrate these; for the whole Sacred Scripture, from beginning to end, proves them, and, in short, teaches nothing else but to shun evils, and do goods, and to believe in the Lord God. Besides, without these three there is not any religion, for religion is of the life; and life is to shun evils and do goods, and man cannot do goods and shun evils except as of himself. Wherefore if these three are removed from the church, the Sacred Scripture, together with religion, is likewise removed at the same time: which being removed the church is not a church. For a further account of the faith of the New Church, in its universal and particular form, see below (n. 116, 117); all which will be demonstrated in the work itself.

IX. The faith of the present day has separated religion from the church, since religion consists in the acknowledgment of One God, and in the worship of Him from the faith of charity.

BRIEF ANALYSIS. What nation is there in the whole world, which has religion and sound reason, that does not know and believe, that there is one God, and that to do evils is contrary to Him, and that to do goods is with Him, and that man must do this from his soul, from his heart, and from his strength, although they inflow from God, and that herein religion consists? Who therefore does not see, that to confess three Persons in the Divinity, and to declare that in good works there is nothing of salvation, is to separate religion from the church? For it is declared that in good works there is not salvation, in these words: That faith justifies without good works [n. 12 (a) (b)]; that works are not necessary to salvation, nor to faith, because salvation and faith are neither preserved nor retained by good works [n. 12 (g) (h) (m) (n)]; consequently, that there is no bond of conjunction between faith and good works. It is indeed said afterwards, that good works nevertheless spontaneously follow faith, as fruit is produced from a tree [n. 13 (i) (n)]. But then who does them, yea, who thinks of them, or who is spontaneously led to perform them, while he knows and believes that they contribute nothing to salvation, and also, that no one can do any good thing towards salvation of himself, and so on? If it is said, that still they have conjoined faith with good works; we reply, this conjunction when closely inspected, is not conjunction, but it is mere adjunction, and this only like a superfluous appendage, that neither coheres nor adheres in any other manner than as a dark background to a picture, from which the picture appears more living. And because religion is of the life, and this consists in good works according to the truths of faith, it is evident that religion is the picture itself, and not the mere appendage; yea, with many it is like the tail of a horse, which because it avails nothing, may be cut off at pleasure. Who can rationally conclude otherwise, while he perceives such expressions as these according to their obvious meaning: That it is a folly to dream that the works of the second table of the Decalogue justify before God [n. 12 (d)]; and these: That if any one believes he shall therefore obtain salvation, because he hath charity, he brings reproach upon Christ [n. 12 (e)]; as also these: That good works are utterly to be excluded, in treating of justification and eternal life [n. 12 (f)]; with more to the same purpose? Who, therefore, when he reads afterwards, that good works necessarily follow faith, and that if they do not follow, the faith is a false and not a true faith [n. 13 (p) (q) (y)], with more to the same purpose, attends to it? or if he attends to it, understands whether such good works are attended with any perception? Yet good flowing forth from man without perception is inanimate as if from a statue. But if we inquire more deeply into the rise of this doctrine, it will appear as though the leading reformers first laid down faith alone as their rule, in order that they might be severed from the Roman Catholics, as mentioned above (n. 21, 22, 23); and that afterwards they adjoined thereto the works of charity, that it might not appear to contradict the Sacred Scripture, but have the semblance of religion, and thus be healed.

X. The faith of the present church cannot be conjoined with charity, and produce any fruits, which are good works.

BRIEF ANALYSIS. Before this is demonstrated, we shall first explain the origin and nature of charity, and the origin and nature of faith, and thus the origin and nature of good works, which are called fruits. Faith is truth, wherefore the doctrine of faith is the doctrine of truth; and the doctrine of truth is of the understanding, and thence of the thought, and from this of the speech; wherefore it teaches what we are to will and do, thud that evils and what evils are to be shunned, and that goods and what goods are to be done. When man does goods then goods thence conjoin themselves with truths, because the will is conjoined with the understanding, for good is of the will, and truth is of the understanding; from this conjunction the affection of good exists, which in its essence is charity, and the affection of truth, which in its essence is faith, and these two united together constitute a marriage. From this marriage good works are produced, as fruits from a tree; and hence they are the fruits of good, and the fruits of truth; the latter are signified in the Word by grapes, but the former by olives.

From this generation of good works, it is evident, that faith alone cannot possibly produce or beget any works, that are called fruits, any more than a woman alone without a man can produce any offspring; wherefore the fruits of faith is an empty expression and word. Besides, in the whole world nothing ever was or can be produced, but from a marriage, one of which has relation to good, and the other to truth, or in the opposite sense, one to evil, and the other to falsity; consequently no works can be conceived, much less be born but from such marriage, good works from the marriage of good and truth, and evil works from the marriage of evil and falsity.

The reason why charity cannot be conjoined with the faith of the present church, and consequently why good works cannot be born from any marriage, is because imputation supplies everything, remits guilt, justifies, regenerates, sanctifies, imparts the life of heaven and thus salvation, and all this freely, without any works of man; what then is charity, which ought to be united with faith, but something superfluous and vain, and a mere addition and supplement to imputation and justification, to which nevertheless it is of no avail? Besides, a faith founded on the idea of three Gods is erroneous, as has been shown above (n. 39, 40); and with an erroneous faith, charity, that in itself is charity, cannot be conjoined. There are two reasons given for believing that there is no bond of union between that faith and charity; the one is, because they make their faith spiritual, but charity natural moral, thinking that there is not given any conjunction of the spiritual with the natural; the other reason is, lest anything of man, and so anything of merit, should inflow into their faith alone, as saving. Furthermore, between charity and that faith there is no bond, but there is with the new faith, which may be seen below (n. 116, 117).

Footnotes
31-1 This relates to the Protestant churches on the continent of Europe.
31-2 The original Latin has "anno 318," in the year 318. There were 318 bishops in attendance; the Council met in the year 325.

De Verbo

I. THE SENSE OF THE LETTER OF THE WORD, IN WHICH IS THE SPIRITUAL SENSE, REPRESENTED. It was given to see great purses, appearing like sacks, in which was hidden silver in great abundance; and, since these sacks were open, it seemed as if anyone might take from the silver placed therein, yea, steal from it; but near the sacks sat two angels who were guards. The place where the sacks were deposited appeared like a manger in a stable. In the next chamber were seen modest virgins together with a chaste wife, and near that chamber were two infants, and it was said that they were not to be played with in a childish manner, but wisely. Afterwards there appeared a harlot, and then a horse lying dead. It was then perceived that thus was represented the sense of the letter of the Word, in which is the spiritual sense. 1-1 Those great purses filled with silver signified the knowledges of truth in great abundance therein. That they were open and yet guarded by angels, signified that everyone may take thence the knowledges of truth, but that care must be taken lest its interior sense in which is nothing but verities be falsified. The manger in the stable where the sacks lay, signified spiritual instruction for the understanding. A manger signifies this, even the one wherein the Lord was laid when born; for a horse signifies the understanding: hence a manger signifies its nourishment. The modest virgins who were seen in the next chamber signified the truths of the church, and the chaste wife signified the conjunction of truth and good which is everywhere in the Word. The infants signified the innocence of wisdom in the Word; they were angels from the third heaven who all appear like infants. The harlot, with the dead horse, signified the falsification of the Word by many at this day, whereby all understanding of truth is destroyed; a harlot signifies falsification, and a dead horse, no understanding of truth.

II. THE WORD INWARDLY IS LIVING. When the Word is read by a man who esteems it holy, its natural sense then becomes spiritual in the second heaven, and celestial in the third heaven, thus it is successively stripped of its natural (sense); the reason is, because the natural, spiritual, and celestial (senses) correspond to each other, and the Word is written by mere correspondences. The natural sense of the Word is such as it is in the sense of the letter, every particular of which becomes spiritual, and afterwards celestial in the heavens; and when it becomes spiritual it then lives in heaven from the light of truth therein, and when it becomes celestial, it lives from the flame of good therein; for spiritual ideas, with the angels of the second heaven, derive their origin from the light existing there, which in its essence is Divine Truth; but the celestial ideas, with the angels of the third heaven, derive their origin from the flame of good, which in its essence is Divine Good. For in the second heaven there is a white light, from which the angels who are in that heaven think, and in the third heaven there is a flaming light, from which the angels who are in that heaven think. The thoughts of angels differ entirely from the thoughts of men; they think by lights either bright white or flamy, which are such that they can never be described in natural language. From this it appears that the Word is inwardly living, consequently that it is not dead, but alive with that man who, while reading the Word, thinks holily concerning it. Moreover, everything of the Word is vivified by the Lord; because with the Lord it becomes life, as the Lord also says in John: The words which I speak unto you, they are spirit and they are life (John 6:63). The life, which by means of the Word flows in from the Lord, is the light of truth in the understanding, and the love of good in the will; this love and that light constitute together the life of heaven, which life with man is called eternal life. The Lord also teaches: God was the Word, in Him was life, and the life was the light of men (John 1:4.)

III. THE DIFFERENCE IN GENERAL BETWEEN THE NATURAL, THE SPIRITUAL, AND THE CELESTIAL. There are three heavens, the lowest, the middle, and the highest; in the lowest heaven they are natural, but their natural is derived either from the spiritual, which is of the middle heaven or from the celestial, which is of the third heaven. In the second heaven they are spiritual, and in the third heaven celestial; there are also intermediate angels who are called spiritual-celestial; many from these are preachers in the highest heaven. [2] The difference between the natural, the spiritual, and the celestial is such, that there is no ratio between them, for which reason the natural can in no wise by any approximation approach towards the spiritual, nor the spiritual towards the natural; hence it is that the heavens are distinct. This it has been given me to know by much experience; I have often been sent among the spiritual angels, and I then spoke with them spiritually, and then, retaining in my memory what I had spoken, when I returned into my natural state, in which every man is in this world, I then wished to bring it forth from the former memory and describe it, but I could not, it was impossible; there were no expressions, nor even ideas of thought, by which I could express it; they were spiritual ideas of thought and spiritual expressions so remote from natural ideas of thought and natural expressions, that they did not approximate in the least. What is wonderful, when I was in that heaven and conversing with the angels, then I knew no otherwise than that I spoke in like manner as I speak with men; but afterwards I found that the thoughts and the discourses were so unlike that they could not be approximated, consequently that there is no ratio between them. [3] There is a similar difference between the spiritual and the celestial. I was told that there is a similar difference, and that it is such, that there is given no ratio or approximation between them; but as I could not be confirmed in this by my own experience, unless I was altogether an angel of the middle heaven, therefore it has been granted to some angels of the middle heaven to be with angels of the third heaven, and then to think and speak there with them, also to retain in their memory what they had been thinking and speaking, and afterwards to return into their own heaven; and they told me from that heaven that they were not able to express a single idea or a single word of their former state, and that it was impossible, and lastly they said, that there is no ratio nor any approximation between them. [4] It has accordingly been sometimes granted me to be among the angels of the middle and of the highest heaven, and to hear them conversing with one another, at which time I was in an interior natural state, removed from worldly and corporeal things, namely, when first waking after sleep; then I heard things unutterable and inexpressible, as we read happened with Paul; and sometimes I was let into the perception and understanding of the subjects they were conversing upon; the subjects they conversed upon were full of arcana concerning the Lord, redemption, regeneration, providence, and other similar things: after which it was given me to understand that I could not utter nor describe them by any spiritual or celestial expression, but that nevertheless they could be described even to their rational comprehension by words of natural language. And it was told me that there is not any Divine arcana which may not be perceived, and even expressed naturally, although more generally and imperfectly; and that they who, in a natural manner, by means of their rational understanding, perceive those things from the affection of truth, afterwards, when they become spirits, can perceive and speak of them in a spiritual manner, and when they become angels, in a celestial manner, but no others. For one Divine truth naturally perceived and loved, is like a crystal or porcelain vessel, which is afterwards filled with wine, and with such wine as the nature of the truth was, and as it were of such a taste as the affection of the truth was. [5] That there is such a difference, which may be termed unlimited, between the natural, the spiritual, and the celestial, may clearly appear from the difference between the thoughts of men and angels, as well as from the difference of their speech and operations, and also from the difference of their writings; from all which, as from so many confirmations, it will appear what the quality is of each, and in what manner the perfections in everything ascend and pass from the world into heaven and from heaven to heaven. [6] As regards thoughts: all the thoughts of man, together with the single ideas thereof, derive something from space, time, person, and matter, which appear in natural light or the light of the world, for nothing can be thought without light, in like manner as nothing can be seen without light, and natural light or the light of the world is dead, because it is from its sun, which is pure fire; nevertheless the light of heaven everywhere and constantly flows into and vivifies that light, communicating perception and understanding of the subject. The light of the world alone cannot give anything perceptive and intellectual, or present any natural or rational light [lumen]; but the light of the world gives and presents it from the light of heaven, because the light of heaven is from its sun, which is the Lord, and thence life itself. The influx of heavenly light into the light of the world is like the influx of the cause into the effect; the nature of this influx shall be explained elsewhere. From this it appears what the quality of natural thought is, or what quality the ideas of men's thoughts are, namely, that they inseparably cohere with space, time, with what is personal, and material; consequently, such thoughts or ideas of thoughts are very limited and bounded and thus gross, and to be called material. But the thoughts of the angels of the middle heaven are all without space, time, or what is personal, and material, for which reason they are unlimited and unbounded; the objects of their thoughts are spiritual like the thoughts themselves, for which reason they think concerning those objects spiritually and not naturally. But with regard to the angels of the highest heaven, they have no thoughts, but perceptions of the things which they hear and see; instead of thoughts they have affections, which with them are varied in like manner as thoughts are varied with the spiritual angels. [7] As regards speech: the speech of men is according to their ideas of thoughts, for the ideas of thought become expressions when they pass into speech; for which reason the speech of man in every expression partakes of space, time, what is personal, and material. But the speech of the angels of the middle heaven is also like the ideas of their thought, for the words of speech express them. But the speech of the angels of the highest heaven is from the variation of their affections; but when they are speaking with the spiritual angels they speak in a similar manner, but not so when conversing with each other. Since such is the speech of angels, and such the speech of men, therefore their speech differs so much that they have nothing in common; their difference is such that a man cannot understand a single expression of an angel, nor an angel a single expression of a man. I have heard the speech of angels, and retained the expressions, and I afterwards examined whether any expression coincided with any word of the speech or languages of men, and there was not one. Spiritual speech is the same with all, and is implanted in every man, and he comes into it as soon as he becomes a spirit. As regards writing, it is similar to their speech. The writing of the spiritual angels as to the letters resembles the writing of men in the world, but every letter signifies a thing, so that you would say if you saw it in a natural state, that it consisted merely of letters; but writings in the highest heaven have no resemblance as to letters, for with them letters are drawn in various curvatures, not unlike the letters of the Hebrew language, but everywhere inflected, and not consisting merely of lines. Every letter involves a thing, of which they have a perception from affection, and not from thought. Hence it is that the natural comprehends nothing of spiritual writing, nor the spiritual of natural writing; neither does the spiritual comprehend anything of celestial writing, nor the celestial of spiritual writing, unless he is with the spiritual. [8] Their operations, which are many, are similar, for every one is in some work. How the spiritual work cannot be described to the natural; nor can it be described to the spiritual, how the celestial angels work; for they differ as much as in their thoughts, speech, and writings. [9] From these things it is evident, what the difference is between the natural, the spiritual, and the celestial, that it is such that they do not at all agree except by correspondences; which is also the reason that men do not know that they are in consociation with spirits, and spirits that they are in consociation with men, when nevertheless the consociation is continual; for man cannot live a single instant, unless he is in the midst of spirits as to his thoughts and affections; neither can a spirit or an angel live a single moment unless he is with man; the reason is, because there is a perpetual conjunction from firsts to ultimates, thus from the Lord to man; and conjunction from creation is effected by correspondences, and flows in through angels and spirits. Everything celestial flows into the spiritual, and the spiritual into the natural, and terminates and subsists in the ultimate of this, which is the corporeal and material. Without such an ultimate, into which the intermediates flow, there is no subsistence, otherwise than like a house built in the air; wherefore the basis and the foundation of the heavens is the human race. [10] No angel knows that there is such a difference between the natural, the spiritual, and the celestial; the reason is, because an angel does not change his state, nor pass from a spiritual into a natural state, and thus be able to explore the differences. I have spoken with them on this subject, and they said they did not know the differences. They believed that they thought, spoke, wrote, and worked in the same manner as in the world. But the difference was shown them by this, that they changed states, and thought first in one state, then in the other by turns, then in like manner that they spoke by turns in one state and then in another, and further that they read their writings in a spiritual state and in a natural state, and in like manner worked, then they found that there is such a difference as cannot be described. On this subject it was granted me to instruct the angels themselves, because it has been granted me to be alternately in both worlds, and from the one to explore the other, and they all afterwards confessed that it was so. [11] But the similitude of the natural, spiritual, and celestial states is in such things as are objects of sight, taste, smell, and hearing, also the sense of touch of various kinds. In their sight they appear like men in the world. Their garments so appear, also their houses, and gardens, or paradises, as also fields, likewise land and water, food and drink of various kinds, besides animals of the earth, the flying things of heaven, and fishes in waters, of various kinds and of various species. Their speech is heard as in the world, likewise singing and musical modulations. Taste is similar, and also odor; in a word, everything that appears and is perceived by any of the senses. But still those things are from a spiritual origin, and therefore they think of them spiritually and give them spiritual names. But even all these things, in what manner they appear and are perceived in the middle and highest heaven, as to the excellence of their forms and harmonies, and as to their perfections, which are supereminent and transcendent, can only be described in an imperfect manner, only as it were by the most perfect things in the world, which nevertheless are imperfect, respectively to those things which are in heaven.

IV. THE WORD IS HOLY, EVEN AS TO SYLLABLES AND POINTS. Once there was sent me from heaven a little paper written over with Hebrew letters, but written as with the most ancient people, with whom the letters which at this day are in some part rectilinear, were at that time curved, with little horns turning upwards. The angel who was with me said that he knew whole meanings from the letters themselves; that every letter had its own meaning, and that they knew that meaning from the curves of the lines in each letter, besides they knew the subject from each letter by itself. He then explained to me what [A] signified, and what _ [H]; what those letters meant separately, and what when combined; that _, which is in ____ [Jehovah], and which was added to the names of Abraham and Sarai, signified what is infinite and eternal. And thus the Word is so written in many places, whereby when it is read by a Jew or a Christian in the Hebrew text, it may be known in the third heaven what the very letters signify. For the angels of the third heaven have the Word written in such letters, and they read it according to the letters. They said that in the sense extracted from the letters, the Word treats of the Lord alone. The reason for this is that the curvatures in the letters derive their origin from the flow of heaven, in which the angels of the third heaven are, above all others. Wherefore these angels are skilled in that writing from what is implanted in them, because they are in the order of heaven, and live altogether according to it. They also explained in my presence the sense of the Word (Ps. 32:2), from the letters or syllables alone, saying that their meaning was, in a summary, that the Lord is merciful, even to those who do evil. They added that the vowels there are for the sake of the sound, which corresponds to the affection, and that they cannot utter the vowels i and e, but for i they pronounce y or eu, and for e pronounce eu, and that the vowels a, o and u are in use with them, because these vowels give a full sound, while i and e have a close sound. 4-1 They said further that they do not pronounce any consonants with aspiration, but with a smooth sound, and that the aspirated letters, as _ [dh] and _ [qh] and others, do not mean anything to them, except when uttered with a smooth sound, and that for this reason most aspirated letters have also a point within, which signifies that they are to be uttered with a smooth sound. They added that roughness, or aspiration, in the letters is in use in the spiritual heaven, because there they are in truths, and by means of truths in understanding; but in the celestial heaven all are in the good of love and thence in wisdom, and truth admits of roughness, but not good. From these things it may be evident what is signified by the Lord's saying, that not a jot, tittle, or little curve shall pass from the Law (Matt. 5:18; Luke 16:17); and it is also plain that it was of the Divine providence of the Lord that all the letters of the Word in the Hebrew text were counted by the Masorites.

V. THE SPIRITUAL SENSE OF THE WORD AND ITS NATURAL SENSE. I have spoken at times with spirits who did not wish to know anything about the spiritual sense of the Word, saying that its natural sense is the only sense of the Word, and that this is holy because it is from God; and they asserted that if the spiritual sense were to be accepted, the Word in the letter would become nothing. There were many who insisted upon this, but they were answered from heaven that the Word without the spiritual sense within it would not be Divine; and because the spiritual sense is its soul, it is thence Divine, yea, living, for without it the letter would be as it were dead; the very holiness of the Word consists in this. The Word may thus be compared to the Divine Man who is the Lord, in whom there is not only the Divine natural, but also the Divine spiritual and the Divine celestial; it is on this account that the Lord calls Himself the Word. And the angels said that the very holiness of the Word is in the sense of its letter, and that this is more holy than the other senses, which are internal, because it is the complex and containant of the rest, and is like the body living from the soul. Thus the Word in the sense of the letter, or the natural, is in its fullness, and also in its power; and by means of it man is in conjunction with the heavens, which, without the sense of the letter, would be separated from man. Who does not know and acknowledge that the Word in its bosom is spiritual? But where the spiritual is stored up, has hitherto lain concealed. [2] But because the spirits who stood for the sense of the letter alone, were not willing to be convinced by these reasons, the angels brought forward innumerable passages from the natural sense which could never be comprehended without the spiritual sense. As in the Prophets, where mere names are heaped up; where many kinds of animals are mentioned such as lions, bears, oxen, bullocks, dogs, foxes, owls, ijim, dragons; as also mountains and forests, besides many other things which would have no meaning without the spiritual sense. What, for instance, should be understood by the dragon who is described as red, having seven heads, and upon the heads seven diadems, and who by his tail drew down the third part of the stars of heaven and who sought to devour the offspring which the woman was about to bring forth; and that two wings of a great eagle were given to the woman, that she might fly into the desert, where the dragon cast after her water as a river out of his mouth. Again, without the spiritual sense it could not be known what should be understood by the two beasts of the dragon: the one ascending out of the sea, like a leopard, with feet as of a bear, and a mouth as of a lion, and the other beast ascending from the earth, of which it is spoken in the Apocalypse (12 and 13). Again, what is there meant in the sixth chapter of the Apocalypse, by the horses which went forth when the Lamb opened the seals of the book: first a white horse, afterwards a red one, then a black, and finally a pale horse; besides all the other things in that book? Also what is meant in Zachariah by the four horns and the four artificers (Chapter 2); by the lampstand and the two olive trees near it (Chapter 4); by the four chariots going forth between two mountains to which were horses, red, black, white, and grizzled (Chapter 6)? Or, again, in Daniel viii., what is meant by the ram and the he-goat, and by their horns with which they fought each other; and by the four beasts ascending from the sea (Chap. 7), besides similar things elsewhere in great abundance? In order that they might still further be convinced, the angels quoted what the Lord said to His disciples, in Matthew (Chap. 24), about the consummation of the age and His coming, which could be understood by no one without the spiritual sense. [3] That the spiritual sense is in each and all of the things or the Word, was also confirmed by certain things said by the Lord which could not be comprehended unless they were understood spiritually, as that no one should call his father on earth, father, nor any one, teacher, or master, because one is their Father, Teacher, and Master (Matt. 13:7-10); also that they should not judge, lest they be judged (Matt. 7:1, 2); and that a husband and wife are not two, but one flesh (Matt. 19:5, 6), when yet in the natural sense they are not one flesh; neither is it forbidden to judge concerning a companion and neighbor as to his natural life, for this is of importance in society; but it is forbidden to judge of him as to his spiritual life, for this is known to the Lord alone. So too the Lord did not forbid calling a father, father, neither a teacher, teacher, nor a master, master, in the natural sense, but in the spiritual sense, in which there is only one Father, Teacher, and Master: so in other cases. [4] From these illustrations the spirits were convinced that there is a spiritual sense within the natural sense of the Word, and that still the very holiness of the Word is in the sense of its letter, because all the interior senses of the Word are in that in their fullness. Moreover it was confirmed that in the sense of the letter all things which teach the way to salvation, thus to life and faith, stand forth clearly, also that every doctrine of the church is to be drawn from the sense of the letter of the Word and confirmed thereby, and not by the pure spiritual sense; for conjunction with heaven, and through heaven with the Lord, is not given by this sense alone, but by the sense of the letter; and the Divine influx of the Lord through the Word is from firsts through ultimates.

   VI. THE WORD, AND NATURAL THEOLOGY: THIS THEOLOGY IS NOTHING WITHOUT THE WORD, AND UNLESS DERIVED FROM IT. THE EXCELLENCE OF THE STYLE IN THE WORD. I once heard a grave dispute among spirits who in the world had been learned, some of them from the Word and some from natural light alone; the latter insisted that natural theology is sufficient, and that this can teach, yea, enlighten man, without the Word, and enable him to discern that there is a God, that there is a heaven and a hell, and that the soul has immortality and thus eternal life; but the former ones said that the Word alone teaches and gives light on these subjects. The spirits who were for natural theology alone, greatly infested those who were for the Word, and this for several days: thinking at heart, and at last saying, that the Word is not anything, that it is written in a style so simple and at the same time so obscure, in very many places, that no one can be taught, and still less be enlightened by it, and that the writings of the learned by far surpass it, as for instance the writings of Cicero, Seneca, and of some of the learned at this day. But reply was made to them, that the style of the Word is more excellent than the style of all the learned in the whole world, since in the former there is not a sentence, nor even a word or a letter, which does not contain within itself something of the Lord and thence something of heaven and the church. For the Word is from God, and thence in its bosom it is spiritual, and this Divine lies hidden there interiorly, as the soul is hidden in the body; and when man reads it devoutly, this Divine is unfolded in order before the angels, who are affected by the spiritual sanctity unfolded therein, and this is communicated to man. Hence it is clear that the very style of the Word, however simple it may appear, is infinitely superior to any style of the most learned in the world; for the latter, although the sense may be both elegant and sublime, still it does not effect communication with heaven, and thus, compared with the style of the Word, it is of no value at all. [2] The spirits who were in favor of natural theology heard these things indeed, but still rejected them, because in the world they had utterly despised the Word, and those who despise the Word in the world, and confirm their contempt by passages from it, continue to despise it after death; for every principle adopted and confirmed in the world concerning God and the Word, remains enrooted after death, neither can it be torn out. Since therefore these spirits did not communicate with heaven, but with hell, they began to conjoin themselves with certain satans there, till at length they and the satans spoke in concert, and gnashing with their teeth breathed the destruction of the soul of those who were in favor of the Word. Yet they could avail nothing at all, for the Lord was on the side of those who were for the Word, and satans on the side of those who were against it; wherefore the former were received into heaven, but the latter were cast down into hell. [3] The angels afterwards said of natural theology, that without the Word it reveals nothing, but only confirms those things which are known in the doctrine of the church from the Word; and that confirmations from nature by means of rational light corroborate spiritual truths, for the reason that everyone has some natural idea of spiritual things, by which he retains them in memory, and thence brings them forth into the thought, and turns them over and airs them rationally. Wherefore, if confirmations are added from nature, the truth is corroborated. But yet care should be taken lest falsity be seized upon instead of truth, since what is false may be confirmed by the ingenious, equally as well as what is true; and thereby what is heretical may be confirmed even to the destruction of truth itself. [4] They added that no one from natural theology can enter into spiritual theology, but that everyone from spiritual theology can enter into natural theology, because the latter entrance is of Divine order, but the former against Divine order; for the natural is gross and impure, while the spiritual is subtle and pure. To enter from the gross and impure into the subtle and pure is not granted. But, conversely, angels can look down beneath them and see all things which are there, while no one from below can see the things which are in the heavens. Yea, an angel can see a spirit who is grosser than himself, but the spirit cannot see the angel who is purer than himself. When therefore, as is often the case, such spirits ascend into heaven where angels are, they see no one, nor even their homes, and so go away saying that the place is empty and a desert. [5] It is similar with the Word. They who do not believe in the Word from the Word, can by no means believe anything Divine from nature; for the Lord teaches: They have Moses and the prophets; let them hear them. If they hear not Moses and the prophets, neither will they be persuaded, if one shall have risen from the dead (Luke 16:29, 31). So would it be if one wished to believe from nature alone, rejecting the Word. Some of the ancients, who were pagans, as Aristotle, Cicero, and others, wrote concerning the existence of God and the immortality of the soul, but they did not know this from their own natural light, but from the religion of the ancients who had a Divine revelation, which was successively handed down to the Gentiles.

VII. THE SPIRITUAL SENSE OF THE WORD. CORRESPONDENCES. Each and all things which are in nature, correspond to spiritual things; similarly each and all things which are in the human body, as may be seen in two articles in the work on Heaven and Hell. But it is not known at this day what correspondence is, but in the most ancient times the science of correspondences was the science of sciences, thus the universal science, so that the most ancient people wrote all their manuscripts and books by correspondences. The fables of the most ancient times and the hieroglyphics of the Egyptians are nothing else: the book of Job, which is a book of the Ancient Church, is full of correspondences. [2] All the ancient churches were churches representative of heavenly things; all their rites and also their statutes, according to which their worship was instituted, consisted of nothing but correspondences. Similarly the church with the sons of Jacob; the burnt offerings and sacrifices with all their particulars, were correspondences; likewise the tabernacle with the single things therein, as also their feasts, such as the feast of unleavened bread, the feast of tabernacles, and the feast of first fruits, and also all their statutes and judgments; and because correspondences are such things as exist in the ultimates of nature, and because all things of nature correspond, and the things which correspond also signify, therefore the sense of the letter of the Word consists of nothing but correspondences. The Lord also, because He spoke from His Divine, and spoke the Word, spoke therefore also by correspondences. What is from the Divine, and in itself is Divine, in the ultimate falls into such things as correspond to Divine, celestial and spiritual things, thus such as in their bosom conceal and signify celestial and spiritual things. What, further, correspondences are, may be seen in the Arcana Coelestia, in which the correspondences which are in Genesis and in Exodus are explained. And again a collection of citations from that work concerning correspondences, may be seen in the Doctrine of the New Jerusalem and in the treatise on Heaven and Hell. The spiritual or internal sense of the Word is nothing else than the sense of the letter unfolded according to correspondences; for it teaches the spiritual which is perceived by angels in the heavens, while man in the world is thinking in a natural way of that which he reads in the Word. [3] I have heard and perceived from heaven that the men of the Most Ancient Church, who are those meant in the spiritual sense of the first chapters of Genesis by Adam and Eve, were so consociated with the angels of heaven, that they could speak with them by correspondences, and hence the state of their wisdom was such that whatever they saw on earth, they perceived at the same time spiritually, thus conjointly with the angels. It was told me that Enoch, of whom mention is made in Genesis (Chap. 5:21-24), with his associates, collected correspondences from the mouth of those people, and transmitted the knowledge of them to posterity. From this it came to pass, that the science of correspondences not only was known, but was also cultivated, in many kingdoms of Asia, and especially in Egypt, Assyria and Babylon, Syria, Mesopotamia, Arabia, and also in Canaan. From thence it was carried over to Greece, but was there turned into fables, as may be sufficiently evident from what is told of Olympus, Helicon and Pindus near Athens, and also of the winged horse called Pegasus, as, that with the hoof he broke open a fountain, by which the nine virgins [the Muses], established their seats. For a mountain, and thus Helicon, from correspondence signifies the higher heaven; the hill under the mountain, which was Pindus, signifies the heaven below it; the winged horse, or Pegasus, signifies the understanding enlightened by the spiritual; the fountain signifies intelligence and learning, and the nine virgins signify the knowledges of truth and the sciences. Similar were the rest of the things which are called fabulous, which were written by the most ancient writers in Greece, and which were collected together and described by Ovid in his Metamorphoses. [4] But when the representatives of the church in the course of time were turned into idolatries, then by the Divine Providence of the Lord that science was successively obliterated, and with the Israelitish and Jewish nation it was altogether destroyed and extinguished. The worship of that nation was indeed altogether representative, but still they did not know what any representative thing signified. For they were altogether natural men, and hence they were neither able nor willing to know anything about the spiritual man and about his faith and love, consequently nothing about correspondences. [5] That the idolatries of the nations in ancient times derived their origin from the science of correspondences amongst them, was because all things that appear upon the earth have a correspondence, as not only trees, but also cattle and birds of every kind, as well as fishes, and the rest. The ancients, who were in the science of correspondences, made themselves images, which corresponded to spiritual things, and they were delighted with those things, because they signified such things as are of heaven and thence of the church, they therefore not only placed them in their temples, but also in their houses, not for the purpose of adoration, but for the recollection of the heavenly thing that was signified, thence in Egypt there were set up calves, oxen, serpents, boys, old men, virgins, and many other things. For a calf signified the innocence of the natural man, oxen affections of the natural man, serpents the prudence of the sensual man, a boy innocence, old men wisdom, virgins affections for truth, and so on. After the science of correspondences was there lost, their posterity, who were ignorant what the images and likenesses set up by the ancients signified, began to worship them as holy, and finally as deities, because they were placed in and near the temples. The Egyptian hieroglyphics are from the same origin. So was it also with other nations, as with the Philistines in Ashdod, where was Dagon, formed like a man above and like a fish below, which image was so contrived because a man signifies rational intelligence, and a fish natural knowledge. From similar origin was the worship of the ancients in gardens and groves according to the kinds of trees, as also their sacred worship upon mountains; for gardens and groves signified spiritual intelligence, and each tree something thereof, as the olive its good of love, the vine its truth of the doctrine of faith, the cedar its rational, and so on. A mountain signified heaven, and therefore the worship of the most ancient people was upon mountains. That the science of correspondences remained with many oriental nations until the coming of the Lord, may be evident from the wise men from the East, who came to the Lord when He was born. Therefore a star went before them, and they brought with them gold, frankincense, and myrrh. It was also said to the shepherds, in order that they might know that it was the Lord Himself, that it should be a sign unto them, that they should see Him in a manger, wrapped in swaddling clothes, because there was no place in the inn. "The star" which went before the wise men signified knowledge from heaven, for stars in the Word signify knowledges. "The gold" signified celestial good, "frankincense" spiritual good, and "myrrh" natural good; all worship being from these three. "The manger" in which the infant Lord was found by the shepherds, signifies spiritual nourishment, because horses, which are fed from a manger, signify intellectual things. "The inn" where there was no place signified the Jewish Church, in which at that time there was no spiritual nourishment, because everything of the Word and thence everything of worship with them, had then been adulterated and perverted. Hence it is said that this would be for a sign to them that it was the Lord (Luke 2:12). Nevertheless, the science of correspondences was altogether none with the Israelitish and Jewish nation, although all things of their worship, and all the statutes and judgments given to them, and all things of the Word, were pure correspondences. The reason was that that nation was idolatrous in heart, and such that it did not even wish to know that anything of their worship signified anything celestial and spiritual. For they wished that all these things should be holy from themselves and with them in externals. Wherefore if spiritual and celestial things had been disclosed to them, they would not only have rejected, but would also have profaned them. For this reason heaven was closed to them so that they scarcely knew that they were to live after death. That this is so, is manifestly evident. They do not acknowledge the Lord, although the whole Sacred Scripture prophesied concerning Him, and predicted Him they rejected Him for this sole reason, that He taught them of the heavenly kingdom, and not concerning an earthly kingdom, for they wanted a Messiah who would exalt them above all nations in the whole world, and they did not wish any Messiah who would provide for their eternal salvation. Moreover, they say the Word contains in itself many arcana, which are called mystical, but they do not wish to know that these treat of the Lord and His Kingdom; but they do wish to know when it is said that they are concerning gold and alchemy. [6] That this science was not disclosed after those times, was because the Christians in the primitive church were very simple, that it could not be disclosed to them, for if disclosed, it would have been of no use to them, nor would it have been comprehended. After those times darkness arose over the entire Christian world, on account of the Papacy, which at length became Babylon, and they who are of Babel, and have confirmed themselves in its falsities, are for the most part natural, sensual men, and these are neither able nor willing to apprehend what is spiritual, thus what is the correspondence of natural things with spiritual. 7-1 But after the Reformation, because they began to make a distinction between faith and charity, and to worship one God under three Persons, the three Gods, whom they only named one, heavenly truths were then concealed from them, lest if revealed they should falsify them and bend them to faith alone, and none of them to charity and love. If therefore the spiritual sense of the Word had then been revealed, they would have shut heaven to themselves even by the falsification of its truths. [7] For everyone is allowed to understand the sense of the letter of the Word in simplicity, provided he does not confirm the appearances of truth which are there, so far as to destroy genuine truth; for to interpret the Word as to its spiritual sense from falsities of doctrine, closes heaven, and does not open it; but to interpret the spiritual sense from truths of doctrine, opens heaven, because that is the sense in which the angels are, and so man by means of it thinks together with angels, and thus conjoins them to himself in his intellectual mind. But if a man is in falsities of doctrine and wishes to explore the spiritual sense from some knowledge of correspondences, he falsifies it. It is otherwise if man is already in genuine truths; that sense agrees with truths and appears from them, because that sense is in the light of heaven. Cloud on the other hand agrees with falsities, and if anything of this truth should appear, instead of the light of heaven thick darkness would arise, for angels turn themselves away from him, and so close heaven to him. The spiritual sense of the Word is meant by the inner garment of the Lord, which was without seam, and which the soldiers were not permitted to divide; but the natural sense of the Word, which is the sense of its letter, is meant by His outer garments, which the soldiers divided. Garments in the Word signify truths, and the Lord's garments Divine truth, wherefore also the garments of the Lord, when He was transfigured before Peter, James, and John, appeared shining white, like light. [8] At this day the spiritual sense of the Word has been revealed from the Lord, because the doctrine of genuine truth has now been revealed, which doctrine is partly contained in the Doctrine of the New Jerusalem, and now in the small works, which are being given to the public; 7-2 and because that doctrine, and no other, agrees with the spiritual sense of the Word, therefore that sense, together with the science of correspondences, has now for the first time been disclosed. That sense is also signified by the Lord's appearing in the clouds of heaven with glory and power (Matt. 24:30, 31), in which chapter it treats of the consummation of the age, by which is meant the last time of the church. By the cloud of heaven, there and elsewhere in the Word, is signified the Word in the letter, which there, in respect to the spiritual sense, is as a cloud. But by the glory there, as also elsewhere in the Word, is signified the Word in the spiritual sense, which also is the Divine truth in light; and by the power is signified its power in the Word. The revelation of the Word as to the spiritual sense was also promised in Revelation, where that sense is meant by the "White Horse" (Chapter 19:11 to 14), and by the great supper of God, to which all were invited and gathered together (Rev. 19:17). By many that sense will not be acknowledged for a long time. Those alone who are in the falsities of doctrine, especially in regard to the Lord, and who do not admit truths, will not acknowledge this is meant by the beast and by the kings of the earth, who make war with the one sitting upon the white horse (Rev. 19:19). By "the beast" are meant the Roman Catholics, as in Rev. 17:3, and by "the kings of the earth" are meant the Reformed who are in falsities of doctrine. The mystical things which some seek in the Word, are nothing else than the spiritual and celestial senses.

VIII. THE MARRIAGE OF THE LORD WITH THE CHURCH, WHICH IS THE MARRIAGE OF GOOD AND TRUTH IN THE WORD. It is known that the Lord is called in the Word the Bridegroom and Husband, and the church the bride and wife. That the Lord and the church are so called, is because of the conjunction of good and truth with everyone who is in heaven, and who is in the church, in whom is the church; for the Lord flows in with an angel and with a man of the church from the good of love and charity. The angel and the man of the church who is in the good of love and charity, receives the Lord in the truths of doctrine and of faith which he has from the Word. Thereby conjunction is effected, which is called the heavenly marriage. This marriage is in the single things of the Word, and because it is in the single things, the Word itself may be called the heavenly marriage. That there is such a marriage in the single things of the Word has been shown in many places in the Arcana Coelestia, and also in the Doctrine of the New Jerusalem, where it treats of the Word. That there is such a marriage there, can be seen only by those who study its internal or spiritual sense, for everywhere, and conspicuously in the prophets, there are two expressions for one thing, of which one refers to good, thus to the Lord, and the other to truth, thus to the church. This is clearly seen by one who has a knowledge of correspondences, for there are senses and words which correspond to good, and there are correspondences which correspond to truths. Hence now there is a conjunction of the Lord with heaven and with the church by means of the Word. [2] Since there is a marriage in the Word, therefore there is in it a spiritual sense and there is a celestial sense: the spiritual sense for those who are in the Lord's spiritual kingdom, who constitute all the lower heavens; and the celestial sense for those who are in the Lord's celestial kingdom, who constitute all the higher heavens. The angels of the spiritual kingdom are in the truths of the Word, but the angels of the celestial kingdom are in the goods of the Word. When therefore a man reads the Word with reverence, spiritual angels according to correspondences perceive truths therein, and celestial angels perceive goods; but, and this is an arcanum, the celestial angels do not perceive the goods therein immediately from man, but mediately through the spiritual angels. The reason is, that scarcely any one in the Christian world at this day is in the good of celestial love, but only some are in truths; wherefore the good of love cannot pass immediately from man to the celestial angels, of whom the third heaven consists, but passes mediately through the spiritual angels, of whom the second heaven is composed. The marriage of the Lord with the church thus exists also in the heavens by means of the Word, for the Word in its spiritual sense treats of the church, but in the celestial sense, of the Lord. Therefore the spiritual angels apply all things to the church, but the celestial angels all things to the Lord. Hence heaven is compared by the Lord to a marriage, and is also called a marriage, and hence the Word effects that marriage. But this is an arcanum, which can be perceived only obscurely by man, while it is clearly perceived by an angel of heaven. [3]

The celestial angels can apply to the Lord all things which spiritual angels apply to the church, because the Lord is the all of the church.

IX. THEY WHO HAVE FOR AN END MAGNIFICENCE AND HONORS IN THE WORLD AND ALSO IN HEAVEN, AND THOSE WHO HAVE FOR AN END WEALTH AND GAIN IN THE WORLD, AND THOSE WHO HAVE FOR AN END THE FAME OF LEARNING, DO NOT SEE AND DO NOT FIND ANYTHING OF GENUINE TRUTH IN THE WORD. It has been given me to speak with many in the spiritual world who believed that they would shine as stars in heaven, because, as they said, they held the Word holy, often read it, gathered many things from it, and by it confirmed the dogmas of their faith, and hence were esteemed learned in the world, and themselves believed with others that they would be Michaels and Raphaels. But many of them having been explored as to the love from which they studied the Word, it was found that some had done so from the love of self, that they might appear great in the world, and be worshipped as primates of the church; some that they might obtain the fame of learning, and so be promoted to honors; some that they might gain wealth, and some that they might preach learnedly. Afterwards when examined to see whether they had learned anything of genuine truth from the Word, it was found that they knew nothing whatever, except that which is obvious to everyone in the sense of the letter, and nothing of genuine truth which might serve interiorly for doctrine. This was because themselves and the world had been their ends, but not the Lord and heaven, and when such are the ends, then man with his mind clings to self and the world, and continually thinks from his proprium, which is in thick darkness as to all things of heaven. For the proprium of man is mere evil and falsity therefrom; wherefore the man who looks to self, honor, fame, or gain, in reading the Word, cannot be led by the Lord away from the proprium and thus be elevated into the light of heaven, and so cannot receive any influx from the Lord through heaven. [2] Many such have been seen and they every one earnestly desired heaven, and they were also admitted into heaven; but when they came thither, they were examined as to whether they knew anything of truth, as it is with angels; and they knew nothing except the bare words of the sense of the letter, and had no interior understanding of them whatever. Therefore they appeared in the eyes of the angels stripped of their garments and as if naked, and thus they were sent down below. Some of them in the light of heaven were deprived of the sight of the understanding, and soon of the sight of the eyes; and then they were seized with anguish of heart, and were thus led away below, still however retaining pride in their own merit. This is the lot of those who study the Word and have honor, fame, and gain for their end. It is entirely different with those who study the Word from the affection of truth, or who, in reading the Word, take delight in truth because it is truth. These have for an end the love of God and the love of the neighbor, and for themselves, they have life as an end. All these because they love truth receive an influx from the Lord, and see and find genuine truths in the Word; for they are enlightened as to the understanding, and perceive truths in enlightenment as from themselves, though they are not from themselves; and after death they are taken up into heaven, where truth is in its own light, and there they become spiritual and angels.

X. THE ULTIMATE SENSE OF THE WORD, 10-1 WHICH IS THE

SENSE OF THE LETTER ONLY, CORRESPONDS TO THE BEARD, AND TO THE HAIRS OF THE HEAD, ON A MAN ANGEL. That the hairs of the head and the beard correspond to the Word in its ultimates, may seem strange when first said or heard, but this correspondence has its cause in this, that all things of the Word correspond with all things of heaven, and heaven with all things of man; for heaven in its complex is before the Lord as one man, concerning which correspondence see what is shown in the work on Heaven and Hell [n. 87-102, 307]. [2] That all things of the Word correspond to all things of heaven, has been given me to perceive from this, that the separate chapters in the prophetic Word correspond to individual societies of heaven; for when I read through the prophetic books of the Word from Isaiah to Malachi, it was given me to see that societies of heaven were called forth in their order and perceived the spiritual sense corresponding to them. Hence, from these and other proofs, it was, made plain to me that there is a correspondence of the whole heaven with the Word in its series. Now because there is such a correspondence of the Word with heaven, and heaven in whole and in part corresponds to man, thence it is that the ultimate of the Word corresponds to the ultimates of man. The ultimate of the Word is the sense of the letter, and the ultimates of man are the hairs of the head and beard. [3] Therefore it is that men who have loved the Word even in its ultimates, after death when they become spirits appear with becoming hair, and angels likewise. The same when they become angels also let the beard grow. But on the other hand all they who have despised the sense of the letter of the Word, after death when they become spirits appear bald. This is a sign also that they are without truths, and therefore, that they may not be in shame before others, they cover the head with a tiara. [4] Because the hairs and the beard signify the ultimate of heaven, and hence the ultimates also of Divine truth or the Word, therefore the Ancient of Days is described as having the hair of His head like clean wool (Dan. 7:9). In like manner is described the Son of man, or the Lord as to the Word (Rev. 1:14). So too the strength of Samson was in his hair, and when his hair was cut off, he became weak. Nazariteship also depended on the hair, for by a Nazarite was represented the Lord as to His ultimates, thus also heaven in ultimates. This was why the forty-two boys were torn by the bears, because they called Elisha bald (2 Kings 2:23, 24). [5] Elisha, like Elijah and the other prophets, represented the Lord as to the Word, and the Word without its ultimate sense, which is the sense of the letter, is not the Word; for the sense of the letter of the Word is like a vessel filled with noble wine, wherefore when the vessel is broken, all the wine is spilled. The sense of the letter is also like the bones and skin with man, which being taken away, the whole man would fall asunder. Therefore it is that the stability, yea the power of the whole Word rests in its ultimate sense, which is the sense of the letter, for this sense sustains and contains all the Divine truth therein. [6] Since baldness signifies no truth, because it has no ultimate, therefore they of the Jewish Church, when they left Jehovah and rejected the Word, are called bald, as in Jeremiah: Every head is bald, and every beard is cut off (Jer. 48:37). On the heads is baldness, and the beard is cut off (Isa. 15:2). That he should shave the head and beard with a razor (Ezek. 5:1). Shame shall be upon all faces, and baldness upon all heads (Ezek. 7:18). Every head was made bald (Ezek. 29:18); as also elsewhere (Amos 8:10; Micah 1:16). [7] But the sense of the Word which is called the sense of the letter, corresponds in its ultimates to the hair of the head, and for the rest it corresponds to the various parts in man, as his head, breast, loins, and feet; but where there are these correspondences in that sense, the Word is as it were clothed, and it therefore corresponds to the clothing of those parts, for garments in general signify truths, and also actually correspond to them. But yet many things in the sense of the letter of the Word are naked, as without clothing, and these correspond to the face of man, and also to his hands, which parts are bare. These parts of the Word serve for the doctrine of the church, because in themselves they are spiritual natural truths. Whence it may be evident that there is no lack, but that man can find and see naked truths even in the letter of the Word.

XI. THE WISDOM OF THE ANGELS OF THE THREE HEAVENS IS FROM THE LORD BY MEANS OF THE WORD, TO WHICH THE SENSE OF ITS LETTER SERVES AS A SUPPORT AND BASIC. I have heard from heaven that there was immediate revelation with the most ancient people on this earth, and that therefore they had no written Word; but after their times, when immediate revelation could neither be given nor received without danger to their souls, lest the communication and conjunction of men with the heavens should be intercepted and perish, it pleased the Lord to reveal Divine truth by means of the Word, which was written solely by correspondences. It is therefore of such a nature in the ultimate sense, that it comprehends within itself the wisdom of the angels of the three heavens. This wisdom does not appear in our Word, but yet it is within it, and how it is within it shall be briefly told. There are three heavens, one beneath another, and under them is the world. In the highest heaven is angelic wisdom in the highest degree, which is called celestial wisdom; in the middle heaven is angelic wisdom in the middle degree, which is called spiritual wisdom; but in the lowest heaven is angelic wisdom in the lowest degree, which is called spiritual and celestial natural. In the world, because that is below the heavens, is wisdom in the lowest degree, which is called natural. All these degrees of wisdom are in the Word which is in the world, but in simultaneous order, for successive order in its descent becomes simultaneous. Therefore that which is simultaneous becomes the complex of all its successive degrees. The highest in successive order becomes the inmost in simultaneous order, the middle becomes the middle there, and the ultimate the ultimate there. Such a simultaneous order is the Word in the world. In its inmost is the Lord as a sun, from which Divine truth and Divine good, light and flame, radiate and propagate themselves through immediates even to ultimates. Next in that simultaneous order is the Divine celestial, such as is in the highest or third heaven, from which the angels there have wisdom. Then follows the Divine spiritual, such as is in the middle or second heaven, from which the angels there have wisdom. After that succeeds the Divine spiritual natural, and celestial natural, such as is in the ultimate or first heaven, from which the angels there have wisdom. The ultimate border of this simultaneous order is made by the Divine natural, such as is in the world, from which men have wisdom. This ultimate girds about, binds together, and thus contains the interiors, that they may not flow away; thus it serves also as a support. Such is our Word in the sense of the letter, in general and also in every part. When therefore this is read with reverence by man, then its interiors are unbound and unfolded, and each heaven draws therefrom its own, spiritual angels their Divine spiritual, and celestial angels their Divine celestial, from which they have their wisdom. That our Word is such has not only been declared and heard from heaven, but has also been shown and confirmed by much experience. The Divine let down by the Lord into the world, could not but pass through the heavens in their order, and exist in the world, so formed that it might in like order return through the heavens to the Lord, from whom it proceeded.

XII. ENLIGHTENMENT BY MEANS OF THE WORD. Every man who is in the spiritual affection of truth, that is, who loves truth itself because it is truth, is enlightened by the Lord when he reads the Word; but not the man who reads it from mere natural affection of truth, which is called the desire of knowing. The latter does not see anything except what agrees with his love, or with the principles which he has either himself adopted, or derived from others by hearing or reading. In a few words therefore it shall be told whence and with what man there is enlightenment by means of the Word. That man has enlightenment who shuns evils because they are sins, and because they are against the Lord, and against His Divine laws. With this man and with no other, the spiritual mind is opened, and so far as it is opened, the light of heaven enters, from which light is all enlightenment in the Word. For man then has a will for good, and this will, when it is determined to that use, becomes in the understanding first the affection of truth, then the perception of truth, soon by means of rational light the thought of truth, thus decision and conclusion, which as it passes thence into the memory, also passes into the life, and so remains. This is the way of all enlightenment in the Word, and also the way of reformation and regeneration of man. But first the memory must needs have knowledges both of spiritual and natural things, for these are the stores into which the Lord operates by means of the light of heaven, and the fuller these are and freer from confirmed falsities, the more enlightened is the perception given and the clearer the conclusion. For the Divine operation does not fall into a man who is empty and void, as for example one who does not know that the Lord is pure love and pure mercy, good itself, and truth itself, and that love itself and good itself are such in their essence that they cannot do evil to anyone, neither be angry nor revengeful; or who does not know that the Word in the sense of the letter is written in many places from appearances. Such a man cannot be enlightened by the Word where it is said of Jehovah that He is wrathful and angry, and that to Him belong fire and fury, that His wrath burns, even to the lowest hell-as in David; that there is no evil in the city which Jehovah hath not done, as in Amos (3:6); that He would rejoice to do evil as He had rejoiced to do good (Deut. 28:63); that He leads into temptations, as in the Lord's prayer; and similarly in other places.

XIII. HOW MUCH MEDIATE REVELATION, WHICH IS EFFECTED THROUGH THE WORD, SURPASSES IMMEDIATE REVELATION, WHICH IS EFFECTED THROUGH SPIRITS. It is believed that man might be more enlightened and become more wise if he should have immediate revelation through speech with spirits and with angels, but the reverse is the case. Enlightenment by means of the Word is effected by an interior way, while enlightenment by immediate revelation is effected by an exterior way. The interior way is through the will into the understanding, the exterior way is through the hearing into the understanding. Man is enlightened through the Word by the Lord so far as his will is in good, but man may be instructed and as it were enlightened through the hearing, though the will is in evil; and what enters into the understanding with a man whose will is in evil, is not within, but without him. It is only in the memory and not in the life, and what is without a man and not in his life, is gradually separated, if not before, yet after death, for the will which is in evil either casts it out, or suffocates it, or falsifies and profanes it. For the will makes the life of man, and continually acts into the understanding, and regards as extraneous that which is from the memory in the understanding. On the other hand the understanding does not act into the will, but only teaches in what manner the will should act. Wherefore, were a man to know from heaven all things which even angels ever know or if he were to know all things that are in the Word, and that are in all the doctrines of the church, and moreover all that the Fathers have written and councils decreed, and yet his will be in evil, he would after death be looked upon as one who knows nothing, because he does not will what he knows. In such case because evil hates truths, the man himself casts them out, and in their place adopts falsities agreeing with the evil of his will. [2] Moreover, no leave is given to any spirit or even angel, to instruct any man on this earth in Divine truths, but the Lord Himself teaches everyone through the Word, and teaches him so far as the man receives good from the Lord in the will, and this the man receives so far as he shuns evils as sins. Again, every man is in a society of spirits as to his affections and thoughts thence, in which he is as one with them, wherefore spirits speaking with man speak from his affections and according to them. Man cannot speak with other spirits unless the societies in which he is, be first removed, which cannot be done except by the reformation of his will. Because every man is in society with spirits who are of the same religion with himself, therefore spirits speaking with him confirm all things which he has made a part of his religion. Thus enthusiastic spirits confirm all things of enthusiasm with the man, Quaker spirits all things of Quakerism, Moravian spirits all things of Moravianism, and so on. Hence come confirmations of falsity which can never be extirpated. From this it is plain that mediate revelation, which is effected through the Word, is better than immediate revelation, which takes place through spirits. As for myself, I have not been allowed to take anything from the mouth of any spirit, nor from the mouth of any angel, but from the mouth of the Lord alone.

XIV. THE WORD IN THE HEAVENS. The Word is in all the heavens. It is read there as in the world and they preach from it, for it is the Divine truth from which the angels have intelligence and wisdom; since without the Word no one knows anything of the Lord, of love and faith, of redemption, or of any other arcana of heavenly wisdom. Yea, without the Word there would be no heaven, as without the Word there would be no church in the world, thus there would be no conjunction with the Lord. That there is no such thing as natural theology without revelation, and in the Christian world without the Word, has been shown above. If it cannot exist in the world, neither can it exist after death, for such as a man is as to his religion in the world, such he is as to his religion after death when he becomes a spirit; and the whole heaven does not consist of any angels created before the world, or with the world, but of those who have been men, and were then interiorly angels. These through the Word come in heaven into spiritual wisdom, which is interior wisdom, because the Word there is spiritual. [2] The Word in the spiritual kingdom of the Lord is not like the Word in the world; in the world the Word is natural, but in that kingdom it is spiritual. The difference is as that between its natural sense and its spiritual sense, and what this spiritual sense is has been shown in many places in the Arcana Coelestia, where all things in Genesis and Exodus have been explained according to that sense. Such is the difference that no word is the same; instead of names there are in the spiritual sense things, instead of numbers and historical facts are things relating to the church. But, what is wonderful, when an angel reads the Word in heaven, he knows not otherwise than that it is like the Word which he read in the world. The reason is that he no longer has any natural ideas, but in their place spiritual ideas, and the natural and the spiritual are so conjoined by correspondences that they make, as it were, one. When therefore one comes from what is natural into what is spiritual, it appears to him as if it were the same. Yea, an angel does not know that he is wiser than he had been in the world, although he has wisdom so supereminent as to be ineffable in comparison. Nor can he know the distinction, because in his spiritual state he knows nothing of his natural state, in which he was in the world. Neither can he compare and discriminate them, because he does not return into his former state, and so make a comparison. Nevertheless an angel is perfected in wisdom continually, in heaven more than in the world, because he is in purer affection for spiritual truth. [3] But the Word in the celestial kingdom of the Lord is of far greater excellence and wisdom than is the Word which is in His spiritual kingdom; and they differ in a degree similar to that of the difference between the natural Word which is in the world, and the spiritual Word of which we have been speaking; for in that Word there is an inmost sense, which is called the celestial, in which all things of the Word treat of the Lord alone. In this Word instead of Jehovah is read the Lord, and instead of Abraham, Isaac, and Jacob, also instead of David, Moses, Elijah, and the other prophets, the Lord is named, and His Divine as meant by them is distinguished by peculiar marks. By the names of the tribes of Israel, which are twelve, and also by the names of the apostles in the Word, something of the Lord as to the church is read; and so throughout. From this it has been made plain to me that the whole Sacred Scripture in its inmost sense treats of the Lord alone. There is a like difference between those two Words, the spiritual and the celestial, as between the thoughts which are of the understanding, and the affections, which are of the will; for the angels of the celestial kingdom are in love toward the Lord, and thence in the affection of good, and the angels of the spiritual kingdom are in faith in the Lord, and thence in the perception of truth. [4] The spiritual Word and the celestial Word differ also as to the writing. The writing of the spiritual Word is of letters which are similar to the type letters in our world, but every letter expresses a meaning. If, therefore, you should see that writing, you would not understand a single expression, for it is written letter next to letter in a continuous series, with little lines and points above and below, being written according to spiritual speech, which has nothing in common with natural speech. The angels, in proportion as they are wiser, see in their Word so written, more interior arcana than simpler angels see. The hidden things therein appear clearly before the eyes of the wise, but not before, the eyes of the simple; in like manner as with our Word, though still more so, in which also the wise see more than the simple. But the writing of the celestial Word is composed of letters unknown in the world. They are indeed alphabetic letters, but each one is made up of curved lines, with little horns above and below, and there are dots or points in the letters, and also below and above them. It was said that the most ancient people on this earth had such writing, agreeing in some respects, but only slightly, with Hebrew writing. By such writing are expressed the affections of love, so that it involves more arcana than they themselves can utter, and they express these unutterable arcana which they perceive from their Word, by representations. The wisdom which lies hid in this Word, transcends the wisdom which is in the spiritual Word as thousands to one. [5] That the difference between the three Words, the natural, the spiritual, and the celestial, may be understood, let us take for illustration the first chapters of Genesis, which treat of Adam, his wife, and paradise. In the natural Word which is in the world, is described the creation of the world and the first creation of man, and its and his pleasures and earthly delights; and by the persons named after him even to the flood, are meant his posterity, and by the numbers their ages. But in the spiritual Word, which is with the angels of the spiritual kingdom, are not meant those things, but in the first chapter is described the reformation and regeneration of the men of the Most Ancient Church, which is also called the new creation. In the second chapter, by "paradise" is described the intelligence of the men of that church; by "Adam" and his "wife," that church itself, and by their posterity, even to the flood, are described the changes of state of that church, until it declined, and finally its destruction by the flood. But in the celestial Word, or in the Word which is with the angels in the celestial kingdom of the Lord, in the first chapter is described the glorification of the Lord's Human. Instead of "paradise" is described His Divine wisdom; by "Adam" himself is there meant the Lord as to the Divine itself, and at the same time the Divine Human; and by his "wife," the church, which is called "Chavah" [Eve], from life, because it has life from the Lord. Of her Adam said that she was his "bone" and his "flesh," and that they were "one flesh," because the church is from the Lord and of Him, and as one with Him. By the names which are the posterity of Adam, are there described the successive states of reception of the Lord, and of conjunction with Him, by the men of that church, even until there was no longer any reception, and therefore no conjunction. [6] When therefore these first chapters of our Word are read by upright men, and especially when they are read by little boys and girls, and they are affected with joy from the state of the creation of all things, and from paradise, then those senses are evolved, and the spiritual angels understand them according to their Word, and the celestial angels according to theirs, without knowing that the man or child is reading it; for those senses are evolved in their order, because they correspond, and correspondences are such from creation. From these things it is plain what the Word is in its bosom, namely, that there are in it three senses, the ultimate which is natural for man, and which in many places treats of worldly things, and where it treats of Divine things, still they are described by such things as are in the world; a middle sense which is spiritual, in which are described such things as relate to the church; and an inmost sense which is celestial, in which are contained such things as relate to the Lord. For all nature is a theater representative of the Lord's kingdom, and the Lord's kingdom, which is heaven, and the church, is a theater representative of the Lord Himself; for as the Lord glorified His Human, so also He regenerates man, and as He regenerates man, so also He created him. [7] From this it may be evident what is the nature of the Word in its bosom. The natural Word, such as is in the world, in Christendom, contains within itself both the spiritual Word and the celestial Word; for the spiritual sense of our Word is the Word in the heavens which constitute the Lord's spiritual kingdom; and the celestial sense of our Word, which is its inmost sense, is the Word in the heavens which constitute the Lord's celestial kingdom. Consequently in our natural Word is contained both the spiritual Word and the celestial Word; but in the spiritual Word and the celestial Word is not contained the natural Word. For this reason the Word of our world is the most full of the Divine wisdom, and therefore more holy than the Words of the heavens.

XV. THE ANCIENT WORD THAT IS LOST. That there was a Word with the ancients, written like our Word by mere correspondences, but that this has been lost, has been told me by angels of the third heaven. They said further that this Word is still preserved with them, and is in use among the ancients in that heaven, whose Word it was when they were in the world. Those ancients, with whom that Word is still in use in the heavens, were in part from the land of Canaan and its borders, and also from certain kingdoms in Asia, as from Syria, Mesopotamia, Arabia, Chaldea, Assyria, and Egypt, from Sidon and Tyre, the inhabitants of all of which kingdoms were in representative worship, and thus in a knowledge of correspondences. Their wisdom at that time was from that knowledge, since by it they had communication with the heavens, and interior perception, and also many had converse with spirits. But because that Word was full of such correspondences, which remotely signified heavenly things, and for that reason in the course of time began to be falsified by many, therefore from the Divine providence of the Lord it gradually passed out of sight, and another Word was given, which was written by correspondences less remote, and this through the prophets with the sons of Israel. In this Word, however, the names of places in the land of Canaan and in Asia round about, were retained and kept their signification. For this reason, the posterity of Abraham from Jacob were introduced into the land of Canaan, and the Word in which those places were to be named was there written. [2] That there was such a Word with the ancients is plain also in Moses, by whom it is mentioned and something is taken from it (Num. 21:14-27). The historicals of that Word were called the Wars of Jehovah, and the propheticals the Enunciations. From the historicals of that Word Moses took these words: Wherefore it is said in the Book of the Wars of Jehovah, At Vaheb in Suphah, and the streams of Arnon, and the channel of the streams that descend towards the dwelling of Ar, and reach to the border of Moab (Num. 21:14, 15). By "the Wars of Jehovah" are there meant and described the combats of the Lord with the hells and victories over them, when He should come into the world. The same combats are also meant and described in many places in the historicals of our Word, as in the wars of Joshua with the nations of the land of Canaan, in the wars of the judges, and in the wars of David and the rest of the kings. [3] From the propheticals of that Word these words were taken by Moses: Wherefore the prophetic enunciations say, Come ye to Heshbon, let the city of Sihon be built and established, for a fire has gone out of Heshbon, a flame from the city of Sihon: it hath devoured Ar of Moab, the possessors of the high places of Arnon. Woe to thee, Moab! Thou hast perished, O people of Chemosh. He hath given his sons as fugitives, and his daughters into captivity, unto Sihon king of the Amorites. With darts we have destroyed them. Heshbon is perished even unto Dibon, and we have laid them waste even unto Nophah, which is even unto Medeba (Num. 21:27-30). That these propheticals were called Enunciations, and not Proverbs or the makers of proverbs, as the translators render it, may be evident from the signification of the word maschalim in the Hebrew language, which means not only proverbs, but also prophetic enunciations, as may appear elsewhere in Numbers (23:7, 18; 24:3, 15), where it is said that Balaam put forth his enunciation, which also was a prophecy, yea, concerning the Lord. His enunciation is there called a maschal, in the singular. Furthermore, those things which are described by Moses in those citations are prophecies, but they are not proverbs. [4] That that Word was in like manner Divine, or Divinely inspired, is plain in Jeremiah, where are almost the same words, as follows: A fire has gone forth out of Heshbon, and a flame from the midst of Sihon, and hath devoured the corner of Moab, and the crown of the head of the sons of tumult. Woe unto thee, O Moab! the people of Chemosh hath perished; for thy sons are carried away into captivity, and thy daughters into captivity (Jer. 48:45, 46). Besides these, a prophetic book of that ancient Word, called the Book of Jasher, or the Book of the Upright, is also cited by David (2 Sam. 1:18), and by Joshua (Josh. 10:13); from which it is plain that the historic statement there about the sun and moon, was a prophecy from that book. It has moreover been told me that the first seven chapters of Genesis are so manifestly extant in that same Word, that not a little word is wanting. [5] The religious systems of many nations have been derived from that ancient Word and carried elsewhere, as from the land of Canaan and from various parts of Asia into Greece and from there into Italy, and through Ethiopia and Egypt into certain kingdoms of Africa. In Greece, however, out of correspondences they made fables, and out of the Divine attributes they made so many gods, the greatest of whom they called Jove, from Jehovah.

XVI. THE GENTILES, AND PEOPLES OUTSIDE OF THE CHURCH, WHO HAVE NOT THE WORD, AND THEREFORE KNOW NOTHING OF THE LORD AND OF REDEMPTION. They who have the Word are few as compared with those who have not the Word. The Word is found only in Europe with the Christians who are called the Reformed. The Word is indeed with the Roman Catholics, but it is not read, and the kingdoms devoted to that religion, as France, Spain, Portugal, Italy, more than half of Germany, and also of Hungary, as well as Poland, do not read it. The Word is also but little read in Russia, but yet it is believed to be holy. Communication through the Word. Only in England, Holland, certain duchies in Germany, and in Sweden and Denmark is the Word taught and preached; but in Asia, Africa, and the Indies, with the Gentiles, who are more numerous than the Reformed Christians, the Word is unknown. But that the Word might not be lost, it has been provided by the Lord that the Jewish nation, with whom is the Word of the Old Testament in its original tongue, should still survive and dwell dispersed through much of the earth. Though this nation denies that the Lord is the Messiah or Christ, foretold by the prophets, and though it is evil in heart, yet the reading of the Word by them has communication with certain heavens; for correspondences communicate, whatever the quality of the person who reads, if only he acknowledges the Word to be Divine. This is the case today, as formerly; for when Moses, Abraham, Isaac, and Jacob, David, Elias, and many others named in the Word, are adored by them as deities, then the heavens perceive the Lord, instead of these persons, not knowing the person in the world from whom that holy of worship proceeds. Such is the conjunction of heaven with man by means of the Word.

XVII. [BY MEANS OF THE WORD THOSE ALSO HAVE LIGHT WHO ARE OUT OF THE CHURCH AND HAVE NOT THE WORD.] The case is thus: there cannot be any conjunction with heaven, unless somewhere on the earth there is a church where the Word is, and by it the Lord is known; for the Lord is the God of heaven and earth, and without the Lord there is no salvation. It is enough that there be somewhere on the earth a church where the Word is. Though it consist of comparatively few, still by means of it, the Lord is present everywhere in the whole world, and by means of it heaven is conjoined to the human race, for conjunction is effected by means of the Word. But without the Word somewhere in the world there would not be conjunction with anyone. The reason of the presence of the Lord and of the conjunction of heaven with the inhabitants of the earth everywhere by means of the Word, is, that the whole heaven is before the Lord as one man, and likewise the church, and it is also actually a man, because the Lord is heaven and also the church. In that man the church where the Word is read and thereby, the Lord is known, is like the heart and lungs; and as from those two fountains of life in the human body all the rest of the members and viscera subsist and live, so also all those in the world who have a religion in which one God is worshipped, and who constitute the members and viscera of that Greatest Man which is heaven and the church, subsist and live. For, by means of the Word in the church, though it be among comparatively few, life is given to the rest from the Lord through heaven, as from the heart and lungs to the members and viscera of the whole body. The communication is also similar. This is the reason that Christians with whom the Word is read, constitute the breast of that man and are also in the midst of all; round about them are the Roman Catholics, around these are the Mohammedans who acknowledge the Lord as the Greatest Prophet and as the Son of God, behind them are the Africans, and the Gentiles and people of Asia and the Indies constitute the outmost circumference. All who are in that man look also towards the middle region. Moreover in that middle region where, as already said, are the Christians who have the Word, is the greatest light, because light in the heavens is the Divine truth proceeding from the Lord as the sun. The light thence, as from its center, propagates itself to all the borders, and enlightens. Hence the Gentiles and peoples outside of the church are enlightened also by means of the Word, for all the light of truth with man is from the Lord through heaven. [2] As it is in the whole heaven, so also is it in every society of heaven, for each society of heaven is a heaven in smaller form, and also is in the sight of the Lord as one man, in regard to which see the work on Heaven and Hell [n. 41-87]. There also they who are in the midst in like manner relate to the heart and lungs, and with them is the greatest light. The light itself and the perception of truth thereby propagates itself from that middle portion towards the borders in every direction, and makes their spiritual life. It was also shown me that when those who were in the midst, who constituted the province of the heart and lungs, and with whom therefore was the greatest light, were taken away, those who were round about were in shade, and in so little perception of truth that it was scarcely any at all. But as soon as they returned, the light was seen as before, and there was perception of truth as before. [3] From this it may be seen that the Word which is in the church of the Reformed, enlightens all nations and peoples by spiritual communication, which is of this nature; also that it is provided by the Lord that in this earth there may always be a church where the Word is read. When therefore the Word was almost rejected by the Roman Catholics, by the Divine providence of the Lord the Reformation was effected, and in that the Word was again received, and it was also regarded as holy by a noble nation among the Papists. [4] Since without the Word there is no knowledge of the Lord, thus no salvation, therefore when the Word was altogether adulterated and falsified with the Jewish nation, and hence as it were made of none effect, it pleased the Lord to come into the world and not only to fulfill the Word, but also to renew and restore it, and so again to give light to the inhabitants of this earth, according to the words of the Lord in John: In the beginning was the Word, and the Word was with God, and God was the Word. In Him was life, and the life was the light of men. And the light appeareth in the darkness. He was the true light, which lighteth every man coming into the world (John 1:1, 4-5, 9). In the same: Jesus said, I am the light of the world: he that followeth Me shall not walk in the darkness, but shall have the light of life (John 8:12). And in Matthew: The people which sat in darkness saw a great light; and to them which sat in the region and shadow of death, to them did light spring up (Matt. 4:16). [5] Since it has been foretold that in the end of this church darkness would also arise, from a lack of knowledge and acknowledgment of the Lord, that He is the God of heaven and earth; and from the separation of faith from charity, whereby the genuine understanding of the Word has perished; therefore it has pleased the Lord now to reveal the spiritual sense of the Word, and to show that the Word treats in that sense of the Lord and of the church, yea, of them only, and to show many other things by which the light of truth, almost extinguished, may be restored. That the light of truth at the end of this church would be extinguished, is meant by the words of the Lord in Matthew: Immediately after the affliction of those days, the sun shall be darkened, and the moon shall not give her light, and the stars shall fall from heaven, and the powers of the heavens shall be shaken: and then they shall see the Son of man, coming in the clouds of heaven, with glory and power (Matt. 24:29, 30). By the "sun" is here meant the Lord as to the Divine love, by the "moon" the Lord as to faith, by the "stars" the Lord as to knowledges of good and truth, by "clouds" the sense of the letter of the Word, and by "glory" its spiritual sense, and by the "Son of man" the Lord as to the Word.

XVIII. THE CONJUNCTION OF HEAVEN WITH THE MAN OF THE CHURCH, BY MEANS OF THE SENSE OF THE LETTER OF THE WORD.

From much experience it has been given me to know that the Word opens heaven to man, that is, that when man reads the Word or speaks from it, communication is effected with heaven. I have read the prophetic Word through from Isaiah even to Malachi, and it was given to perceive that every chapter, yea every verse, was perceived in some heavenly society. And because the spiritual sense and not the sense of the letter is communicated, therefore the angels of the society did not know that these things came from any man. Such things as are inwardly in the Word appear to them as if they thought them from themselves. [2] There were with me African spirits, from Abyssinia. Their ears were once opened so that they heard singing in a certain temple in the world, from the Psalms of David, and they were affected with such delight that they sang together with the singers. But soon their ears were closed, and they did not hear from there the singing of anyone; and then they were affected with still greater delight, because spiritual; and at the same time they were filled with intelligence, because the Psalm in the spiritual sense treated of the Lord, and of redemption by Him. The delight of their hearts' joy was for a little time communicated with a certain heavenly society from the Christian world, and that society came thereby into similar delight. Hence it was plain, that communication with the whole heaven is given by means of the Word. [3] I pass over a thousand other experiences by which I have been convinced that the sense of the letter of our Word produces that effect, yea, that the spiritual sense without its companion, the natural sense, does not communicate with heaven. The reason of this is, that the Lord flows in from firsts through ultimates, therefore from Himself into the natural sense of the Word, and from that calls forth, or evolves its spiritual and celestial senses, and thus enlightening, teaches and leads the angels; wherefore the Lord is called in the Word "the First and the Last." [4] From this it is plain that the doctrine of the church, unless it be gathered and confirmed from the sense of the letter of the Word, has no power, because it does not communicate; but doctrine from the sense of the letter and together with it does have power.

XIX. THE TRUTHS WHICH ARE CALLED TRUTHS OF FAITH, AND THE GOODS WHICH ARE CALLED GOODS OF LOVE, ARE INEFFABLY INCREASED IN THE INTERNAL SENSES, THUS IN THE HEAVENS. THE QUALITY OF THE NATURAL SENSE WITHOUT THE SPIRITUAL AND CELESTIAL SENSES, AND THE REVERSE. The reason of this is, that natural things are effects from spiritual, and spiritual things are effects from celestial, and the effect consists of so many things which are causes, that do not appear before the eyes, as may be said to reach to infinity. The effect is gross, and the cause enters every effect and composes it as its own general, in which are particulars and single things altogether beyond the sphere of the sight of the eye. [2] It is comparatively like a tree, which appears before the eyes luxuriant with branches, leaves, and fruits. All these are effects, but if you could examine a branch within as to the filaments, or a leaf as to fibers, or the fruit as to each and all things of it which are invisible, and the seed as to its invisible parts, of which the tree with all its members consists, you would see how innumerable and indescribable things lie hidden from the eyes. Once a flower was opened before the angels as to its interiors, which are called spiritual, and when they saw they said that there was within as it were a whole paradise,

consisting of indescribable things. [3] It is also like the human body with all its
members and organs that appear before the eye, as compared with its interiors,
where are so many organic forms, by pure arcana of all the sciences making so
many bodies from one, even so that you might say that into it are gathered
arcana of all the sciences, as Physics, Chemistry, Mechanics, Geometry,
Acoustics, Optics, which arcana of the sciences can in no wise be explored,
because not comprehended. Such is the internal with respect to the external, or
the spiritual with respect to the natural, and the celestial with respect to the
spiritual. The natural in itself regarded is nothing else than an external form,
which is called the effect of spiritual things; and the spiritual is an external
form, which is called the effect of celestial things; wherefore everything spiritual
is from the celestial, and everything natural is from the spiritual. From this it
is plain how it is to be understood that truth is the form of good, that good has
its quality in truths, because form is in them, and without form quality is
lacking; and that truth exists from good as from its own living cause; and that
if you remove good from truths, it is as if you should take the kernel from an
almond, the truth being like its shell; or as if you should take out the pulp from
fruit, and leave only the skin. Hence truth without good is turned into what is
fantastic, which appears externally like truth, but is empty within. So is the
natural without the spiritual, and also the spiritual without the celestial. [4]
Because there are ineffable things in the spiritual which do not appear in the
natural, and innumerable things in the celestial, therefore it is plain what is the
nature of the natural, the spiritual, and the celestial, that they are ineffable
with respect to one another. They follow after one another, as knowledge,
intelligence, and wisdom; wherefore also men on earth, because they are in
natural light, are called by the angels knowing, while angels of the Lord's
spiritual kingdom are called intelligent; and angels of the Lord's celestial
kingdom are called wise. [5] The Word in the sense of the letter may be
compared to a tree, surrounded with cortex or bark, entire, and endowed with
vegetative life, and the spiritual sense may be compared to its nutrition from
various juices and essences, partly ascending from the ground, partly imbibed
from the air and ether, by means of the heat and light of the sun. If the sense
of the letter alone existed, and not at the same time the spiritual sense and the
celestial sense, the Word would be as a tree without sap, or as the bark alone
without wood; but with those senses it is like a tree in its perfect state; indeed
in a tree all the sap passes from the root through the bark or cortex, wherefore
when that is taken away the tree dries up. Such would be the case with the
spiritual sense of the Word without its natural sense.

    XX. ALL THE HOLINESS OF THE WORD IS IN THE SENSE OF THE
LETTER, AND THERE IS NO HOLINESS IN ITS SPIRITUAL SENSE
WITHOUT THE SENSE OF THE LETTER. The spiritual sense without the
sense of the letter would be like a house without a foundation, thus like a house
in the air. It would be like the human body without its skins, all things of which
would be dissipated. As all the interiors of the body have a connection with the
peritoneum, the pleura, and the skins, so the spiritual sense of the Word is
connected with the sense of the letter. The spiritual sense without the sense of
the letter would be like the contents without that which contains, thus like wine
without a containing vessel. The case is similar with the spiritual without the

natural, or the heaven of angels and their wisdom without the human race and the church therein, and its intelligence from the sense of the letter. The sense of the letter of the Word with man makes that connection, and that conjunction. This also was the reason why the Lord came into the world, for all of the sense of the letter of the Word had been so falsified by the Jews that there was no longer an ultimate of Divine truth in man. Therefore the Lord came into the world and put on the Human, that He might also become the Word in the sense of the letter, or the Divine truth in ultimates; wherefore it is said that "the Word became flesh" (John 1:14). [2] The case is similar with the power of Divine truth. All power in the spiritual world belongs to the Divine truth proceeding from the Lord. What this power of Divine truth there is, may be illustrated by many things from experience, of which experience some things may be adduced; and all the power of Divine truth resides in the sense of the letter of the Word. In the spiritual sense without the sense of the letter there is no power, but all in the sense of the letter in which is the spiritual sense. Wherefore when spirits quote anything from the sense of the letter, manifest communication with heaven is effected, but not if they quote anything from the spiritual sense without the sense of the letter. [3] Therefore all answers from heaven have been made, and are made, through such things as are of the sense of the letter. For this reason the Urim and Thummim in the breastplate of Aaron, his outmost vesture, represented the sense of the letter. For the same reason in Revelation the foundations of the New Jerusalem are enumerated as of twelve precious stones, and moreover of pearls, which also signified the sense of the letter. In like manner the cherubim above the mercy seat signified the sense of the letter; wherefore responses were given by this to Moses and Aaron. [4] The order in which the interior things of Divine truth rest, from which the angels have wisdom, is simultaneous order, for which reason the sense of the letter is the containant. [5] Therefore all things of the doctrine of the church are to be confirmed by the sense of the letter of the Word, and whatever of doctrine is not confirmed from the sense of the letter of the Word has no power. Doctrine confirmed by the sense of the letter as to genuine truth, has power. The appearance of Divine truth also has power, though less, so far as it can agree with genuine truth; but the sense of the letter of the Word falsified has no power. It closes and does not open heaven.

XXI. THE SPIRITUAL SENSE. No one can see the spiritual sense except from the doctrine of genuine truth; from this doctrine the spiritual sense can be seen, when there is some knowledge of correspondences. He who is in false doctrine cannot see anything of the spiritual sense. He draws out and applies the correspondences which he sees to the falsities of his doctrine; and thus he can still more falsify the Word. Wherefore the true spiritual sense of the Word is from the Lord alone. This is the reason why it is not permitted anyone in the natural world, nor in the spiritual world, to investigate the spiritual sense of the Word from the sense of its letter, unless he is wholly in the doctrine of Divine truth and in enlightenment from the Lord, wherefore from the doctrine of Divine truth confirmed from the sense of the letter of the Word, the spiritual sense can be seen, but doctrine can never first be seen from the spiritual sense. He thinks falsely who says with himself, I know many correspondences, I can know the true doctrine of the Divine Word, the spiritual sense will teach it to me. This cannot be done. But, as has been said, let him say with himself, I know the doctrine of Divine truth, now I can see the spiritual sense, provided I know correspondences. But still this must be in enlightenment from the Lord, because the spiritual sense is Divine truth itself in its light, and is meant by glory, and the sense of the letter by a cloud in passages in the Word where these are mentioned. [2] That there is a spiritual sense in the Word is to be confirmed by ten passages in the Prophetic Word, likewise in the Evangelists, and also in Revelation, which passages are to be adduced, and it is to be shown that they would have no meaning without the spiritual sense.

XXII. IT IS BETTER FOR MAN IN MANY PASSAGES TO UNDERSTAND THE WORD ACCORDING TO THE LETTER. For example, in what the Lord says concerning cities, concerning the successive states of the church, in the Prophets in many passages, as concerning Tyre, in Revelation, and concerning paradise; for the reason that the angels are then in the spiritual sense with man.

XXIII. THE WORD. [1] Various things concerning the marriage of good and truth in the Word, to be shown from passages therein. [2] There are chapters and expressions peculiarly pertaining to good, and others to truth. [3] When pertaining to celestial good and truth, as where Judah is treated of; and to spiritual good and truth, as where Israel is treated of. [4] Each chapter has reference to one society, and many to all. [5] In some passages there is a sense from the letters alone, concerning which. [6] Numbers and names of persons and places signify things, of which examples are to be given.

XXIV. THE WORD IN HEAVEN. They have the Word in the spiritual kingdom in its higher region so written that it may be more and more intelligently understood by one who is intelligent, but simply by one who is simple, in which Word stands forth both interior and exterior intelligence, and the interior is written. This is effected by various points above the letters, the points signifying affections, and the series of points expressing the interior things of intelligence continuously to the more intelligent. This Word was seen by me, that is, something of it was seen. Something also of the Word of the celestial kingdom was seen, in which still more arcana were described, but by various curves and spirals above and within the letters, which are peculiar to the celestial kingdom. These arcana are very transcendent, nor can they be comprehended by an angel of the spiritual kingdom, nor even thought of; wherefore it was said to them that they can no more approximate to the wisdom of angels of the celestial kingdom than can those who are in a natural sphere approximate to the intelligence of angels of the spiritual kingdom; and how far this transcends has frequently been tried. From experience it was made evident to me, that the intelligence of angels of the spiritual kingdom is ineffable and incomprehensible to those who are in the natural kingdom; and that the wisdom of the angels of the celestial kingdom is incomprehensible and ineffable to those who are in the spiritual kingdom. But as to the Divine wisdom of the Lord, this so transcends all wisdom that no ratio can be given; for all the intelligence and wisdom of angels is finite, but the Divine wisdom of the Lord is infinite; and there is no ratio between the finite and the infinite. The intelligence and wisdom of angels is finite, because angels are recipients, and all recipients are created, and so finite.

XXVI. 26-1 [THE WORD WITH THE SPIRITUAL ANGELS.] Exploration was made as to how the spiritual angels express the words of their speech, and it was found that they express or speak them according to ideas, and from the ideas of the things which they signify, as when they express or speak of a horse and chariot, then they express them by a word which is significative, as a horse from ideas of the understanding, and a chariot from ideas of doctrine from the Word; and in like manner in other cases; so that they speak from the correspondence of those things which they see in like manner as men. In a word, they give names to them from correspondence. [2] It was therefore now disclosed to them, a thing they had not known, that they have correspondences in the words of their speech; and it was disclosed by their examining in the natural with me their ideas concerning those things in a spiritual state. In a word, the words of speech of their tongue were all formed from correspondences. [3] Inquiry was made as to how they write, "horses harnessed to a chariot." They said that they write only l, and that that letter expresses it. Inquiry was then made how they write "the understanding of doctrine," and they said in like manner by l, but that they are then in a higher thought. From this also it was plain that there are correspondences in the words of their language, but that few of them had attended to this, just as few in this world attend to spiritual light, when the light of the understanding is spoken of, or illumination and enlightenment; and to fire or spiritual heat when heavenly fire is spoken of, as that which enkindles hearts, not knowing that fire and heat therefrom correspond to love, which is of the heart, that is, to the will, and light to truth, which is of the understanding. 26-2

Footnotes

1-1 [MARGINAL NOTE.] The sense of the letter is the foundation of the wall of Jerusalem and the twelve precious stones there; these are the Urim and Thummin upon the ephod of Aaron.

4-1 We are to understand by all these vowels their Continental, not their English sounds.

7-1 [MARGINAL NOTE.] For thus they would be convinced that by Peter is not meant Peter, also that the Word even to its inmosts is Divine; and that a papal decree is of no account in comparison.

7-2 The Four Leading Doctrines.--TR.

10-1 [MARGINAL NOTE.] From the correspondence of natural things with spiritual, the ultimate sense of the word is meant by the twelve precious stones or which the foundations of the wall of the New Jerusalem consisted.

26-1 No number 25 is found.

26-2 The manuscript ends here.

God the Savior

1. The theology of the whole Christian world is founded on the worship of three Gods.

2. God is one in essence and Person.

3. In Him is a Trinity, and this must not be distinguished into Persons.

4. The Divine attributes constitute His essence.

5. These are many, and also succeeding.

6. The succeeding Divine attributes are creation and preservation, redemption and salvation, reformation and regeneration.

7. These are Divine, but that they are not as God is in Himself.

8. The one God willed to become a natural Man, and thus a full Man, for many reasons, the primary of which was the redemption of angels and men.

9. Passages from Scripture showing that there is one God.

10 He is the Redeemer and Savior.

11. He came into the world.

12. As to His Human, He called Himself Jesus Christ.

13. Jehovah Himself came into the world and became the Savior and Redeemer.

14. The one God is not only the Creator, but also the Redeemer and Regenerator.

15. As to the Divine truth, He descended and took upon Himself the Human, is confirmed in John, Chap. 1. Also, that He was from eternity, also from His nativity, Luke 1.

16. Passages from the sacred Scripture showing that He is the truth and the light; also, that He is the Word and that He fulfilled the whole of it.

17. All things were made by him.

18. In the spiritual sense, Divine truth is called the Son of God.

19. Divine truth is meant by Messiah, Christ, King, the Anointed, and David.

20. Divine truth is meant by angel and by one sent.

21. Divine truth is meant by glory.

22. In no other way could all things in the heavens and in the hells have been reduced into order.

23. In no other way could He destroy the old church and institute a new church.

24. In no other way could He admit temptations into Himself, and suffer.

25. In no other way could He be in the state of exinanition and pray to God the Father as though absent.

26. In no other way could He become Redemption and Justice from His own power.

27. Thus, in no other way could He unite the Human to the Divine and the reverse, and thus add the Human in time to the Divine from eternity.

28. In no other way could He be and become one with the Father.

29. All things which are in the Divine are together in the Human.

30. The Lord glorified His Human in the order in which He makes man spiritual, or an angel. Concerning the two states of man's regeneration.

31. Thus He made His Human Divine.

32. Thus He became the First and the Last, thus the all in all.

33. The Divine operation is from firsts through lasts, and because, in the church, lasts had failed, therefore, He made Himself the Last.

34. Man cannot be conjoined with God except by means of a visible and

accessible Human.

35. Every male is born, as to his spiritual origin, from truth as a seed.

36. The reason why men have not hitherto perceived this, and why consequently there have been so many opinions about the human nature of Christ, is because men have had no distinct understanding concerning the nature of good and truth and of their marriage, nor concerning the nature of the will and the understanding, nor of the soul and the body.

37. The virgin also, of whom He was born, signifies the church as to the affection of truth.

38. It was necessary for Him to be born of a virgin in legitimate marriage with Joseph.

39. Christ alone is man from eternity and natural man in time.

40. In Him everything is Divine from the Divine in itself.

41. He alone is to be approached, that there may be salvation.

42. He must be approached immediately, and if He is approached mediately, communication is intercepted.

43. Here may be adduced those passages, which treat of the "great affliction," and the things which follow.

44. To worship three Gods is to worship none.

45. No one comes to God or is conjoined to Him, unless the Human be approached; otherwise God is not accessible.

46. Because God the Father is the Redeemer as to the Human.

47. In order that there may be conjunction, there must be a visible God, thus one accessible and fixed; this is not so apparent to Christians, but it is to all others.

48. The Divine truth suffered.

Interaction of the Soul and Body

Concerning the interaction between the soul and the body, or the operation of one into the other, and of one with the other, there are three opinions and traditions, which are hypotheses. The first is called Physical Influx, the second Spiritual Influx, and the third Pre-established Harmony. The first, which is called Physical Influx, is from the appearances of the senses and the fallacies therefrom, since it appears as if the objects of sight, which affect the eyes, flow into thought and produce it; in like manner that speech, which moves the ears, flows into the mind and introduces ideas there; and similarly with the senses of smell, taste, and touch. Since the organs of these senses first receive the impressions from contact with the world, and according as they are affected the mind appears to think and also to will; for this reason the ancient philosophers and scholastics believed that influx was derived from these organs into the soul, and thus they adopted the hypothesis of physical or natural influx. [2] The second hypothesis, which is called Spiritual Influx, by some occasional influx, is from order and its laws; since the soul is a spiritual substance, and therefore purer, prior, and interior, but the body is material, and therefore grosser, posterior, and exterior; and it is according to order that purer should flow into grosser, prior into posterior, and interior into exterior, thus spiritual into material, and not the reverse. Consequently it is of order that the thinking mind should flow into the sight according to the state induced on the eyes from objects, which state the mind also disposes at will; and likewise the perceptive mind into the hearing according to the state induced on the ears from speech. [3] The third hypothesis, which is called Pre-established Harmony, is from the appearances and fallacies of reason, since the mind in its operation acts together and at the same time with the body. But yet every operation is first successive and afterward simultaneous. Successive operation is influx, and simultaneous operation is harmony; as when the mind thinks and afterward speaks, or when it wills and afterward acts. It is therefore a fallacy of reason to establish simultaneous operation and to exclude successive. Besides these three opinions concerning the interaction of the soul and the body, no fourth is possible, for either the soul must operate on the body, or the body on the soul, or both continually together.

Since spiritual influx is from order and its laws, as was said, therefore this influx has been acknowledged and received by the wise in the learned world in preference to the other two hypotheses. All that which is from order is truth, and truth manifests itself by the light implanted in it, even in the shade of reason, in which hypotheses are. But there are three things that involve this hypothesis in shade; ignorance of what the soul is, ignorance of what the spiritual is, and ignorance of what influx is; therefore these three must first be unfolded before reason sees the truth itself. For hypothetical truth is not truth itself, but only a conjecture of truth. It is as a picture on the wall seen at night by the light of the stars, on which the mind induces various forms according to its fancy. It is otherwise when the light of the sun after the dawn shines upon it, and disposes and brings to view not only its generals, but also its particulars. So out of the shade of truth in which this hypothesis is, truth is opened when it is known what the spiritual is and what is its quality in comparison with the natural, also what the human soul is and its quality, as well as the nature of the influx that flows into the soul and through it into the perceptive and thinking mind, and from this into the body. [2] But these things cannot be explained except by one to whom it has been granted by the Lord to associate with angels in the spiritual world and at the same time with men in the natural world. And because this has been granted to me, I have been able to describe both the spiritual and the natural, and their nature; which has been done in the work on Conjugal Love, the spiritual is described there in the Relation (n. 326-399); the human soul (n. 315); influx (n. 380); and more fully (n. 415-422). Who does not know, or may not know, that the good of love and the truth of faith flow from God into man, and that they flow into his soul, and are felt in his mind, and flow out from his thought into his speech, and from his will into his actions? [3] That spiritual influx, and its origin and derivation, are from this, will be manifested in the following order: I. There are two worlds, the spiritual world, where spirits and angels are, and the natural world, where men are. II. The spiritual world existed and subsists from its own sun, and the natural world from its sun. III. The sun of the spiritual world is pure love from Jehovah God, who is in the midst of it. IV. From that sun proceed heat and light, and the heat proceeding from it is in its essence love, and the light thence is in its essence wisdom. V. Both that heat and that light flow into man, the heat into his will, where it produces the good of love, and the light into his understanding, where it produces the truth of wisdom. VI. These two, heat and light, or love and wisdom, flow conjointly from God into the soul of man, and through this into his mind, its affections and thoughts, and from these into the senses, speech, and actions of the body. VII. The sun of the natural world is pure fire, and by means of this sun the world of nature existed and subsists. VIII. Therefore everything which proceeds from this sun, regarded in itself, is dead. IX. The spiritual clothes itself with the natural, as a man clothes himself with a garment. X. Spiritual things thus clothed in a man enable him to live as a rational and moral man, thus a spiritually natural man. XI. The reception of that influx is according to the state of love and wisdom with man. XII. The understanding in man can be elevated into the light, that is, into the wisdom in which the angels of heaven are, according to the cultivation of his reason; and his will can be elevated in like manner into heat, that is, into love, according to the deeds of his life; but the love of the will is not elevated, except so far as man wills and does those things which the wisdom of the understanding teaches. XIII. It is altogether otherwise with beasts. XIV. There are three degrees in the spiritual world, and three degrees in the natural world, according to which all influx takes place. XV. Ends are in the first degree, causes in the second, and effects in the third. XVI. From these things it is evident what is the quality of spiritual influx from its origin to its effects. Each of these propositions shall now be briefly illustrated.

I. There are two worlds, the spiritual world, where spirits and angels are, and the natural world, where men are. That there is a spiritual world, in which spirits and angels are, distinct from the natural world in which men are, has hitherto been deeply hidden even in the Christian world. The reason is, because no angel has descended and taught it by word of mouth, and no man has ascended and seen it. Lest therefore from ignorance of that world, and the uncertain faith concerning heaven and hell resulting from it, man should be infatuated to such a degree as to become an atheistic naturalist, it has pleased the Lord to open the sight of my spirit, and to elevate it into heaven, and also to let it down into hell, and to present to view the quality of both. [2] Thence it has thus been manifested to me that there are two worlds, which are distinct from each other; one in which all things are spiritual, which is therefore called the spiritual world, and the other in which all things are natural, and thence is called the natural world; and that spirits and angels live in their own world, and men in theirs; and also that every man passes by death from his own world into the other, and in this he lives to eternity. A knowledge of both of these worlds must be given first, in order that influx, which is here treated of, may be disclosed from its beginning; for the spiritual world flows into the natural world, and actuates it in all its parts, both with men and with beasts, and also constitutes the vegetative activity in trees and herbs.

II. The spiritual world existed and subsists from its own sun, and the natural world from its own sun. That there is one sun of the spiritual world and another of the natural world, is because those worlds are altogether distinct; and a world derives its origin from its sun; for a world in which all things are spiritual cannot arise from a sun all things from which are natural, for thus there would be physical influx, which however is contrary to order. That the world existed from the sun, and not the reverse, is manifest from the effect of the cause, namely, that the world, in each and every part subsists by means of the sun; and subsistence demonstrates existence, wherefore it is said that subsistence is perpetual existence; from which it is evident, that if the sun were removed, its world would fall into chaos, and this chaos into nothing. [2] That in the spiritual world there is a sun other than that in the natural world, I can testify, for I have seen it. It appears fiery like our sun, of a nearly similar magnitude, it is distant from the angels as our sun is from men; but it does not rise nor set, but stands immovable at a middle altitude between the zenith and the horizon, whence the angels have perpetual light and perpetual spring. [3] The man of reason, who knows nothing concerning the sun of the spiritual world, easily goes astray in his idea of the creation of the universe, which, when he deeply considers it, he perceives no otherwise than as being from nature; and as the origin of nature is the sun, no otherwise than as being from its sun as a creator. Moreover no one can apprehend spiritual influx, unless he also knows its origin; for all influx is from a sun, spiritual influx from its sun, and natural influx from its sun. The internal sight of man, which is that of his mind, receives influx from the spiritual sun, but his external sight, which is that of his body, receives influx from the natural sun; and both conjoin themselves together in operation, in like manner as the soul conjoins itself with the body. [4] From these things it is evident into what blindness, thick darkness, and foolishness they may fall who know nothing about the spiritual world and its sun: into blindness, because the mind that depends on the sight of the eye alone becomes in its reasonings like a bat, which flies by night here and there to a suspended cloth; into thick darkness, because the sight of the mind, when the sight of the eye flows into it from within, is deprived of all spiritual light, and becomes like an owl; into foolishness, because the man still thinks, but from natural things concerning spiritual things, and not the reverse; thus insanely, stupidly, and foolishly.

III. The sun of the spiritual world is pure love, from Jehovah God, who is in the midst of it. Spiritual things cannot proceed from any other source than from love, and love cannot proceed from any other source than from Jehovah God, Who is love itself. Wherefore the sun of the spiritual world, from which all spiritual things flow forth as from their fountain, is pure love from Jehovah God, Who is in the midst of it. That sun itself is not God, but is from God, and is the nearest sphere around Him from Him. By means of this sun the universe was created by Jehovah God; by which universe are meant all worlds in the aggregate which are as many as the stars in the expanse of our heaven. [2] That creation was effected by means of that sun, which is pure love, thus by Jehovah God, is because love is the very esse of life, and wisdom is the existere of life therefrom, and all things were created from love by wisdom. This is meant by these words in John: The Word was with God, and God was the Word, all things were made by Him, and without Him nothing was made which was made; and the world was made by Him (1:1, 3, 10). "The Word" there is the Divine truth; thus also the Divine wisdom; wherefore also the Word is there called the light which enlightens every man (verse 9), in like manner as does the Divine wisdom by Divine truth. [3] Those who derive the origin of worlds from any other source than from the Divine love through the Divine wisdom, are deluded like persons of disordered brain, who see specters as men, phantoms as lights, and imaginary beings as real figures. For the created universe is a connected work, from love by wisdom. You will see this if you are able to investigate the connections of things in their order from firsts to lasts. [4] As God is one, so also the spiritual sun is one; for the extension of space cannot be predicated of spiritual things, which are the derivations of that sun; and essence and existence without space is everywhere in spaces without space; thus the Divine love is from the beginning of the universe to all its boundaries. That the Divine fills all things, and by filling preserves all things in the state in which they were created, reason sees remotely, and closely so far as it knows the quality of love as it is in itself, with its conjunction with wisdom for the perception of ends, its influx into wisdom for the exhibition of causes; and its operation through wisdom for the production of effects.

IV. From that sun proceed heat and light, and the heat proceeding from it is in its essence love, and the light thence is in its essence wisdom. It is known that in the Word, and thence in the common language of preachers, the Divine love is expressed by fire, as that heavenly fire fills the heart and kindles holy desires to worship God. The reason is because fire corresponds to love, and therefore signifies it. From this it is that Jehovah God was seen as fire in the bush before Moses, and in like manner on Mount Sinai before the sons of Israel; and that it was commanded that fire should be perpetually kept upon the altar, and that the lights of the lamp stand in the tabernacle should be lighted every evening. This was because fire signified love. [2] That there is heat from that fire is clearly evident from the effects of love; for a man is kindled, grows warm, and is inflamed, as his love is exalted into zeal, or into the wrath of anger. The heat of the blood, or the vital heat of men, and of animals in general, is from no other source than from the love, which constitutes their life. Nor is infernal fire anything else than love opposite to heavenly love. This then is the reason that the Divine love appears to the angels as the sun in their world, fiery like our sun, as was said above, and that the angels are in heat according to their reception of love from Jehovah God through that sun. [3] It follows from this that the light there is in its essence wisdom; for love and wisdom are indivisible, like esse and existere, for love exists through wisdom and according to it. This is very much as it is in our world, in that, in the time of spring, heat unites itself with light, and produces germinations and at length fructifications. Furthermore, everyone knows that spiritual heat is love, and spiritual light is wisdom, for a man grows warm according as he loves, and his understanding is in light according as he is wise. [4] I have often seen that spiritual light. It immensely exceeds natural light in brightness and also in splendor, for it is as brightness and splendor themselves, and appears like bright and dazzling snow, as the garments of the Lord appeared when He was transfigured (Mark 9:3; Luke 9:29). Since light is wisdom, therefore the Lord calls Himself: The Light which enlightens every man (John 1:9). And says in other places that: He is the Light itself (John 3:19; 8:12; 12:35, 36, 46). That is, that He is the Divine truth itself, which is the Word, thus wisdom itself. [5] It is believed that natural light which is also rational light, is from the light of our world; but it is from the light of the sun of the spiritual world; for the sight of the mind flows into the sight of the eye, thus also the lights, and not the reverse. If the reverse took place, there would be physical influx and not spiritual influx.

V. Both that heat and that light flow into man, the heat into his will, where it produces the good of love, and the light into his understanding, where it produces the truth of wisdom. It is known that all things universally have relation to good and truth, and that there is not given a single entity in which there is not what has relation to those two. From this it is that in man there are two receptacles of life, one which is the receptacle of good, which is called the will, and another which is the receptacle of truth, which is called the understanding; and as good is of love, and truth is of wisdom, the will is the receptacle of love, and the understanding is the receptacle of wisdom. That good is of love, is because what a man loves, this he wills, and when he does it he calls it good; and that truth is of wisdom, is because all wisdom is from truths; yea, the good which a wise man thinks, is truth, and this becomes good when he wills it and does it. [2] He who does not rightly distinguish between these two receptacles of life, which are the will and the understanding, and does not form a clear notion concerning them, vainly endeavors to know spiritual influx; for there is influx into the will, and there is influx into the understanding; there is an influx of the good of love into man's will, and there is an influx of the truth of wisdom into his understanding, both of them from Jehovah God immediately through the sun in the midst of which He is, and mediately through the angelic heaven. These two receptacles, the will and the understanding, are as distinct as heat and light; for the will receives the heat of heaven, which in its essence is love, and the understanding receives the light of heaven, which in its essence is wisdom, as was said above. [3] There is an influx from the human mind into the speech, and there is an influx into the actions; the influx into the speech is from the will through the understanding, but the influx into the actions is from the understanding through the will. They who know only of the influx into the understanding, and not at the same time into the will, and who reason and conclude from this, are like one-eyed persons, who see the objects on one side only, and not at the same time on the other; and like maimed persons, who do their work awkwardly with one hand only; and like the lame who hobble on one foot with a crutch. From these few things it is made plain, that spiritual heat flows into man's will, and produces the good of love, and that spiritual light flows into his understanding, and produces the truth of wisdom.

VI. Those two, namely heat and light, or love and wisdom, flow conjointly from God into the soul of man, and through this into his mind, its affections and thoughts, and from these into the senses, speech, and actions of the body. The spiritual influx hitherto treated of by men of learning, is the influx from the soul into the body, and not any influx into the soul, and through that into the body; although it is known that all the good of love, and all the truth of faith, flow from God into man, and that nothing of them is from man; and those things which flow in from God, flow directly into his soul and through the soul into the rational mind, and through this into those things which constitute the body. If anyone investigates spiritual influx in any other manner, he is like one who stops up the source of a fountain, and still seeks there for unfailing waters; or like one who deduces the origin of a tree from the root and not from the seed; or like one who examines derivatives without the beginning. [2] For the soul is not life in itself, but is a recipient of life from God, Who is life in itself; and all influx is of life, thus from God. This is meant by this passage: Jehovah God breathed into the nostrils of the man the soul of lives, and the man became a living soul (Gen. 2:7). "To breathe into the nostrils the soul of lives," signifies to implant the perception of good and truth. And the Lord also says of Himself: As the Father hath life in Himself, so hath He given also to the Son to have life in Himself (John 5:26). "Life in Himself" is God; and the life of the soul is life that flows in from God. [3] Now because all influx is of life, and life operates through its receptacles, and the inmost or first of the receptacles in man is his soul, therefore, that influx may be rightly perceived, it is necessary to begin from God, and not from an intermediate station. If the beginning were from an intermediate station, the doctrine of influx would be like a chariot without wheels, or like a ship without sails. Since it is so, therefore in the preceding articles the sun of the spiritual world has been treated of, in the midst of which is Jehovah God (n. 5); and the influx thence of love and wisdom, thus of life (n. 6, 7). [4] The reason that life from God flows into man through the soul, and through this into his mind, that is, into its affections and thoughts, and from these into the senses, speech, and actions of the body, is because these are of life in successive order; for the mind is subordinate to the soul, and the body is subordinate to the mind. And the mind has two lives, one of the will and another of the understanding. The life of the will is the good of love, the derivations of which are called affections, and the life of the understanding is the truth of wisdom, the derivations of which are called thoughts. By these together the mind lives. But the senses, speech, and actions are the life of the body; that these are from the soul through the mind, follows from the order in which they are; and from this they manifest themselves before a wise man without investigation. [5] The human soul, because it is a superior spiritual substance, receives influx immediately from God; but the human mind, because it is an inferior spiritual substance, receives influx from God mediately through the spiritual world; and the body, because it is from the substances of nature, which are called material, receives influx from God mediately through the natural world. That the good of love and the truth of wisdom flow from God into the soul of man conjointly, that is, united into one, but that they are divided by man in their progression, and are conjoined only with those who suffer themselves to be led by God, will be seen in the following articles.

VII. The sun of the natural world is pure fire, and by means of this sun the world of nature existed and subsisted. That nature and its world, by which are meant the atmospheres, and the earths which are called planets, among which is the terraqueous globe on which we dwell, and also each and all of the things which yearly adorn its surface, subsist solely from the sun, which constitutes their center, and which by the rays of its light and the temperings of its heat is everywhere present, everyone knows with certainty from experience, from the testimony of the senses, and from the writings which treat of the way in which the world has become inhabited. And as the perpetual subsistence of these things is from the sun, reason may with certainty conclude that their existence also is thence; for perpetually to subsist is perpetually to exist as they first existed. From this it follows that the natural world was created by Jehovah God secondarily through this sun. [2] That there are spiritual things and that there are natural things, which are entirely distinct from each other, and that the origin and maintenance of spiritual things is from a sun which is pure love, in the midst of which is the Creator and founder of the universe, Jehovah God, has been heretofore shown; but that the origin and maintenance of natural things is from a sun which is pure fire, and that the latter is from the former, and both from God, follows of itself, as the posterior follows from the prior, and the prior from the first. [3] That the sun of nature and its worlds is pure fire, all its effects clearly show; as the concentration of its rays into a focus by optical instruments, from which proceeds fire burning with vehemence and also flame; the nature of its heat, which is similar to heat from elementary fire; the graduation of that heat according to its angle of incidence, whence are the varieties of climate, and also the four seasons of the year; besides many things, from which reason, by the senses of its body, may confirm the truth that the sun of the natural world is mere fire, and also that it is fire in its purity itself. [4] Those who know nothing concerning the origin of spiritual things from their own sun, but only concerning the origin of natural things from theirs, can scarcely avoid confounding spiritual things and natural things, and concluding, through the fallacies of the senses and thence of the reason, that spiritual things are nothing but pure natural things, and that from the activity of the latter, excited by light and heat, wisdom and love arise. Those, because they see nothing else with their eyes, and smell nothing else with their nostrils, and breathe nothing else with their breast than nature, therefore ascribe all rational things to it also, and thus absorb naturalism, as a sponge does waters. But these may be compared to charioteers who yoke the horses behind the chariot and not before it. [5] It is otherwise with those who distinguish between spiritual things and natural things, and deduce the latter from the former; these also perceive that the influx of the soul into the body is spiritual, and that natural things, which are of the body, serve the soul for vehicles and means, that it may produce its effects in the natural world. If you conclude otherwise, you may be likened to a crab, which in walking assists its progress with its tail, and draws its eyes backward at every step; and your rational sight may be compared to the sight of the eyes of Argus in the back of his head, when those in his forehead were asleep. These persons also believe themselves to be Arguses when they reason; for they say, Who does not see that the origin of the universe is from nature? and what then is God but the inmost extension of nature? and the like irrational things; of which they boast more than the wise do of rational things.

VIII. Therefore everything which proceeds from this sun, regarded in itself, is dead. Who does not see from the reason of his understanding, if this is a little elevated above the sensual things of the body, that love regarded in itself is alive, and that the appearance of its fire is life, and, on the contrary, that elementary fire regarded in itself is respectively dead; consequently, that the sun of the spiritual world, because it is pure love, is alive: and that the sun of the natural world, because it is pure fire, is dead; and similarly all things which proceed and exist from them? [2] There are two things which produce all the effects in the universe, Life and Nature, and they produce them according to order when life from within actuates nature. It is otherwise when nature from within brings life to act, which takes place with those who place nature, which in itself is dead, above and within life, and thence who strive solely after the pleasures of the senses and the lusts of the flesh, and care nothing for the spiritual things of the soul and the truly rational things of the mind. Such persons, on account of that inversion, are they who are called "the dead"; such are all atheistic naturalists in the world, and all satans in hell. [3] They are also called "the dead" in the Word, as in David: They joined themselves to Baal-peor, and ate the sacrifices of the dead (Ps. 106:28). The enemy persecuteth my soul, he maketh me to sit in darkness like the dead of the world (Ps. 143:3). To hear the groaning of the bound, and to open to the sons of death (Ps. 102:20). And in Revelation: I know thy works, that thou hast a name that thou livest, but thou art dead; be watchful and establish the things which remain that are ready to die (3:1, 2). [4] They are called "the dead," because spiritual death is damnation, and damnation is the lot of those who believe that life is from nature, and thus that the light of nature is the light of life, and thereby hide, suffocate, and extinguish every idea of God, of heaven, and of eternal life. Such persons are like owls, which see light in darkness and darkness in light, that is, falsities as truths and evils as goods; and because the delights of evil are the delights of their hearts, they are not unlike those birds and beasts which devour the bodies of the dead as dainties, and perceive the fetid odors from sepulchers as balsams. Such persons also do not see any other influx than physical or natural; if notwithstanding they affirm influx to be spiritual, this is not done from any idea of it but from the mouth of a teacher.

IX. The spiritual clothes itself with the natural, as a man clothes himself with a garment. It is known that in every operation there is an active and a passive; and that from the active alone nothing exists, and nothing from the passive alone. It is the same with the spiritual and the natural; the spiritual, because it is a living force, is active, and the natural, because it is a dead force, is passive. Hence it follows that whatever has existed in this solar world from the beginning, and afterwards exists every moment, is from the spiritual through the natural, and this not only in the subjects of the animal kingdom, but also in the subjects of the vegetable kingdom. [2] Another similar thing is also known, namely, that in everything which is effected there is a principal and an instrumental, and that these two, when anything is done, appear as one, although they are distinctly two; wherefore this also is one of the canons of wisdom, that the principal cause and the instrumental cause make together one cause; so also do the spiritual and the natural. That these two in producing effects appear as one, is because the spiritual is within the natural as the fibre is within the muscle, and as the blood is within the arteries; or as the thought is within the speech, and the affection in sounds; and it makes itself felt by means of the natural. From these things, but still as if through a lattice, it is evident that the spiritual clothes itself with the natural, as a man clothes himself with a garment. [3] The organic body with which the soul clothes itself is here likened to a garment, because it clothes the soul, and the soul also puts off the body, and casts it away as exuviae when by death it emigrates from the natural world into its own spiritual world. For the body grows old like a garment; but not the soul, because this is a spiritual substance, which has nothing in common with the changes of nature, which progress from their beginnings to their ends, and are periodically terminated. [4] They who do not consider the body as the vesture or covering of the soul, and as being in itself dead, and only adapted to receive the living forces flowing in through the soul from God, cannot help concluding, from fallacies, that the soul lives by itself, and the body by itself, and that there is a preestablished harmony between the lives of the two; or even that the life of the soul flows into the life of the body, or the life of the body into the life of the soul, and thus they conceive influx as either spiritual or natural; when yet it is a truth which is proved by everything that is created, that what is posterior does not act from itself, but from what is prior, from which it proceeded; thus that neither does this act from itself, but from something still prior; and thus that nothing acts except from the First which acts from itself, thus from God. Besides, there is only one life, and this is not capable of being created, but is eminently capable of flowing into forms organically adapted to its reception. Such forms are each and all of the things in the created universe. [5] It is believed by many that the soul is life, and thus, that a man, because he lives from the soul, lives from his own life, thus from himself, and therefore not by an influx of life from God; but these cannot help tying a sort of Gordian knot of fallacies, and entangling in it all the judgments of their mind, whence are mere insanities in spiritual things; or constructing a labyrinth, from which the mind can never, by any thread of reason, retrace its way and extricate itself; they also actually let themselves down as it were in caverns under the earth, where they dwell in eternal darkness. [6] For from such a belief proceed innumerable fallacies, each of which is horrible; as that God transfused and transcribed Himself into men, and that thus every man is a sort of Deity, which lives from itself, and thus that he does good and is wise from himself; likewise that he possesses faith and charity in himself, and thus derives them from himself, and not from God; besides many monstrous beliefs such as prevail with those in hell, who, when they were in the world, believed that nature lived, or produced life by its own activity. When these look towards heaven they see its light as mere thick darkness. I once heard the voice of one saying from heaven, that if a spark of life in man were his own, and not of God in him, there would be no heaven, nor anything therein, and hence that there would not be any church on earth, and consequently no life eternal. More upon this subject may be consulted in the Relation inserted in the work on Conjugal Love (n. 132-136).

X. Spiritual things, thus clothed in a man, enable him to live as a rational and moral man, thus a spiritually natural man. From the principle established above, that the soul clothes itself with a body as a man clothes himself with a garment, this follows as a conclusion. For the soul flows into the human mind, and through this into the body, and carries life with it, which it continually receives from the Lord, and thus transfers it mediately into the body, where by the closest union it makes the body as it were to live. Thence from a thousand testimonies of experience, it is evident that the spiritual united to the material, as a living force with a dead force, causes man to speak rationally and to act morally. [2] It appears as if the tongue and lips speak from a certain life in themselves, and that the arms and hands act in a like manner; but it is the thought, which in itself is spiritual, that speaks, and the will, which likewise is spiritual, that acts, and each through its own organs, which in themselves are material, because taken from the natural world. That it is so appears in the day, provided this is attended to: remove thought from speech, is not the mouth dumb in a moment? also remove will from action, do not the hands rest in a moment? [3] The union of spiritual things with natural, and the appearance of life therefrom in material things, may be compared to generous wine in a clean sponge, and to the sweet must in a grape, and to the savory liquor in an apple, and also to the aromatic odor in cinnamon. The fibers containing all these things are matters which neither taste nor are fragrant from themselves, but from the fluids in and between them; wherefore if you squeeze out those juices, they are dead filaments. So are the organs proper to the body, if life is taken away. [4] That man is rational from the union of spiritual things with natural, is evident from the analytical processes of his thought; and that he is moral from the honorableness of his conduct and the graces of his bearing. These he has from the faculty of receiving influx from the Lord through the angelic heaven, where is the very abode of wisdom and love, thus of rationality and morality. From these things it is perceived, that what is spiritual and what is natural, being united in man, cause him to live a spiritually natural man. The reason that he lives in a similar and yet dissimilar manner after death, is because his soul is then clothed with a substantial body, as in the natural world it was clothed with a material body. [5] It is believed by many that the perceptions and thoughts of the mind, because they are spiritual, flow in naked, and not through organized forms. But those dream thus who have not seen the interiors of the head, where perceptions and thoughts are in their beginnings; and that the brains are there, interwoven and composed of the cineritious and medullary substances, and that there are glands, cavities, septa, and the meninges and matres, which surround them all; and that a man thinks and wills sanely or insanely according to the sound or perverted state of all those things; thence that he is rational and moral according to the organic formation of his mind. For nothing could be predicated of the rational sight of man, which is the understanding, without forms organized for the reception of spiritual light, just as nothing could be predicated of the natural sight without the eyes; and so in other instances.

XI. The reception of that influx is according to the state of love and wisdom with a man. That a man is not life, but an organ recipient of life from God, and that love together with wisdom is life, also that God is love itself and wisdom itself, and thus life itself, has been demonstrated above. Thence it follows that so far as a man loves wisdom, or so far as wisdom in the bosom of love is with him, so far he is an image of God, that is, a receptacle of life from God; and, on the contrary, so far as he is in opposite love, and thence in insanity, so far he does not receive life from God, but from hell, which life is called death. [2] Love itself and wisdom itself are not life, but are the esse of life, but the delights of love and the pleasantnesses of wisdom, which are affections, constitute life, for the esse of life exists by these. The influx of life from God carries with it those delights and pleasantnesses just as does the influx of light and heat in springtime, into human minds, and also into birds and beasts of every kind, yea into plants, which then germinate and become prolific; for the delights of love and the pleasantnesses of wisdom expand minds and adapt them to reception, as joys and gladness expand the face and adapt it to the influx of the cheerfulness of the soul. [3] The man who is affected with the love of wisdom, is like the garden in Eden, in which are two trees, the one of life and the other of the knowledge of good and evil. The tree of life is the reception of love and wisdom from God, and the tree of the knowledge of good and evil is the reception of them from himself. But the latter is insane, and still believes that it is wise like God, while the former is truly wise, and believes that no one is wise but God alone, and that man is wise so far as he believes this, and more wise so far as he feels that he wills it. But more on this subject may be seen in the Relation inserted in the work on Conjugial Love (n. 132-136). [4] I will here add an arcanum confirming these things from heaven. All the angels of heaven turn their forehead to the Lord as a sun, and all the angels of hell turn the back of the head to Him; and the latter receive influx into the affections of their will, which in themselves are lusts, and make the understanding favor them; but the former receive influx into the affections of their understanding, and make the will favor them. Hence these are in wisdom, but the others are in insanity; for the human understanding dwells in the cerebrum, which is under the forehead, and the will in the cerebellum, which is in the back of the head. [5] Who does not know that a man who is insane from falsities, favors the cupidities of his own evil, and confirms them by reasons from the understanding; and that a wise man sees from truths the quality of the cupidities of his will, and curbs them? A wise man does this because he turns his face to God, that is, he believes in God, and not in himself; but an insane man does the other thing because he turns his face from God, that is, he believes in himself, and not in God. To believe in himself is to believe that he loves and is wise from himself, and not from God, and this is signified by eating of the tree of the knowledge of good and evil; but to believe in God is to believe that he loves and is wise from God, and not from himself, and this is to eat of the tree of life (Rev. 2:7). [6] From these things, but still only as in the light of the moon by night, it may be perceived that the reception of the influx of life from God is according to the state of love and wisdom with a man. This influx may further be illustrated by the influx of light and heat into plants, which blossom and bear fruit according to the structure of the fibers which form them, thus according to reception. It may also be illustrated by the influx of the rays of light into precious stones, which modify them into colors according to the situation of the parts composing them, thus also according to reception; and likewise by optical glasses and by drops of rain, which exhibit rainbows according to the incidences, refractions, and thus the receptions of light. The case is similar with human minds as to spiritual light, which proceeds from the Lord as a sun, and perpetually flows in, but is variously received.

XII. The understanding in a man can be elevated into the light, that is, into the wisdom in which the angels of heaven are, according to the cultivation of his reason; and in like manner his will can be elevated into the heat of heaven, that is, into love, according to the deeds of his life; but the love of the will is not elevated except so far as the man wills and does those things which the wisdom of the understanding teaches. By the human mind are meant its two faculties, which are called the understanding and the will. The understanding is the receptacle of the light of heaven, which in its essence is wisdom, and the will is the receptacle of the heat of heaven, which in its essence is love, as was shown above. These two, wisdom and love, proceed from the Lord, as a sun, and flow into heaven universally and particularly, whence the angels have wisdom and love; and they also flow into this world universally and particularly, whence men have wisdom and love. [2] But these two united proceed from the Lord, and likewise united flow into the souls of angels and men, but they are not received united in their minds. Light which makes the understanding is first received there, and love which constitutes the will is received gradually. This also is of providence, because every man is to be created anew, that is, reformed, and this is effected through the understanding; for from infancy he must acquire the knowledges of truth and good, which will teach him to live well, that is, to will and act rightly. Thus the will is formed through the understanding. [3] For the sake of this end, there is given to man the faculty of elevating his understanding almost into the light in which the angels of heaven are, that he may see what he ought to will and thence to do, in order that he may be prosperous in the world for a time, and be happy after death to eternity. He becomes prosperous and happy if he procures for himself wisdom, and keeps his will under obedience to it; but unprosperous and unhappy if he subjects his understanding under obedience to his will. The reason is, because the will from birth inclines to evils, even to enormous ones; wherefore unless it were curbed by the understanding, a man would rush into heinous things, yea, from his inborn savage nature, he would depopulate and slaughter for the sake of himself all those who do not favor and indulge him. [4] Furthermore, unless the understanding could be separately perfected, and the will by means of it, a man would not be a man, but a beast. For without that separation, and without the ascent of the understanding above the will, he would not be able to think, and from thought to speak, but only to express his affection by sounds; neither would he be able to act from reason, but only from instinct; still less would he be able to know the things which are of God, and God by means of them, and thus to be conjoined to Him, and to live to eternity. For a man thinks and wills as from himself, and this as from himself is the reciprocal of conjunction; for there cannot be conjunction without a reciprocal, just as there cannot be conjunction of the active with the passive without reaction. God alone acts, and man suffers himself to be acted on, and he reacts in all appearance as from himself, though interiorly it is from God. [5] From these things rightly perceived it may be seen what is the quality of the love of a man's will if it is elevated by means of the understanding, and what is its quality if it is not elevated; consequently, what is the quality of the man. But this quality of a man if the love of his will is not elevated by means of the understanding shall be illustrated by comparisons. He is like an eagle which flies on high, and as soon as it sees the food below which is the object of its desire, as chickens, young swans, yea, young lambs, swoops down in a moment and devours them. He is also like an adulterer, who conceals a harlot in a cellar below, and by turns goes up to the highest part of the house, and talks wisely with those who dwell there about chastity, and by turns hastens away from his companions, and indulges his lasciviousness below with his harlot. [6] He is also like a thief on a tower, who there pretends to keep watch, but who, as soon as he sees an object of plunder below, hastens down and seizes it. He may also be compared to marsh-flies, which fly in a column over the head of a running horse, but which fall down when the horse stops, and immerse themselves in their marsh. Such is the man whose will or love is not elevated by means of the understanding, for he then stands still below at the foot, immersed in the unclean things of nature and the lusts of the senses. It is altogether otherwise with those who subdue the allurements of the cupidities of the will by means of the wisdom of the understanding. With these the understanding afterwards enters into a conjugial covenant with the will, thence wisdom with love, and they dwell together above with delights.

XIII. It is altogether otherwise with beasts. Those who judge from the mere appearance to the senses of the body, conclude that beasts have will and understanding as well as men, and hence that the only distinction is that man can speak, and thus describe what he thinks and desires, while beasts can only express this by sounds. Yet beasts have not will and understanding, but only an image of each, which the learned call an analog. [2] That a man is a man, is because his understanding can be elevated above the desires of his will, and thus can know and see them from above, and also moderate them; but a beast is a beast because its desires impel it to do whatever it does. Wherefore a man is a man in that his will is under obedience to his understanding; but a beast is a beast in that its understanding is under obedience to its will. From these things this conclusion follows, that the understanding of man, because it receives the light that flows in from heaven, and apprehends and perceives this as its own, and from it thinks analytically with all variety, altogether as from itself, is alive, and thence a true understanding; and that the will of man, because it receives the inflowing love of heaven, and from it acts as from itself, is alive, and is thence truly will; but the contrary is the case with beasts. [3] Wherefore those who think from the lusts of the will are likened to beasts, and also in the spiritual world they appear at a distance as beasts; they also act like beasts, with this difference only, that they can act otherwise if they will. But those who restrain the lusts of their will by means of the understanding, and therefore act rationally and wisely, appear in the spiritual world as men, and are angels of heaven. [4] In a word, the will and the understanding in beasts always cohere; and because the will in itself is blind, for it is of heat and not of light, it makes the understanding blind also. Hence a beast does not know and understand its own actions; and yet it acts, for it acts from an influx from the spiritual world; and such action is instinct. [5] It is believed that a beast thinks from the understanding what it does, but this is not so; it is impelled to act only from natural love, which is in it from creation, with the assistance of the senses of its body. That a man thinks and speaks is solely because his understanding can be separated from his will, and can be elevated even into the light of heaven; for the understanding thinks, and thought speaks. [6] That beasts act according to the laws of order inscribed on their nature, and some beasts as it were morally and rationally, differently from many men, is because their understanding is blind obedience to the desires of their will, and therefore they are not able to pervert these by depraved reasonings, as men do. It is to be observed, that by the will and the understanding of beasts in the foregoing statements, is meant an image and analog of them. Analogs are so named from appearance. [7] The life of a beast may be compared with a somnambulist who walks and acts from the will while the understanding is in a deep sleep; and also with a blind man who walks through the streets with a dog leading him; and also with a foolish person, who from custom and the habit thence acquired does his work according to rules; likewise with a person void of memory, and therefore deprived of understanding, who still knows or learns how to clothe himself, to eat dainties, to love the sex, to walk the streets from house to house, and to do such things as soothe the senses and gratify the flesh, by the allurements and pleasures of which he is carried along, though he does not think, and therefore cannot speak. [8] From these things it is plain how much they are deceived who believe that beasts enjoy rationality, and are only distinguished from men by the external figure, and by their not being able to give utterance to the rational things which they hide within. From which fallacies many even conclude that if man lives after death beasts also will live after death, and, on the contrary, that if beasts do not live after death neither will man; besides many dreams arising from ignorance about the will and the understanding, and also about degrees, by means of which, as by a ladder, the mind of man mounts up to heaven.

XIV. There are three degrees in the spiritual world, and three degrees in the natural world, hitherto unknown, according to which all influx takes place. It is discovered, by the investigation of causes from effects, that there are degrees of two kinds, one in which are things prior and posterior, and another in which are things greater and less. The degrees which distinguish things prior and posterior are to be called degrees of altitude, and also discrete degrees; but the degrees by which things greater and less are distinguished from each other are to be called, degrees of latitude, and also continuous degrees. [2] Degrees of altitude, or discrete degrees, are like the generations and compositions of one thing from another; as, for example, of any nerve from its fibers, and of any fiber from its fibrils; or of any piece of wood, stone, or metal from its parts, and of any part from its particles. But degrees of latitude or continuous degrees are like the increments and decrements of the same degree of altitude as to breadth, length, height, and depth; as of greater and smaller volumes of water, or air, or ether; and as of large and small masses of wood, stone, or metal. [3] All and each of the things in both worlds, the spiritual and the natural, are, from creation, in degrees of both these kinds. The whole animal kingdom in this world is in those degrees both in general and in particular; and the whole vegetable kingdom and the whole mineral kingdom likewise; as also is the expanse of atmospheres from the sun even to the earth. [4] There are therefore three atmospheres discretely distinct according to the degrees of altitude, both in the spiritual world and in the natural world, because each world has its sun; but the atmospheres of the spiritual world, by virtue of their origin, are substantial, and the atmospheres of the natural world, by virtue of their origin, are material. And because the atmospheres descend from their origins according to those degrees, and are the containants, and, as it were, the carriers of light and heat, it follows that there are three degrees of light and heat. And because light in the spiritual world in its essence is wisdom, and heat there in its essence is love, as was shown above in its own article, it follows also that there are three degrees of wisdom and three degrees of love, hence three degrees of life; for they are graded by those things through which they pass. [5] Hence it is that there are three angelic heavens: a highest, which is also called the third heaven, where are the angels of the highest degree; a middle, which is also called the second heaven, where are the angels of the middle degree; and a lowest, which is also called the first heaven, where are the angels of the lowest degree. Those heavens are also distinguished according to the degrees of wisdom and love. Those who are in the lowest heaven are in the love of knowing truths and goods; those who are in the middle heaven are in the love of understanding them; and those who are in the highest heaven are in the love of being wise, that is, of living according to those things which they know and understand. [6] Since the angelic heavens are distinguished into three degrees, therefore the human mind is also distinguished into three degrees, because the human mind is an image of heaven, that is, it is a heaven in the least form. Hence it is that man can become an angel of one of those three heavens, and this is effected according to his reception of wisdom and love from the Lord: an angel of the lowest heaven if he receives only the love of knowing truths and goods; an angel of the middle heaven if he receives the love of understanding them; and an angel of the highest heaven if he receives the love of being wise, that is, of living according to them. That the human mind is distinguished into three regions, according to the three heavens, may be seen in the Relation inserted in the work on Conjugial Love (n. 270). From these things it is evident that all spiritual influx to man and into man descends from the Lord through these three degrees, and that it is received by man according to the degree of wisdom and love in which he is. [7] The knowledge of these degrees is of the greatest use at the present day; since many, because they do not know them, subsist and inhere in the lowest degree, in which are the senses of their body, and from ignorance, which is intellectual thick darkness, cannot be elevated into spiritual light, which is above them. Hence naturalism invades them, as it were spontaneously, as soon as they enter on any investigation and inquiry concerning the human soul and mind, and its rationality, and still more if they inquire concerning heaven and the life after death. Thus they become comparatively like those who stand in the marketplaces with telescopes in their hands, looking at the sky, and utter vain predictions; and also like those who chatter and also reason concerning every object they see, and everything they hear, without there being in it anything rational from the understanding. But such persons are like butchers, who believe themselves to be skilled in anatomy, because they have examined the viscera of oxen and sheep outwardly but not inwardly. [8] But it is a truth, that to think from the influx of natural light, not enlightened by the influx of spiritual light, is nothing else than dreaming, and to speak from such thought is to talk nonsense. But more concerning these degrees may be seen in the work on The Divine Love and The Divine Wisdom (n. 173-281).

XV. Ends are in the first degree, causes in the second, and effects in the third. Who does not see that the end is not the cause, but that it produces the cause, and that the cause is not the effect, but that it produces the effect; consequently that they are three distinct things which follow in order? The end with man is the love of his will, for what a man loves, this he proposes to himself and intends; the cause with him is the reason of his understanding, for by means of it the end seeks for mediate or efficient causes; and the effect is the operation of the body from them and according to them. Thus there are three things in man, which follow each other in order, in like manner as the degrees of altitude follow each other. When these three things appear in act, then the end is inwardly in the cause, and the end through the cause is in the effect, wherefore the three coexist in the effect. On this account it is said in the Word, that everyone shall be judged according to his works; for the end, or the love of his will, and the cause, or the reason of his understanding, are together in the effects, which are the works of his body; thus the quality of the whole man is in them. [2] They who do not know these things, and do not thus distinguish the objects of reason, cannot avoid terminating the ideas of their thought in the atoms of Epicurus, the monads of Leibniz, or in the simple substances of Wolff, and thus they close up their understandings as with a bolt, so that they cannot even think from reason concerning spiritual influx, because they cannot think concerning any progression; for the author says concerning his simple substance, that if it is divided it falls into nothing. Thus the understanding stands still in its first light, which is merely from the senses of the body, and does not advance a step further. Hence it is not known but that the spiritual is a subtle natural, and that beasts have a rational as well as men, and that the soul is a breath of wind such as is breathed forth from the breast when a person dies; besides many things which are not of light but of thick darkness. [3] Since all things in the spiritual world and all things in the natural world proceed according to these degrees, as was shown in the preceding article, it is evident that intelligence properly consists in knowing and distinguishing them, and seeing them in their order. By means of these degrees, also, every man is known as to his quality, when his love is known; for, as was said above, the end which is of the will, and the causes which are of the understanding, and the effects which are of the body, follow from his love, as a tree from its seed, and as fruit from the tree. [4] There are three kinds of loves, the love of heaven, the love of the world, and the love of self; the love of heaven is spiritual, the love of the world is material, and the love of self is corporeal. When the love is spiritual, all the things which follow from it, as forms from their essence, derive their spiritual nature; similarly if the principal love is the love of the world or of wealth, and thus is material, all the things which follow from it, as derivatives from their principle derive their material nature; likewise if the principal love is the love of self, or of eminence above all others, and thus is corporeal, all the things which follow from it derive their corporeal nature. The reason is, because the man who is in this love regards himself alone, and thus immerses the thoughts of his mind in his body. Wherefore, as was just now said, he who knows the ruling love of anyone, and at the same time the progression of ends to causes and of causes to effects, which three things follow in order according to the degrees of altitude, knows the whole man. Thus the angels of heaven know everyone with whom they speak; they perceive his love from the tone of his speech; and they see his image from his face, and his character from the gestures of his body.

XVI. From these things it is evident what is the quality of spiritual influx from its origin to its effects. Spiritual influx has hitherto been deduced from the soul into the body, but not from God into the soul and thus into the body. This has been done, because no one knew anything concerning the spiritual world, and concerning the sun there, from which all spiritual things flow as from their fountain, and thus nothing concerning the influx of spiritual things into natural things. [2] Now because it has been granted me to be in the spiritual world and in the natural world at the same time, and thus to see each world and each sun, I am obliged by my conscience to manifest these things; for what is the use of knowing, unless what is known to one be also known to others? Without this, what is knowing but collecting and storing up riches in a casket, and only looking at them occasionally and counting them over, without any thought of use from them? Spiritual avarice is nothing else. [3] But that it may be fully known what and of what quality spiritual influx is, it is necessary to know what the spiritual is in its essence, and what the natural is, and also what the human soul is. Lest therefore this short treatise should be defective through ignorance of these things, it is important to consult some Relations inserted in the work on Conjugial Love; concerning the spiritual, in the Relation there (n. 326-329); concerning the human soul (n. 315); and concerning the influx of spiritual things into natural things (n. 380); and more fully (n. 415-422).

To these things I will add this Relation. After these things were written, I prayed to the Lord that I might be permitted to converse with disciples of Aristotle, and at the same time with disciples of Descartes, and with disciples of Leibnitz, in order that I might draw forth the opinions of their minds concerning the interaction between the soul and the body. After my prayer, there were present nine men, three Aristotelians, three Cartesians, and three Leibnitzians; and they stood around me, the admirers of Aristotle on the left side, the followers of Descartes on the right, and the supporters of Leibnitz behind. Quite a distance away, and at intervals from each other, were seen three persons as it were crowned with laurel, and I knew from an inflowing perception that they were those three great leaders or teachers themselves. Behind Leibnitz stood one holding in his hand the skirt of his garment, and I was told that it was Wolff. Those nine men, when they beheld one another, at first saluted and spoke to one another in a courteous tone. [2] But presently there arose from below a spirit with a torch in his right hand, which he shook before their faces, whereupon they became enemies, three against three, and looked at one another with a fierce countenance; for they were seized with the lust of disputing and discussing. Then the Aristotelians, who were also scholastics, began to speak, saying, Who does not see that objects flow in through the senses into the soul, as one enters through the doors into a chamber, and that the soul thinks according to such influx? When a lover sees a beautiful virgin or his bride, does not his eye sparkle and carry the love of her into the soul? When a miser sees bags of money, does he not burn for them with every sense, and thence convey this order into the soul, and excite the cupidity of possessing them? When a proud man hears his praises from another, does he not prick up his ears, and do not these transmit those praises to the soul? Are not the senses of the body like outer courts, through which alone there is entrance to the soul? From these things and innumerable others like them, who can conclude otherwise than that influx is from nature, or is physical? [3] To these statements the followers of Descartes, who had held their fingers on their foreheads, and now withdrew them, replied, saying, Alas, you speak from appearances. Do you not know that the eye does not love a virgin or a bride from itself, but from the soul? Likewise that the senses of the body do not covet the bags of money from themselves, but from the soul? and similarly that the ears do not seize on the praises of flatterers in any other manner? Is it not perception that causes sensation? and perception is of the soul, and not of the organs. Tell, if you can, what else makes the tongue and lips to speak but the thought? and what else makes the hands to work but the will? and thought and will are of the soul, and not of the body. Thus what makes the eye to see, and the ears to hear, and the other organs to feel, but the soul? From these things, and innumerable others like them, everyone whose wisdom is above the sensual things of the body, concludes, that there is no influx of the body into the soul, but of the soul into the body, which we call occasional, and also spiritual influx. [4] When these had been heard, the three men who stood behind the former triads, who were the supporters of Leibnitz, lifted up their voices, saying, We have heard the arguments on both sides, and have compared them, and we have perceived that in many particulars the latter are stronger than the former, and that in many others the former are stronger than the latter; wherefore if it is permitted, we will settle the dispute. And on being asked how, they said, There is not any influx of the soul into the body, nor of the body into the soul, but there is a unanimous and instantaneous operation of both together, which a celebrated author has distinguished by a beautiful name, calling it preestablished harmony. [5] Hereupon there appeared again the spirit with the torch in his hand, but now in his left, and he shook it at the back of their heads, whence their ideas of everything became confused and they cried out together, Neither our soul nor body knows what part to take, wherefore let us decide this dispute by lot, and we will favor the lot which comes out first. And they took three pieces of paper, and wrote on one of them, physical influx, on another spiritual influx, and on the third, preestablished harmony; and they put these three pieces into a hat. Then they chose one of their number to draw, and he, putting in his hand, took hold of that on which was written spiritual influx; and when this was seen and read, they all said, yet some with a clear and flowing, some with a faint and smothered voice, Let us favor this because it came out first. [6] But then an angel suddenly stood by, and said, Do not believe that the paper in favor of spiritual influx came out by chance, but from providence; for you do not see its truth because you are in confused ideas, but the truth itself presented itself to the hand of him that drew the lots, that you might favor it.

I was once asked how from a philosopher I became a theologian; and I answered, In the same manner that fishermen were made disciples and apostles by the Lord; and that I also from early youth had been a spiritual fisherman. On hearing this the inquirer asked, What is a spiritual fisherman? I replied that a fisherman in the spiritual sense of the Word, signifies a man who investigates and teaches natural truths, and afterwards spiritual truths rationally. [2] To the question, How is this demonstrated? I said, From these passages in the Word: Then the waters shall fail from the sea, and the river shall be dried up and become dry, therefore the fishers shall mourn, and all that cast a hook into the sea shall be sad (Isa. 19:5, 8). In another place: Upon the river whose waters were healed, the fishers stood from Engedi; they were there in the spreading forth of nets; according, to its kind was their fish, as the fish of the great sea, exceeding many (Ezek. 47:9-10). And in another place: The saying of Jehovah, Behold, I will send to many fishers, who shall fish the sons of Israel (Jer. 16:16). Thence it is evident, why the Lord chose fishermen for disciples, and said: Come ye after Me, and I will make you fishers of men (Matt. 4:18-19; Mark 1:16-17). And to Peter after he had caught a multitude of fishes: From henceforth thou shalt catch men (Luke 5:9-10). [3] Afterwards I demonstrated the origin of this signification of fishermen from The Apocalypse Revealed; namely, because "water" signifies natural truths (n. 50, 932); likewise "a river" (n. 409, 932); "fish," those who are in natural truths (n. 405); and thence "fishermen" signify those who investigate and teach truths. [4] On hearing this my interrogator raised his voice and said, Now I can understand why the Lord called and chose fishermen to be His disciples, and therefore I do not wonder that He has also called and chosen you, since, as you have said, you were from early youth a fisherman in a spiritual sense, that is, an investigator of natural truths; that you are now an investigator of spiritual truths, is because these are founded on the former. To this he added, because he was a man of reason, that the Lord alone knows who is adapted to receive and to teach those things which are of His New Church, whether someone among the primates, or someone among their servants. Moreover, what theologian among Christians does not first study philosophy at college, before he is inaugurated as a theologian; and from what other source has he intelligence? [5] At last he said, Since you are become a theologian, explain what is your theology. I replied, These are the two principles of it, That God is one, and that there is a conjunction of charity and faith. To which he replied, Who denies these? I answered, The theology of the present day, when interiorly examined.

The New Jerusalem and its Heavenly Doctrine

Section 1

THE NEW HEAVEN AND THE NEW EARTH, AND WHAT IS MEANT BY THE NEW JERUSALEM. It is written in the Apocalypse: I saw a New Heaven and a New Earth; for the first heaven and the first earth were passed away. And I saw the holy city, New Jerusalem, coming down from God out of heaven, prepared as a bride before her husband. The city had a wall, great and high, which had twelve gates, and at the gates twelve angels, and names written thereon, which are the names of the twelve tribes of Israel. And the wall of the city had twelve foundations, in which were the names of the twelve apostles of the Lamb. The city itself lieth four-square, and the length is as great as the breadth. And he measured the city with the reed, twelve thousand stadia; the length and the breadth and the height of it were equal. And he measured the wall thereof, a hundred forty-four cubits, the measure of a man, which is, of an angel. And the wall of it was of jasper; and the city itself was pure gold, like unto pure glass; and the foundations of the wall of the city were of every precious stone. The twelve gates were twelve pearls. And the street of the city was pure gold, as it were pellucid glass. The glory of God did lighten it, and the lamp of it was the Lamb. The nations which were saved shall walk in the light of it; and the Kings of the earth shall bring their glory and honor into it. (21:1, 2, 12-24.) The man who reads these things, understands them only according to the sense of the letter; namely, that the visible heaven and earth will perish, and a new heaven will exist, and that the holy city Jerusalem, answering to the measures above described, will descend upon the new earth; but the angels understand these things altogether differently; namely, what man understands naturally, they understand spiritually; and as the angels understand, so they signify; and this is the internal or spiritual sense of the Word. In the internal or spiritual sense, "a New Heaven and a New Earth" means a New Church, both in the heavens and on the earth, which will be more particularly spoken of hereafter. "The city Jerusalem coming down from God out of heaven" signifies its heavenly doctrine; "the length," "the breadth," and "the height," which are equal, signify all the goods and truths of that doctrine in the aggregate. By "the wall" of it is meant the truths which protect it; "the measure of the wall," which is "a hundred forty-four cubits, which is the measure of a man, that is, of an angel," signifies all those protecting truths in the aggregate, and their quality. "The twelve gates" of pearl mean introductory truths; "the twelve angels at the gates" signify the same. "The foundations of the wall" which are "of every precious stone," mean the knowledges on which that doctrine is founded. "The twelve tribes of Israel," and "the twelve apostles," mean all things of the church in general and in particular. The city and its streets being of "gold like unto pure glass," signifies the good of love from which the doctrine and its truths are pellucid. "The nations" who are saved, and "the kings of the earth" who bring glory and honor into it, mean all of the church who are in goods and truths. "God" and "the Lamb" mean the Lord as to the Divine itself and the Divine Human. Such is the spiritual sense of the Word, to which the natural sense, which is that of the letter, serves as a basis; but still these two senses, the spiritual and the natural, form a one by correspondences. It is not the design of the present work to show that there is such a spiritual meaning in the afore-mentioned passages, but the proof of it may be seen in the Arcana Coelestia, in the following places: In the Word by "land" [earth] the church is signified, particularly when it is applied to the land of Canaan (n. 662, 1066, 1067, 1262, 1413, 1607, 2928, 3355, 4447, 4535, 5577, 8011, 9325, 9643). Because by "land" in the spiritual sense is meant the nation dwelling therein, and its worship (n. 1262), "the people of the land" signify those who are of the spiritual church (n. 2928). "A New Heaven and a New Earth" signify something new in the heavens and on earth, as to goods and truths, thus as to those things that relate to the church in each (n. 1733, 1850, 2117, 2118, 3355, 4535, 10373). What is meant by "the first heaven and the first earth" which passed away, may be seen in Last Judgment and Babylon Destroyed, from beginning to end, but particularly n. 65 to 72. "Jerusalem" signifies the church as to doctrine (n. 402, 3654, 9166). "Cities" signify doctrines which are of the church and religion (n. 402, 2449, 2712, 2943, 3216, 4492, 4493). "The wall of a city" signifies the truth of doctrine defending (n. 6419). "The gates of a city" signify truths introducing to doctrine, and through doctrine to the church (n. 2943, 4477, 4492, 4493). "The twelve tribes of Israel" represented, and thence signified, all the truths and goods of the church in general and in particular, thus all things of faith and love (n. 3858, 3926, 4060, 6335). The same is signified by "the Lord's twelve apostles" (n. 2129, 3272, 3354, 3488, 3858, 6397). When it is said of the apostles, that "they shall sit upon twelve thrones, and judge the twelve tribes of Israel," it signifies that all are to be judged according to the goods and truths of the church, thus by the Lord from whom they are (n. 2129, 6397). "Twelve" signifies all things in the aggregate (n. 577, 2089, 2129, 2130, 3272, 3858, 3913). Also "a hundred forty-four" signifies the same because that number is the product of twelve multiplied by twelve (n. 7973); "twelve thousand" has also the same signification (n. 7973). All numbers in the Word signify things (n. 482, 487, 647, 648, 755, 813, 1963, 1988, 2075, 2252, 3252, 4264, 6175, 9488, 9659, 10217, 10253). Numbers multiplied into each other have the same signification as the simple numbers from which they arise by multiplication (n. 5291, 5335, 5708, 7973). "Measure" signifies the quality of a thing as to truth and good (n. 3104, 9603, 10262). "The foundations of a wall" signify the knowledges of truth on which doctrinals are founded (n. 9643). "Quadrangular" or "square" signifies what is perfect (n. 9717, 9861). "Length" signifies good and its extension, and "breadth" truth and its extension (n. 1613, 9487). "Precious stones" signify truths from good (n. 114, 9863, 9865). What "the precious stones" in the Urim and Thummim signify, both in general and in particular (n. 3862, 9864, 9866, 9891, 9895, 9905). What the "jasper" of which the wall was built signifies (n. 9872). "The street of the city" signifies the truth of doctrine from good (n. 2336). "Gold" signifies the good of love (n. 113, 1551, 1552, 5658, 6914, 6917, 9510, 9874, 9881). "Glory" signifies the Divine truth, such as it is in heaven, and the intelligence and wisdom thence (n. 4809, 5068, 5922, 8267, 8427, 9429, 10574). "Nations" signify those in the church who are in good, and, in the abstract sense, the good of the church (n. 1059, 1159, 1258, 1261, 1285, 1416, 1849, 4574, 7830, 9255, 9256). "Kings" signify those in the church who are in truths, and thence abstractly the truth of the church (n. 1672, 2015, 2069, 4575, 5044). The rites at the coronation of kings, involve such things as are of the Divine truth, but the knowledge of these things is at this day lost (n. 4581, 4966).

Before the New Jerusalem and its doctrine are treated of, something shall be said of the New Heaven and the New Earth. What is meant by "the first heaven and the first earth," which passed away, is shown in the small work Last Judgment and Babylon Destroyed. Immediately after that event, that is, after the Last Judgment was completed, a New Heaven was created or formed by the Lord. This heaven was formed of all those who, from the coming of the Lord to the present time, had lived the life of faith and charity, since these alone were forms of heaven. For the form of heaven, according to which all consociations and communications therein are effected, is the form of the Divine truth from the Divine good proceeding from the Lord; and this form man as to his spirit acquires by a life according to the Divine truth. That the form of heaven is thence may be seen in the work on Heaven and Hell (n. 200-212), and that all the angels are forms of heaven (n. 51-58, and 73-77). From these things it may be known, who they are of whom the New Heaven consists; and thereby what its quality is, namely, that it is altogether unanimous. For he who lives the life of faith and charity, loves another as himself, and by love conjoins him to himself, and thus reciprocally and mutually; for in the spiritual world, love is conjunction. Wherefore, when all act thus, then from many, yea from innumerable individuals consociated according to the form of heaven, unanimity exists, and they become as one; for then nothing separates and divides, but everything conjoins and unites.

Since this heaven was formed of all those who had been such from the coming of the Lord until the present time, it follows that it is composed both of Christians and of Gentiles; but chiefly of all infants from the whole world, who have died since the Lord's coming; for all these were received by the Lord, and educated in heaven, and instructed by the angels, and reserved, that they, together with the others, might constitute the New Heaven; whence it may be concluded how great that heaven is. That all who die in infancy are educated in heaven, and become angels, may be seen in the work on Heaven and Hell (n. 329-345). And that heaven is formed of Gentiles as well as of Christians (n. 318-328).

Moreover, with respect to this New Heaven, it is to be known, that it is distinct from the ancient heavens which were formed before the coming of the Lord; but still they together with this are so arranged that they form one heaven. The reason why this New Heaven is distinct from the ancient heavens, is because in the ancient churches there was no other doctrine than the doctrine of love and charity; and then they did not know of any doctrine of faith separated from love and charity. Hence also it is that the ancient heavens constitute higher expanses, while the New Heaven constitutes an expanse beneath them; for the heavens are expanses one above another. In the highest expanse those dwell who are called celestial angels, many of whom were of the Most Ancient Church; they who are there are called celestial angels from celestial love, which is love to the Lord. In the expanse beneath them are those who are called spiritual angels, most of whom were of the Ancient Church; they are called spiritual angels from spiritual love, which is charity towards the neighbor. Below these are the angels who are in the good of faith; these are they who have lived the life of faith. To live the life of faith, is to live according to the doctrine of their church; and to live is to will and to do. All these heavens, however, form a one, by mediate and immediate influx from the Lord. But a more full idea of these heavens may be obtained from what is said of them in the work on Heaven and Hell, and particularly in the article which treats of the Two Kingdoms into which the heavens in general are distinguished (n. 20-28); and in the article concerning the Three Heavens (n. 29-40); concerning mediate and immediate influx, in the extracts from Arcana Coelestia (after n. 603); and concerning the Most Ancient and Ancient Churches in the small work on The Last Judgment and Babylon Destroyed (n. 46).

These things are concerning the New Heaven; something shall now be said concerning "the New Earth." By "the New Earth" is meant the New Church on the earth; for when a former church ceases to exist, then a new one is established by the Lord. For it is provided by the Lord that there should always be a church on earth, since by means of the church there is a conjunction of the Lord with the human race, and of heaven with the world; for there the Lord is known, and there are the Divine truths by which man is conjoined to Him. That a New Church is at this time being established, may be seen in the small work on The Last Judgment (n. 74). The reason why a New Church is signified by "the New Earth" arises from the spiritual sense of the Word; for in that sense, by the "earth" no particular country is meant, but the nation dwelling there, and its Divine worship; this, in the spiritual sense, being what answers to earth in the natural sense. Moreover, by "earth" in the Word, when there is no name of any particular country affixed to the term, is signified the land of Canaan; and in the land of Canaan a church had existed from the most ancient times; in consequence of which, all the places therein, and in the adjacent countries, with the mountains and rivers, which are mentioned in the Word, became representative and significative of the things which are the internals of the church, and which are called its spiritual things. Hence it is, as was said, that "earth" in the Word, because it means the land of Canaan, signifies the church; in like manner here by "the New Earth"; from this comes the custom in the church to speak of the heavenly Canaan, by which is meant heaven. That "the land of Canaan," in the spiritual sense of the Word, signifies the church, is shown in the Arcana Coelestia, in various places, of which the following are here adduced: The Most Ancient Church, which was before the flood, and the Ancient Church, which was after the flood, were in the land of Canaan (n. 567, 3686, 4447, 4454, 4516, 4517, 5136, 6516, 9325). Then all places in that land became representative of such things as are in the kingdom of the Lord, and in the church (n. 1585, 3686, 4447, 5136). Therefore Abraham was commanded to go thither, since with his posterity from Jacob, a representative church might be established, and that the Word might be written, the ultimate of which should consist of representatives and significatives which are there (n. 3686, 4447, 5136, 6516). Hence it is that "earth" and "the land of Canaan," when they are mentioned in the Word, signify the church (n. 3038, 3481, 3705, 4447, 4517, 5757, 10568).

What is meant by "Jerusalem" in the spiritual sense of the Word, shall also be briefly stated. "Jerusalem" means the church itself as to doctrine, because there in the land of Canaan, and in no other place, were the temple, the altar, the sacrifices, and thus Divine worship itself. On this account, also, three festivals were celebrated there every year, to which every male throughout the whole land was commanded to go. This, then, is the reason why "Jerusalem," in the spiritual sense, signifies the church as to worship, or, what is the same, as to doctrine; for worship is prescribed in doctrine, and is performed according to it. The reason why it is said, "The holy city, New Jerusalem, descending from God out of heaven," is because, in the spiritual sense of the Word, "a city" [civitas] and "a town" [urbs], signify doctrine, and "the holy city" the doctrine of Divine truth, since Divine truth is what is called "holy" in the Word. It is called "the New Jerusalem" for the same reason that "the earth" is called "new"; because, as was observed above, "the earth" signifies the church, and "Jerusalem," the church as to doctrine; which is said "to descend from God out of heaven," because all Divine truth, whence doctrine is derived, descends out of heaven from the Lord. That "Jerusalem" does not mean a city, although it was seen as a city, manifestly appears from its being said that: Its height was, as its length and breadth, twelve thousand stadia (Rev. 21:16). And that the measure of its wall, which was a hundred forty-four cubits, was the measure of a man, that is, of the angel (Rev. 21:17). Also from its being said that: It was prepared as a Bride adorned for her Husband (verse 2). And afterwards the angel said: Come, I will show thee the Bride, the Lamb's Wife: and he showed me that great city, the holy Jerusalem (verses 9, 10). The church is called in the Word "the Bride" and "the Wife" of the Lord; she is called "the Bride" before conjunction, and "the Wife" after conjunction. As may be seen in the Arcana Coelestia (n. 3103, 3105, 3164, 3165, 3207, 7022, 9182).

To add a few words respecting the doctrine which is delivered in the following pages. This, also, is from heaven, because it is from the spiritual sense of the Word, and the spiritual sense of the Word is the same with the doctrine that is in heaven; for there is a church in heaven as well as on earth. In heaven there are the Word and doctrine from the Word, there are temples there, and preaching in them; there are also both ecclesiastical and civil governments there: in a word, the only difference between the things which are in heaven, and those which are on earth, is, that in heaven all things exist in a state of greater perfection, since those who are there are spiritual, and spiritual things immensely exceed in perfection those that are natural. That such things exist in heaven may be seen in the work concerning Heaven and Hell throughout, particularly in the article concerning Governments in Heaven (n. 213-220); and also in the article on Divine Worship in Heaven (n. 221-227). From these things it may be evident what is meant by "the holy city, New Jerusalem, was seen to descend from God out of heaven." But I proceed to the doctrine itself, which is for the New Church, and which is called Heavenly Doctrine, because it was revealed to me out of heaven; to deliver this doctrine is the design of the present book.

INTRODUCTION TO THE DOCTRINE. The end of the church is when there is no faith because there is no charity. This is shown in the small work on The Last Judgment and Babylon Destroyed (n. 33-39 seq.). Because the churches in the Christian world have separated themselves from each other solely by such things as are of faith, when yet there is no faith where there is no charity, I will, by way of introduction to the doctrine which follows, make some observations concerning the doctrine of charity with the ancients. It is said "the churches in the Christian world," and by them is meant the churches with the Reformed or Evangelical and not the Papists, since the Christian church is not there; for where the church exists the Lord is adored and the Word is read; whereas, with the Papists, they adore themselves instead of the Lord; they forbid the Word to be read by the people; and affirm the Pope's decree to be equal, yea, even above it.

The doctrine of charity, which is the doctrine of life, was the doctrine itself in the ancient churches. Concerning these churches see in Arcana Coelestia (n. 1238, 2385). And that doctrine conjoined all churches, and thereby formed one church out of many. For they acknowledged all those as men of the church who lived in the good of charity, and called them brethren, however they might differ respecting truths, which at this day are called matters of faith. In these they instructed one another, which was among their works of charity; nor were they indignant if one did not accede to the opinion of another, knowing that everyone receives truth so far as he is in good. Because the ancient churches were such, therefore they were interior men; and because they were interior men they excelled in wisdom. For they who are in the good of love and charity, as to the internal man, are in heaven, and as to that are in an angelic society which is in similar good. Hence they enjoy an elevation of mind towards interior things, and, consequently, they are in wisdom; for wisdom can come from no other source than from heaven, that is, through heaven from the Lord; and in heaven there is wisdom, because there they are in good. Wisdom consists in seeing truth from the light of truth; and the light of truth is the light which is in heaven. But in process of time that ancient wisdom decreased; for as mankind removed themselves from the good of love to the Lord, and of love towards the neighbor, which love is called charity, they removed themselves in the same proportion from wisdom because, in the same proportion, they removed themselves from heaven. Hence it was that man, from being internal, became external, and this successively; and when he became external, he became also worldly and corporeal. When such is his quality, he cares but little for the things of heaven; for the delights of earthly loves, and the evils which, from those loves, are delightful to him, then possess him entirely. And then the things which he hears concerning the life after death, concerning heaven and hell, in a word, concerning spiritual things, are as it were out of him, and not within him, as nevertheless they ought to be. Hence also it is, that the doctrine of charity, which with the ancients was held in such high estimation, is at this day among the things that are lost. For who, at this day, knows what charity is, in the genuine sense of the term, and what, in the same sense, is meant by our neighbor? whereas, that doctrine not only teaches this, but innumerable things besides, of which not a thousandth part is known at this day. The whole Sacred Scripture is nothing else than the doctrine of love and charity, which the Lord also teaches, when He says: Thou shalt love the Lord thy God with all thy heart, and with all thy soul, and with all thy mind; this is the first and great commandment; the second is like unto it, thou shalt love thy neighbor as thyself: on these two commandments hang all the law and the prophets (Matt. 22:37-39). "The law and the prophets" in each and all things are the Word.

In the following doctrine we will annex to each section extracts from the

Arcana Coelestia, because in these the same things are more fully explained.

I. GOOD AND TRUTH. All things in the universe, which are according to Divine order, have relation to good and truth. There is nothing in heaven, and nothing in the world, which has not relation to these two; the reason is, because both good and truth proceed from the Divine from Whom all things are.

Hence it appears that there is nothing more necessary for man to know than what good and truth are; how the one has respect to the other; and how one is conjoined to the other. But such knowledge is especially necessary for the man of the church; for as all things of heaven have relation to good and truth, so also have all things of the church, because the good and truth of heaven are also the good and truth of the church. It is on this account that a beginning is made from good and truth.

It is according to Divine order that good and truth should be conjoined, and not separated; thus, that they should be one, and not two; for they proceed in conjunction from the Divine, and are conjoined in heaven, and therefore they should be conjoined in the church. The conjunction of good and truth is called, in heaven, the heavenly marriage, for all there are in this marriage. Hence it is that in the Word heaven is compared to a marriage, and that the Lord is called the Bridegroom and Husband, but heaven, and also the church, are called the Bride and Wife. That heaven and the church are so called, is because they who are therein receive Divine good in truths.

All the intelligence and wisdom which the angels have is from that marriage, and not any of it from good separate from truth, nor from truth separate from good. It is the same with the men of the church.

Because the conjunction of good and truth is an image of marriage, it is plain that good loves truth, and truth, in its turn, loves good, and that one desires to be conjoined with the other. The man of the church, who has not such love and such desire, is not in the heavenly marriage, consequently the church as yet is not in him; for the conjunction of good and truth constitutes the church.

Goods are manifold; in general there is spiritual good and natural good, and both are conjoined in genuine moral good. As goods are manifold, so also are truths, because truths are of good, and are the forms of good.

As it is with good and truth, so it is in the opposite with evil and falsity; namely, as all things in the universe, which are according to Divine order, have relation to good and truth, so all things which are contrary to Divine order have relation to evil and falsity. Again, as good loves to be conjoined to truth, and vice versa, so evil loves to be conjoined to falsity, and vice versa. And again, as all intelligence and wisdom are born from the conjunction of good and truth, so all insanity and folly are born from the conjunction of evil and falsity. The conjunction of evil and falsity is called the infernal marriage.

Since evil and falsity are opposite to good and truth, it is plain that truth cannot be conjoined to evil, nor good to the falsity of evil; if truth be adjoined to evil, it is truth no longer, but falsity, because it is falsified; and if good be adjoined to the falsity of evil, it is good no longer, but evil, because it is adulterated. But falsity which is not of evil may be conjoined to good.

No one who is in evil, and thence in falsity from confirmation and life, can know what good and truth is, for he believes his own evil to be good, and thence he believes his falsity to be truth; but everyone who is in good and thence in truth from confirmation and life may know what evil and falsity are. The reason of this is, because all good and its truth is, in its essence, heavenly, and what is not heavenly in its essence is still from a heavenly origin; but all evil and its falsity is in its essence infernal, and what is not infernal in its essence has nevertheless its origin from thence; and all that is heavenly is in light, but all that is infernal is in darkness.

FROM THE ARCANA COELESTIA. Each and all things in the universe have relation to good and truth, and to evil and falsity; those things which are and are done according to Divine order, to good and truth; but those which are opposite to Divine order, to evil and falsity (n. 2452, 3166, 4390, 4409, 5232, 7256, 10122). Consequently everything in man has reference to the understanding and will, since the understanding is the recipient of truth, or of falsity; and the will the recipient of good, or of evil (n. 10122). At this day it is little known what truth in its genuine essence is, because it is little known what good is, when nevertheless all truth is from good, and all good is by truths (n. 2507, 3603, 4136, 9186, 9995). There are four kinds of men: 1. Those who are in falsities from evil; and those who are in falsities not from evil. 2. Those who are in truths without good. 3. Those who are in truths, and by them look and tend to good. 4. Those who are in truths from good. But each of these shall be spoken of in particular.

[1]. Of those who are in falsities from evil, and of those who are in falsities not from evil; thus of falsities from evil, and of falsities not from evil. There are innumerable kinds of falsities, namely, as many as there are evils; and the origins of evils, and thence of falsities, are many (n. 1188, 1212, 4729, 4822, 7574). There is falsity from evil, or falsity of evil; and there is evil from falsity, or evil of falsity, and again falsity thence, thus derivative (n. 1679, 2243). From one falsity, especially if it is in the place of a principle, there flow falsities in a continual series (n. 1510, 1511, 4717, 4721). There is falsity from the cupidities of the love of self and of the world; and there is falsity from the fallacies of the senses (n. 1295, 4729). There are falsities of religion, and there are falsities of ignorance (n. 4729, 8318, 9258). There is falsity in which there is good, and falsity in which there is not good (n. 2863, 9304, 10109, 10302). There is what is falsified (n. 7318, 7319, 10648). All evil has falsity with it (n. 7577, 8094). Falsity from the cupidities of the love of self is the very falsity of evil; and the worst kinds of falsities are thence (n. 4729). Evil is heavy, and has in itself a tendency to fall into hell, but not so falsity, unless derived from evil (n. 8279, 8298). Good is turned into evil, and truth into falsity, when it descends from heaven into hell, because as it were into a gross and impure atmosphere (n. 3607). Falsities from evil appear as mists and foul waters over the hells (n. 8137, 8138, 8146). They who are in the hells speak falsities from evil (n. 1695, 7351, 7352, 7357, 7392, 7699). They who are in evil cannot but think falsities, when they think from themselves (n. 7437). More is said concerning evil of falsity (n. 2408, 4818, 7272, 8265, 8279); and concerning falsities of evil (n. 6359, 7272, 9304, 10302). Every falsity may be confirmed, and when confirmed appears as truth (n. 5033, 6865, 8521, 8780). Therefore everything should be examined to see whether it is true before it is confirmed (n. 4741, 7012, 7680, 7950, 8521). Care should be taken that the falsities of religion be not confirmed, because the persuasion of falsity arises thence, which adheres to man after

death (n. 845, 8780). How hurtful the persuasion of falsity is (n. 794, 806, 5096, 7686). Good cannot flow into truths so long as man is in evil (n. 2434). Goods and truths are so far removed from man as he is in evil, and thereby in falsities (n. 3402). The greatest care is taken by the Lord lest truth be conjoined to evil, and the falsity of evil to good (n. 3110, 3116, 4416, 5217). Profanation arises from such mixture (n. 6348). Truths exterminate falsities, and falsities truths (n. 5207). Truths cannot be deeply received so long as incredulity reigns (n. 3399). How truths may be falsified, from examples (n. 7318). The evil are permitted to falsify truths, the reason (n. 7332). Truths are falsified by the evil, by being applied and thus turned aside to evil (n. 8094, 8149). Truth is said to be falsified when it is applied to evil, which is done especially by fallacies and appearances in externals (n. 7334, 8062). The evil are allowed to assault truth, but not good, because they can falsify truth by various interpretations and applications (n. 6677). Truth falsified from evil, is contrary to truth and good (n. 8062). Truth falsified from evil has a grievous stench in the other life (n. 7319). More is said concerning the falsification of truth (n. 7318, 7319, 10648). There are falsities of religion which agree with good, and others which disagree (n. 9258, 9259). Falsities of religion, if they do not disagree with good, do not produce evil, except with those who are in evil (n. 8318). Falsities of religion are not imputed to those who are in good, but to those who are in evil (n. 8051, 8149). Truths not genuine, and also falsities, may be consociated with genuine truths with those who are in good, but not with those who are in evil (n. 3470, 3471, 4551, 4552, 7344, 8149, 9298). Falsities and truths are consociated by appearances from the sense of the letter of the Word (n. 7344). Falsities are made true by good, and grow soft when they are applied and turned to good, and evil is removed (n. 8149). Falsities of religion with those who are in good, are received by the Lord as truths (n. 4736, 8149). Good whose quality is from the falsity of religion, is accepted by the Lord, if there is ignorance, and therein innocence, and a good end (n. 7887). Truths with man are appearances of truth and good imbued with fallacies; but nevertheless the Lord adapts them to genuine truths with the man who lives in good (n. 2053). Falsities in which is good are given with those who are out of the church, and thence in ignorance of truth; also with those who are within the church where are falsities of doctrine (n. 2589-2604, 2861, 2863, 3263, 3778, 4189, 4190, 4197, 6700, 9256). Falsities in which there is not good are more grievous with those who are within the church, than with those who are out of the church (n. 7688). Truths and goods are taken away from the evil in the other life, and given to the good, according to the words of the Lord: To him that hath shall be given that he may abound; and from him who hath not shall be taken away that which he hath (Matt. 25:29, n. 7770).

[2]. Of those who are in truths, and not in good; consequently of truths without good. Truths without good are not in themselves truths because they have no life, for all the life of truths is from good (n. 3603). Thus they are as a body without a soul (n. 8530, 9154). The knowledges of truth and good which are only in the memory and not in the life, are believed by them to be truths (n. 5276). The truths are not appropriated to man, nor become his own, which he only knows and acknowledges from causes which proceed from the love of self and the world (n. 3402, 3834). But those are appropriated, which he

acknowledges for the sake of truth itself and good (n. 3849). Truths without good are not accepted by the Lord (n. 4368); neither do they save (n. 2261). They who are in truths without good, are not of the church (n. 3963). Neither can they be regenerated (n. 10367). The Lord does not flow into truths except through good (n. 10367). Of the separation of truth from good (n. 5008, 5009, 5022, 5028). The quality of truth without good, and its quality from good (n. 1949, 1950, 1964, 5951); from comparisons (n. 5830). Truth without good is morose (n. 1949-1951, 1964). In the spiritual world it appears hard (n. 6359, 7068); and pointed (n. 2799). Truth without good is as the light of winter, in which all things of the earth are torpid, and nothing is produced; but truth from good is as the light of spring and summer, in which all things flourish and are produced (n. 2231, 3146, 3412, 3413). Such a wintry light is turned into dense darkness when light flows in from heaven; and that then they who are in those truths come into blindness and stupidity (n. 3412, 3413). They who separate truths from good are in darkness, and in ignorance of truth and in falsities (n. 9186). From falsities they cast themselves into evils (n. 3325, 8094). The errors and falsities into which they cast themselves (n. 4721, 4730, 4776, 4783, 4925, 7779, 8313, 8765, 9222). The Word is shut to them (n. 3773, 4783, 8780). They do not see and attend to all those things which the Lord spoke concerning love and charity, thus concerning good (n. 2051, 3416). They know not what good is, nor what heavenly love and charity are (n. 2471, 3603, 4136, 9995). They who know the truths of faith, and live in evil, in the other life abuse truths to domineer thereby; concerning their quality and lot there (n. 4802). Divine truth condemns to hell, but Divine good elevates to heaven (n. 2258). Divine truth terrifies, not so Divine good (n. 4180). What it is to be judged from truth, and to be judged from good (n. 2335).

[3]. Of those who are in truths, and by them look and tend to good; thus of truths by which there is good. What man loves, this he wills, and what man loves or wills this he thinks, and confirms in various ways: what man loves or wills, this he calls good, and what man thence thinks and confirms in various ways, this he calls truth (n. 4070). Hence it is, that truth becomes good, when it becomes of the love or will, or when man loves and wills it (n. 5526, 7835, 10367). And because the love or the will is the very life of man, truth does not live with man when he only knows it, and thinks it, but when he loves and wills it, and from love and will does it (n. 5595, 9282). Thence truths receive life, consequently from good (n. 2434, 3111, 3607, 6077). Thence the life of truths is from good, and they have no life without good (n. 1589, 1947, 1997, 3180, 3579, 4070, 4096, 4097, 4736, 4757, 4884, 5147, 5928, 9154, 9667, 9841, 10729); illustrated (n. 9154). When truths may be said to have acquired life (n. 1928). Truth when it is conjoined to good, is appropriated to man because it becomes of his life (n. 3108, 3161). That truth may be conjoined to good, there must be consent from the understanding and will; when the will also consents, then there is conjunction (n. 3157, 3158, 3161). When man is regenerated, truths enter with the delight of affection, because he loves to do them, and they are reproduced with the same affection because the two cohere (n. 2474, 2487, 3040, 3066, 3074, 3336, 4018, 5893, 7967). The affection which is of love always adjoins itself to truths according to the uses of life, and that affection is reproduced with the truths, and the truths are reproduced with the affection (n.

3336, 3824, 3849, 4205, 5893, 7967). Good acknowledges nothing else for truth than what agrees with the affection which is of the love (n. 3161). Truths are introduced by delights and pleasantnesses that agree therewith (n. 3502, 3512). All genuine affection of truth is from good, and according to it (n. 4373, 8349, 8356). Thus there is an insinuation and an influx of good into truths, and conjunction (n. 4301). And thus truths have life (n. 7917, 7967). Because the affection which is of love always adjoins itself to truths according to the uses of life, good acknowledges its own truth, and truth its own good (n. 2429, 3101, 3102, 3161, 3179, 3180, 4358, 5407, 5835, 9637). Thence is the conjunction of truth and good, concerning which (n. 3834, 4096, 4097, 4301, 4345, 4353, 4364, 4368, 5365, 7623-7627, 7752-7762, 8530, 9258, 10555). Truths also acknowledge each other, and are mutually consociated (n. 9079). This is from the influx of heaven (n. 9079). Good is the esse of life, and truth the existere of life thence; and thus good has its existere of life in truth, and truth its esse of life in good (n. 3049, 3180, 4574, 5002, 9154). Hence every good has its own truth, and every truth its own good, because good without truth does not exist, and truth without good is not (n. 9637). Good has also its form and quality from truths, and that truth is the form and quality of good (n. 3049, 4574, 6916, 9154). And thus truth and good ought to be conjoined that they may be something (n. 10555). Hence good is in the perpetual endeavor and desire of conjoining truths to itself (n. 9206, 9495); illustrated (n. 9207). And truths in like manner with good (n. 9206). The conjunction is reciprocal, of good with truth, and of truth with good (n. 5365, 8516). Good acts, and truth reacts, but from good (n. 3155, 4380, 4757, 5928, 10729). Truths regard their own good, as the beginning and end (n. 4353). The conjunction of truth with good is as the progression of man's life from infancy, as he first imbibes truths scientifically, then rationally, and at length makes them of his life (n. 3203, 3665, 3690). It is also as with offspring that is conceived, is in the womb, is born, grows up, and becomes wise (n. 3298, 3299, 3308, 3665, 3690). It is also like seeds and soil (n. 3671). And as with water and bread (n. 4976). The first affection of truth is not genuine, but as man is perfected it is purified (n. 3040, 3089). Nevertheless goods and truths, not genuine, serve for introducing goods and truths that are genuine, and afterwards the former are left behind (n. 3665, 3690, 3974, 3982, 3986, 4145). Moreover man is led to good by truths, and not without truths (n. 10124, 10367). If man does not learn or receive truths, good cannot flow in, thus man cannot become spiritual (n. 3387). The conjunction of good and truth takes place according to the increase of knowledge (n. 3141). Truths are received by everyone according to his capacity (n. 3385). The truths of the natural man are scientifics (n. 3293, 3309, 3310). Scientifics and knowledges are as vessels (n. 6004, 6023, 6052, 6071, 6077). Truths are vessels of good, because they are recipients (n. 1496, 1900, 2063, 2261, 2269, 3318, 3365, 3368). Good flows into man by an internal way, or that of the soul, but truths by an external way, or that of hearing and sight; and they are conjoined in his interiors by the Lord (n. 3030, 3098). Truths are elevated out of the natural man, and implanted in good in the spiritual man; and thus truths become spiritual (n. 3085, 3086). And afterwards they flow thence into the natural man, spiritual good flowing immediately into the good of the natural, but mediately into the truth of the natural (n. 3314, 3573, 4563); illustrated (n. 3314, 3576, 3616, 3969, 3995). In a word, truths are conjoined to good with man, so far and in such manner as man is in good as to life (n. 3834, 3843). Conjunction is effected in one manner with the celestial, and in another with the spiritual (n. 10124). More concerning the conjunction of good and truth, and how it is effected (n. 3090, 3203, 3308, 4096, 4097, 4345, 4353, 5365, 7623-7627). And how spiritual good is formed by truths (n. 3470, 3570).

[4]. Of those who are in truths from good, consequently of truths from good. Of the difference between truth that leads to good, and truth which proceeds from good (n. 2063). Truth is not essentially truth, any further than as it proceeds from good (n. 4736, 10619); because truth has its esse from good (n. 3049, 3180, 4574, 5002, 9144); and its life (n. 2434, 3111, 6077); and because truth is the form or quality of good (n. 3049, 4574, 5951, 9154). Truth is altogether as good with man, in the same ratio and degree (n. 2429). In order that truth may be truth, it must derive its essence from the good of charity and innocence (n. 3111, 6013). The truths which are from good are spiritual truths (n. 5951). Truth makes one with good when it proceeds from good, even so that both together are one good (n. 4301, 4337, 7835, 10252, 10266). The understanding and will make one mind and one life, when the understanding proceeds from the will, because the understanding is the recipient of truth, and the will, of good, but not when man thinks and speaks otherwise than he wills (n. 3623). Truth from good is truth in will and act (n. 4337, 4353, 4385, 4390). When truth proceeds from good, good has its image in truth (n. 3180). In the whole heaven and world, and in the single things thereof, there is an image of marriage (n. 54, 718, 747, 917, 1432, 2173, 2516, 5194). Particularly between truth and good (n. 1904, 2173, 2508). Because all things in the universe have relation to truth and good, in order that they may be anything, and to their conjunction, in order that anything may be produced (n. 2452, 3166, 4390, 4409, 5232, 7256, 10122, 10555). The ancients also instituted a marriage between truth and good (n. 1904). The law of marriage is, that two be one, according to the words of the Lord (n. 10130, 10168, 10169). Love truly conjugial descends and exists from heaven, from the marriage of truth and good (n. 2728, 2729). Man is so far wise, as he is in good and thence in truths, but not so far as he knows truths and is not in good (n. 3182, 3190, 4884). The man who is in truths from good, is actually elevated from the light of the world into the light of heaven, consequently from what is obscure into what is clear; but on the other hand, he is in the light of the world, and what is obscure, so long as he knows truths and is not in good (n. 3190, 3192). Man does not know what good is, before he is in it, and knows from it (n. 3325, 3330, 3336). Truths increase immensely when they proceed from good (n. 2846, 2847, 5345). Of which increase (n. 5355). This increase is as fructification from a tree, and multiplication from seeds from which whole gardens are produced (n. 1873, 2846, 2847). Wisdom increases in a like degree, and this to eternity (n. 3200, 3314, 4220, 4221, 5527, 5859, 10303). The man also who is in truths from good is in a like degree enlightened, and he is so far in enlightenment when he reads the Word (n. 9382, 10548-10550, 10691, 10694). The good of love is as fire, and truth thence as light from that fire (n. 3195, 3222, 5400, 8644, 9399, 9548, 9684). In heaven truths from good shine (n. 5219). Truths from good, by which is wisdom, increase according to the quality and quantity of the love of good;

and on the other hand, falsities from evil, according to the quality and quantity of the love of evil (n. 4099). The man who is in truths from good comes into angelic intelligence and wisdom, and they lie hid in his interiors so long as he lives in the world, but they are opened in the other life (n. 2494). The man, who is in truths from good, becomes an angel after death (n. 8747). Truths from good are like generations (n. 9079). They are disposed in series (n. 5339, 5343, 5530, 7408, 10303, 10308). The arrangement of truths from good compared with the fibers and blood-vessels in the body; and thence with their textures and forms, according to the uses of life (n. 3470, 3570, 3579, 9154). Truths from good form as it were a city, and this from the influx of heaven (n. 3584). The truths which are of the principal love are in the midst; and the rest are more or less remote from thence according to their degrees of disagreement (n. 3993, 4551, 4552, 5530, 6028). Conversely with the evil (n. 4551, 4552). Truths when they proceed from good are arranged in the form of heaven (n. 4302, 4904, 5339, 5343, 5704, 6028, 10303). And this according to the order in which are the angelic societies (n. 10303). All truths when they proceed from good are conjoined to one another by a certain affinity, and they are as derivations of families from one father (n. 2863). All truth has a sphere of extension into heaven, according to the quality and quantity of the good from which it is (n. 8063). The marriage of good and truth is the church and heaven with man (n. 2731, 7752, 7753, 9224, 9995, 10122). Of the delight and happiness of those with whom good is in truths (n. 1470). Truths from good, in conjunction, present an image of man (n. 8370). Man is nothing but his own good, and truth thence derived; or evil, and falsity thence derived (n. 10298). A summary: Faith is by truths (n. 4353, 4997, 7178, 10367). Charity towards the neighbor is by truths (n. 4368, 7623, 7624, 8034). Love to the Lord is by truths (n. 10143, 10153, 10310, 10578, 10645). Conscience is by truths (n. 1077, 2053, 9113). Innocence is by truths (n. 3183, 3494, 6013). Purification from evils is by truths (n. 2799, 5954, 7044, 7918, 9088, 10229, 10237). Regeneration is by truths (n. 1555, 1904, 2046, 2189, 9088, 9959, 10028). Intelligence and wisdom are by truths (n. 3182, 3190, 3387, 10064). The beauty of angels, and also of men, as to the interiors which are their spirits, is by truths (n. 553, 3080, 4985, 5199). Power against evils and falsities is by truths (n. 3091, 4015, 10488). Order, such as it is in heaven, is by truths (n. 3316, 3417, 3570, 4104, 5339, 5343, 6028, 10303). The church is by truths (n. 1798, 1799, 3963, 4468, 4672). Heaven is with man by truths (n. 3690, 9832, 9931, 10303). Man becomes man by truths (n. 3175, 3387, 8370, 10298). Nevertheless all these things are by truths from good, and not by truths without good; and good is from the Lord (n. 2434, 4070, 4736, 5147). All good is from the Lord (n. 1614, 2016, 2904, 4151, 9981).

   All good and truth is from the Lord. The Lord is good itself and truth itself (n. 2011, 4151, 10336, 10619). The Lord, as to both the Divine and the Human, is the Divine good of the Divine love; and from Him proceeds Divine truth (n. 3704, 3712, 4180, 4577). The Divine truth proceeds from the Divine good of the Lord, comparatively as light from the sun (n. 3704, 3712, 4180, 4577). The Divine truth proceeding from the Lord appears in the heavens as light, and forms all the light of heaven (n. 3195, 3223, 5400, 8694, 9399, 9548, 9684). The light of heaven, which is the Divine truth united to the Divine good, enlightens both the sight and the understanding of angels and spirits (n. 2776, 3138).

Heaven is in light and heat, because it is in truth and good, for the Divine truth is light there, and the Divine good is heat there (n. 3643, 9399, 9400); and in the work on Heaven and Hell (n. 126-140). The Divine truth proceeding from the Divine good of the Lord, forms the angelic heaven and arranges it in order (n. 3038, 9408, 9613, 10716, 10717). The Divine good united to the Divine truth, which is in the heavens, is called the Divine truth (n. 10196). The Divine truth proceeding from the Lord is the only reality (n. 6880, 7004, 8200). By Divine truth all things were made and created (n. 2803, 2894, 5272, 7678). All power belongs to the Divine truth (n. 8200). Man from himself can do nothing of good, and think nothing of truth (n. 874-876). The rational of man cannot perceive Divine truth from itself (n. 2196, 2203, 2209). Truths which are not from the Lord, are from the proprium of man, and they are not truths, but only appear as truths (n. 8868). All good and truth is from the Lord, and nothing from man (n. 1614, 2016, 2904, 4151, 9981). Goods and truths are so far goods and truths, as they have the Lord in them (n. 2904, 3061, 8480). Of the Divine truth proceeding immediately from the Lord, and of the Divine truth proceeding mediately through the angels, and of their influx with man (n. 7055, 7056, 7058). The Lord flows into good with man, and by good into truths (n. 10153). He flows in by good into truths of every kind, and particularly into genuine truths (n. 2531, 2554). The Lord does not flow into truths separate from good, and no parallelism exists between the Lord and man, with respect to them, but with respect to good (n. 1831, 1832, 3514, 3564). To do good and truth for the sake of good and truth is to love the Lord, and to love the neighbor (n. 10336). They who are in the internal of the Word, of the church, and of worship, love to do good and truth for the sake of good and truth; but they who are in the external of these, without the internal, love to do good and truth for the sake of themselves and the world (n. 10683). What it is to do good and truth for the sake of good and truth, illustrated by examples (n. 10683).

Of the various kinds of goods and truths. There is an infinite variety, and one thing is never exactly the same as another (n. 7236, 9002). There is also an infinite variety in the heavens (n. 684, 690, 3744, 5598, 7236). Varieties in the heavens are varieties of good, and thence is the distinction of all therein (n. 3519, 3744, 3804, 3986, 4005, 4067, 4149, 4263, 7236, 7833, 7836, 9002). These varieties are from truths, which are manifold, by which everyone has good (n. 3470, 3519, 3804, 4149, 6917, 7236). Thence all the angelic societies in the heavens, and every angel in a society are distinguished from each other (n. 690, 3241, 3519, 3804, 3986, 4067, 4149, 4263, 7236, 7833, 7836). But they all act in unity by love from the Lord, and thereby regard one end (n. 457, 3986). In general, goods and truths are distinguished according to degrees, into natural, spiritual, and celestial (n. 2069, 3240). In general, there are three degrees of good, and consequently of truth, according to the three heavens (n. 4154, 9873, 10270). The goods and thence the truths in the internal man, are of a threefold kind, and so also in the external (n. 4154). There is natural good, civil good, and moral good (n. 3768). Natural good, into which some are born, is not good in the other life, unless made spiritual good (n. 2463, 2464, 2468, 3408, 3469, 3470, 3508, 3518, 7761). Of natural spiritual good; and of that which is not spiritual (n. 4988, 4992, 5032). There is intellectual truth, and scientific truth (n. 1904, 1911, 2503).

That wisdom is from good by truths. In what manner the rational is conceived and born with man (n. 2094, 2524, 2557, 3030, 5126). This is effected by an influx of the Lord through heaven into the knowledges and sciences which are with man, and thence is elevation (n. 1895, 1899-1901). Elevation is according to uses, and the love of them (n. 3074, 3085, 3086). The rational is born through truths, hence such as they are, such is the rational (n. 2094, 2524, 2557). The rational is opened and formed by truths from good; and it is shut and destroyed by falsities from evil (n. 3108, 5126). Man is not rational by this that he can reason on any subject, but that he can see and perceive whether a thing be true or not (n. 1944). Man is not born into any truth, because not born into good; but he is to learn and imbibe both (n. 3175). It is with difficulty that man can receive genuine truths, and thence become wise, on account of the fallacies of the senses, the persuasions of falsity, and the reasonings and doubts thence (n. 3175). Man first begins to be wise, when he begins to be averse to reasonings against truths, and to reject doubts (n. 3175). The unenlightened human rational laughs at interior truths, from examples (n. 2654). Truths with man are called interior when they are implanted in his life, and not in consequence of his knowing them, although they may be truths which are called interior (n. 10199). In good there is the faculty of becoming wise, whence those who have lived in good in the world come into angelic wisdom after their departure out of the world (n. 5527, 5859, 8321). There are innumerable things in every good (n. 4005). Innumerable things may be known from good (n. 3612). Concerning the multiplication of truth from good (n. 5345, 5355, 5912). The good of infancy by truths, and by a life according to them, becomes the good of wisdom (n. 3504). There is the affection of truth and the affection of good (n. 1904, 1997). What is the quality of those who are in the affection of truth, and what is the quality of those who are in the affection of good (n. 2422, 2429). Who are able to come into the affection of truth, and who are not able (n. 2689). All truths are arranged in order under a general affection (n. 9094). The affection of truth and the affection of good in the natural man are as brother and sister; but in the spiritual man, as husband and wife (n. 3160). Pure truths are not given with man, nor even with an angel, but only with the Lord (n. 3207, 7902). Truths with man are appearances of truth (n. 2053, 2519). The first truths with man are appearances of truth from the fallacies of the senses, which nevertheless are successively put off, as he is perfected as to wisdom (n. 3131). Appearances of truth with the man who is in good are received by the Lord for truths (n. 2053, 3207). What, and of what quality the appearances of truth are (n. 3207, 3357-3362, 3368, 3404, 3405, 3417). The sense of the letter of the Word in many places is according to appearances (n. 1838). The same truths with one man are more true, with another less so, and with another false, because falsified (n. 2439). Truths are also truths according to the correspondence between the natural and the spiritual man (n. 3128, 3138). Truths differ according to the various ideas and perceptions concerning them (n. 3470, 3804, 6917). Truth when it is conjoined to good, vanishes out of the memory because it then becomes of the life (n. 3108). Truths cannot be conjoined to good except in a free state (n. 3158). Truths are conjoined to good by temptations (n. 3318, 4572, 7122). There is in good a continual endeavor of arranging truths in order, and of restoring its state thereby (n. 3610). Truths appear undelightful when the communication with good is intercepted (n. 8352). Man can scarcely distinguish between truth and good, because he can scarcely distinguish between thinking and willing (n. 9995). Good is called in the Word the "brother" of truth (n. 4267). Also in a certain respect good is called "lord," and truth, "servant" (n. 3409, 4267).

II. THE WILL AND THE UNDERSTANDING. Man has two faculties which make his life; one is called the Will, and the other the Understanding. These faculties are distinct from each other, but are so created that they may be one; and when they are one they are called the Mind. Of these, then, the human mind consists; and the whole life of man is there.

As all things in the universe, which are according to Divine order, have relation to good and truth, so all things with man have relation to the will and the understanding; for good with man is of his will, and truth with him is of his understanding; for these two faculties, or these two lives of man, are their receptacles and subjects. The will is the receptacle and subject of all things of good, and the understanding the receptacle and subject of all things of truth. Goods and truths with man are nowhere else; and because goods and truths with man are nowhere else, so neither are love and faith elsewhere; for love is of good, and good is of love; and faith is of truth, and truth is of faith.

Since, then, all things in the universe have relation to good and truth, and all things of the church to the good of love and the truth of faith; and since man is man from those two faculties, therefore they also are treated of in this doctrine; otherwise man could have no distinct idea of them, on which to found his thought.

The will and the understanding also constitute the spirit of man; for his wisdom and intelligence, and his life in general, reside in them; the body is only obedience.

Nothing is more important to know than how the will and the understanding make one mind. They make one mind as good and truth make one; for there is a similar marriage between the will and the understanding as there is between good and truth. What is the quality of that marriage may fully appear from what has been quoted above, concerning good and truth, namely, as good is the very esse of a thing, and truth the existere of a thing thence derived, so the will with man is the very esse of his life, and the understanding the existere of life thence; for good, which is of the will, forms and renders itself visible in the understanding.

They who are in good and truth have will and understanding, but they who are in evil and in falsity have not will and understanding; but instead of will they have cupidity, and instead of understanding they have science. For the truly human will is the receptacle of good, and the understanding is the receptacle of truth; for which reason will cannot be predicated of evil, nor can understanding be predicated of falsity, because they are opposites, and opposites destroy each other. Hence it is, that the man who is in evil and thence in falsity, cannot be called rational, wise, and intelligent. With the evil, also, the interiors of the mind, in which the will and the understanding principally reside, are closed. It is believed that the evil also have will and understanding, because they say that they will, and that they understand; but their willing is only cupidity, and their understanding is only knowing.

FROM THE ARCANA COELESTIA Spiritual truths cannot be

comprehended, unless the following universals are known: I. All things in the universe have relation to good and truth, and to the conjunction of both, in order that they may be anything; consequently to love and faith, and their conjunction. II. With man there is will and understanding, and the will is the receptacle of good, and the understanding the receptacle of truth, and all things with man have relation to those two, and to their conjunction, as all things relate to good and truth, and their conjunction. III. There is an internal man and an external, and they are distinct one from the other like heaven and the world, and nevertheless that they ought to make one, in order that man may be truly man. IV. The light of heaven is that in which the internal man is, and the light of the world that in which the external is; and the light of heaven is the Divine truth itself, from which is all intelligence. V. There is a correspondence between the things which are in the internal, and those which are in the external man; and consequently they appear in each under a different form, so that they can only be discerned by the science of correspondences. Unless these and many other things are known, it is impossible to form any ideas concerning spiritual and celestial things, but such as are incongruous; and thus the scientifics and knowledges, which are of the external man, without these universals, can be of little service to the rational man for understanding and growth. Hence it appears, how necessary scientifics are. Concerning those universals, much is said in the Arcana Coelestia.

Man has two faculties, one which is called the will, and the other the understanding (n. 35, 641, 3539, 3623, 5969, 10122). Those two faculties constitute the very man (n. 10076, 10109, 10110, 10264, 10284). The quality of man is according to those two faculties with him (n. 7342, 8885, 9282, 10264, 10284). By them also man is distinguished from beasts, by reason that the understanding of man may be elevated by the Lord, and see Divine truths, and in like manner his will may be elevated and perceive Divine goods; and thus man may be conjoined to the Lord by those two faculties, which make him; but that the case is otherwise with beasts (n. 4525, 5114, 5302, 6323, 9231). And since man may thus be conjoined to the Lord, he cannot die as to his interiors, which are his spirit, but he lives forever (n. 5302). Man is not man from his form, but from good and truth, which are of his will and understanding (n. 4051, 5302). As all things in the universe relate to good and truth, so do all things in man to the will and the understanding (n. 803, 10122). For the will is the receptacle of good, and the understanding is the receptacle of truth (n. 3332, 3623, 5835, 6065, 6125, 7503, 9300, 9930). It amounts to the same, whether you say truth or faith, for faith is of truth, and truth is of faith; and it amounts to the same whether you say good or love, for love is of good, and good is of love; for what a man believes, that he calls true; and what he loves, that he calls good (n. 4353, 4997, 7178, 10122, 10367). Hence it follows that the understanding is the recipient of faith, and the will the recipient of love; and that faith and love are in man, when they are in his understanding and will, for the life of man is nowhere else (n. 7179, 10122, 10367). And since the understanding of man is capable of receiving faith in the Lord, and the will of receiving love to the Lord, that by faith and love he may be conjoined to the Lord, and whoever is capable of conjunction with the Lord by faith and love, cannot die to eternity (n. 4525, 6323, 9231). Love is conjunction in the spiritual world (n. 1594, 2057, 3939,

4018, 5807, 6195, 6196, 7081, 7086, 7501, 10130). The will of man is the very esse of his life, because it is the receptacle of good, and the understanding is the existere of life thence derived, because it is the receptacle of truth (n. 3619, 5002, 9282). Thus the life of the will is the principal life of man, and the life of the understanding proceeds therefrom (n. 585, 590, 3619, 7342, 8885, 9282, 10076, 10109, 10110); comparatively as light proceeds from fire or flame (n. 6032, 6314). Whatever things enter into the understanding, and at the same time into the will, are appropriated to man, but not those which are received in the understanding alone (n. 9009, 9069, 9071, 9133, 9182, 9386, 9393, 10076, 10109, 10110). Those things become of the life of man, which are received in the will, and thence in the understanding (n. 8911, 9069, 9071, 10076, 10109, 10110). Every man also is loved and esteemed by others according to the good of his will and thence of his understanding; for he who wills well and understands well is loved and esteemed, and he who understands well and does not will well, is rejected and is held in low estimation (n. 8911, 10076). Man also after death remains such as his will and the understanding are (n. 9069, 9071, 9386, 10153) and those things which are of the understanding, and not at the same time of the will, then vanish, because they are not in man's spirit (n. 9282). Or, what amounts to the same, man after death remains as his love and its faith are, or as his good and its truth are; and the things which are of the faith and not at the same time of the love, or the things which are of truth and not at the same time of good, vanish, because they are not in the man, thus not man's (n. 553, 2363, 10153). Man is capable of comprehending with the understanding what he does not do from the will, or he may understand what he does not will, because it is against his love (n. 3539). The will and the understanding constitute one mind (n. 35, 3623, 5835, 10122). Those two faculties of life ought to act as one, that man may be man (n. 3623, 5835, 5969, 9300). How perverted a state they are in, whose understanding and will do not act as one (n. 9075). Such is the state of hypocrites, the deceitful, flatterers, and simulators (n. 2426, 3573, 4799, 8250). The will and the understanding are reduced to one in another life, and there it is not allowable to have a divided mind (n. 8250). Every doctrinal of the church has its own ideas by which its quality is perceived (n. 3310). The understanding of the doctrinal is according to those ideas, and without an intellectual idea, man would only have an idea of words, and none of things (n. 3825). The ideas of the understanding extend themselves widely into the societies of spirits and angels round about (n. 6599, 6600-6605, 6609, 6613). The ideas of man's understanding are opened in another life, and appear to the life as to their quality (n. 1869, 3310, 5510). Of what quality the ideas of some appear (n. 6200, 8885). All the will of good and the understanding of truth is from the Lord, but not so the understanding of truth separate from the will of good (n. 1831, 3514, 5482, 5649, 6027, 8685, 8701, 10153). It is the understanding which is enlightened by the Lord (n. 6222, 6608, 10659). The Lord grants to those who are enlightened, to see and understand truth (n. 9382, 10659). The enlightening of the understanding is various, according to the states of man's life (n. 5221, 7012, 7233). The understanding is enlightened as far as man receives truth in the will, that is, as far as he wills to act according thereto (n. 3619). They have their understanding enlightened who read the Word from the love of truth and from the love of the uses of life; but not they who read it from the love of fame, honor, and gain (n. 9382, 10548, 10549, 10551). Enlightenment is an actual elevation of the mind into the light of heaven (n. 10330); from experience (n. 1526, 6608). Light from heaven is the enlightenment of the understanding, as light from the world is to the sight (n. 1524, 5114, 6608, 9128). The light of heaven is the Divine truth, from which is all wisdom and intelligence (n. 3195, 3222, 5400, 8644, 9399, 9548, 9684). It is the understanding of man which is enlightened by that light (n. 1524, 3138, 3167, 4408, 6608, 8707, 9128, 9399, 10569). The understanding is such as are the truths from good, of which it is formed (n. 10064). The understanding is that which is formed by truths from good, but not what is formed by falsities from evil (n. 10675). The understanding consists in seeing truths, the causes of things, their connections, and consequences in regular order, from those things which are of experience and science (n. 6125). The understanding consists in seeing and perceiving whether a thing be true, before it is confirmed, but not in being able to confirm everything (n. 4741, 7012, 7680, 7950, 8521, 8780). The light of confirmation without a previous perception of truth, is natural light, and may be possessed even by those who are not wise (n. 8780). To see and perceive whether a thing be true before it is confirmed, is only given with those who are affected with truth for the sake of truth, consequently who are in spiritual light (n. 8780). Every dogma even what is false, may be confirmed, even so as to appear true (n. 2243, 2385, 4677, 4741, 5033, 6865, 7950). How the rational is conceived and born with man (n. 2094, 2524, 2557, 3030, 5126). It is from the influx of the light of heaven from the Lord through the internal man into theknowledges and sciences, which are in the external, and an elevation thence (n. 1895, 1899, 1902). The rational is born by truths, and not by falsities; consequently according to the quality of the truths, such is the rational (n. 2094, 2524, 2557). The rational is opened and formed by truths from good, and it is shut and destroyed by falsities from evil (n. 3108, 5126). A man is not rational who is in falsities from evil; and consequently a man is not rational from being able to reason upon every subject (n. 1944). Man scarcely knows how to distinguish between the understanding and the will, because he scarcely knows how to distinguish between thinking and willing (n. 9995). Many more things concerning the will and the understanding may be known and concluded from what has been just adduced concerning good and truth, provided the will be perceived instead of good, and the understanding instead of truth, for the will is of good, and the understanding is of truth.

    III. THE INTERNAL AND THE EXTERNAL MAN. Man is so created as to be in the spiritual world and in the natural world at the same time. The spiritual world is where the angels are, and the natural world where men are. As man is so created, there has been given to him an internal and an external; an internal by which he is in the spiritual world, and an external by which he is in the natural world. His internal is what is called the internal man, and his external is what is called the external man.

    Every man has an internal and an external; but they differ with the good and the evil. With the good, the internal is in heaven, and in its light, and the external is in the world, and in its light, which light with them is illumined by the light of heaven, so that the internal and the external act as one, like the efficient cause and the effect, or like what is prior and what is posterior. But with the evil, the internal is in the world, and in its light; as is also the external; for which reason they see nothing from the light of heaven, but only from the light of the world, which they call the light of nature. Hence it is that to them the things of heaven are in thick darkness, whilst the things of the world are in light. From this it is manifest that the good have both an internal and an external man, but that the evil have not an internal man, but only an external.

The internal man is called the spiritual man, because it is in the light of heaven, which light is spiritual; and the external man is called the natural man, because it is in the light of the world, which light is natural. The man whose internal is in the light of heaven, and whose external is in the light of the world, is a spiritual man as to both; but the man whose internal is not in the light of heaven, but only in the light of the world, in which is his external also, is a natural man as to both. The spiritual man is called in the Word "living," but the natural man is called "dead."

The man whose internal is in the light of heaven, and his external in the light of the world, thinks both spiritually and naturally; but then his spiritual thought flows into his natural thought, and is there perceived. But the man whose internal and external are in the light of the world, does not think spiritually, but materially; for he thinks from such things as are in the nature of the world, all which are material. To think spiritually is to think of things themselves as they are in themselves, to see truths in the light of truth, and to perceive goods from the love of good; also, to see the qualities of things, and to perceive their affections, abstractly from matter. But to think materially is to think, see, and perceive them together with matter, and in matter, thus in a gross and obscure manner respectively.

The internal spiritual man, regarded in himself, is an angel of heaven; and, also, during his life in the body, is in society with angels, although he does not then know it; and after his separation from the body, he comes among the angels. But the merely natural internal man, regarded in himself, is a spirit, and not an angel; and, also, during his life in the body, is in society with spirits, but with those who are in hell, among whom he also comes after his separation from the body.

The interiors, with those who are spiritual men, are also actually elevated towards heaven, for that is what they primarily regard; but the interiors which are of the mind with those who are merely natural, are actually turned to the world, because that is what they primarily regard. The interiors, which are of the mind [mens], are turned with everyone to that which he loves above all things; and the exteriors which are of the mind [animus], are turned the same way as the interiors.

They who have only a general idea concerning the internal and the external man, believe that it is the internal man which thinks and wills, and the external which speaks and acts; because to think and to will is internal, and to speak and to act thence is external. But it is to be known that when man thinks intelligently and wills wisely, he then thinks and wills from a spiritual internal; but when man does not think intelligently, and will wisely, he thinks and wills from a natural internal. Consequently, when a man thinks well concerning the Lord, and those things which are of the Lord, and well concerning the neighbor, and those things which are of the neighbor, and wills well to them, he then thinks and wills from a spiritual internal, because he then thinks from the faith of truth and from the love of good, thus from heaven. But when man thinks and wills wickedly concerning them, he then thinks and wills from a natural internal, because he thinks and wills from the faith of falsity and from the love of evil, thus from hell. In a word, so far as man is in love to the Lord, and in love towards the neighbor, so far he is in a spiritual internal, from which he thinks and wills, and from which also he speaks and acts; but so far as man is in the love of self, and in the love of the world, so far he is in a natural internal, from which he thinks and wills, and from which also he speaks and acts.

It is so provided and ordered by the Lord, that so far as man thinks and wills from heaven, so far the internal spiritual man is opened and formed. It is opened into heaven even to the Lord, and the formation is according to those things which are of heaven. But, on the contrary, so far as man does not think and will from heaven, but from the world, so far the internal spiritual man is closed, and the external is opened. The opening is into the world, and the formation is to those things which are of the world.

They with whom the internal spiritual man is opened into heaven to the Lord, are in the light of heaven, and in enlightenment from the Lord, and thence in intelligence and wisdom; these see truth because it is truth, and perceive good because it is good. But they with whom the internal spiritual man is closed, do not know that there is an internal man, and much less what the internal man is; neither do they believe that there is the Divine, nor that there is a life after death; consequently they do not believe the things which are of heaven and of the church. And because they are only in the light of the world and in the enlightenment thence, they believe in nature as the Divine, they see falsity as truth, and they perceive evil as good.

He whose internal is so far external, that he believes nothing but what he can see with his eyes and touch with his hands, is called a sensual man; this is the lowest natural man, and is in fallacies concerning all the things which are of the faith of the church.

The internal and the external, which have been treated of, are the internal and the external of the spirit of man; his body is only a superadded external, within which they exist; for the body does nothing from itself, but from its spirit which is in it. It is to be known that the spirit of man, after its separation from the body, thinks and wills, speaks and acts, the same as before; to think and to will is its internal, and to speak and to act is its external; concerning which, see in the work on Heaven (n. 234-245, 265-275, 432-444, 453-484).

FROM THE ARCANA COELESTIA. Of the internal and the external with man. It is known in the Christian world, that man has an internal and an external, or an internal man and an external man; but it is little known what is the quality of the one and of the other (n. 1889, 1940). The internal man is spiritual, and the external is natural (n. 978, 1015, 4459, 6309, 9701-9709). How the internal man which is spiritual is formed to the image of heaven; and the external which is natural to the image of the world; and man was therefore called by the ancients a microcosm (n. 3628, 4523, 4524, 6057, 6314, 9706, 10156, 10472). Thus in man the spiritual world and natural world are conjoined

(n. 6057, 10472). Thence man is such that he can look up towards heaven, and down towards the world (n. 7601, 7604, 7607). When he looks upwards, he is in the light of heaven and sees thence; but when he looks downwards, he is in the light of the world and sees thence (n. 3167, 10134). There is given with man a descent from the spiritual world into the natural (n. 3702, 4042). The internal man which is spiritual, and the external man which is natural, are altogether distinct (n. 1999, 2018, 3691, 4459). The distinction is such as exists between cause and effect, and between prior and posterior, and there is no continuity (n. 3691, 4154, 5145, 5146, 5711, 6275, 6284, 6299, 6326, 6465, 8603, 10076, 10099, 10181). Consequently that the distinction is like that between heaven and the world, or between the spiritual and the natural (n. 4292, 5032, 5620, 5639). The interiors and exteriors of man are not continuous, but distinct according to degrees, and each degree is terminated (n. 3691, 4145, 5114, 6326, 6465, 8603, 10099). He who does not perceive the distinctions of the interiors and the exteriors of man according to degrees, and does not understand the quality of those degrees, cannot comprehend the internal and the external of man (n. 5146, 6465, 10099, 10181). The things of a higher degree are more perfect than those of a lower degree (n. 3405). There are three degrees in man answering to the three heavens (n. 4154). The exteriors are more remote from the Divine with man, and therefore they are respectively obscure, and of a general nature (n. 6451). And they are also respectively not in order (n. 996, 3855). The interiors are more perfect, because nearer to the Divine (n. 5146, 5147). In the internal there are thousands and thousands of things, which in the external appear as one general thing (n. 5707). Thence thought and perception is clearer in proportion as it is interior (n. 5920). Hence it follows that man ought to be in internals (n. 1175, 4464). The interiors of the mind, with the man who is in love and charity, are actually elevated by the Lord, and otherwise they would look downwards (n. 6952, 6954, 10330). Influx and enlightenment from heaven with man, is an actual elevation of the interiors by the Lord (n. 7816, 10330). Man is elevated when he advances to spiritual things (n. 9922). As far as man is elevated from externals towards interiors, so far he comes into light, consequently into intelligence; and this is what is meant by being withdrawn from sensual things, according to the saying of the ancients (n. 6183, 6313). Elevation from the external to the interiors, is like that from mist into light (n. 4598). Influx from the Lord is through the internal man into the external (n. 1940, 5119). Interiors can flow into exteriors, but not the contrary; consequently that influx is spiritual and not physical, namely, from the spiritual man into the natural, and not from the natural man into the spiritual (n. 3219, 5119, 5259, 5427, 5428, 5477, 6322, 9109, 9110). The Lord from the internal, where there is peace, governs the external, where there is turbulence (n. 5396). The internal can see all things in the external, but not the reverse (n. 1914, 1953, 5427, 5428, 5477). When man lives in the world, he thinks from the internal in the external, consequently his spiritual thought flows into his natural, and there presents itself naturally (n. 3679). When man thinks well, it is from the internal or spiritual in the external or natural (n. 9704, 9705, 9707). The external man thinks and wills according to conjunction with the internal (n. 9702, 9703). There is an interior and an exterior thought; the quality of the one and the other (n. 2515, 2552, 5127, 5141, 5168, 6007). The thought and affection in the internal is not perceived by man during his life in the world, but only that which is in the external therefrom (n. 10236, 10240). But in the other life externals are taken away, and man is then let into his own internals (n. 8870). It then becomes manifest what is the quality of his internals (n. 1806, 1807). The internal produces the external (n. 994, 995). And the internal then invests itself with such things as enable it to produce its effects in the external (n. 6275, 6284, 6299); and by which it may live in the external (n. 1175, 6275). The Lord conjoins the internal or spiritual man to the external or natural man, when He regenerates him (n. 1577, 1594, 1904, 1999). The external or natural man is then reduced into order through the internal or spiritual man, and is subordinated (n. 9708). The external must be subordinate and subject to the internal (n. 5077, 5125, 5128, 5786, 5947, 10272). The external is so created, that it may serve the internal (n. 5947). The internal must be lord, and the external its minister, and in a certain respect its servant (n. 10471). The external ought to be in correspondence with the internal, that there may be conjunction (n. 5427, 5428, 5477). What the quality of the external is when it corresponds with the internal, and what when it does not correspond (n. 3493, 5422, 5423, 5427, 5428, 5477, 5511). In the external man there are things which correspond and agree with the internal, and there are things which do not correspond and agree (n. 1563, 1568). The external has its quality from the internal (n. 9912, 9921, 9922). How great the beauty of the external man is, when it is conjoined with the internal (n. 1590). And how great its foulness when not conjoined (n. 1598). Love to the Lord and charity towards the neighbor conjoin the external man with the internal (n. 1594). Unless the internal man be conjoined with the external, there is no fructification (n. 3987). The interiors successively flow into the exteriors, even into the extreme or ultimate, and they there exist and subsist together (n. 634, 6239, 9215, 9216). They not only flow in successively, but also form in the ultimate what is simultaneous, in what order (n. 5897, 6451, 8603, 10099). All the interiors are held in connection from the first, through the ultimate (n. 9828). Thence also in the ultimates are strength and power (n. 9836). And therefore responses and revelations were made from the ultimates (n. 9905, 10548). Thence also the ultimate is more holy than the interiors (n. 9824). Hence also in the Word, "first and last" signify all and every particular, thus the whole (n. 10044, 10329, 10335). The internal man is open to him who is in Divine order, but shut to him who is not in Divine order (n. 8513). There is no conjunction of heaven with the external man without the internal (n. 9380). Evils and the falsities of evil shut the internal man, and cause man to be only in externals (n. 1587, 10492). Especially evils from the love of self (n. 1594). The interiors are shut even to the sensual, which is the ultimate, if the Divine is denied (n. 6564). With the intelligent and learned of the world, who from the sciences confirm themselves against the things of heaven and the church, the internal is shut more than with the simple (n. 10492). Because the internal man is in the light of heaven, and the external in the light of the world, therefore they who are in the external without the internal, that is, they with whom the internal is shut, do not care for the internal things of heaven and the church (n. 4464, 4946). In the other life they cannot at all endure internal things (n. 10694, 10701, 10707). They believe nothing (n. 10396, 10400, 10411, 10429). They love themselves and the world above all things (n. 10407, 10412, 10420). Their interiors, or the things which are of their thought and affection, are vile, filthy, and profane, howsoever they may appear in externals (n. 1182, 7046, 9705, 9707). The ideas of their thought are material, and not at all spiritual (n. 10582). The quality further described of those whose internal that looks heavenward is shut (n. 4459, 9709, 10284, 10286, 10429, 10472, 10492, 10602, 10683). So far as the internal, which is spiritual, is opened, so far truths and goods are multiplied; and so far as the internal, which is spiritual, is shut, so far truths and goods vanish (n. 4099). The church is in the internal spiritual man, because that is in heaven, and not in the external without it (n. 10698). Hence the external church with man is nothing without the internal (n. 1795). External worship without internal worship is no worship (n. 1094, 1175). Concerning those who are in the internal of the church, of worship, and of the Word; of those who are in the external in which is the internal; and of those who are in the external without the internal (n. 10683). The external without the internal is hard (n. 10683). The merely natural man is in hell, unless he be made spiritual by regeneration (n. 10156). All who are in the external without the internal, or with whom the spiritual internal is shut, are in hell (n. 9128, 10483, 10489). The interiors of man are actually turned according to his loves (n. 10702). In each and all things there must be an internal and an external that they may subsist (n. 9473). "Above" and "high" in the Word, signifies the internal (n. 1725, 2148, 4210, 4599). Thence in the Word higher is interior, and lower is exterior (n. 3084).

Of the natural and the spiritual. How perverse it is that the world at this day attributes so much to nature, and so little to the Divine (n. 3483). Why it is so (n. 5116). When nevertheless each and every particular in nature not only exists, but likewise continually subsists from the Divine, and through the spiritual world (n. 775, 8211). Divine, celestial, and spiritual things terminate in nature (n. 4240, 4939). Nature is the ultimate plane whereon they stand (n. 4240, 5651, 6275, 6284, 6299, 9216). Celestial, spiritual, and natural things follow and succeed each other in order; so do Divine things with them, because they are from the Divine (n. 880, 4938, 4939, 9992, 10005, 10017, 10068). Celestial things are the head, spiritual things the body, and natural things the feet (n. 4938, 4939). They also inflow in an order similar to that wherein they follow and succeed each other (n. 4938, 4939). The good of the inmost or third heaven is called celestial, the good of the middle or second heaven is called spiritual, and the good of the ultimate or first heaven is called spiritual natural, whence it may be known what is the celestial, spiritual, and natural (n. 4279, 4286, 4938, 4939, 9992, 10005, 10017, 10068); and in the work on Heaven and Hell (n. 20-28, 29-40). All things of the natural world are from the Divine through the spiritual world (n. 5013). Consequently the spiritual is in every natural thing, just as the efficient cause is in the effect (n. 3562, 5711); or as effort is in motion (n. 5173), and as the internal is in the external (n. 3562, 5326, 5711). And since the cause is the very essential in the effect, as effort is in motion, and the internal in the external; hence it follows, that the spiritual, and consequently the Divine, is the very essential in the natural (n. 2987-3002, 9701-9709). Spiritual things are presented to view in the natural, and the things manifested are representatives and correspondences (n. 1632, 2987-3002). Hence all nature is a theater representative of the spiritual world, that is, of heaven (n. 2758, 2999, 3000, 4939, 8848, 9280). All things in nature are disposed in order and series according to ends (n. 4104). This is from the spiritual world, that is, from heaven, because ends, which are uses, reign there (n. 454, 696, 1103, 3645, 4054, 7038). Man is so created that Divine things descending according to order into nature, may be perceived in him (n. 3702). With every man, who is in Divine order, there is an internal and an external, his internal is called the spiritual, or the spiritual man, and his external is called the natural, or the natural man (n. 978, 1015, 4459, 6309, 9701-9709). The spiritual man is in the light of heaven, and the natural man in the light of the world (n. 5965). The natural man can discern nothing from himself, but from the spiritual (n. 5286). The natural is like a face in which the interiors see themselves, and thus man thinks (n. 5165). The spiritual man thinks in the natural, consequently naturally, so far as it comes to the sensual perception of the natural (n. 3679, 5165, 6284, 6299). The natural is the plane, in which the spiritual terminates (n. 5651, 6275, 6284, 6299, 9216). The spiritual sees nothing, unless the natural be in correspondence (n. 3493, 3620, 3623). The spiritual or internal man can see what is being done in the natural or external, but not the contrary, because the spiritual flows into the natural, and not the natural into the spiritual (n. 3219, 4667, 5119, 5259, 5427, 5428, 5477, 6322, 9109, 9110). The natural man from his own light, which is called the light [lumen] of nature, knows nothing concerning God, nor concerning heaven, nor concerning the life after death; neither does he believe, if he hears of such things, unless spiritual light, which is light from heaven, flows into that natural light [lumen] (n. 8944). The natural man of himself, by birth, is opposite to the spiritual man (n. 3913, 3928). Therefore as long as they are opposite to each other, man feels it grievous to think of spiritual and celestial things, but delightful to think of natural and corporeal things (n. 4096). He nauseates the things of heaven, and even the bare mention of anything spiritual, from experience (n. 5006, 9109). Merely natural men regard spiritual good and truth as a servant (n. 5013, 5025). When nevertheless the natural man ought to be subordinate to the spiritual man, and serve him (n. 3019, 5168). The spiritual man is said to serve the natural, when the latter from the intellectual principle seeks confirmations of the objects of his concupiscence, particularly from the Word (n. 3019, 5013, 5025, 5168). How merely natural men appear in another life, and what is the quality of their state and lot there (n. 4630, 4633, 4940-4952, 5032, 5571). The truths, which are in the natural man, are called scientifics and knowledges (n. 3293). The imagination of the natural man, when viewed in itself, is material, and his affections are like those of beasts (n. 3020). But there is a genuine thinking and imaginative principle from the internal or spiritual man when the natural man sees, acts, and lives therefrom (n. 3493, 5422, 5423, 5427, 5428, 5477, 5510). The things which are in the natural man, respectively to those which are in the spiritual man, are general (n. 3513, 5707); and consequently obscure (n. 6686). There is an interior and an exterior natural with man (n. 3293, 3294, 3793, 5118, 5126, 5497, 5649). There is also a medium between them (n. 4570, 9216). The discharges of the spiritual man are made into the natural, and by it (n. 9572). They who do good merely from a natural disposition, and not from religion, are not received in heaven (n. 8002, 8772).

Of the light of heaven in which the spiritual man is. There is great light in

the heavens (n. 1117, 1521, 1533, 1619-1632). The light in the heavens exceeds
the meridian light on earth by many degrees (n. 1117, 1521, 4527, 5400, 8644).
That light has been often seen by me (n. 1522, 4527, 7174). The light which the
angels of the inmost or third heaven have is as the light from the sun, but the
light which the angels of the second heaven have is as the light from the moon
(n. 1529, 1530). The light in the inmost heaven is flamy, but in the second
heaven it is bright white (n. 9570). All light in the heavens is from the Lord as
a sun there (n. 1053, 1521, 3195, 3341, 3636, 3643, 4415, 9548, 9684, 10809).
The Lord is the sun of the angelic heaven, and His Divine love is that sun (n.
1521, 1529, 1530, 1531, 1837, 4321, 4696, 7078, 7083, 7173). The Divine truth
proceeding from the Lord in the heavens appears as light, and constitutes all
the light of heaven; and consequently that light is spiritual light (n. 3195, 3322,
5400, 8644, 9399, 9548, 9684). Therefore the Lord in the Word is called light (n.
3195). Because that light is the Divine truth, there is in it Divine wisdom and
intelligence (n. 3195, 3485, 3636, 3643, 3993, 4302, 4413, 4415, 9548, 9684).
How light from the Lord flows into the heavens, illustrated by the circles of rays
round the sun (n. 9407). That the Lord is a sun to the heavens, and from Him
is all the light there may be seen in the work on Heaven and Hell (n. 116-125).
And the light from that sun is the Divine truth, and the heat from it the Divine
good of the Divine love (n. 126-140). The light of heaven enlightens both the
sight and the understanding of angels and spirits (n. 2776, 3138). They have
light there according to their understanding and wisdom (n. 1524, 3339).
Testified from the Word (n. 1529, 1530). There are as many differences of light
in the heavens as there are angelic societies (n. 4414); since there are perpetual
varieties in the heavens as to good and truth, thus as to wisdom and
intelligence (n. 684, 690, 3241, 3744, 3745, 5598, 7236, 7833, 7836). Heaven's
being in light and heat signifies its being in wisdom and in love (n. 3643, 9399,
9400). The light of heaven enlightens the understanding of man (n. 1524, 3138,
3167, 4408, 6608, 8707, 9128, 9399, 10569). Man, when he is elevated from the
sensual, comes into a milder light [lumen], and at length into celestial light [lux]
(n. 6313, 6315, 9407). There is elevation into the light of heaven when man
comes into intelligence (n. 3190). What great light was perceived, when I have
been withdrawn from worldly ideas (n. 1526, 6608). The sight of the internal
man is in the light of heaven, and therefore man is able to think analytically
and rationally (n. 1532). The light of heaven from the Lord is always present
with man, but it flows in only so far as he is in truths from good (n. 4060, 4214).
That light is according to truth from good (n. 3094). Truths shine in the
spiritual world (n. 5219). Spiritual heat and spiritual light make the true life of
man (n. 6032). The light of the world is for the external man, and the light of
heaven for the internal (n. 3223, 3324, 3337). The light of heaven flows into
natural light [lumen] and the natural man is so far wise as he receives that
light (n. 4302, 4408). There is a correspondence between those lights (n. 3225).
The things which are in the light of heaven cannot be seen from the light of the
world with man, which is called his natural light [lumen]; but the things in the
light of the world may be seen from the light of heaven (n. 9577). Whence it
follows, that they who are only in the light of the world, which is called natural
light [lumen], do not perceive those things which are of the light of heaven (n.
3108). To those who are in falsities from evil, the light of heaven is thick

darkness (n. 1783, 3337, 3413, 4060, 6907, 8197). The light of the world with the evil is glowing, and so far as it glows, so far the things which are of the light of heaven are dark to them (n. 6907). The light of the world does not appear to the angels (n. 1521, 1783, 1880). In the heavens all light is from the Lord, and all shade from the ignorance and proprium of the angels and spirits; hence the modifications and variegations of light and shade, which are colors there (n. 3341). Concerning the variegations of light by the Urim and Thummim (n. 3862). The light of those who are in faith separate from charity is snowy, and like the light of winter (n. 3412, 3413). That light is turned into mere darkness on the influx of light from heaven (n. 3412). Of the light of those who are in a persuasive faith, and in a life of evil (n. 4416). Of what quality the light appears with those who are in intelligence from the proprium, and what with those who are in intelligence from the Lord (n. 4419). There is light [lumen] in the hells, but fatuous (n. 1528, 3340, 4214, 4418, 4531). This light is as light from a coal fire (n. 1528, 4418, 4531). They who are in the hells appear to themselves in their own light as men, but in the light of heaven as devils and monsters (n. 4532, 4533, 4674, 5057, 5058, 6605, 6626). All things in the light of heaven appear according to their true quality (n. 4674). The hells are said to be in thick darkness and darkness, because they are in falsities from evils (n. 3340, 4418, 4531). "Darkness" signifies falsities, and "thick darkness" the falsity of evil (n. 1839, 1860, 7688, 7711).

Of the sensual man, who is the lowest degree natural (spoken of in the doctrine above, n. 45). The sensual is the ultimate of the life of man, adhering to and inhering in his corporeal (n. 5077, 5767, 9212, 9216, 9331, 9730). He who judges and concludes concerning everything from the bodily senses, and who believes nothing but what he can see with his eyes and touch with his hands, saying that these are something, and rejecting all things else, is a sensual man (n. 5094, 7693). Such a man thinks in outmosts, and not interiorly in himself (n. 5089, 5094, 6564, 7693). His interiors are shut, so that he sees nothing of truth therein (n. 6564, 6844, 6845). In a word, he is in gross natural light, and thus perceives nothing which is from the light of heaven (n. 6201, 6310, 6564, 6598, 6612, 6614, 6622, 6624, 6844, 6845). Consequently he is interiorly against the things which are of heaven and the church (n. 6201, 6316, 6844, 6845, 6948, 6949). The learned, who have confirmed themselves against the truths of the church, are sensual (n. 6316). Sensual men reason sharply and shrewdly, because their thought is so near their speech as to be almost in it, and because they place all intelligence in discourse from the memory alone (n. 195, 196, 5700, 10236). But they reason from the fallacies of the senses, with which the common people are captivated (n. 5084, 6948, 6949, 7693). Sensual men are more crafty and malicious than others (n. 7693, 10236). The avaricious, adulterers, the voluptuous, and the deceitful especially are sensual (n. 6310). Their interiors are foul and filthy (n. 6201). By means thereof they communicate with the hells (n. 6311). They who are in the hells are sensual in proportion to their depth (n. 4623, 6311). The sphere of infernal spirits conjoins itself with man's sensual from behind (n. 6312). They who reasoned from the sensual, and thereby against the truths of faith, were called by the ancients serpents of the tree of knowledge (n. 195-197, 6398, 6949, 10313). The sensual of man, and the sensual man himself, is further described (n. 10236). And the

extension of the sensual with man (n. 9731). Sensual things ought to be in the
last place, not in the first, and with a wise and intelligent man they are in the
last place and subject to the interiors; but with an unwise man they are in the
first place, and have dominion; these are they who are properly called sensual
(n. 5077, 5125, 5128, 7645). If sensual things are in the last place, and are
subject to the interiors, a way is opened through them to the understanding,
and truths are refined by a kind of extraction (n. 5580). The sensual things of
man stand nearest to the world, and admit things that flow from the world, and
as it were sift them (n. 9726). The external or natural man communicates with
the world by means of those sensuals, and with heaven by means of rationals
(n. 4009). Thus sensual things administer those things which are serviceable to
the interiors of man (n. 5077, 5081). There are sensual things ministering to the
intellectual part, and likewise to the will part (n. 5077). Unless the thought is
elevated from sensual things, man possesses but little wisdom (n. 5089). A wise
man thinks above the sensual (n. 5089, 5094). Man, when his thought is
elevated above sensual things, comes into a clearer light [lumen], and at length
into heavenly light [lux] (n. 6183, 6313, 6315, 9407, 9730, 9922). Elevation
above sensual things, and withdrawal from them, was known to the ancients
(n. 6313). Man with his spirit may see the things which are in the spiritual
world, if he can be withdrawn from the sensual things of the body, and elevated
by the Lord into the light of heaven (n. 4622). The reason is, because the body
does not feel, but the spirit in the body; and so far as the spirit perceives in the
body, so far is the perception gross and obscure, consequently in darkness; but
so far as not in the body, so far is the perception clear and in the light (n. 4622,
6614, 6622). The ultimate of the understanding is the sensual scientific, and the
ultimate of the will the sensual delight, concerning which see n. 9996. What is
the difference between the sensual things that are common with beasts, and
those that are not common with them (n. 10236). There are sensual men who
are not evil, inasmuch as their interiors are not so much closed; concerning
whose state in another life (see n. 6311).

Section 2

But charity extends itself much more widely than to the poor and indigent; for charity consists in doing what is right in every work, and our duty in every office. If a judge does justice for the sake of justice, he exercises charity; if he punishes the guilty and absolves the innocent, he exercises charity, for thus he consults the welfare of his fellow-citizens and of his country. The priest who teaches the truth, and leads to good, for the sake of truth and good, exercises charity. But he who does such things for the sake of self and the world, does not exercise charity, because he does not love the neighbor, but himself.

The case is the same in all other instances, whether a man be in any office or not; as with children towards parents, and with parents towards children; with servants towards masters, and with masters towards servants; with subjects towards the king, and with a king towards subjects: whoever of these does his duty from a principle of duty, and what is just from a principle of justice, exercises charity.

The reason why such things belong to love towards the neighbor, or charity, is because, as was said above, every man is the neighbor, but in a different manner. A less and greater society is more the neighbor; our country is still more the neighbor; the Lord's kingdom still more; and the Lord above all; and in a universal sense, good, which proceeds from the Lord, is the neighbor; consequently also sincerity and justice. Wherefore he who does any good for the sake of good, and he who acts sincerely and justly for the sake of sincerity and justice, loves the neighbor and exercises charity; for he does so from the love of what is good, sincere, and just, and consequently from the love of those in whom good, sincerity, and justice are.

Charity therefore is an internal affection, from which man wills to do good, and this without remuneration; the delight of his life consists in doing it. With them who do good from internal affection, there is charity in each thing which they think and speak, and which they will and do; it may be said that a man and an angel, as to his interiors, is charity, when good is his neighbor. So widely does charity extend itself.

They who have the love of self and of the world for an end, cannot in any wise be in charity; they do not even know what charity is; and they cannot at all comprehend that to will and do good to the neighbor without reward as an end, is heaven in man, and that there is in that affection a happiness as great as that of the angels of heaven, which is ineffable; for they believe, if they are deprived of the joy from the glory of honors and riches, that nothing of joy can be given them any longer; when yet it is then that heavenly joy first begins, which infinitely transcends the other.

FROM THE ARCANA COELESTIA. Heaven is distinguished into two kingdoms, one of which is called the celestial kingdom, and the other the spiritual kingdom; the love in the celestial kingdom is love to the Lord, and is called celestial love; and the love in the spiritual kingdom is love towards the neighbor, or charity, and is called spiritual love (n. 3325, 3653, 7257, 9002, 9835, 9961). Heaven is distinguished into two kingdoms, see the work on Heaven and Hell (n. 20-28); and the Divine of the Lord in the heavens is love to Him, and charity towards the neighbor (n. 13-19, in the same). It cannot be known what good is and what truth is, unless it be known what love to the Lord and love towards the neighbor are, because all good is of love, and all truth is of good (n. 7255, 7366). To know truths, to will truths, and to be affected with them for the sake of truths, that is, because they are truths, is charity (n. 3876, 3877). Charity consists in an internal affection of doing truth, and not in an external affection without an internal one (n. 2429, 2442, 3776, 4899, 4956, 8033). Thus charity consists in performing uses for the sake of uses (n. 7038, 8253). Charity is the spiritual life of man (n. 7081). The whole Word is the doctrine of love and charity (n. 6632, 7262). It is not known at this day what charity is (n. 2417, 3398, 4776, 6632). Nevertheless man may know from the light of his own reason, that love and charity make the man (n. 3957, 6273). Also that good and truth agree together, and that one is of the other, and so also love and faith (n. 7627). The Lord is the neighbor in the highest sense, because He is to be loved above all things; and hence all is the neighbor which is from Him, and in which he is, thus good and truth (n. 2425, 3419, 6706, 6819, 6823, 8124). The distinction of neighbor is according to the quality of good, thus according to the presence of the Lord (n. 6707-6710). Every Man and every society, also our country and the church, and, in the universal sense, the kingdom of the Lord, are the neighbor, and to do good to them according to the quality of their state from the love of good, is to love the neighbor; thus the neighbor is their good, which is to be consulted (n. 6818-6824, 8123). Civil good, which is justice, and moral good, which is the good of life in society, and is called sincerity, are also the neighbor (n. 2915, 4730, 8120-8122). To love the neighbor does not consist in loving his person, but in loving that with him from which he is, consequently good and truth (n. 5028, 10336). They who love the person, and not that which is with him from which he is, love evil as well as good (n. 3820). And they do good to the evil as well as to the good, when nevertheless doing good to the evil is doing evil to the good, which is not loving the neighbor (n. 3820, 6703, 8120). The judge who punishes the evil that they may be amended, and that the good may not be contaminated by them, loves the neighbor (n. 3820, 8120, 8121). To love the neighbor is to do what is good, just, and right, in every work and in every office (n. 8120-8122). Hence charity towards the neighbor extends itself to each and every thing which man thinks, wills, and does (n. 8124). To do what is good and true is to love the neighbor (n. 10310, 10336). They who do this love the Lord, who in the highest sense is the neighbor (n. 9210). The life of charity is a life according to the commandments of the Lord; and to live according to Divine truths is to love the Lord (n. 10143, 10153, 10310, 10578, 10645). Genuine charity is not meritorious (n. 2027, 2343, 2400, 3887, 6388-6393). Because it is from internal affection, consequently from the delight of the life of doing good (n. 2373, 2400, 3887, 6388-6393). They who separate faith from charity, in another life hold faith and the good works which they have done in the external form as meritorious (n. 2373). They who are in evils from the love of self or the love of the world, do not know what it is to do good without remuneration, thus what that charity is which is not meritorious (n. 8037). The doctrine of the Ancient Church was the doctrine of life, which is the doctrine of charity (n. 2385, 2417, 3419, 3420, 4844, 6628). Thence they had intelligence and wisdom (n. 2417, 6629, 7259-7262). Intelligence and wisdom increase immensely in the other life with those who have lived a life of charity in the world (n. 1941, 5859). The Lord flows in with Divine truth into charity, because into the essential life of man (n. 2063). The man with whom charity and faith are conjoined is like a garden; but like a desert with whom they are not conjoined (n. 7626). Man recedes from wisdom in proportion as he recedes from charity; and they who are not in charity, are in ignorance concerning Divine truths, however wise they think themselves (n. 2417, 2435). The angelic life consists in performing the goods of charity, which are uses (n. 454). The spiritual angels, who are they that are in the good of charity, are forms of charity (n. 553, 3804, 4735). All spiritual truths regard charity as their beginning and end (n. 4353). The doctrinals of the church effect nothing unless they regard charity as their end (n. 2049, 2116). The presence of the Lord with men and angels is according to their state of love and charity (n. 549, 904). Charity is the image of God (n. 1013). Love to the Lord, consequently the Lord, is within charity, although man does not know it (n. 2227, 5066, 5067). They who live a life of charity are accepted as citizens both in the world and in heaven (n. 1121). The good of charity is not to be violated (n. 2359). They who are not in charity cannot acknowledge and worship the Lord except from hypocrisy (n. 2132, 4424, 9833). The forms of hatred and of charity cannot exist together (n. 1860).

To the above shall be added some particulars concerning the doctrine of love to the Lord, and the doctrine of charity, as it was held by the ancients with whom the church was, in order that the former quality of that doctrine, which at this day exists no longer, may he known. The particulars are extracted from the Arcana Coelestia (n. 7257-7263). The good which is of love to the Lord, is called celestial good; and the good which is of love towards the neighbor, or charity, is called spiritual good. The angels who are in the inmost or third heaven, are in the good of love to the Lord, being called celestial angels; but the angels of the middle or second heaven, are in the good of love towards the neighbor, being called spiritual angels. The doctrine of celestial good, which is that of love to the Lord, is of most wide extent, and at the same time most full of arcana; being the doctrine of the angels of the inmost or third heaven, which is such, that if it were delivered from their mouths, scarcely a thousandth part of it would be understood: the things also which it contains are ineffable. This doctrine is contained in the inmost sense of the Word; but the doctrine of spiritual love, in the internal sense. The doctrine of spiritual good, which is that of love towards the neighbor, is also of wide extent and full of arcana, but much less so than the doctrine of celestial good, which is that of love to the Lord. That the doctrine of love towards the neighbor, or charity, is of wide extent, may appear from the fact, that it reaches to all the things which man thinks and wills, consequently to all which he speaks and does, even to the most minute particulars; and also from the fact, that charity does not exist alike with two different persons, and that no two persons are alike the neighbor. As the doctrine of charity was so extensive, therefore the ancients, with whom it was the very doctrine of the church, distinguished charity towards the neighbor into several classes, which they again subdivided, and gave names to each class, and taught how charity was to be exercised towards those who are in one class, and towards those who are in another; and thus they reduced the doctrine and the exercises of charity into order, that they might fall distinctly into the understanding. The names which they gave to those towards whom they were to exercise charity were many; some they called "the blind," some "the lame," some "the maimed," some "the poor," some "the miserable," and "afflicted," some "the fatherless," some "widows," but in general they called them "the hungry," to whom they should give to eat; "the thirsty," to whom they should give to drink; "strangers," whom they should take in; "the naked," whom they should clothe; "the sick," whom they should visit, and "the bound in prison," to whom they should come. Who they were whom they meant by these particulars, has been made known already in the Arcana Coelestia, as whom they meant by "the blind" (n. 2383, 6990); by "the lame" (n. 4302); "the poor" (n. 2129, 4459, 4958, 9209, 9253, 10227); "the miserable" (n. 2129); "the afflicted" (n. 6663, 6851, 9196); "the fatherless" (n. 4844, 9198-9200) and "widows" (n. 4844, 9198, 9200); "the hungry" (n. 4958, 10227); "the thirsty" (n. 4958, 8568); "the strangers" (n. 4444, 7908, 8007, 8013, 9196, 9200); "the naked" (n. 1073, 5433, 9960); "the sick" (n. 4958, 6221, 8364, 9031); "the bound in prison" (n. 5037, 5038, 5086, 5096). It may be seen that the whole doctrine of charity is comprehended in the offices towards those who are called by the Lord "the hungry," "the thirsty," "strangers," "the naked," "the sick," and "the bound in prison" Matt. 25:34-36 and the verses following) [n. 4954-4959]. These names were given from heaven to the ancients who were of the church, and by those who were so named they understood those who were spiritually such. Their doctrine of charity not only taught who these were, but also the quality of the charity to be exercised towards each. Hence it is, that the same names are in the Word, and signify those who are such in the spiritual sense. The Word in itself is nothing but the doctrine of love to the Lord, and of charity towards the neighbor, as the Lord also teaches: Thou shalt love the Lord thy God with all thy heart, and with all thy soul, and with all thy mind; this is the first and great commandment. The second is like unto it, Thou shalt love thy neighbor as thyself. On these two commandments hang all the law and the prophets (Matt. 22:37-40). "The law and the prophets" are the whole Word (n. 2606, 3382, 6752, 7643). The reason why those same names are in the Word, is that the Word, which is in itself spiritual, might in its ultimate be natural; and because they who are in external worship are to exercise charity towards such as are so named, and they who are in internal worship towards such spiritually understood; thus that the simple might understand and do the Word in simplicity, and the wise, in wisdom; also, that the simple, by the externals of charity, might be initiated into its internals.

VII. FAITH. No one can know what faith is in its essence, unless he knows what charity is, because where there is no charity there is no faith, for charity makes one with faith as good does with truth. For what man loves or holds dear, this to him is good, and what man believes, this to him is truth; whence it is plain that there is a like union of charity and faith, as there is of good and truth; the quality of which union may appear from what has been said above concerning Good and Truth.

The union of charity and faith is also like that of the will and the understanding with man; for these are the two faculties which receive good and truth, the will receiving good and the understanding truth; thus, also, these two faculties receive charity and faith, since good is of charity and truth is of faith. Everyone knows that charity and faith are with man, and in him, and because they are with man, and in him, they must be in his will and understanding, for all the life of man is therein, and from thence. Man has also memory, but this is only the outer court, where those things are collected together which are to enter into the understanding and the will. Thence it is evident that there is a like union of charity and faith, as there is of the will and the understanding; the quality of which union may appear from what has been said above concerning the Will and the Understanding.

Charity conjoins itself with faith with man, when man wills that which he knows and perceives; to will is of charity, and to know and perceive is of faith. Faith enters into man, and becomes his, when he wills and loves that which he knows and perceives; meanwhile it is without him.

Faith does not become faith with man, unless it becomes spiritual, and it does not become spiritual, unless it becomes of the love; and it then becomes of the love, when man loves to live truth and good, that is, to live according to those things which are commanded in the Word.

Faith is the affection of truth from willing truth because it is truth; and to will truth because it is truth is the spiritual itself of man; for it is abstracted from the natural, which is to will truth not for the sake of truth, but for the sake of one's own glory, reputation, or gain. Truth withdrawn from such things is spiritual, because it is from the Divine. That which proceeds from the Divine is spiritual, and this is conjoined to man by love, for love is spiritual conjunction.

Man may know, think, and understand much, but when he is left to himself alone, and meditates, he rejects from himself those things which do not agree with his love; and therefore he also rejects them after the life of the body when he is in the spirit, for that only remains in the spirit of man which has entered into his love: other things after death are regarded as foreign, and because they are not of his love he casts them out. It is said in the spirit of man, because man lives a spirit after death.

An idea concerning the good which is of charity, and concerning the truth which is of faith, may be formed from the light and heat of the sun. When the light which proceeds from the sun is conjoined to heat, as is the case in the time of spring and summer, then all things of the earth germinate and flourish; but when there is no heat in the light, as in the time of winter, then all things of the earth become torpid and die; also spiritual light is the truth of faith, and spiritual heat is love. From these things an idea may be formed concerning the man of the church, what his quality is when faith with him is conjoined to charity, namely, that he is like a garden and paradise; and what his quality is when faith with him is not conjoined to charity, that he is like a desert and earth covered with snow.

The confidence or trust, which is said to be of faith, and is called saving faith itself, is not spiritual confidence or trust, but natural, when it is of faith alone. Spiritual confidence or trust has its essence and life from the good of love, but not from the truth of faith separate. The confidence of faith separate is dead; wherefore true confidence cannot be given with those who lead an evil life. The confidence also that salvation is on account of the Lord's merit with the Father, whatever a man's life may have been, is not from truth. All those who are in spiritual faith have confidence that they are saved by the Lord, for they believe that the Lord came into the world to give eternal life to those who believe and live according to the precepts which He taught, and that He regenerates them, and renders them fit for heaven, and that He alone does this from pure mercy without the aid of man.

To believe those things which the Word teaches, or which the doctrine of the church teaches, and not to live according to them, appears as if it were faith, and some also assert that they are saved by it; but by this alone no one is saved, for it is persuasive faith, the quality of which shall now be stated.

Faith is persuasive, when the Word and the doctrine of the church are believed and loved, not for the sake of truth and of a life according to it, but for the sake of gain, honor, and the fame of erudition, as ends; wherefore they who are in that faith, do not look to the Lord and to heaven, but to themselves and the world. They who in the world aspire after great things, and covet many things, are in a stronger persuasion that what the doctrine of the church teaches is true than they who do not aspire after great things and covet many things: the reason is, because the doctrine of the church is to the former only a means to their own ends, and so far as the ends are coveted, so far the means are loved, and are also believed. But the case in itself is this: so far as they are in the fire of the loves of self and of the world, and from that fire speak, preach, and act, so far they are in that persuasion, and then they know no other than that it is so; but when they are not in the fire of those loves, then they believe little, and many not at all. Thence it is evident, that persuasive faith is a faith of the mouth and not of the heart, thus that in itself it is not faith.

They who are in persuasive faith do not know, from any internal enlightenment, whether the things which they teach be true or false; yea, neither do they care, provided they be believed by the common people; for they are in no affection of truth for the sake of truth. Wherefore they recede from faith, if they are deprived of honors and gains, provided their reputation be not endangered. For persuasive faith is not inwardly with man, but stands without, in the memory only, out of which it is taken when it is taught. Wherefore also that faith with its truths vanishes after death; for then there remains only that faith which is inwardly in man, that is, which is rooted in good, thus which has become of the life.

They who are in persuasive faith are meant by these in Matthew: Many will say to me in that day, Lord, Lord, have we not prophesied by Thy name, and by Thy name cast out demons, and in Thy name done many virtues? But then I will confess to them, I have not known you, ye workers of iniquity (7:22, 23). Also in Luke: Then will ye begin to say, We have eaten before Thee, and have drunk, and Thou hast taught in our streets; but He will say, I say to you, I have not known you whence you are; depart from Me all ye workers of iniquity (13:26, 27). They are meant also by the five foolish virgins who had no oil in their lamps, in Matthew: At length came those virgins, saying, Lord, Lord, open to us; but He answering will say, Verily I say unto you, I have not known you (Matt. 25: 11, 12). "The oil in the lamps" is the good of love in faith.

FROM THE ARCANA COELESTIA. They who do not know that all things in the universe have relation to truth and good, and to the conjunction of both, that anything may be produced, do not know that all things of the church have relation to faith and love, and to the conjunction of both, that the church may be with man (n. 7752-7762, 9186, 9224). All things in the universe, which are according to Divine order have relation to good and truth, and to their conjunction (n. 2452, 3166, 4390, 4409, 5232, 7256, 10122, 10555). Truths are of faith and goods are of love (n. 4352, 4997, 7178, 10367). This is the reason that good and truth have been treated of in this doctrine; wherefore from what has been adduced, it may be concluded respecting faith and love; and it may be known what their quality is when they are conjoined, and what it is when they are not conjoined, by putting love in the place of good, and faith in the place of truth, and making applications accordingly. They who do not know that each and all things in man have relation to the understanding and will, and to the conjunction of both, in order that man may be man, do not know clearly that all things of the church have relation to faith and love, and to the conjunction of both, in order that the church may be with man (n. 2231, 7752-7754, 9224, 9995, 10122). Man has two faculties, one of which is called the understanding and the other the will (n. 641, 803, 3623, 3539). The understanding is designed for receiving truths, thus the things of faith; and the will for receiving goods, thus the things of love (n. 9300, 9930, 10064). This is the reason why the will and the understanding have been also treated of in this doctrine; for from what has been adduced, conclusions may be drawn respecting faith and love, and it may be known what their quality is when they are conjoined, and what it is when they are not conjoined, by thinking of love in the will, and faith in the understanding. They who do not know that man has an internal and an external, or an internal and an external man, and that all things of heaven have relation to the internal man, and all things of the world to the external, and that their conjunction is like the conjunction of the spiritual world and the natural world, do not know what spiritual faith and spiritual love are (n. 4392, 5132, 8610). There is an internal and an external man, and the internal is the spiritual man, and the external the natural (n. 978, 1015, 4459, 6309, 9701-9709). Faith is so far spiritual, thus so far faith, as it is in the internal man; and love likewise (n. 1594, 3987, 8443). And so far as the truths which are of faith are loved, so far they become spiritual (n. 1594, 3987). This is the reason why the internal and the external man have been treated of, for from what has been adduced, conclusions may be drawn respecting faith and love, what their quality is when they are spiritual, and what when they are not spiritual; consequently how far they are of the church, and how far they are not of the church.

Faith separate from love or charity is like the light of winter, in which all things on earth are torpid, and no harvests, fruits, or flowers, are produced; but faith with love or charity is like the light of spring and summer, in which all things flourish and are produced (n. 2231, 3146, 3412, 3413). The wintry light of faith separate from charity is changed into dense darkness when light from heaven flows in; and they who are in that faith then come into blindness and stupidity (n. 3412, 3413). They who separate faith from charity, in doctrine and life, are in darkness, thus in ignorance of truth, and in falsities, for these are darkness (n. 9186). They cast themselves into falsities, and into evils thence (n.

3325, 8094). The errors and falsities into which they cast themselves (n. 4721, 4730, 4776, 4783, 4925, 7779, 8313, 8765, 9224). The Word is shut to them (n. 3773, 4783, 8780). They do not see or attend to all those things which the Lord so often spoke concerning love and charity, and concerning their fruits, or goods in act, concerning which (n. 1017, 3416). Neither do they know what good is, nor thus what celestial love is, nor what charity is (n. 2517, 3603, 4136, 9995). Faith separate from charity is no faith (n. 654, 724, 1162, 1176, 2049, 2116, 2343, 2349, 2417, 3849, 3868, 6348, 7039, 7342, 9783). Such a faith perishes in the other life (n. 2228, 5820). When faith alone is assumed as a principle, truths are contaminated by the falsity of the principle (n. 2335). Such persons do not suffer themselves to be persuaded, because it is against their principle (n. 2385). Doctrinals concerning faith alone destroy charity (n. 6353, 8094). They who separate faith from charity were represented by Cain, by Ham, by Reuben, by the firstborn of the Egyptians, and by the Philistines (n. 3325, 7097, 7317, 8093). They who make faith alone saving, excuse a life of evil, and they who are in a life of evil have no faith, because they have no charity (n. 3865, 7766, 7778, 7790, 7950, 8094). They are inwardly in the falsities of their own evil, although they do not know it (n. 7790, 7950). Therefore good cannot be conjoined with them (n. 8981, 8983). In the other life they are against good, and against those who are in good (n. 7097, 7127, 7317, 7502, 7545, 8096, 8313). Those who are simple in heart and yet wise, know what the good of life is, thus what charity is, but not what faith separate is (n. 4741, 4754). All things of the church have relation to good and truth, consequently to charity and faith (n. 7752-7754). The church is not with man before truths are implanted in his life, and thus become the good of charity (n. 3310). Charity constitutes the church, and not faith separate from charity (n. 809, 916, 1798, 1799, 1834, 1844). The internal of the church is charity (n. 1799, 7755). Hence there is no church where there is no charity (n. 4766, 5826). The church would be one if all were regarded from charity, although men might differ as to the doctrinals of faith and the rituals of worship (n. 1285, 1316, 1798, 1799, 1834, 1844, 2385, 2982, 3267, 3451). How much of good would be in the church if charity were regarded in the first place, and faith in the second (n. 6269, 6272). Every church begins from charity, but in process of time turns aside to faith, and at length to faith alone (n. 1834, 1835, 2231, 4683, 8094). There is no faith at the last time of the church, because there is no charity (n. 1843). The worship of the Lord consists in a life of charity (n. 8254, 8256) The quality of the worship is according to the quality of the charity (n. 2190). The men of the external church have an internal if they are in charity (n. 1100, 1102, 1151, 1153). The doctrine of the ancient churches was the doctrine of life, which is the doctrine of charity, and not the doctrine of faith separate (n. 2385, 2417, 3419, 3420, 4844, 6628, 7259-7262). The Lord inseminates and implants truth in the good of charity when he regenerates man (n. 2063, 2189, 3310). Otherwise the seed, which is the truth of faith, cannot take root (n. 880). Then goods and truths increase, according to the quality and quantity of the charity received (n. 1016). The light of a regenerate person is not from faith, but from charity by faith (n. 854). The truths of faith, when man is regenerated, enter with the delight of affection, because he loves to do them, and they are reproduced with the same affection, because they cohere (n. 2484, 2487, 3040, 3066, 3074, 3336, 4018, 5893). They who live in love to the Lord, and in charity towards the neighbor, lose nothing to eternity, because they are conjoined to the Lord; but it is otherwise with those who are in separate faith (n. 7506, 7507). Man remains such as is his life of charity, not such as his faith separate (n. 8256). All the states of delight of those who have lived in charity, return in the other life, and are increased immensely (n. 823). Heavenly blessedness flows from the Lord into charity, because into the very life of man; but not into faith without charity (n. 2363). In heaven all are regarded from charity, and none from faith separate (n. 1258, 1394). All are associated in the heavens according to their loves (n. 7085). No one is admitted into heaven by thinking, but by willing good (n. 2401, 3459). Unless doing good is conjoined with willing good and with thinking good, there is no salvation, neither any conjunction of the internal man with the external (n. 3987). The Lord, and faith in Him, are received by no others in the other life, than those who are in charity (n. 2343). Good is in the perpetual desire and consequent endeavor of conjoining itself with truths, and charity with faith (n. 9206, 9207, 9495). The good of charity acknowledges its own truth of faith, and the truth of faith its own good of charity (n. 2429, 3101, 3102, 3161, 3179, 3180, 4358, 5807, 5835, 9637). Hence there is a conjunction of the truth of faith and the good of charity, concerning which (n. 3834, 4096, 4097, 4301, 4345, 4353, 4364, 4368, 5365, 7623-7627, 7752-7762, 8530, 9258, 10555). Their conjunction is like a marriage (n. 1904, 2173, 2508). The law of marriage is that two be one, according to the Word of the Lord (n. 10130, 10168, 10169). So also faith and charity (n. 1094, 2173, 2503). Therefore faith which is faith, is, as to its essence, charity (n. 2228, 2839, 3180, 9783). As good is the esse of a thing, and truth the existere thence, so also is charity the esse of the church, and faith the existere thence (n. 3409, 3180, 4574, 5002, 9145). The truth of faith lives from the good of charity, thus a life according to the truths of faith is charity (n. 1589, 1947, 2571, 4070, 4096, 4097, 4736, 4757, 4884, 5147, 5928, 9154, 9667, 9841, 10729). Faith cannot be given but in charity, and if not in charity, there is not good in faith (n. 2261, 4368). Faith does not live with man when he only knows and thinks the things of faith, but when he wills them, and from will does them (n. 9224). There is no salvation by faith, but by a life according to the truths of faith, which life is charity (n. 379, 389, 2228, 4663, 4721). They are saved who think from the doctrine of the church that faith alone saves, if they do what is just for the sake of justice, and good for the sake of good, for thus they are still in charity (n. 2442, 3242, 3459, 3463, 7506, 7507). If a mere cogitative faith could save, all would be saved (n. 2361, 10659). Charity constitutes heaven with man, and not faith without it (n. 3513, 3584, 3815, 9832, 10714, 10715, 10721, 10724). In heaven all are regarded from charity, and not from faith (n. 1258, 1394, 2361, 4802). The conjunction of the Lord with man is not by faith, but by a life according to the truths of faith (n. 9380, 10143, 10153, 10310, 10578, 10645, 10648). The Lord is the tree of life, the goods of charity the fruits, and faith the leaves (n. 3427, 9337). Faith is the "lesser luminary," and good the "larger luminary" (n. 30-38). The angels of the Lord's celestial kingdom do not know what faith is, so that they do not even name it, but the angels of the Lord's spiritual kingdom speak of faith, because they reason concerning truths (n. 202, 203, 337, 2715, 3246, 4448, 9166, 10786). The angels of the Lord's celestial kingdom say only yea, yea or nay, nay, but the angels of the Lord's spiritual kingdom reason whether it be so or not so, when there is discourse concerning spiritual truths, which are of faith (n. 2715, 3246, 4448, 9166, 10786), where the Lord's words are explained: Let your discourse be yea, yea, nay, nay; what is beyond these is from evil (Matt. 5:37). The reason why the celestial angels are such, is, because they admit the truths of faith immediately into their lives, and do not deposit them first in the memory, as the spiritual angels do; and hence the celestial angels are in the perception of all things of faith (n. 202, 585, 597, 607, 784, 1121, 1387, 1398, 1442, 1919, 5113, 5897, 6367, 7680, 7877, 8521, 8780, 9936, 9995, 10124). Trust or confidence, which in an eminent sense is called saving faith, is given with those only who are in good as to life, consequently with those who are in charity (n. 2982, 4352, 4683, 4689, 7762, 8240, 9239-9245). Few know what that confidence is (n. 3868, 4352). What difference there is between believing those things which are from God, and believing in God (n. 9239, 9243). It is one thing to know, another to acknowledge, and another to have faith (n. 896, 4319, 5664). There are scientifics of faith, rationals of faith and spirituals of faith (n. 2504, 8078). The first thing is the acknowledgment of the Lord (n. 10083). All that flows in with man from the Lord is good (n. 1614, 2016, 2751, 2882, 2883, 2891, 2892, 2904, 6193, 7643, 9128). There is a persuasive faith, which nevertheless is not faith (n. 2343, 2682, 2689, 3427, 3865, 8148). It appears from various reasonings as though faith were prior to charity, but this is a fallacy (n. 3324). It may be known from the light of reason, that good, consequently charity, is in the first place, and truth, consequently faith, in the second (n. 6273). Good, or charity, is actually in the first place, or is the first of the church, and truth, or faith, is in the second place, or is the second of the church, although it appears otherwise (n. 3324, 3325, 3330, 3336, 3494, 3539, 3548, 3556, 3570, 3576, 3603, 3701, 3995, 4337, 4601, 4925, 4926, 4928, 4930, 5351, 6256, 6269, 6272, 6273, 8042, 8080, 10110). The ancients disputed concerning the first or primogeniture of the church, whether it be faith or whether it be charity (n. 367, 2435, 3324).

The twelve disciples of the Lord represented the church as to all things of faith and charity in the complex, as did also the twelve tribes of Israel (n. 2129, 3354, 3488, 3858, 6397). Peter, James, and John represented faith, charity, and the goods of charity in their order (n. 3750). Peter represented faith (n. 4738, 6000, 6073, 6344, 10087, 10580). And John represented the goods of charity, see the preface to the eighteenth and twenty-second chapters of Genesis. That there would be no faith in the Lord, because no charity, in the last time of the church, was represented by Peter's thrice denying the Lord before the cock crew the third 122-1 time; for Peter there, in a representative sense, is faith; (n. 6000, 6073). "Cock crowing," as well as "twilight," signifies in the Word the last time of the church (n. 10134). And "three" or "thrice," signifies what is complete to the end (n. 2788, 4495, 5159, 9198, 10127). The like is signified by the Lord's saying to Peter, when Peter saw John follow the Lord: What is it to thee, Peter? follow thou Me, John; for Peter had said of John, What is this? (John 21:21, 22); (n. 10087). John lay on the breast of the Lord, because he represented the good of charity (n. 3934, 10081). That the good of charity constitutes the church, is also signified by the words of the Lord from the cross to John: Jesus saw His mother, and the disciple whom He loved, who stood by, and He said to His mother, Woman, behold thy son: and He said to that disciple, Behold thy mother; and from that hour that disciple took her to himself (John 19:26, 27).

"John" signifies the good of charity, and "woman" and "mother," the church; and the whole passage signifies that the church will be where the good of charity is; that "woman" in the Word means the church (see n. 252, 253, 749, 770, 3160, 6014, 7337, 8994). And likewise "mother" (n. 289, 2691, 2717, 3703, 4257, 5580, 8897, 10490). All the names of persons and places in the Word signify things abstractly from them (n. 768, 1888, 4310, 4442, 10329).

VIII. PIETY. It is believed by many, that spiritual life, or the life which leads to heaven, consists in piety, in external sanctity, and in the renunciation of the world; but piety without charity, and external sanctity without internal sanctity, and a renunciation of the world without a life in the world, do not constitute spiritual life; but piety from charity, external sanctity from internal sanctity, and a renunciation of the world with a life in the world, constitute it.

Piety consists in thinking and speaking piously, in devoting much time to prayers, in behaving humbly at that time, in frequenting temples and harkening devoutly to the preaching there, in frequently every year receiving the Sacrament of the Supper, and in performing the other parts of worship according to the ordinances of the church. But the life of charity consists in willing well and doing well to the neighbor, in acting in every work from justice and equity, from good and truth, and in like manner in every office; in a word, the life of charity consists in performing uses. Divine worship primarily consists in this life, but secondarily in the former; wherefore he who separates one from the other, that is, who lives the life of piety, and not at the same time the life of charity, does not worship God. He thinks indeed of God, but not from God but from himself, for he thinks continually of himself, and nothing of the neighbor; and if he thinks of the neighbor, he holds him in low estimation, if he be not also such as himself. And likewise he thinks of heaven as a reward, thence in his mind there is merit, and also the love of self, as also contempt or neglect of uses, and thus of the neighbor, and at the same time he cherishes a belief that he is blameless. Hence it may appear that the life of piety, separate from the life of charity, is not the spiritual life which should be in Divine worship. (Compare Matt. 6:7, 8.)

External sanctity is like such piety, and especially 125-1 consists in this, that man places all Divine worship in sanctity when he is in temples; but this is not holy with man unless his internal be holy; for such as man is as to his internal, such he also is as to his external, for this proceeds from the former as action does from its spirit; wherefore external sanctity without internal sanctity is natural and not spiritual. Hence it is that external sanctity is given with the evil as well as with the good; and they who place the whole of worship therein are for the most part empty; that is, without the knowledges of good and truth. And yet goods and truths are the real sanctities which are to be known, believed and loved, because they are from the Divine, and thus the Divine is in them. Internal sanctity, therefore, consists in loving good and truth for the sake of good and truth, and justice and sincerity for the sake of justice and sincerity. So far also as man thus loves them, so far he is spiritual, and also his worship, for so far also he is willing to know them and to do them; but so far as man does not thus love them, so far he is natural, and his worship also, and so far also he is not willing to know them and do them. External worship without internal may be compared with the life of the respiration without the life of the heart; but external worship from internal may be compared with the life of the respiration conjoined to the life of the heart.

But as to what relates to the renunciation of the world: it is believed by many, that to renounce the world, and to live in the spirit and not in the flesh, is to reject worldly things, which are chiefly riches and honors; to be continually engaged in pious meditation concerning God, concerning salvation, and concerning eternal life; to lead a life in prayers, in the reading of the Word and pious books; and also to afflict one's self: but this is not renouncing the world; but to renounce the world is to love God and to love the neighbor; and God is loved when man lives according to His commandments, and the neighbor is loved when man performs uses. Therefore in order that man may receive the life 126-1 of heaven, it is altogether necessary that he should live in the world, and in offices and business there. A life abstracted from worldly things is a life of thought and faith separate from the life of love and charity, in which life the will of good and the doing of good to the neighbor perishes. And when this perishes, spiritual life is as a house without a foundation, which either sinks down successively, or becomes full of chinks and cracks, or totters till it falls.

That to do good is to worship the Lord, appears from the Lord's words: Everyone who heareth My words and doeth them, I will liken to a prudent man who built a house upon a rock; but he who heareth My words and doeth them not, I will liken to a foolish man who built a house upon the sand, or upon the ground without a foundation (Matt. 7:24-27; Luke 6:47-49).

Hence now it is manifest, that a life of piety so far avails, and is accepted by the Lord, as a life of charity is conjoined to it; for this is the primary, and such as this is, such is that. Also, that external sanctity so far avails, and is accepted by the Lord, as it proceeds from internal sanctity for such as this is, such is that. And also, that the renunciation of the world so far avails, and is accepted by the Lord, as it is practiced in the world; for they renounce the world who remove the love of self and the world, and act justly and sincerely in every office, in every business, and in every work, from an interior, thus from a heavenly origin; which origin is in that life when man acts well, sincerely, and justly, because it is according to the Divine laws.

FROM THE ARCANA COELESTIA. A life of piety without a life of charity, is of no avail, but when united therewith aids (n. 8252, seq.). External sanctity without internal sanctity is not holy (n. 2190, 10177). Of the quality of those in another life, who have lived in external sanctity, and not from internal (n. 951, 952). There is an internal and external of the church (n. 1098). There is internal worship and external worship, and the quality of each (n. 1083, 1098, 1100, 1151, 1153). Internals are what make worship (n. 1175). External worship without internal is no worship (n. 1094, 7724). There is an internal in worship, if man's life is a life of charity (n. 1100, 1151, 1153). Man is in true worship when he is in love and charity, that is, when he is in good as to life (n. 1618, 7724, 10242). The quality of worship is according to good (n. 2190). Worship itself consists in a life according to the precepts of the church from the Word (n. 7884, 9921, 10143, 10153, 10196, 10645). True worship is from the Lord with man, not from man himself (n. 10203, 10299). The Lord desires worship from man for the sake of man's salvation, and not for the sake of his own glory (n. 4593, 8263, 10646). Man believes that the Lord desires worship for the sake of glory; but they who thus believe know not what Divine glory is, nor that it consists in the salvation of the human race, which man has when he attributes nothing to himself, and when he removes his proprium by humiliation; because the Divine is then first able to flow in (n. 4347, 4593, 5957, 7550, 8263, 10646). Humiliation of heart with man exists from an acknowledgment of himself, which is, that he is nothing but evil, and that he can do nothing from himself; and from a consequent acknowledgment of the Lord, which is, that nothing but good is from the Lord, and that the Lord can do all things (n. 2327, 3994, 7478). The Divine cannot flow in except into a humble heart, since so far as man is in humiliation, so far he is absent from his proprium, and thus from the love of self (n. 3994, 4347, 5957). Hence the Lord does not desire humiliation for His own sake, but for man's sake, that man may be in a state for receiving the Divine (n. 4347, 5957). Worship is not worship without humiliation (n. 2327, 2423, 8873). The quality of external humiliation without internal (n. 5420, 9377). The quality of humiliation of heart, which is internal (n. 7478). There is no humiliation of heart with the evil (n. 7640). They who have not charity and faith are in external worship without internal worship (n. 1200). If the love of self and of the world reigns interiorly with man, his worship is external without internal, however it may appear in the external form (n. 1182, 10307-10309). External worship in which the love of self reigns inwardly, as is the case with those who are of Babylon, is profane (n. 1304, 1306-1308, 1321, 1322, 1326). To imitate heavenly affections in worship, when man is in evils from the love of self, is infernal (n. 10309). What the quality of external worship is when it proceeds from internal, and when it does not, may be seen and concluded from what has been said and adduced above concerning the INTERNAL and the EXTERNAL MAN. Concerning those who renounce the world and those who do not renounce it, their quality, and their lot in the other life, may be seen in the work on Heaven and Hell, under the following heads: Of the Rich and Poor in Heaven (n. 357-365); and of the Life that leads to Heaven (n. 528-535).

IX. CONSCIENCE. Conscience is formed with man from the religious principle in which he is, according to its reception inwardly in himself.

Conscience, with the man of the church, is formed by the truths of faith from the Word, or from doctrine out of the Word, according to their reception in the heart; for when man knows the truths of faith, and comprehends them in his own manner, and then wills them and does them, he then acquires conscience. Reception in the heart is reception in the will, for the will of man is what is called the heart. Hence it is that they who have conscience, speak from the heart the things which they speak, and do from the heart the things which they do. They have also an undivided mind, for they act according to that which they understand and believe to be true and good.

A more perfect conscience can be given with those who are enlightened in the truths of faith more than others, and who are in a clear perception above others, than with those who are less enlightened, and are in obscure perception.

In a true conscience is man's spiritual life itself, for there his faith is conjoined to charity. On which account to act from conscience is to them to act from their spiritual life; and to act against conscience is to them to act contrary to that life of theirs. Hence it is that they are in the tranquillity of peace, and in internal happiness, when they act according to conscience, and in intranquillity and pain, when they act against it. This pain is what is called remorse of conscience.

Man has a conscience of what is good, and a conscience of what is just. The conscience of what is good is the conscience of the internal man, and the conscience of what is just is the conscience of the external man. The conscience of what is good consists in acting according to the precepts of faith from internal affection; but the conscience of what is just consists in acting according to civil and moral laws from external affection. They who have the conscience of what is good, have also the conscience of what is just; but they who have only the conscience of what is just, are in a faculty of receiving the conscience of what is good; and they also do receive it when they are instructed.

Conscience, with those who are in charity towards the neighbor, is the conscience of truth, because it is formed by the faith of truth; but with those who are in love to the Lord, it is the conscience of good, because it is formed by the love of truth. The conscience of these is a superior conscience, and is called the perception of truth from good. They who have the conscience of truth, are of the Lord's spiritual kingdom; but they who have the superior conscience, which is called perception, are of the Lord's celestial kingdom.

But let examples illustrate what conscience is. He who has possession of another man's goods, whilst the other is ignorant of it, and thus can retain them without fear of the law, or of the loss of honor and reputation, and he still restores them to the other, because they are not his own, he has conscience, for he does what is good for the sake of what is good, and what is just for the sake of what is just. Again, if anyone can obtain an office, but knows that another, who also desires it, would be more useful to his country, and gives way to the other for the sake of the good of his country, he has a good conscience. So in other cases.

From these instances it may be concluded, what quality they are of who have not conscience; they are known from the opposite. Thus, they who for the sake of any gain make what is unjust appear as just, and what is evil appear as good, and vice versa, have not conscience. Neither do they know what conscience is, and if they are instructed what it is, they do not believe; and some are not willing to know. Such are those who do all things for the sake of themselves and the world.

They who have not received conscience in the world, cannot receive it in the other life; thus they cannot be saved. The reason is, because they have no plane into which heaven, that is, the Lord through heaven, may flow in, and by which He may operate, and lead them to Himself. For conscience is the plane and receptacle of the influx of heaven.

FROM THE ARCANA COELESTIA. Of Conscience. They who have no conscience, do not know what conscience is (n. 7490, 9121). There are some who laugh at conscience, when they hear what it is (n. 721). Some believe that conscience is nothing; some that it is a sad, doleful, natural something, arising from bodily or worldly causes; and some that it is an effect of religion on the minds of the common people (n. 950). Some know not that they have conscience, when yet they have it (n. 2380). The good have conscience, but not the evil (n. 831, 965, 7490). They who are in love to God and in love towards the neighbor have conscience (n. 2380). Conscience is especially with those who are regenerated by the Lord (n. 977). They who are in truths alone, and not in a life according to them, have no conscience (n. 1076, 1077, 1919). They who do good from natural good, and not from religion, have no conscience (n. 6208). Man's conscience is from the doctrine of his church, or from some religious principle, and is according thereto (n. 9112). Conscience is formed with man from those things which are of his religion, and which he believes to be truths (n. 1077, 2053, 9113). Conscience is an internal bond, by which man is held to thinking, speaking, and doing good; and by which he is withheld from thinking, speaking, and doing evil; and this is not for the sake of self and the world, but for the sake of good, truth, justice, and uprightness (n. 1919, 9120). Conscience is an internal dictate, that one ought to do so or not so (n. 1919, 1935). Conscience is in its essence a conscience of what is true and right (n. 986, 8081). The new will with the spiritual regenerate man is conscience (n. 927, 1023, 1043, 1044, 4299, 4328, 4493, 9115, 9596). The spiritual life of man is from conscience (n. 9117). There is a true conscience, a spurious conscience, and a false conscience, concerning which (n. 1033). Conscience is more true, in proportion as it is formed from more genuine truths (n. 2053, 2063, 9114). In general, conscience is two-fold, interior and exterior, and interior conscience is of spiritual good, which in its essence is truth, and exterior conscience is of moral and civil good, which in its essence is sincerity and justice, in general, uprightness (n. 5140, 6207, 10296). Pain of conscience is anxiety of mind on account of injustice, insincerity, and any evil, which a man believes to be against God, and against the good of the neighbor (n. 7217). If anxiety is felt when a man thinks evil, it is from conscience (n. 5470). Pain of conscience is an anguish felt on account of the evil which man does, and also on account of the privation of good and truth (n. 7217). Since temptation is a combat of truth and falsity in the interiors of man, and since in temptations there is pain and anxiety, therefore no others are admitted into spiritual temptations, but those who have conscience (n. 847). They who have conscience speak and act from the heart (n. 7935, 9114). They who have conscience do not swear in vain (n. 2842). They who have conscience are in interior blessedness when they do what is good and just according to conscience (n. 9118). They who have conscience in the world, have conscience in the other life, and are there amongst the happy (n. 965). The influx of heaven flows into conscience with man (n. 6207, 6213, 9122). The Lord rules the spiritual man by conscience, which is an internal bond (n. 1835, 1862). They who have conscience, have interior thought; but they who have no conscience, have only exterior thought (n. 1919, 1935). They who have conscience, think from the spiritual, but they who have no conscience, think only from the natural (n. 1820). They who have no conscience, are only external men (n. 4459). The Lord rules those who have no conscience by external bonds, which are all those things which are of the love of self and of the world, and which thence relate to the fear of the loss of reputation, honor, office, gain, wealth, and the fear of the law, and of the loss of life (n. 1077, 1080, 1835). They who have no conscience, and yet suffer themselves to be ruled by these external bonds, are capable of discharging the duties of high offices in the world, and of doing good, as well as those who have conscience; but the former do it in an external form, and from external bonds, whereas the latter do it in an internal form, and from internal bonds (n. 6207). They who have no conscience would destroy conscience with those who have it (n. 1820). They who have no conscience in the world, have no conscience in the other life (n. 965, 9122). Hence those who are in hell have no torment of conscience for their evils in the world (n. 965, 9122). Who and of what quality, and how troublesome, the scrupulously conscientious are, and what they correspond to in the spiritual world (n. 5386, 5724). They who are in the Lord's spiritual kingdom, have conscience, and it is formed in their intellectual part (n. 863, 865, 875, 895, 927, 1043, 1044, 1555, 2256, 4328, 4493, 5113, 6367, 8521, 9596, 9915, 9995, 10124). It is otherwise with those who are in the Lord's celestial kingdom (n. 927, 2256, 5113, 6367, 8521, 9915, 9995, 10124).

Of Perception. Perception consists in seeing what is true and good by influx from the Lord (n. 202, 895, 7680, 9128). Perception is given only with those who are in the good of love from the Lord to the Lord (n. 202, 371, 1442, 5228). Perception is given with those in heaven who, whilst they lived in the world, brought the doctrinals of the church which are from the Word immediately into the life, and who did not first commit them to memory; thus the interiors of their minds were formed to the reception of the Divine influx; and thence their understanding is in heaven in continual enlightenment (n. 104, 495, 503, 521, 536, 1616, 1791, 5145). They know innumerable things, and are wise beyond measure (n. 2718, 9543). They who are in perception, do not reason concerning the truths of faith, and if they reasoned their perception would perish (n. 586, 1398, 5897). They who believe that they know and are wise from themselves, cannot have perception (n. 1386). The learned do not comprehend what this perception is, from experience (n. 1387). They who are in the Lord's celestial kingdom, have perception; but they who are in the spiritual kingdom, have no perception, but conscience in its place (n. 805, 2144, 2145, 8081). They who are in the Lord's celestial kingdom do not think from faith, like those in the Lord's spiritual kingdom, because they who are in the celestial kingdom are in perception from the Lord of all things of faith (n. 202, 597, 607, 784, 1121, 1387, 1398, 1442, 1919, 7680, 7877, 8780). Wherefore the celestial angels say concerning the truths of faith only, Yea, yea, or Nay, nay, because they perceive them and see them; but the spiritual angels reason concerning the truths of faith, whether a thing be so or not (n. 2715, 3246, 4448, 9166, 10786); where the words of the Lord are explained: Let your discourse be Yea, yea, Nay, nay: what is beyond these is from evil (Matt. 5:37). The celestial angels, because they know the truths of faith from perception, are not even willing to name faith (n. 202, 337). The distinction between the celestial angels and the spiritual angels (n. 2088, 2669, 2708-2715, 3235, 3240, 4788, 7068, 8521, 9277, 10295). Of the perception of those who were of the Most Ancient Church, which was a celestial church (n. 125, 597, 607, 784, 895, 1121, 5121). There is interior and exterior perception (n. 2145, 2171, 2831, 5920). There is in the world a perception of what is just and equitable, but rarely a perception of spiritual truth and good (n. 2831, 5937, 7977). The light of perception is altogether different from the light of confirmation; and it is not like it, although it may appear so to some persons (n. 8521, 8780).

X. FREEDOM. All freedom is of love, for what man loves, this he does freely; hence also all freedom is of the will, for what man loves, this he also wills; and because love and the will make the life of man, so also does freedom. From these things it may appear what freedom is, namely, it is that which is of the love and the will, and thence of the life of man. Hence it is, that what a man does from freedom, appears to him as if from his own proprium.

To do evil from freedom, appears as freedom, but it is slavery, because that freedom is from the love of self and from the love of the world, and these loves are from hell. Such freedom is actually turned into slavery after death, for the man who has been in such freedom then becomes a vile servant in hell. But to do good from freedom is freedom itself, because it is from love to the Lord and from love towards the neighbor, and these loves are from heaven. This freedom also remains after death, and then becomes freedom indeed, for the man who has been in such freedom, becomes in heaven like a son of the house. This the Lord thus teaches: Everyone that doeth sin is the servant of sin; the servant abideth not in the house forever: the son abideth forever; if the Son shall have made you free, you shall be truly free (John 8:34-36). Now, because all good is from the Lord, and all evil from hell, it follows that freedom consists in being led by the Lord, and slavery is being led by hell.

That man has the freedom of thinking evil and falsity, and also of doing it, so far as the laws do not withhold him, is in order that he may be capable of being reformed; for goods and truths are to be implanted in his love and will, so that they may become of his life, and this cannot be done unless he have the freedom of thinking evil and falsity as well as good and truth. This freedom is given to every man by the Lord, and so far as he does not love evil and falsity, so far, when he thinks what is good and true, the Lord implants them in his love and will, consequently in his life, and thus reforms him. What is inseminated in freedom, this also remains, but what is inseminated in a state of compulsion, this does not remain, because what is from compulsion is not from the will of the man, but from the will of him who compels. Hence also it is, that worship from freedom is pleasing to the Lord, but not worship from compulsion; for worship from freedom is worship from love, but worship from compulsion is not so.

The freedom of doing good, and the freedom of doing evil, though they appear alike in the external form, are as different and distant from each other as heaven and hell are: the freedom of doing good also is from heaven, and is called heavenly freedom; but the freedom of doing evil is from hell, and is called infernal freedom; so far, also, as man is in the one, so far he is not in the other, for no one can serve two lords (Matt. 6:24); which also appears from hence, that they who are in infernal freedom believe that it is slavery and compulsion not to be allowed to will evil and think falsity at their pleasure, but they who are in heavenly freedom abhor willing evil and thinking falsity, and would be tormented if they were compelled to do so.

Because acting from freedom appears to man as if from his own proprium, therefore heavenly freedom may also be called the heavenly proprium, and infernal freedom may be called the infernal proprium. The infernal proprium is that into which man is born, and this is evil; but the heavenly proprium is that into which man is reformed, and this is good.

From this it may appear what Free-will is; namely, that it consists in doing good from choice or will, and that they are in that freedom who are led by the Lord; and they are led by the Lord who love good and truth for the sake of good and truth.

Man may know what is the quality of the freedom in which he is, from the delight which he feels when he thinks, speaks, acts, hears, and sees; for all delight is of love.

FROM THE ARCANA COELESTIA. All freedom is of love or affection, for what a man loves, he does freely (n. 2870, 3158, 8987, 8990, 9585, 9591). As freedom is of love, it is the life of everyone (n. 2873). There is heavenly freedom and infernal freedom (n. 2870, 2873, 2874, 9589, 9590). Heavenly freedom is of the love of good and truth (n. 1947, 2870, 2872). And because the love of good and truth is from the Lord, that being led by the Lord is true freedom (n. 892, 905, 2872, 2886, 2890-2892, 9096, 9586, 9587-9591). Man by regeneration is introduced into heavenly freedom by the Lord (n. 2874, 2875, 2882, 2892). Man ought to be in freedom, that he may be regenerated (n. 1937, 1947, 2876, 2881, 3145, 3158, 4031, 8700). Otherwise the love of good and truth cannot be implanted in and appropriated to man, so as to appear his own (n. 2877, 2879, 2880, 2888). Nothing is conjoined to man which is done in compulsion (n. 2875, 8700). If man could be reformed by compulsion, all would be saved (n. 2881). Compulsion is hurtful in reformation (n. 4031) Worship from freedom is worship, but not worship from compulsion (n. 1947, 2880, 7349, 10097). Repentance should take place in a free state, and what is done in a forced state is of no avail (n. 8392). What forced states are (n. 8392). Man is allowed to act from the freedom of reason, in order that good may be provided for him, and therefore man is in the freedom of thinking and willing, and even of doing evil, so far as the laws do not forbid (n. 10777). Man is kept by the Lord between heaven and hell, and thus in equilibrium, that he may be in freedom for the sake of reformation (n. 5982, 6477, 8209, 8987). What is inseminated in freedom remains, but not what is inseminated in compulsion (n. 9588, 10777). Therefore freedom is never taken away from anyone (n. 2876, 2881). No one is compelled by the Lord (n. 1937, 1947). How the Lord leads man by means of freedom into good; by means of freedom he turns him from evil, and bends him to good, so gently and tacitly that the man knows no other than that all proceeds from himself (n. 9587). To compel himself is from liberty, but not to be compelled (n. 1937, 1947). Man ought to compel himself to resist evil (n. 1937, 1947, 7914). And also to do good as from himself, but still to acknowledge that it is from the Lord (n. 2883, 2891, 2892, 7914). Man has a stronger freedom in the combats of temptations in which he conquers, since he then interiorly compels himself to resist evils, although it appears otherwise (n. 1937, 1947, 2881). There is freedom in every temptation, but this freedom is interiorly with man from the Lord; and he therefore combats and wills to conquer, and not to be overcome, which he would not do without freedom (n. 1937, 1947, 2881). The Lord does this by means of an affection of truth and good impressed on the internal man, the man himself not knowing (n. 5044). Infernal freedom consists in being led by the loves of self and of the world, and their lusts (n. 2870, 2873). They who are in hell do not know any other freedom (n. 2871). Heavenly freedom is as far from infernal freedom as heaven is from hell (n. 2873, 2874). Infernal freedom in itself regarded is slavery (n. 2884, 2890). Because it is slavery to be led by hell (n. 9586, 9589-9591). All freedom is as the proprium, and according to it (n. 2880). Man receives a heavenly proprium from the Lord by regeneration (n.

1937, 1947, 2882, 2883, 2891). The nature of the heavenly proprium (n. 164, 5660, 8480). This proprium appears to man as his own, but it is not his, but the Lord's with him (n. 8497). They who are in this proprium are in true liberty, because true liberty consists in being led by the Lord and His proprium (n. 892, 905, 2872, 2886, 2890-2892, 4096, 9586, 9587, 9589-9591).

Freedom originates from the equilibrium between heaven and hell, and man, without freedom, cannot be reformed, is shown in the work on Heaven an Hell, in the articles concerning that equilibrium (n. 589-596), and concerning freedom (n. 597 to the end); but for the sake of instruction respecting what freedom is, and to show that man is reformed by means of it, I will here quote the following extracts from that work. "It has been shown, that the equilibrium between heaven and hell is an equilibrium between the good which is from heaven and the evil which is from hell; and thus it is a spiritual equilibrium, which in its essence is freedom. The reason that spiritual equilibrium is, in its essence, freedom, is, because it is an equilibrium between good and evil, and between truth and falsity, which are spiritual things; wherefore, the power of willing either good or evil, and of thinking either truth or falsity, and of choosing the one in preference to the other, is freedom. This freedom is given to everyone by the Lord, nor is it ever taken away from him. In its origin, indeed, it does not belong to man, but to the Lord, because it is from the Lord; but, nevertheless, it is given to man, together with life, as his own: and it is given him to this end, that he may be reformed and saved; for without freedom there can be no reformation and salvation. Everyone who takes any rational view of things may see, that man has freedom to think either ill or well, sincerely or insincerely, justly or unjustly; and also, that he is at liberty to speak and to act well, sincerely, and justly, but is withheld from speaking and acting ill, insincerely, and unjustly, by spiritual, moral, and civil laws, by which his external is kept in bonds. From these things it is evident, that the spirit of man, which is that which thinks and wills: is in freedom. Not so the external of man, which speaks and acts, except in conformity with the above-mentioned laws. The reason that man cannot be reformed, unless he is in freedom, is because he is born into evils of all kinds. These must be removed, in order that he may be saved; and they cannot be removed, unless he sees them in himself, and acknowledges them; and afterwards ceases to will them, and at length holds them in aversion. It is then that they are first removed. This could not be done, unless man possessed in him good as well as evil; for he is capable, from good, of seeing evils, but not, from evil, of seeing goods. The spiritual goods which man can think, he learns from infancy by reading the Word and hearing sermons; and he learns moral and civil goods from life in the world. This is the first reason why man ought to be in freedom. Another is, that nothing is appropriated to man, but what he does from an affection that is of his love; other things may indeed enter his mind, but no further than into his thought; and not into his will; and what does not enter into the will does not become his own, for the thought draws its ideas from the memory, but the will from the life itself. Nothing that man ever does or thinks is free, but what proceeds from this will, or, what is the same thing, from an affection belonging to his love. Whatever a man wills or loves, he does freely; in consequence of which, a man's freedom, and the affection which is that of his love or of his will, are one: on which account, therefore, man must have freedom, in order that he may be affected by truth and good, or love them, and that they may become as it were his own. In a word, whatever does not enter man in freedom, does not remain, because it is not of his love or will; and whatever is not of a man's love or will is not of his spirit: for the esse of the spirit of man is his love or will. "That man may be in freedom, as necessary to his being reformed, he is conjoined, as to his spirit, with heaven and with hell; for spirits from hell, and angels from heaven, are with every man. By the spirits from hell, man is held in his evil; but by the angels from heaven, he is held in good by the Lord. Thus he is in spiritual equilibrium, that is, in freedom. That angels from heaven, and spirits from hell, are adjoined to every man, may be seen in the Section on the Conjunction of Heaven with the Human Race" (n. 291-302).

XI. MERIT. They who do good that they may merit, do not do good from the love of good, but from the love of reward, for he who wills to merit, wills to be rewarded; they who do so, regard and place their delight in the reward, and not in good; wherefore they are not spiritual, but natural.

Footnotes

122-1 Swedenborg has "tertio," third, the Greek is second, see Mark 14:30, 72. In AC 10134 Swedenborg has "bis," twice.

125-1 In the original edition the following words were omitted by the printer, which Swedenborg afterward in a letter supplied to the publisher, "et praecipue consistit in eo, quod homo ponat omnem cultum Divinum in sancto cum est in templis;" and especially consist in this, that man places all Divine worship in sanctity when he is in temples.

126-1 The translator has "light" here, a misreading of the Latin "vitam."

Section 3

To do good, which is good, must be from the love of good, thus for the sake of good. They who are in that love are not willing to hear of merit, for they love to do, and perceive satisfaction therein, and, on the other hand, they are sorrowful if it be believed that what they do is for the sake of anything of themselves. This is almost like those who do good to their friends for the sake of friendship; to a brother for the sake of brotherhood, to wife and children for the sake of wife and children, to the country for the sake of the country, thus from friendship and love. They who think well, also say and insist, that they do not do good for the sake of themselves, but for the sake of others.

They who do good for the sake of reward, do not do good from the Lord, but from themselves, for they regard themselves in the first place, because they regard their own good; and the good of the neighbor, which is the good of fellow-citizens, of human society, of the country, and of the church, they regard no otherwise than as a means to an end. Hence it is, that the good of the love of self and of the world lies concealed in the good of merit, and that good is from man and not from the Lord, and all good which is from man is not good; yea, so far as self and the world lies concealed in it, it is evil.

Genuine charity and genuine faith is without any merit, for good itself is the delight of charity, and truth itself is the delight of faith; wherefore they who are in that charity and faith know what good not meritorious is, but not they who are not in charity and faith.

That good is not to be done for the sake of reward, the Lord Himself teaches in Luke: If ye love those who love you, what grace have you? for sinners do the same; rather love your enemies, and do good, and lend, hoping for nothing; then shall your reward be great, and ye shall be the sons of the Most High (6:32-35). That man cannot do good that is good from himself, the Lord also teaches in John: A man cannot take anything unless it be given Him from heaven (3:27). And in another place: Jesus said, I am the vine, ye are the branches: as the branch cannot bear fruit from itself, unless it shall abide in the vine, so neither can ye unless ye shall abide in Me: He who abideth in Me and I in him, he beareth much fruit, for except from Me ye cannot do anything (15:4-8).

Because all good and truth are from the Lord, and nothing of them from man, and because good from man is not good, it follows that merit belongs to no man, but to the Lord alone. The merit of the Lord consists in this, that from his own power He has saved the human race, and also, that He saves those who do good from Him. Hence it is that in the Word, he is called "just" to whom the merit and justice of the Lord are ascribed, and he is called "unjust" to whom are ascribed his own justice and the merit of self.

The delight itself, which is in the love of doing good without an end to reward, is a reward which remains to eternity, for heaven and eternal happiness are insinuated into that good by the Lord.

To think and believe that they who do good will come into heaven, and also that good is to be done in order that they may come into heaven, is not to regard reward as an end, thus neither is it to place merit in works; for even they who do good from the Lord think and believe so, but they who thus think, believe and do, and are not in the love of good for the sake of good, have regard to reward as an end, and place merit in works.

FROM THE ARCANA COELESTIA. Merit and justice belong to the Lord alone (n. 9715, 9979). The merit and justice of the Lord consist in His having saved the human race by His own power (n. 1813, 2025, 2026, 2027, 9715, 9809, 10019). The good of the Lord's justice and merit is the good which reigns in heaven, and is the good of His Divine love from which He saved the human race (n. 9486, 9979). No man can of himself become justice, nor claim it by any right (n. 1813). The quality of those in the other life who claim justice to themselves (n. 942, 2027). In the Word, the man to whom the justice and merit of the Lord are ascribed, is called "just;" and the man to whom his own justice and merit are ascribed, "unjust" (n. 5069, 9263). Whoever is once just from the Lord, will be continually just from Him; for justice never becomes man's own, but is continually the Lord's (n. 3686). They who believe in the justification taught in the church, know little of regeneration (n. 5398). Man is so far wise as he ascribes all goods and truths to the Lord, and not to himself (n. 10227). As all good and truth which are good and truth are from the Lord, and nothing is from man, and as good from man is not good, it follows that merit belongs to no man, but to the Lord alone (n. 9975, 9981, 9988). They who enter heaven put off all merit of their own (n. 4007). And they do not think of reward for the good they have done (n. 6478, 9174). They who think from merit so far do not acknowledge all things to be of mercy (n. 6478, 9174). They who think from merit, think of reward and remuneration, and therefore to will to merit is to will to be remunerated (n. 5660, 6392, 9975). Such persons cannot receive heaven in themselves (n. 1835, 8478, 9977). Heavenly happiness consists in the affection of doing good, without an end of remuneration (n. 6388, 6478, 9174, 9984). In the other life so far as anyone does good without an end of remuneration, so far happiness inflows with increase from the Lord; and it is immediately dissipated when remuneration is thought of (n. 6478, 9174). Good is to be done without an end of remuneration (n. 6392, 6478); illustrated (n. 9981). Genuine charity is without anything meritorious (n. 2343, 2371, 2400, 3887, 6388-6393). Because it is from love, thus from the delight of doing good (n. 3816, 3887, 6388, 6478, 9174, 9984). "Reward" in the Word, means the delight and happiness in doing good to others without an end of reward, and this delight and happiness is felt and perceived by those who are in genuine charity (n. 3816, 3956, 6388). They who do good for the sake of reward, love themselves and not the neighbor (n. 8002, 9210). "Mercenaries," in the spiritual sense of the Word, mean those who do good for the sake of reward (n. 8002). They who do good for the sake of remuneration, in the other life desire to be served, and are never contented (n. 6393). They despise the neighbor, and are angry at the Lord Himself, because they do not receive a reward, saying that they have merited it (n. 9976). They who have separated faith from charity, in the other life make their faith, and also the good works which they have done in an external form, thus for the sake of themselves, meritorious (n. 2371). Further particulars respecting the quality of those in the other life who have placed merit in works (n. 942, 1774, 1877, 2027). They are there in the lower earth, and appear to themselves to cut wood (n. 1110, 4943, 8740). Because wood, especially shittim wood, signifies the good of merit in particular (n. 2784, 2812, 9472, 9486, 9715, 10178). They who have done good for the sake of remuneration, are servants in the Lord's kingdom (n. 6389, 6390). They who place merit in works, fall in temptations (n. 2273, 9978). They who are in the loves of self and of the world, do not know what it is to do good without a view to remuneration (n. 6392).

XII. REPENTANCE AND THE REMISSION OF SINS. He who would be saved must confess his sins, and do the work of repentance.

To confess sins, is to know evils, to see them in one's self, to acknowledge them, to make himself guilty, and to condemn himself on account of them. When this is done before God, it is the confession of sins.

To do the work of repentance, is to desist from sins after he has thus confessed them, and from a humble heart has made supplication for remission, and to live a new life according to the precepts of charity and faith.

He who only acknowledges universally that he is a sinner, and makes himself guilty of all evils, and yet does not explore himself, that is, see his own sins, makes confession, but not the confession of repentance; he, because he does not know his own evils, lives afterwards as he did before.

He who lives the life of charity and faith does the work of repentance daily; he reflects upon the evils which are with him, he acknowledges them, he guards against them, he supplicates the Lord for help. For man of himself continually lapses, but he is continually raised by the Lord, and led to good. Such is the state of those who are in good. But they who are in evil lapse continually, and are also continually elevated by the Lord, but are only withdrawn from falling into the most grievous evils, to which of themselves they tend with all their endeavor.

The man who explores himself that he may do the work of repentance, must explore his thoughts and the intentions of his will, and must there explore what he would do if it were permitted him, that is, if he were not afraid of the laws, and of the loss of reputation, honor, and gain. There the evils of man reside, and the evils which he does in the body are all from thence. They who do not explore the evils of their thought and will, cannot do the work of repentance, for they think and will afterwards as they did before, and yet to will evils is to do them. This is to explore one's self.

Repentance of the mouth and not of the life is not repentance. Sins are not remitted by repentance of the mouth, but by repentance of the life. Sins are continually remitted to man by the Lord, for He is mercy itself, but sins adhere to man, however he may suppose that they are remitted; nor are they removed from him but by a life according to the precepts of true faith. So far as he lives according to them, so far sins are removed; and so far as they are removed, so far they are remitted.

It is believed that sins are washed away, or are washed off, as filth is by water, when they are remitted; but sins are not washed away, but they are removed; that is, man is withheld from them when he is kept in good by the Lord; and when he is kept in good, it appears as if he were without them, thus as if they were washed away; and so far as man is reformed, so far he is capable of being kept in good. How man is reformed will be shown in the following doctrinal concerning regeneration. He who believes that sins are in any other manner remitted, is much deceived.

The signs that sins are remitted, that is, removed, are these which follow. They whose sins are remitted, perceive a delight in worshiping God for the sake of God, and in serving their neighbor for the sake of their neighbor, thus in doing good for the sake of good, and in speaking truth for the sake of truth; they are unwilling to claim merit by anything of charity and faith; they shun and are averse to evils, as enmities, hatreds, revenges, adulteries, and the very thoughts of such things with intention. But the signs that sins are not remitted, that is, removed, are these which follow. They whose sins are not remitted, worship God not for the sake of God, and serve the neighbor not for the sake of the neighbor, thus they do not do good and speak truth for the sake of good and truth, but for the sake of themselves and the world; they wish to claim merit by their deeds; they perceive nothing undelightful in evils, as in enmity, in hatred, in revenge, in adulteries; and they think of them and concerning them in all license.

The repentance which takes place in a free state is of avail, but that which takes place in a state of compulsion is of no avail. States of compulsion are states of sickness, states of dejection of mind from misfortune, states of imminent death, as also every state of fear which takes away the use of reason. He who is evil, and in a state of compulsion promises repentance, and also does good, when he comes into a free state returns to his former life of evil; it is otherwise with the good.

After a man has explored himself, and acknowledged his sins, and has done the work of repentance, he must remain constant in good even to the end of life. For if he afterwards relapses into his former life of evil and embraces it, he then profanes, for he then conjoins evil with good; whence his latter state becomes worse than his former, according to the words of the Lord: When the unclean spirit goes out from a man, he walks through dry places, seeking rest, but doth not find; then he saith, I will return into my house whence I went out; and when he cometh and findeth it empty, and swept, and adorned for him, then he goeth away, and adjoineth to himself seven other spirits worse than himself, and, entering in, they dwell there, and the latter things of the man become worse than the first (Matt. 12:43-45).

From Arcana Coelestia: Of sin or evil. There are innumerable kinds of evil and falsity (n. 1188, 1212, 4818, 4822, 7574). There is evil from falsity, there is falsity from evil, and evil and falsity again from thence (n. 1679, 2243, 4818). The nature and quality of the evil of falsity (n. 2408, 4818, 7272, 8265, 8279). The nature and quality of the falsity of evil (n. 6359, 7272, 9304, 10302). Of blamable evils, and of those which are not so blamable (n. 4171, 4172). Of evils from the understanding and of evils from the will (n. 9009). The difference between transgression, iniquity and sin (n. 6563, 9156). All evils adhere to man (n. 2116). Evils cannot be taken away from man, but man can only be withheld from them, and kept in good (n. 865, 868, 887, 894, 1581, 4564, 8206, 8393, 8988, 9014, 9333, 9446-9448, 9451, 10057, 10059). To be withheld from evil and kept in good, is effected by the Lord alone (n. 929, 2406, 8206, 10060). Thus evils and sins are only removed, and this is effected successively (n. 9334-9336). This is done by the Lord by means of regeneration (n. 9445, 9452-9454, 9938). Evils shut out the Lord (n. 5696). Man ought to abstain from evils, that he may receive good from the Lord (n. 10109). Good and truth inflow in proportion as man is withheld from evils (n. 2388, 2411, 10675). To be withheld from evil and kept in good, constitutes remission of sins (n. 8391, 8393, 9014, 9444-9450). The signs whether sins are remitted or not (n. 9449, 9450). It is a consequence of the remission of sins to look at things from good and not from evil (n. 7697). Evil and sin are a separation and turning away from the Lord; and this is signified by "evil" and "sin" in the Word (n. 4997, 5229, 5474, 5746, 5841, 9346); they are and signify separation and aversion from good and truth (n. 7589). They are and signify what is contrary to Divine order (n. 4839, 5076). Evil is damnation and hell (n. 3513, 6279, 7155). It is not known what hell is, unless it be known what evil is (n. 7181). Evils are as it were heavy, and fall of themselves into hell; and so also falsities that are from evil (n. 8279, 8298). It is not known what evil is unless it be known what the love of self and the love of the world are (n. 4997, 7178, 8318). All evils are from those loves (n. 1307, 1308, 1321, 1594, 1691, 3413, 7255, 7376, 7488, 7489, 8318, 9335, 9348, 10038, 10742). All men whatever are born into evils of every kind, even so that their proprium is nothing but evil (n. 210, 215, 731, 874-876, 987, 1047, 2307, 2308, 3518, 3701, 3812, 8480, 8550, 10283, 10284, 10731). Man must therefore be born again or regenerated, in order to receive a life of good (n. 3701). Man casts himself into hell when he does evil from consent, afterwards from purpose, and at last from delight (n. 6203). They who are in evil of life, are in the falsities of their own evil, whether they know it or not (n. 7577, 8094). Evil would not be appropriated to man, if he believed, as is really the case, that all evil is from hell, and all good from the Lord (n. 4151, 6206, 6324, 6325). In the other life evils are removed from the good and goods from the evil (n. 2256). All in the other life are let into their interiors, thus the evil into their evils (n. 8870). In the other life evil contains its own punishment, and good its own reward (n. 696, 967, 1857, 6559, 8214, 8223, 8226, 9048). Man is not punished in the other life for hereditary evils, as he is not to blame for these, but for his actual evils (n. 966, 2308). The interiors of evil are foul and filthy, however they may appear otherwise in an external form (n. 7046). Evil is attributed in the Word to the Lord, and yet nothing but good proceeds from Him (n. 2447, 6071, 6991, 6997, 7533, 7632, 7677, 7926, 8227, 8228, 8632, 9306). So also anger (n. 5798, 6997, 8284, 8483, 9306, 10431). Why it is so said in the Word (n. 6071, 6991, 6997, 7632, 7643, 7679, 7710, 7926, 8282, 9010, 9128). What is signified by "bearing iniquity," where it is predicated of the Lord (n. 9937, 9965). The Lord turns evil into good with the good who are infested and tempted (n. 8631). To leave man from his own liberty to do evil, is permission (n. 1778). Evils and falsities are governed by the laws of permission by the Lord; and they are permitted for the sake of order (n. 7877, 8700, 10778). The permission of evil by the Lord is not as of one who wills, but as of one who does not will, but who cannot bring aid on account of the end (n. 7877).

    Of Falsity. There are innumerable kinds of falsity, namely, as many as there are evils, and evils and falsities are according to their origins, which are many (n. 1188, 1212, 4729, 4822, 7574). There is falsity from evil, or the falsity of evil; and there is evil from the falsity, or the evil of falsity; and falsity again from thence (n. 1679, 2243). From one falsity that is assumed as a principle, falsities flow in a long series (n. 1510, 1511, 4717, 4721). There is falsity from the lusts of the love of self and of the world; and there is falsity from the fallacies of the senses (n. 1295, 4729). There are falsities of religion; and there are falsities of ignorance (n. 4729, 8318, 9258). There is falsity which contains good, and falsity which does not contain good (n. 2863, 9304, 10109, 10302). There is what is falsified (n. 7318, 7319, 10648). The quality of the falsity of evil (n. 6359, 7272, 9304, 10302). The quality of the evil of falsity (n. 2408, 4818, 7272, 8265, 8279). The falsities from evil appear like mists, and impure waters over the hells (n. 8138, 8146, 8210). Such waters signify falsities (n. 739, 790, 7307). They who are in hell speak falsities from evil (n. 1695, 7351, 7352, 7357, 7392, 7699). They who are in evil cannot do otherwise than think what is false when they think from themselves (n. 7437). There are falsities of religion which agree with good, and falsities which disagree (n. 9258). Falsities of religion, if they do not disagree with good, do not produce evil but with those who are in evil of life (n. 8318). Falsities of religion are not imputed to those who are in good, but to those who are in evil (n. 8051, 8149). Every falsity may be confirmed, and then it appears like truth (n. 5033, 6865, 8521, 8780). Care should be taken lest falsities of religion be confirmed, since the persuasion of falsity principally arises from thence (n. 845, 8780). How hurtful the persuasion of falsity is (n. 794, 806, 5096, 7686). A persuasion of falsity is perpetually exciting such things as confirm falsities (n. 1510, 1511, 2477). They who are in the persuasion of falsity are interiorly bound (n. 5096). In the other life, they who are in a strong persuasion of falsity, when they approach others, close up their rational, and as it were suffocate it (n. 3895, 5128). Truths which are not genuine, and also falsities, may be consociated with genuine truths; but falsities which contain good, and not falsities in which is evil (n. 3470, 3471, 4551, 4552, 7344, 8149, 9298). Falsities which contain good are received by the Lord as truths (n. 4736, 8149). The good which has its quality from falsity is accepted by the Lord, if there is ignorance, and therein is innocence and a good end (n. 7887). Evil falsifies truth, because it draws aside and applies truth to evil (n. 8094, 8149). Truth is said to be falsified, when it is applied to evil by confirmations (n. 8602). Falsified truth is contrary to truth and good (n. 8602). For further particulars respecting the falsification of truth (see n. 7318, 7319, 10648).

Of the Profane and Profanation, spoken of above at (n. 169). Profanation is a commixture of good and evil, as also of truth and falsity in man (n. 6348). None can profane goods and truths, or the holy things of the church and the Word, except those who first acknowledge, believe, and still more live according to them, and afterwards recede from and do not believe, and who live to themselves and the world (n. 593, 1008, 1010, 1059, 3398, 3399, 3898, 4289, 4601, 8394, 10287). He who believes truths in his childhood, and afterwards does not believe them, profanes lightly; but he who confirms truths in himself and after that denies them, profanes grievously (n. 6959, 6963, 6971). They who believe truths, and live evilly, commit profanation; as also they who do not believe truths and live holily (n. 8882). If man, after repentance of heart, relapses to his former evils, he profanes, and then his latter state is worse than his former (n. 8394). Those in the Christian world who defile the holy things of the Word by unclean thoughts and discourses, profane (n. 4050, 5390). There are various kinds of profanation (n. 10287). They who do not acknowledge holy things cannot profane them, still less they who do not know them (n. 1008, 1010, 1059, 9188, 10287). They who are within the church, can profane holy things, but not they who are out of it (n. 2051). The Gentiles, because out of the church, and who do not have the Word, cannot profane (n. 1327, 1328, 2051, 9021). Neither can the Jews profane the holy interior things of the Word and the church, because they do not acknowledge them (n. 6963). Therefore interior truths were not revealed to the Jews, for if they had been revealed and acknowledged, they would have profaned them (n. 3398, 3479, 6963). Profanation is meant by the words of the Lord above quoted at n. 169: When the unclean spirit goes out of a man, he walks through dry places, seeking rest, but finding none; then he saith, I will return into my house from whence I went out; and when he comes and finds it empty, and swept, and garnished, then he goes away, and takes to himself seven other spirits worse than himself, and entering in they dwell there, and the latter things of the man become worse than the first (Matt. 12:43-45). "The unclean spirit going out of a man," signifies the repentance of him who is in evil; his "walking through dry places and not finding rest" signifies that to such a person, a life of good is of that quality; "the house" into which he returned, and which he found empty, swept, and garnished, signifies the man himself, and his will, as being without good. "The seven spirits" which he took to himself and with whom he returned, signify evil conjoined to good; "his state then being worse than his former," signifies profanation. This is the internal sense of these words, for the Lord spoke by correspondences. The same thing is meant by the words of the Lord to the man whom He healed in the Pool of Bethesda: Behold, thou art made whole; sin no more, lest a worse thing come unto thee (John 5:14). Also by these words of the Lord: He hath blinded their eyes, and hardened their heart; that they should not see with their eyes, nor understand with their heart, and be converted, and I should heal them (John 12:40). "To be converted and healed," signifies to profane, which takes place when truth and good are acknowledged, and afterwards rejected, which would have been the case if the Jews had been converted and healed. The lot of profaners in the other life is the worst of all, because the good and truth which they have acknowledged remain, and also the evil and falsity; and because they cohere, a tearing asunder of the life takes place (n. 571, 582, 6348). The greatest care is therefore taken by the Lord, to prevent profanation (n. 2426, 10287). Therefore man is withheld from acknowledgment and faith, if he cannot remain therein to the end of life (n. 3398, 3402). On this account also man is rather kept in ignorance, and in external worship (n. 301-303, 1327, 1328). The Lord also stores up the goods and truths which man has received by acknowledgment, in his interiors (n. 6595). Lest interior truths should be profaned, they are not revealed before the church is at its end (n. 3398, 3399). Wherefore the Lord came into the world, and opened interior truths, when the church was wholly vastated (n. 3398). See what is adduced on this subject in the work on The Last Judgment and Babylon Destroyed (n. 73, 74). In the Word "Babel" signifies the profanation of good, and "Chaldea," the profanation of truth (n. 1182, 1283, 1295, 1304, 1306-1308, 1321, 1322, 1326). These profanations correspond to the prohibited degrees, or foul adulteries, spoken of in the Word (n. 6348). Profanation was represented in the

Israelitish and Jewish church by eating blood, wherefore this was so severely prohibited (n. 1003).

XIII. REGENERATION. He who does not receive spiritual life, that is, who is not begotten anew by the Lord, cannot come into heaven; which the Lord teaches in John: Verily, verily, I say unto thee, except anyone be begotten again, he cannot see the kingdom of God (3:3).

Man is not born of his parents into spiritual life, but into natural life. Spiritual life consists in loving God above all things, and in loving his neighbor as himself, and this according to the precepts of faith, which the Lord has taught in the Word. But natural life consists in loving ourselves and the world more than the neighbor, yea, more than God Himself.

Every man is born of his parents into the evils of the love of self and of the world. Every evil, which by habit has acquired as it were a nature, is derived into the offspring; thus it descends successively from parents, from grandfathers, and from great-grandfathers, in a long series backwards; whence the derivation of evil at length becomes so great, that the whole of man's own life is nothing else but evil. This continual derivation of evil is not broken and altered, except by the life of faith and charity from the Lord.

Man continually inclines to, and lapses into, what he derives from heredity: hence he confirms with himself that evil, and also superadds more from himself. These evils are altogether contrary to spiritual life; they destroy it; wherefore, unless man receives new life, which is spiritual life, from the Lord, thus unless he is conceived anew, is born anew, is educated anew, that is, is created anew, he is damned; for he wills nothing else, and thence thinks nothing else, but what is of self and the world, in like manner as they do in hell.

No man can be regenerated unless he knows such things as are of the new life, that is, of spiritual life. The things which are of the new life, or which are of the spiritual life, are truths which are to be believed and goods which are to be done; the former are of faith, the latter of charity. These things no one can know from himself, for man apprehends only those things which are obvious to the senses, from which he procures to himself a light which is called natural light, from which he sees nothing else than what relates to the world and to self, but not the things which relate to heaven and to God. These he must learn from revelation. As that the Lord, who is God from eternity, came into the world to save the human race; that He has all power in heaven and in earth; that the all of faith and the all of charity, thus all truth and good, is from Him; that there is a heaven, and a hell; and that man is to live to eternity, in heaven if he has done well, in hell if he has done evil.

These and many other things belong to faith, which the man who is regenerating ought to know; for he who knows them, may think them, afterwards will them, and lastly do them, and so have new life. Whilst he who does not know that the Lord is the Savior of the human race, cannot have faith in Him, love Him, and thus do good for the sake of Him. He who does not know that all good is from Him, cannot think that his own salvation is from Him, still less can he will it to be so, thus he cannot live from Him. He who does not know that there is a hell and a heaven, nor that there is eternal life, cannot even think about the life of heaven, nor apply himself to receive it, and so in other cases.

Everyone has an internal man and an external man; the internal is what is called the spiritual man, and the external is what is called the natural man, and each is to be regenerated, that the man may be regenerated. With the man who is not regenerated, the external or natural man rules, and the internal serves; but with the man who is regenerated, the internal or spiritual man rules, and the external serves. Whence it is manifest that the order of life is inverted with man from his birth, namely, that serves which ought to rule, and that rules which ought to serve. In order that man may be saved, this order must be inverted; and this inversion can by no means exist, but by regeneration from the Lord.

What it is for the internal man to rule and the external to serve, and vice versa, may be illustrated by this: If a man places all his good in pleasure, in gain, and in pride, and has delight in hatred and revenge, and inwardly in himself seeks for reasons which confirm them, then the external man rules and the internal serves. But when a man perceives good and delight in thinking and willing well, sincerely, and justly, and in outwardly speaking and doing in like manner, then the internal man rules and the external serves.

The internal man is first regenerated by the Lord, and afterwards the external, and the latter by means of the former. For the internal man is regenerated by thinking those things which are of faith and charity, but the external by a life according to them. This is meant by the words of the Lord: Unless anyone be begotten of water and the spirit, he cannot enter into the kingdom of God (John 3:5). "Water," in the spiritual sense, is the truth of faith, and "the spirit" is a life according to it.

The man who is regenerated is, as to his internal man, in heaven, and is an angel there with the angels, among whom he also comes after death; he is then able to live the life of heaven, to love the Lord, to love the neighbor, to understand truth, to relish good, and to perceive the happiness thence derived.

FROM THE ARCANA COELESTIA. What Regeneration is, and why it is effected. At this day little is known concerning regeneration; the reason (n. 3761, 4136, 5398). Man is born into evils of every kind, and thence as to his proprium by birth, he is nothing but evil (n. 210, 215, 731, 874-876, 987, 1047, 2307, 2308, 3518, 3701, 3812, 8480, 8549, 8550, 8552, 10283, 10284, 10286, 10731). Man's hereditary nature is nothing but evil, see the extracts above in this doctrine (n. 83). Man's proprium is nothing but evil, see the same (n. 82). Man of himself, so far as he is under the influence of his hereditary nature and the proprium, is worse than the brute animals (n. 637, 3175). Therefore of himself he continually looks to hell (n. 694, 8480). Therefore, if man should be led by his own proprium, he could not possibly be saved (n. 10731). Man's natural life is contrary to spiritual life (n. 3913, 3928). The good which he does from himself or from proprium, is not good, because he does it for the sake of self, and the world (n. 8480). Man's proprium must be removed so that the Lord and heaven may be able to be present (n. 1023, 1044). It is actually removed when he is regenerated by the Lord (n. 9334-9336, 9452, 9454, 9938). Therefore he must be created anew, that is, regenerated (n. 8548, 8549, 9452, 9937). "Creating" man, in the Word, signifies to regenerate him (n. 16, 88, 10634). Man is conjoined to the Lord by regeneration (n. 2004, 9338). And consociated with angels in heaven (n. 2474). He does not come into heaven, until he is in a state to be led by the Lord by means of good, which is the case when he is regenerated (n. 8516, 8539, 8722, 9139, 9832, 10367). The external or natural man rules, and the internal man serves, in the man who is not regenerated (n. 3167, 8743). Thus the state of man's life is inverted from his birth, and must be entirely inverted again in order that he may be saved (n. 6507, 8552, 8553, 9258). The end of regeneration is, that the internal or spiritual man may rule, and the external or natural man serve (n. 911, 913). This is actually effected after man is regenerated (n. 5128, 5651, 8743). For after regeneration the love of self and the world no longer reigns, but love to the Lord and towards the neighbor, thus the Lord and not man (n. 8856, 8857). Hence it is plain that man cannot be saved unless he is regenerated (n. 5280, 8548, 8772, 10156). Regeneration is a plane to perfect the life of man to eternity (n. 9334). The regenerate man is perfected to eternity (n. 6648, 10048). The quality of the regenerate and the unregenerate man described (n. 977, 986, 10156).

Who is regenerated. Man cannot be regenerated unless he is instructed in the truths of faith and the goods of charity (n. 677, 679, 711, 8635, 8638-8640, 10729). They who are only in truths and not in good, cannot be regenerated (n. 6567, 8725). No one is regenerated unless he is in charity (n. 989). None can be regenerated but such as have conscience (n. 2689, 5470). Everyone is regenerated according to his faculty of receiving the good of love to the Lord, and of charity towards the neighbor, by the truths of faith from the doctrine of the church, which is from the Word (n. 2967, 2975). Who can be regenerated, and who cannot (n. 2689). They who live the life of faith and charity, and who are not regenerated in the world, are regenerated in the other life (n. 989, 2490).

Regeneration is from the Lord alone. The Lord alone regenerates man, and neither man nor angel contributes thereto (n. 10067). Man's regeneration is an image of the Lord's glorification, that is, as the Lord made His Human Divine, so He makes spiritual the man whom He regenerates (n. 3043, 3138, 3212, 3296, 3490, 4402, 5688, 10057, 10076). The Lord wills to have the whole man whom He regenerates, and not part of him (n. 6138).

Further particular concerning regeneration. Man is regenerated by the truths of faith, and by a life according to them (n. 1904, 2046, 9088, 9959, 10028). This is meant by the words of the Lord: Unless a man be born of water and of the spirit, he cannot enter the Kingdom of God (John 3:5). "Water" signifies the truth of faith, and "spirit" a life according thereto (n. 10240). "Water" in the Word signifies the truth of faith (n. 2702, 3058, 5668, 8568, 10238). Spiritual purification, which is from evils and falsities, is effected by the truths of faith (n. 2799, 5954, 7044, 7918, 9088, 10229, 10237). When man is regenerated, truths are inseminated and implanted in good, that they may become of the life (n. 880, 2189, 2574, 2697). What the quality of truths must be that they may be implanted in good (n. 8725). In regeneration truth is initiated and conjoined to good, and good reciprocally to truth (n. 5365, 8516). How this reciprocal initiation and conjunction is effected (n. 3155, 10067). Truth is implanted in good when it becomes of the will, since it then becomes of the love (n. 10367). There are two states of the man who is regenerated; first, when he is led by truth to good; second, when he acts from good, and from good sees truth (n. 7992, 7993, 8505, 8506, 8510, 8512, 8516, 8643, 8648, 8658, 8685, 8690, 8701, 8772, 9227, 9230, 9274, 9736, 10048, 10057, 10060, 10076). The quality of man's state when truth is in the first place, and good in the second (n. 3610). Hence it appears that when man is regenerating, he looks to good from truth; but when regenerated, he regards truth from good (n. 6247). Thus a turning over as it were takes place, in that the state of man is inverted (n. 6507). But it is to be known, that when man is regenerating, truth is not actually in the first place and good in the second, but only apparently; but when man is regenerated, good is in the first place and truth in the second, actually and perceptibly (n. 3324, 3325, 3330, 3336, 3494, 3539, 3548, 3556, 3563, 3570, 3576, 3603, 3701, 4243, 4245, 4247, 4337, 4925, 4926, 4928, 4930, 4977, 5351, 6256, 6269, 6273, 8516, 10110). Thus good is the first and last of regeneration (n. 9337). Since truth appears to be in the first place and good in the second, when man is regenerating, or, which is the same thing, when man becomes a church, on account of this appearance it was a matter of controversy among the ancients, whether the truth of faith or the good of charity is the first-born of the church (n. 367, 2435). The good of charity is actually the first-born of the church, but the truth of faith only apparently (n. 3325, 3494, 4925, 4926, 4928, 4930, 8042, 8080). "First-born" in the Word signifies the first of the church, to which priority and superiority belongs (n. 3325). The Lord is called thefirst-born, because in Him and from Him is all the good of love, of charity, and of faith (n. 3325). Man ought not to return from the latter state wherein truth is regarded from good, to the former state, wherein good is regarded from truth, and why (n. 2454, 3650-3655, 5895, 5897, 7857, 7923, 8505, 8506, 8510, 8512, 8516, 9274, 10184). Where these words of the Lord are explained: Let not him who is in the field return back to take his garments (Matt. 24:18); also, Whosoever shall then be in the field, let him not return to those things which are behind him. Remember Lot's wife (Luke 17:31, 32); for this is signified by those words. The process of the regeneration of man described, and how it is effected (n. 1555, 2343, 2490, 2657, 2979, 3057, 3286, 3310, 3316, 3332, 3470, 3701, 4353, 5113, 5126, 5270, 5280, 5342, 6717, 8772, 8773, 9043, 9103, 10021, 10057, 10367). The arcana of regeneration are innumerable, since regeneration continues during the whole life of man (n. 2679, 3179, 3584, 3665, 3690, 3701, 4377, 4551, 4552, 5122, 5126, 5398, 5912, 6751, 9103, 9258, 9296, 9297, 9334). Scarcely any of these arcana come to the knowledge and perception of man (n. 3179, 9336). This is what is meant by the words of the Lord: The wind bloweth where it listeth, and thou hearest the sound thereof, but knowest not whence it cometh and whither it goeth; so is everyone that is born of the Spirit (John 3:8). Concerning the process of the regeneration of the man of the spiritual church (n. 2675, 2678, 2679, 2682). And concerning the process of regeneration of the man of the celestial church, with the difference (n. 5113, 10124). The case of the regenerate man is similar to that of an infant, who first learns to speak, then to think, afterwards to live well, until all those things flow from him spontaneously, as from himself (n. 3203, 9296, 9297). Thus he who is regenerated is first led by the Lord as an infant, then as a boy, and afterwards as an adult (n. 3665, 3690, 4377-4379, 6751). When man is regenerated by the Lord, he is first in a state of external innocence, which is his state of infancy, and is afterwards successively led into a state of internal innocence, which is his state of wisdom (n. 9334, 9335, 10021, 10210). The nature and quality of the innocence of infancy, and of the innocence of wisdom (n. 1616, 2305, 2306, 3494, 4563, 4797, 5608, 9301,

10021). A comparison between the regeneration of man, and the conception and formation of an embryo in the womb (n. 3570, 4931, 9258). Therefore "generations and nativities" in the Word signify spiritual generations and nativities, which belong to regeneration (n. 613, 1145, 1255, 2020, 2584, 3860, 3868, 4070, 4668, 6239, 10204). The regeneration of man illustrated by the germinations in the vegetable kingdom (n. 5115, 5116). The regeneration of man represented in the rainbow (n. 1042, 1043, 1053). The internal or spiritual man, and the external or natural man, must each of them be regenerated, and the one by means of the other (n. 3868, 3870, 3872, 3876, 3877, 3882). The internal man must be regenerated before the external, since the internal man is in the light of heaven, and the external man in the light of the world (n. 3321, 3325, 3469, 3493, 4353, 8746, 9325). The external or natural man is regenerated by means of the internal or spiritual (n. 3286, 3288, 3321). Man is not regenerate before the external or natural man is regenerated (n. 8742-8747, 9043, 9046, 9061, 9325, 9334). The spiritual man is shut unless the natural man is regenerated (n. 6299). And it is as it were blind as to the truths and goods of faith and love (n. 3493, 3969, 4353, 4588). When the natural man is regenerated the whole man is regenerated (n. 7442, 7443). This is signified by "the washing of the disciples' feet," and by these words of the Lord: He that is washed hath no need to be washed except as to his feet, and the whole is clean (John 13:9, 10; n. 10243). "Washing" in the Word signifies spiritual washing, which is purification from evils and falsities (n. 3147, 10237, 10241). And "feet" signify those things that are of the natural man (n. 2162, 3761, 3986, 4280, 4938-4952). Therefore "to wash the feet," is to purify the natural man (n. 3147, 10241). How the natural man is regenerated (n. 3502, 3508, 3509, 3518, 3573, 3576, 3579, 3616, 3762, 3786, 5373, 5647, 5650, 5651, 5660). The quality of the natural man when it is regenerated, and when it is not regenerated (n. 8744, 8745). So far as the natural man does not combat with the spiritual man, so far the man is regenerated (n. 3286). When a man is regenerated, the natural man perceives spiritual things by influx (n. 5651). The sensual, which is the ultimate of the natural man, is not regenerated at this day, but man is elevated above it (n. 7442). All who are regenerated are actually elevated from the sensual into the light of heaven (n. 6183, 6454). The nature and quality of the sensual man may be seen in the extracts above (n. 50). Man is regenerated by influx into the knowledges of good and truth which he has (n. 4096, 4097, 4364). When man is regenerated, he is introduced through mediate goods and truths into genuine goods and truths, and afterwards the mediate goods and truths are left, and the genuine succeed in their place (n. 3665, 3686, 3690, 3974, 4063, 4067, 4145, 6384, 9382). Then another order is induced amongst truths and goods (n. 4250, 4251, 9931, 10303). They are disposed according to ends (n. 4104). Thus according to the uses of spiritual life (n. 9297). They who are regenerated undergo many states, and are continually brought more interiorly into heaven, thus nearer to the Lord (n. 6645). The regenerate man is in the order of heaven (n. 8512). His internal is open into heaven (n. 8512, 8513). Man by regeneration comes into angelic intelligence, which, however, lies concealed in his interiors so long as he remains in the world, but is opened in the other life, and his wisdom is then like that of the angels (n. 2494, 8747). The states as to enlightenment of those who are regenerated described (n. 2697, 2701, 2704). By regeneration man receives a new understanding (n. 2657). How the case is with respect to the fructification of good, and the multiplication of truth, with those who are regenerated (n. 984). With a regenerate person truths from good form as it were a constellation by successive derivations, and continually multiply themselves round about (n. 5912). With a regenerate person, truths from good are disposed into such order, that the genuine truths of good, from which, as their parents, the rest proceed, are in the middle, whilst the rest succeed in order according to their relationship and affinities, even to the ultimates, where there is obscurity (n. 4129, 4551, 4552, 5134, 5270). With a regenerate person truths from good are arranged in the form of heaven (n. 3316, 3470, 3584, 4302, 5704, 5709, 6028, 6690, 9931, 10303); and in the work on Heaven and Hell, under the article Concerning the Form of Heaven, according to which are the consociations and communications there (n. 200-212); and Concerning the Wisdom of the Angels of Heaven (n. 265-275). With a regenerate person, there is a correspondence between spiritual things and natural things (n. 2850). His order of life is altogether inverted (n. 3332, 5159, 8995). He is altogether a new man as to his spirit (n. 3212). He appears like the unregenerate man as to externals, but not as to internals (n. 5159). Spiritual good, which is to will and to do good from the affection of the love of good, can only be given to man by means of regeneration (n. 4538). Truths, which enter with affection, are reproduced (n. 5893). Truths, so far as they are deprived of life from the proprium of man, are so far conjoined to good, and receive spiritual life (n. 3607, 3610). So far as evils from the love of self and the love of the world are removed, so far there is life in truths (n. 3610). The first affection of truth with the man who is regenerated is not pure, but is purified successively (n. 3089, 8413). Evils and falsities; with the man who is regenerated, are removed slowly, and not quickly (n. 9334, 9335). The evils and falsities of the proprium of man still remain, and are only removed by regeneration (n. 865, 868, 887, 929, 1581, 2406, 4564, 8206, 8393, 8988, 9014, 9333-9336, 9445, 9447, 9448, 9451-9454, 9938, 10057, 10060). Man can never be so far regenerated as to be called perfect (n. 894, 5122, 6648). Evil spirits dare not assault the regenerate (n. 1695). They who believe the justification taught in the church, know little of regeneration (n. 5398). Man must have freedom, to be capable of being regenerated (n. 1937, 1947, 2876, 2881, 3145, 3146, 3158, 4031, 8700). Man is introduced into heavenly freedom by regeneration (n. 2874, 2875, 2882, 2892). There is no conjunction of good and truth by compulsion, and thus no regeneration (n. 2875, 2881, 4031, 8700). Other particulars respecting freedom as it regards regeneration, may be seen in the doctrine above, where it treats of Freedom. He who is regenerated, must necessarily undergo temptations (n. 3696, 8403). Because temptations take place for the sake of the conjunction of good and truth, and also on account of the conjunction of the internal and the external man (n. 4248, 4272, 5773).

XIV. TEMPTATION. Those only who are being regenerated, undergo spiritual temptations; for spiritual temptations are pains of mind induced by evil spirits, with those who are in goods and truths. While those spirits excite the evils which are with them, there arises the anxiety of temptation. Man does not know whence this anxiety comes, because he does not know his 187-1 origin.

For there are both evil and good spirits with every man; the evil spirits are in his evils, and the good spirits in his goods. When the evil spirits approach they draw forth his evils, while the good spirits, on the contrary, draw forth his goods; whence arise collision and combat, from which the man has interior anxiety, which is temptation. Hence it is plain that temptations are not induced by heaven, but by hell; which is also the faith of the church, which teaches that God tempts no one.

Interior anxieties are also experienced by those who are not in goods and truths; but they are natural, not spiritual anxieties; the two are distinguished by this, that natural anxieties have worldly things for their objects, but spiritual anxieties, heavenly things.

In temptations, the dominion of good over evil, or of evil over good, is contended for. Evil which wills to have dominion, is in the natural or external man, and good is in the spiritual or internal man. If evil conquers, the natural man has dominion; if good conquers, the spiritual has dominion.

These combats are carried on by the truths of faith which are from the Word. From these man must combat against evils and falsities; for if he combats from any other principles, he cannot conquer, because in these alone the Lord is present. 191-1 Because this combat is carried on by the truths of faith, therefore man is not admitted into it until he is in the knowledges of good and truth, and has thence obtained some spiritual life; therefore such combats do not take place till man has arrived at years of maturity.

If man succumbs in temptation, his state after it becomes worse than before, because evil has acquired power over good, and falsity over truth.

Since at this day faith is rare because there is no charity, for the church is at its end, therefore few at this day are admitted into any spiritual temptations; hence it is scarcely known what they are, and to what they are conducive.

Temptations conduce to acquire for good dominion over evil, and for truth dominion over falsity; also to confirm truths, and conjoin them to goods, and at the same time to disperse evils and the falsities thence derived. They serve also to open the internal spiritual man, and to subject the natural man to it; as also to break the loves of self and the world, and to subdue the lusts which proceed from them. When these things are effected, man acquires enlightenment and perception as to what are truth and good, and what falsity and evil are; whence man obtains intelligence and wisdom, which afterwards increase continually.

The Lord alone combats for man in temptations. If man does not believe that the Lord alone combats and conquers for him, he undergoes only external temptation; which is not serviceable to him.

FROM THE ARCANA COELESTIA. Before a summary is given of what is written in the Arcana Coelestia, respecting temptations, something shall first be said concerning them, in order that it may be known still more clearly from whence they proceed. It is called spiritual temptation when the truths of faith which a man believes in his heart, and according to which he loves to live, are assaulted within him, especially when the good of love, in which he places his spiritual life, is assaulted. Those assaults take place in various ways; as by influx of scandals against truths and goods into the thoughts and the will; also by a continual drawing forth, and bringing to remembrance, of the evils which one has committed, and of the falsities which he has thought, thus by inundation of such things; and at the same time by an apparent shutting up of the interiors of the mind, and, consequently, of communication with heaven, by which the capacity of thinking from his own faith, and of willing from his own love, are intercepted. These things are effected by the evil spirits who are present with man; and when they take place, they appear under the form of interior anxieties and pains of conscience; for they affect and torment man's spiritual life, because he supposes that they proceed, not from evil spirits, but from his own interiors. Man does not know that such assaults are 196-1 from evil spirits because he does not know that spirits are present with him, evil spirits in his evils, and good spirits in his goods; and that they are in his thoughts and affections. These temptations are most grievous when they are accompanied with bodily pains; and still more so, when those pains are of long continuance, and no deliverance is granted, even although the Divine mercy is implored; hence results despair, which is the end. Some particulars shall first be adduced from the Arcana Coelestia, concerning the spirits that are with man, because temptations proceed from them. Spirits and angels are with every man (n. 697, 5846-5866). They are in his thoughts and affections (n. 2888, 5846, 5848). If spirits and angels were taken away, man could not live (n. 2887, 5849, 5854, 5993, 6321). Because by spirits and angels man has communication and conjunction with the spiritual world, without which he would have no life (n. 697, 2796, 2886, 2887, 4047, 4048, 5846-5866, 5976-5993). The spirits with man are changed according to the affections of his love (n. 5851). Spirits from hell are in the loves of man's proprium (n. 5852, 5979-5993). Spirits enter into all things of man's memory (n. 5853, 5857, 5859, 5860, 6192, 6193, 6198, 6199). Angels are in the ends from which and for the sake of which man thinks, wills, and acts thus and not otherwise (n. 1317, 1645, 5844). Man does not appear to spirits, nor spirits to man (n. 5885). Thence spirits cannot see what is in our solar world through man (n. 1880). Although spirits and angels are with man, in his thoughts and affections, yet still he is in freedom of thinking, willing, and acting (n. 5982, 6477, 8209, 8307, 10777); and in the work on Heaven and Hell, where the Conjunction of Heaven with the Human Race is treated of (n. 291-302).

Whence and of what quality temptations are. Temptations exist from the evil spirits who are with man, who inject scandals against the goods and truths which a man loves and believes, and likewise they also excite the evils which he has done and the falsities which he has thought (n. 741, 751, 761, 3927, 4307, 4572, 5036, 6657, 8960). Then evil spirits use all sorts of cunning and malice (n. 6666). The man who is in temptations is near to hell (n. 8131). There are two forces which act in temptations, a force from the interior from the Lord, and a force from the exterior from hell (n. 8168). The ruling love of man is assaulted in temptations (n. 847, 4274). Evil spirits attack those things only which are of man's faith and love, thus those things which relate to his spiritual life; wherefore at such times it is about his eternal life (n. 1820). A state of temptations compared with the state of a man among robbers (n. 5246). In temptations angels from the Lord keep man in the truths and goods which are with him, but evil spirits keep him in the falsities and evils which are with him, whence arises a conflict and combat (n. 4249). Temptation is a combat between the internal or spiritual man, and the external or natural man (n. 2183, 4256). Thus between the delights of the internal and external man, which are then opposite to each other (n. 3928, 8351). It takes place on account of the disagreement between those delights (n. 3928). Thus it is concerning the dominion of one over the other (n. 3928, 8961). No one can be tempted unless he is in the acknowledgment, and likewise in the affection of truth and good, because there is otherwise no combat, for there is nothing spiritual to act against what is natural, thus there is no contest for dominion (n. 3928, 4299). Whoever has acquired any spiritual life, undergoes temptations (n. 8963). Temptations exist with those who have conscience, that is, with those who are in spiritual love; but more grievous ones with those who have perception, that is, with those who are in celestial love (n. 1668, 8963). Dead men, that is they who are not in faith and love to God, and in love towards the neighbor, are not admitted into temptations, because they would fall (n. 270, 4274, 4299, 8964, 8968). Therefore very few at this day are admitted into spiritual temptations (n. 8965). But they have anxieties on account of various causes in the world, past, present, or future, which are generally attended with infirmity of mind and weakness of body, which anxieties are not the anxieties of temptations (n. 762, 8164). Spiritual temptations are sometimes attended with bodily pains, and sometimes not (n. 8164). A state of temptation is an unclean and filthy state, inasmuch as evils and falsities are injected, and also doubts concerning goods and truths (n. 5246). Also, because in temptations there are indignations, pains of the mind, and many affections that are not good (n. 1917, 6829). There is also obscurity and doubt concerning the end (n. 1820, 6829). And likewise concerning the Divine Providence and hearing, because prayers are not heard in temptations as they are out of them (n. 8179). And because man when he is in temptation, seems to himself to be in a state of damnation (n. 6097). Because man perceives clearly what is doing in his external man, consequently the things which evil spirits inject and call forth, according to which he thinks of his state; but he does not perceive what is doing in his internal man, consequently the things which flow in by means of angels from the Lord, and therefore he cannot judge of his state therefrom (n. 10236, 10240). Temptations are generally carried to desperation, which is their ultimate (n. 1787, 2694, 5279, 5280, 6144, 7147, 7155, 7166, 8165, 8567). The reasons (n. 2694). In the temptation itself there are also despairings, but that they terminate in a general one (n. 8567). In a state of despair a man speaks bitter things, but the Lord does not attend to them (n. 8165). When the temptation is finished, there is at first a fluctuation between the truth and falsity (n. 848, 857). But afterwards truth shines, and becomes serene and joyful (n. 3696, 4572, 6829, 8367, 8370). They who are regenerated undergo temptations not once only, but many times, because many evils and falsities are to be removed (n. 8403). If they who have acquired some spiritual life do not undergo temptations in the world, they undergo them in the other life (n. 7122). How temptations take place in the other life, and where (n. 537-539, 699, 1106-1113, 1122, 2694, 4728, 4940-4951, 6119, 6928, 7090, 7122, 7127, 7186, 7317, 7474, 7502, 7541, 7542, 7545, 7768, 7990, 9331, 9763). Concerning the state of enlightenment of those who come out of temptation, and are raised into heaven, and their reception there (n. 2699, 2701, 2704). The quality of the temptation from lack of truth, and the desire thereof at the same time (n. 2682, 8352). The temptation of infants in the other life, whereby they learn to resist evils, their quality (n. 2294). The difference between temptations, infestations, and vastations (n. 7474).

How and when temptations take place. Spiritual combats chiefly take place by the truths of faith (n. 8962). Truth is the first of combat (n. 1685). The men of the spiritual church are tempted as to the truths of faith, wherefore with them the combat is by truths; but the men of the celestial church are tempted as to the goods of love, wherefore with them the combat is by goods (n. 1668, 8963). Those who are of the spiritual church, for the most part, do not combat from genuine truths, but from such as they believe to be true from the doctrinals of their church; which doctrinals however ought to be such, as to be capable of being conjoined with good (n. 6765). Whoever is regenerated must undergo temptations, and he cannot be regenerated without them (n. 5036, 8403); and temptations therefore are necessary (n. 7090). The man who is regenerating comes into temptations, when evil endeavors to gain dominion over good, and the natural man over the spiritual man (n. 6657, 8961). And he comes into them when good ought to have the precedence (n. 4248, 4249, 4256, 8962, 8963). They who are regenerated, are first let into a state of tranquillity, then into temptations, and afterwards return into a state of tranquillity of peace, which is the end (n. 3696).

What good is effected by temptations. The effect of temptations, a summary (n. 1692, 1717, 1740, 6144, 8958-8969). By temptations the spiritual or internal man acquires dominion over the natural or external man; consequently good over evil, and truth over falsity; because good resides in the spiritual man, which cannot exist without it, and evil resides in the natural man (n. 8961). Since temptation is a combat between them, it follows that dominion is the object of the contest, that is, whether the spiritual man shall have dominion over the natural man, thus whether good shall have dominion over evil, or vice versa; consequently, whether the Lord or hell shall have dominion over man (n. 1923, 3928). The external or natural man, by means of temptations, receives truths corresponding to the affection thereof in the internal or spiritual man (n. 3321, 3928). The internal spiritual man is opened and conjoined with the external by means of temptations, in order that man as to each may be elevated, and look to the Lord (n. 10685). The internal spiritual man is opened and conjoined with the external by means of temptations, because the Lord acts from the interior, and flows in thence into the external, and removes and subjugates the evils therein, and at the same time subjects and renders it subordinate to the internal (n. 10685). Temptations take place for the sake of the conjunction of good and truth, and the dispersion of the falsities which adhere to truths and goods (n. 4572). Consequently that good is conjoined to truths by temptations (n. 2272). The vessels recipient of truth are softened by temptations, and put on a state receptive of good (n. 3318). Truths and goods, thus the things which belong to faith and charity, are confirmed and implanted by temptations (n. 8351, 8924, 8966, 8967). And evils and falsities are removed, and room made for the reception of goods and truths (n. 7122). By temptations the loves of self and the world, from whence proceed all evils and falsities, are broken (n. 5356). And thus man is humbled (n. 8966, 8967). Evils and falsities are subdued, separated, and removed, but not abolished, by temptations (n. 868). By temptations corporeal things with their lusts are subdued (n. 357, 868). Man by temptations learns what good and truth are, even from their relation to their opposites, which are evils and falsities (n. 5356). He also learns that of himself he is nothing but evil, and that all the good with him is from the Lord, and from His mercy (n. 2334). By the temptations in which man conquers, evil spirits are deprived of the power of rising up against him any further (n. 1695, 1717). The hells dare not rise up against those who have suffered temptations and have conquered (n. 2183, 8273). After temptations in which man has conquered, there is joy arising from the conjunction of good and truth, although the man does not know that the joy is thence (n. 4572, 6829). There is then the enlightenment of the truth which is of faith, and the perception of the good which is of love (n. 8367, 8370). Thence he has intelligence and wisdom (n. 8966, 8967). Truths after temptations increase immensely (n. 6663). And good has the precedence, or is in the first place, and truth in the second (n. 5773). And man, as to his internal spiritual man, is admitted into the angelic societies, thus into heaven (n. 6611). Before a man undergoes temptations, the truths and goods which are with him are arranged in order by the Lord, that he may be able to resist the evils and falsities which are with him, and are excited from hell (n. 8131). In temptations the Lord provides good where the evil spirits intend evil (n. 6574). After temptations the Lord reduces truths with goods into a new order, and arranges them in a heavenly form (n. 10685). The interiors of the spiritual man are arranged into a heavenly form, see the work on Heaven and Hell, in the chapter on the Form of Heaven, according to which are the consociations and communications 199-1 there (n. 200, 212). They who fall in temptations, come into damnation, because evils and falsities conquer, and the natural man prevails over the spiritual man, and afterwards has the dominion; and then the latter state becomes worse than the former (n. 8165, 8169, 8961).

The Lord combats for man in temptations. The Lord alone combats for man in temptations, and man does not combat at all from himself (n. 1692, 8172, 8175, 8176, 8273). Man cannot by any means combat against evils and falsities from himself, because that would be to fight against all the hells, which the Lord alone can subdue and conquer (n. 1692). The hells fight against man, and the Lord for him (n. 8159). Man combats from truths and goods, thus from the knowledges and affections thereof which are with him; but it is not man who combats, but the Lord by them (n. 1661). Man thinks that the Lord is absent in temptations, because his prayers are not heard as they are when out of them, but nevertheless the Lord is then more present with him (n. 840). In temptations man ought to combat as from himself, and not to hang down his hands and expect immediate help; but nevertheless he ought to believe that it is from the Lord (n. 1712, 8179, 8969). Man cannot otherwise receive a heavenly proprium (n. 1937, 1947, 2882, 2883, 2891). The quality of that proprium, that it is not man's, but the Lord's with him (n. 1937, 1917, 2882, 2883, 2891, 8497). Temptation is of no avail, and productive of no good, unless a man believes, at least after the temptations, that the Lord has fought and conquered for him (n. 8969). They who place merit in works, cannot combat against evils, because they combat from their own proprium, and do not permit the Lord to combat for them (n. 9978). They who believe they have merited heaven by their temptations, are with much difficulty saved (n. 2273). The Lord does not tempt, but liberates, and leads to good (n. 2768). Temptations appear to be from the Divine, when yet they are not (n. 4299). In what sense the petition in the Lord's prayer, "Lead us not into temptations," is to be understood, from experience (n. 1875). The Lord does not concur in temptations by permitting them, according to the idea which man has of permission (n. 2768). In every temptation there is freedom, although it does not appear so, but the freedom is interiorly with man from the Lord, and he therefore combats and is willing to conquer, and not to be conquered, which he would not do without freedom (n. 1937, 1947, 2881). The Lord effects this by means of the affection of truth and good impressed on the internal man, although the man does not know it (n. 5044). For all freedom is of affection or love, and according to its quality (n. 2870, 3158, 8987, 8990, 9585, 9591).

Footnotes

187-1 The Latin is "hanc." It probably should be translated "its" or "this."

191-1 The phrase "because in these alone the Lord is present," is more accurately translated "because in other principles the Lord is not present."

196-1 In the original Latin "non" occurs twice in the sentence.

199-1 The phrase "and communications" is found in the 1st Latin edition but not the 2nd. The translator thus omits it.

Section 4

Of the Lord's temptations. The Lord beyond all others 201-1 endured the most grievous and dreadful temptations, which are but little described in the sense of the letter of the Word, but much in the internal sense (n. 1663, 1668, 1787, 2776, 2786, 2795, 2814, 9528). The Lord fought from the Divine love towards the whole human race (n. 1690, 1691, 1812, 1813, 1820). The love of the Lord was the salvation of the human race (n. 1820). The Lord fought from His own power (n. 1692, 1813, 9937). The Lord alone was made justice and merit, by the temptations, and victories which He gained therein from His own power (n. 1813, 2025-2027, 9715, 9809, 10019). By temptations the Lord united the Divine itself, which was in Him from conception, to His Human, and made this Divine, as He makes man spiritual by temptations (n. 1725, 1729, 1733, 1737, 3318, 3381, 3382, 4286). The temptations of the Lord were attended with despair at the end (n. 1787). The Lord, by the temptations admitted into Himself, subjugated the hells, and reduced to order all things in them, and in heaven, and at the same time glorified His Human (n. 1737, 4287, 9315, 9528, 9937). The Lord alone fought against all the hells (n. 8273). He admitted temptations into Himself from thence (n. 2816, 4295). The Lord could not be tempted as to the Divine, because the hells cannot assault the Divine, wherefore He assumed a human from the mother, such as could be tempted (n. 1414, 1444, 1573, 5041, 5157, 7193, 9315). By temptations and victories He expelled all the hereditary from the mother, and put off the human from her, until at length He was no longer her son (n. 2159, 2574, 2649, 3036, 10830). Jehovah, who was in Him from conception, appeared in His temptations as if absent (n. 1815). This was His state of humiliation (n. 1785, 1999, 2159, 6866). His last temptation and victory, by which He fully subjugated the hells, and made His Human Divine, was in Gethsemane and on the cross (n. 2776, 2803, 2813, 2814, 10655, 10659, 10828). "To eat no bread and drink no water for forty days," signifies an entire state of temptations (n. 10686). "Forty years," "months," or "days," signify a plenary state of temptations from beginning to end; and such a state is meant by the duration of the flood, "forty days"; by Moses abiding "forty days" upon Mount Sinai; by the sojourning of the sons of Israel "forty years" in the desert; and by the Lord's temptation in the desert "forty days" (n. 730, 862, 2272, 2273, 8098).

XV. BAPTISM. Baptism was instituted to be a sign that a man is of the church, and as a memorial that he is to be regenerated; for the washing of baptism is nothing else than spiritual washing, which is regeneration.

All regeneration is effected by the Lord, through the truths of faith, and a life according to them. Baptism therefore testifies that the man is of the church, and that he can be regenerated: for in the church the Lord is acknowledged, who alone regenerates, and there also is the Word, which contains the truths of faith, by which regeneration is effected.

This the Lord teaches in John: Except a man be begotten of water and of the spirit, he cannot enter into the kingdom of God (3:5). "Water" in the spiritual sense is the truth of faith from the Word; "the spirit" is a life according to that truth; and "to be begotten" is to be regenerated thereby.

Since everyone who is regenerated also undergoes temptations, which are spiritual combats against evils and falsities, therefore by the water of baptism these also are signified.

As baptism is for a sign and memorial of these things therefore man may be baptized as an infant, and if not then, he may be baptized as an adult.

Let those therefore who are baptized know, that baptism itself does not give faith nor salvation, but it testifies that they may receive faith and be saved, if they are regenerated.

Hence may be seen what is meant by the Lord's words in Mark: He that believeth and is baptized, shall be saved; but he that believeth not shall be condemned (16:16). "He who believeth" is he who acknowledges the Lord, and receives Divine truths from Him through the Word; "he who is baptized" is he who is regenerated by the Lord by means of those truths.

FROM THE ARCANA COELESTIA. Baptism signifies regeneration by the Lord through the truths of faith from the Word (n. 4255, 5120, 9088, 10239, 10386-10388, 10392). Baptism is for a sign that man is of the church, where the Lord is acknowledged, from whom is regeneration, and which has the Word, from which are the truths of faith, by which regeneration is effected (n. 10386-10388). Baptism gives neither faith nor salvation, but testifies that faith and salvation will be received by those who are regenerated (n. 10391). The washings in the ancient churches, and in the Israelitish church, represented and thence signified purifications from evils and falsities (n. 3147, 9088, 10237, 10239). "The washings of garments" signified the purification of the understanding from falsities (n. 5954). "The washing of the feet" signified the purification of the natural man (n. 3147, 10241). What is signified by "the washing of the disciples' feet" by the Lord, is explained (n. 10243). "Waters" signify the truths of faith (n. 28, 2702, 3058, 5668, 8568, 10238). "A fountain" and "a well of living waters" signifies the truths of faith from the Lord, thus the Word (n. 3424). "Bread and water" signify all the goods of love and truths of faith (n. 4976, 9323). "Spirit" signifies the life of truth, or the life of faith (n. 5222, 9281, 9818). What "the spirit" and "the flesh" signify, that "the spirit" signifies life from the Lord, and "flesh," life from man (n. 10283). Hence it is evident what is signified by these words of the Lord: Except a man be begotten of water and the spirit, he cannot enter into the kingdom of God (John 3:5). Namely, that unless man is regenerated by the truths of faith, and by a life according to them, he cannot be saved (n. 10240). All regeneration is effected by the truths of faith, and by a life according to them (n. 1904, 2046, 9088, 9959, 10028). The total washing, which was effected by immersion in the waters of the Jordan, signified regeneration itself, in the same manner as baptism (n. 9088, 10239). What "the waters of Jordan," and "Jordan" signified (n. 1585, 4255). "A flood" and "inundation of waters" signify temptations (n. 660, 705, 639, 756, 790, 5725, 6853). "Baptism" signifies the same (n. 5120, 10389). In what manner baptism was represented from heaven (n. 2299).

XVI. THE HOLY SUPPER. The Holy Supper was instituted by the Lord, that by it there may be conjunction of the church with heaven, thus with the

Lord: therefore it is the most holy thing of worship.

But how conjunction is effected by it is not understood by those who do not know the internal or spiritual sense of the Word, since they do not think beyond the external sense, which is the sense of the letter. It is known from the internal or spiritual sense of the Word, what is signified by the "body" and "blood," and by the "bread" and "wine"; and also what is signified by "eating."

In the spiritual sense, the Lord's "body" or "flesh," and the "bread," signifies the good of love; and the Lord's "blood" and the "wine," the good of faith; and "eating" is appropriation and conjunction. The angels who are with the man who goes to the Sacrament of the Supper, understand those things in no other way, for they perceive all things spiritually. Hence it is, that the holiness of love and the holiness of faith then flow into man from the angels, thus through heaven from the Lord, and hence conjunction is effected.

From these things it is evident, that when man partakes of the bread, which is the body, he is conjoined to the Lord by the good of love to Him from Him; and when he partakes of the wine, which is the blood, he is conjoined to the Lord by the good of faith in Him from Him. But it is to be known that the conjunction with the Lord by the Sacrament of the Supper, is effected with those alone who are in the good of love and faith in the Lord from the Lord. With these there is conjunction by the Holy Supper; with others there is presence, but not conjunction.

Besides, the Holy Supper includes and comprehends the whole of the Divine worship instituted in the Israelitish Church; for the burnt-offerings and sacrifices, in which the worship of that church principally consisted, in one expression were called "bread"; hence also the Holy Supper is its completion. FROM THE ARCANA COELESTIA. Since what is involved in the Holy Supper cannot be known unless it is known what its particulars signify, for they correspond to spiritual things, therefore some passages shall be quoted respecting what is signified by "body" and "flesh," by "bread" and "wine," and by "eating" and "drinking"; as also concerning the sacrifices, wherein the worship of the Israelitish church principally consisted, showing that they were called "bread."

Of Supper. "Dinners" and "suppers" signified consociation by love (n. 3596, 3832, 4745, 5161, 7996). The "paschal supper" signified consociation in heaven (n. 7836, 7997, 8001). "The feast of unleavened bread," or of "the passover," signified deliverance from damnation, by the Lord (n. 7093, 7867, 9286-9292, 10655); in the inmost sense, the remembrance of the glorification of the Lord's Human, because deliverance comes therefrom (n. 10655).

Of Body and Flesh. The Lord's "flesh" signifies the Divine good of His Divine love. that is, of His Divine Human (n. 3813, 7850, 9127, 10283). His "body" has a like signification (n. 2343, 3735, 6135). "Flesh" in general signifies the will or proprium of man, which regarded in itself is evil; but which when vivified by the Lord, signifies good (n. 148, 149, 780, 999, 3813, 8409, 10283). Hence "flesh" in the Word, is the whole man, and every man (n. 574, 1050, 10283). It is said here and in what follows, that these things signify, because they correspond; for whatever corresponds, signifies (see n. 2896, 2979, 2987, 2989, 3002, 3225). The Word is written by mere correspondences, and hence its internal or spiritual sense, the nature of which cannot be known, and scarcely its existence, without a knowledge of correspondences (n. 3131, 3472-3485, 8615, 10687). Therefore there is a conjunction of heaven with the man of the church by the Word (n. 10687). For further particulars on this head see in the work on Heaven and Hell (n. 303-310), where it treats of the Conjunction of Heaven with the Man of the Church by means of the Word.

Of Blood. The Lord's "blood" signifies the Divine truth proceeding from the Divine good of His Divine love (n. 4735, 6978, 7317, 7326, 7846, 7850, 7877, 9127, 9393, 10026, 10033, 10152, 10210). The "blood" sprinkled upon the altar round about, and at its foundation, signified the unition of Divine truth and the Divine good in the Lord (n. 10047). "The blood of grapes" signifies the truth of faith from the good of charity (n. 6378). "A grape" and "a cluster" signify spiritual good, which is the good of charity (n. 5117). "To shed blood" is to offer violence to the Divine truth (n. 374, 1005, 4735, 5476, 9127). What is signified by "blood and water" going out of the Lord's side (n. 9127). What by the Lord's redeeming men by "His blood" (n. 10152).

Of Bread. "Bread," when mentioned in relation to the Lord, signifies the Divine good of the Lord's Divine love, and the reciprocal of the man who eats it (n. 2165, 2177, 3478, 3735, 3813, 4211, 4217, 4735, 4976, 9323, 9545). "Bread" involves and signifies all food in general (n. 2165, 6118). "Food" signifies everything that nourishes the spiritual life of man (n. 4976, 5147, 5915, 6277, 8418). Thus "bread" signifies all celestial and spiritual food (n. 276, 680, 2165, 2177, 3478, 6118, 8410). Consequently, "everything which proceeds out of the mouth of God," according to the Lord's words (Matt. 4:4; n. 681). "Bread" in general signifies the good of love (n. 2165, 2177, 10686). The same is signified by "wheat," of which bread is made (n. 3941, 7605). "Bread and water," when mentioned in the Word, signify the good of love and the truth of faith (n. 9323). Breaking of bread was a representative of mutual love in the ancient churches (n. 5405). Spiritual food is science, intelligence, and wisdom, thus good and truth, because the former are derived from the latter (n. 3114, 4459, 4792, 5147, 5293, 5340, 5342, 5410, 5426, 5576, 5582, 5588, 5655, 8562, 9003). And because they nourish the mind (n. 4459, 5293, 5576, 6277, 8418). Sustenance by food signifies spiritual nourishment, and the influx of good and truth from the Lord (n. 4976, 5915, 6277). The "bread" on the table in the tabernacle, signified the Divine good of the Lord's Divine love (n. 3478, 9545). The "meal-offerings" of cakes and wafers in the sacrifices, signified worship from the good of love (n. 4581, 10079, 10137). What the various meal-offerings signified in particular (n. 7978, 9992-9994, 10079). The ancients, when they mentioned bread, meant all food in general (see Gen. 43:16, 31; Exod. 18:12; Judges 13:15, 16; 1 Sam. 14:28, 29; 20:24, 27; 2 Sam. 9:7, 10; 1 Kings 4:22, 23; 2 Kings 25:29).

Of Wine. "Wine," when mentioned concerning the Lord, signifies the Divine truth proceeding from His Divine good, in the same manner as "blood" (n. 1071, 1798, 6377). "Wine" in general signifies the good of charity (n. 6377). "Must" signifies truth from good in the natural man (n. 3580). Wine is called "the blood of grapes" (n. 6378). "A vineyard" signifies the church as to truth (n. 3220, 9139). The "drink-offering" in the sacrifices, which was wine, signified spiritual good, which is holy truth (n. 1072). The Lord alone is holy, and hence all holiness is from Him (n. 9229, 9680, 10359, 10360). The Divine truth proceeding from the Lord is what is called "holy" in the Word (n. 6788, 8302, 9229, 9820,

10361).

Of Eating and Drinking. "To eat" signifies to be appropriated and conjoined by love and charity (n. 2187, 2343, 3168, 3513, 5643). Hence it signifies to be consociated (n. 8001). "To eat" is predicated of the appropriation and conjunction of good, and "to drink," of the appropriation and conjunction of truth (n. 3168, 3513, 3832, 9412). What "eating and drinking in the Lord's kingdom" signifies (n. 3832). Hence it is, that "to be famished" and "hungry," in the Word, signifies to desire good and truth from affection (n. 4958, 10227). The angels understand the things here spoken of according to their internal or spiritual sense alone, because the angels are in the spiritual world (n. 10521). Hence holiness from heaven flows in with the men of the church, when they receive the Sacrament of the Supper with sanctity (n. 6789). And thence is conjunction with the Lord (n. 3464, 3735, 5915, 10519, 10521, 10522).

Of Sacrifices. "Burnt-offerings" and "sacrifices" signified all things of worship from the good of love, and from the truths of faith (n. 923, 6905, 8680, 8936, 10042). "Burnt-offerings" and "sacrifices" also signified Divine celestial things, which are the internal things of the church, from which worship is derived (n. 2180, 2805, 2807, 2830, 3519). With a variation and difference according to the varieties of worship (n. 2805, 6905, 8936). Therefore there were many kinds of sacrifices, and various processes to be observed in them, and various beasts from which they were (n. 2830, 9391, 9990). The various things which they signified in general, may appear from unfolding the particulars by the internal sense (n. 10042). What "the beasts" which were sacrificed signified in particular (n. 10042). Arcana of heaven are contained in the rituals and processes of the sacrifices (n. 10057). In general they contained the arcana of the glorification of the Lord's Human; and in a respective sense, the arcana of the regeneration and purification of man from evils and falsities; wherefore they were prescribed for various sins, crimes, and purifications (n. 9990, 10022, 10042, 10053, 10057). What is signified by "the imposition of hands" on the beasts which were sacrificed (n. 10023). What by "the inferior parts of the slain beasts being put under their superior parts" in the burnt-offerings (n. 10051). What by "the meal-offerings" that were offered at the same time (n. 10079). What by "the drink-offering" (n. 4581, 10137). What by "the salt" which was used (n. 10300). What by "the altar" and all the particulars of it (n. 921, 2777, 2784, 2811, 2812, 4489, 4541, 8935, 8940, 9388, 9389, 9714, 9726, 9963, 9964, 10028, 10123, 10151, 10242, 10245, 10344). What by "the fire of the altar" (n. 934, 6314, 6832). What by "eating together of the things sacrificed" (n. 2187, 8682). Sacrifices were not commanded, but charity and faith, thus that they were only permitted, shown from the Word (n. 922, 2180). Why they were permitted (n. 2180, 2818). The burnt-offerings and sacrifices, which consisted of lambs, she-goats, sheep, kids, he-goats, and bullocks, were in one word called "Bread," is evident from the following passages: And the priest shall burn it upon the altar; it is the bread of the offering made by fire unto Jehovah (Lev. 3:11, 16). The sons of Aaron shall be holy unto their God, neither shall they profane the name of their God; for the offerings of Jehovah made by fire, the bread of their God, they do offer. Thou shalt sanctify him, for he offered the bread of thy God. A man of the seed of Aaron, in whom there shall be a blemish, let him not approach to offer the bread of his God (Lev. 21:6, 8, 17, 21).

Command the sons of Israel, and say unto them, My offering, My bread, for My sacrifices made by fire for an odor of rest, ye shall observe, to offer unto Me in its stated time (Num. 28:2). He who shall have touched an unclean thing shall not eat of the holy things, but he shall wash his flesh in water; and shall afterwards eat of the holy things, because it is his bread (Lev. 22:6, 7). They who offer polluted bread upon My altar (Mal. 1:7). Hence now, as has been said above (n. 214), the Holy Supper includes and comprehends all of the Divine worship instituted in the Israelitish Church; for the burnt-offerings and sacrifices in which the worship of that church principally consisted were called by the one word "bread." Hence, also, the Holy Supper is its fulfilling. From what has been observed, it may now be seen what is meant by bread in John: Jesus said to them, Verily, verily, I say unto you, Moses gave them not that bread from heaven, but My Father giveth you the true bread from heaven, for the bread of God is He who came down from heaven, and giveth life unto the world. They said unto Lord, evermore give us this bread. Jesus said unto them, I am the bread of life; he that cometh to Me shall never hunger, and he that believeth on Me shall never thirst. He that believeth on Me hath eternal life. I am the bread of life. This is the bread which cometh down from heaven; that anyone may eat thereof, and not die. I am the living bread which came down from heaven; if anyone shall eat of this bread, he shall live forever (John 6:31-35, 47-51). From these passages, and from what has been said above, it appears that "bread" is all the good which proceeds from the Lord, for the Lord Himself is in His own good; and thus that "bread and wine" in the Holy Supper are all the worship of the Lord from the good of love and faith.

To the above shall be added some particulars from the Arcana Coelestia (n. 9127): "He who knows nothing of the internal or spiritual sense of the Word, knows no other than that 'flesh and blood,' when they are mentioned in the Word, mean flesh and blood. But in the internal or spiritual sense, it does not treat of the life of the body, but of the life of man's soul, that is, of his spiritual life, which he is to live to eternity. This life is described in the literal sense of the Word, by things which belong to the life of the body, that is, by `flesh and blood'; and as the spiritual life of man subsists by the good of love and the truth of faith, therefore in the internal sense of the Word the good of love is meant by `flesh,' and the truth of faith by `blood.' These are understood by `flesh and blood,' and by `bread and wine,' in heaven; for `bread' means altogether the same there as `flesh,' and `wine' as `blood.' They who are not spiritual men, do not apprehend this; let such abide therefore in their own faith, only believing that in the Holy Supper, and in the Word, there is holiness, because they are from the Lord, although they may not know where that holiness resides. On the other hand, let those who are endowed with interior perception, consider whether `flesh' means flesh, and `blood,' blood, in the following passages. In the Apocalypse: I saw an angel standing in the sun, and he cried with a great voice, saying unto all the birds that fly in the midst of heaven, come and gather yourselves together to the supper of the great God; that ye may eat the flesh of Kings, and the flesh of commanders of thousands, and the flesh of the mighty, and the flesh of horses and of them that sit on them, and the flesh of all, free and bond, small and great (19:17, 18). Who can understand these words, unless he knows what `flesh,' `kings,' `commanders of thousands,' `the mighty,' 'horses,' 'them that sit on them,' and 'freemen' and 'bondmen,' signify in the internal sense? And in Ezekiel: Thus saith the Lord Jehovah, Say to every bird of heaven, and to every beast of the field, Gather yourselves together and come; gather yourselves together from every side to My sacrifice that I sacrifice for you, a great sacrifice upon the mountains of Israel, that ye may eat flesh and drink blood; ye shall eat the flesh of the mighty, and drink the blood of the princes of the earth; and ye shall eat fat to satiety, and drink blood even to drunkenness, of My sacrifice which I have sacrificed for you: thus shall ye be satisfied at My table, with horse and chariot, with the mighty, and with every man of war; thus will I give My glory among the nations (39:17-21). This passage treats of the calling together of all to the kingdom of the Lord, and in particular of the establishment of the church with the Gentiles; and 'eating flesh and drinking blood,' signify to appropriate to themselves Divine good and Divine truth, thus the holiness which proceeds from the Lord's Divine Human. Who cannot see, that 'flesh' does not here mean flesh; nor 'blood,' blood; as when it said, that 'they should eat the flesh of the mighty,' and 'drink the blood of the princes of the earth'; and that 'they should drink blood even to drunkenness'; also that 'they should be satisfied with horses, with chariots, with mighty men, and with all men of war'? What 'the birds of heaven' and 'the beasts of the field' signify in the spiritual sense, may be seen in the work on Heaven and Hell (n. 110 and the notes). Let us now consider what the Lord said concerning His flesh and His blood, in John: The bread which I will give, is My flesh. Verily, verily, I say unto you, Except ye eat the flesh of the Son of man, and drink His blood, ye have no life in you. Whoso eateth My flesh and drinketh My blood, hath eternal life, and I will raise him up at the last day; for My flesh is meat indeed, and My blood is drink indeed. He that eateth My flesh and drinketh My blood, dwelleth in Me, and I in him. This is the bread which came down from heaven (John 6:50-58). 'The flesh' of the Lord is the Divine good, and His 'blood,' the Divine truth, each from Him, is evident, because these nourish the spiritual life of man; hence it is said, 'My flesh is meat indeed, and My blood is drink indeed,' and as man is conjoined to the Lord by the Divine good and truth, it is also said, 'Whoso eateth My flesh and drinketh My blood, hath eternal life'; and, 'He dwelleth in Me and I in him'; and in the former part of the chapter: Labor not for the food which perisheth, but for that food which endureth to eternal life (John 6:27). 'To abide in the Lord' is to be in love to Him, the Lord Himself teaches in John (15:2-12).

XVII. THE RESURRECTION. Man is so created that as to his internal he cannot die; for he can believe in and also love God, and thus be conjoined to God by faith and love; and to be conjoined to God is to live to eternity.

This internal is with every man who is born; his external is that by which he brings into effect the things which are of his faith and love. The internal is called the spirit, and the external is called the body. The external, which is called the body, is accommodated to the uses in the natural world, this is rejected when man dies; but the internal, which is called the spirit, is accommodated to the uses in the spiritual world, this does not die. This internal is then a good spirit and an angel, if the man had been good in the world; but an evil spirit if man had been evil in the world.

The spirit of man after the death of the body, appears in the spiritual world in a human form, in every respect as in the world. He enjoys the faculty of seeing, of hearing, of speaking, and of feeling, as in the world; and he is endowed with every faculty of thinking, of willing, and of acting, as in the world; in a word, he is a man as to each and every thing, except that he is not encompassed with the gross body which he had in the world. This he leaves when he dies, nor does he ever resume it.

This continuation of life is meant by the resurrection. The reason why men believe that they will not rise again before the Last Judgment, when the whole visible world will perish, is because they have not understood the Word, and because sensual men place all their life in the body, and believe that unless this shall live again, it will be all over with the man.

The life of man after death is the life of his love and the life of his faith; hence such as his love and faith had been, when he lived in the world, such his life will remain to eternity. With those who loved themselves and the world above all things, it is the life of hell; and with those who had loved God above all things, and the neighbor as themselves, it is the life of heaven. The latter are they who have faith; but the former are they who have no faith. The life of heaven is called eternal life; and the life of hell is called spiritual death.

That man lives after death, the Word teaches; as that: God is not the God of the dead, but of the living (Matt. 22:31). Lazarus after death was carried into heaven, but the rich man was cast into hell (Luke 16:22, 23 seq.). Abraham, Isaac, and Jacob are there (Matt. 8:11; 22:31, 32; Luke 20: 37, 38). Jesus said to the robber, Today shalt thou be with Me in paradise (Luke 23:43).

FROM THE WORK ON HEAVEN AND HELL. It is unnecessary here to adduce anything from the Arcana Coelestia, since the things concerning the resurrection and the life of man after death have been fully treated in the work on Heaven and Hell, where they may be seen under the following articles: I. Every Man is a Spirit as to His Interiors (n. 432-444). II. Of Man's Resuscitation from the Dead, and His Entrance into Eternal Life (n. 445-452). III. After Death Man is in a Perfect Human Form (n. 453-460). IV. After Death Man has every Sense, and all the Memory, Thought, and Affection, which He had in the World; and that He Leaves Nothing but His Terrestrial Body (n. 461-469). V. Man after Death is Such as his Life had Been in the World (n. 470-484). VI. The Delights of Everyone's Life are Turned into Corresponding Things (n. 485-490). VII. Of Man's First State after Death (n. 491-498). VIII. Of Man's Second State after Death (n. 499-511). IX. Of Man's Third State after Death, which is a State of Instruction for Those that Come into Heaven (n. 512-520). X. That Heaven and Hell are from the Human Race (311-317). Concerning the Last Judgment, spoken of above at n. 226, see the work on The Last Judgment, and Babylon Destroyed, from the beginning to the end; where it is shown that the Last Judgment will not be attended with the destruction of the world.

XVIII. HEAVEN AND HELL. There are two things which constitute the life of man's spirit, namely, love and faith; love constituting the life of his will, and faith the life of his understanding. The love of good and the faith of truth thence derived, constitute the life of heaven; and the love of evil, and the faith of falsity thence derived, constitute the life of hell.

Love to the Lord and love towards the neighbor constitute heaven; and also faith, so far as it has life from those loves. And because both the love and the faith thence derived, are from the Lord, it is evident that the Lord Himself constitutes heaven.

Heaven is with every man according to his reception of love and faith from the Lord; and they who receive heaven from the Lord while they live in the world, come into heaven after death.

They who receive heaven from the Lord are they who have heaven in themselves, for heaven is in man, as the Lord also teaches: Neither shall they say, The kingdom of God, lo it is here, or lo there, for the Kingdom of God is in you (Luke 17:21).

Heaven is with man in his internal, thus in his willing and thinking from love and faith, and thence in his external, which is in acting and speaking from love and faith. But heaven is not in man's external without the internal; for all hypocrites can act and speak well, but they cannot will and think well.

When man comes into the other life, which takes place immediately after death, it is evident whether heaven is in him or not; but not while he lives in the world. For in the world the external appears, and not the internal, but in the other life the internal is made manifest, because man then lives as to his spirit.

Eternal happiness, which is also called heavenly joy, is imparted to those who are in love and faith in the Lord, from the Lord; for this love and faith have that joy in them; into it the man comes after death who has heaven in him; in the meantime it lies hidden in his internal man. In the heavens there is a communion of all goods; there the peace, the intelligence, the wisdom, and the happiness of all are communicated to each; yet to everyone according to his reception of love and faith from the Lord. Hence it may appear how great is the peace, intelligence, wisdom and happiness in heaven.

As love to the Lord and love towards the neighbor constitute the life of heaven with man, so the love of self and the love of the world, when they reign, constitute the life of hell with him; for these loves are opposite to those. Therefore they with whom the loves of self and of the world reign, can receive nothing from heaven, but what they receive is from hell; for whatever a man loves, and whatever he believes, is either from heaven or from hell.

Those with whom the love of self and the love of the world reign, do not know what heaven and heavenly happiness are; and it appears incredible to them that happiness is given in any other loves than in them. Nevertheless, the happiness of heaven enters so far as the loves of self and the world, regarded as ends, are removed; and the happiness which succeeds on their removal is so great as to exceed all human comprehension.

The life of man cannot be changed after death. It then remains such as it had been. For the quality of man's spirit is in every respect the same as that of his love, and infernal love can never be transcribed into heavenly love, because they are opposite. This is meant by the words of Abraham to the rich man in hell: Between us and you there is a great gulf; so that they which would pass to you cannot; neither can they pass to us from thence (Luke 16:26). Hence it is evident that all who come into hell remain there to eternity; and they who come into heaven remain there to eternity.

Since the subject of heaven and hell has been treated of in a separate work, wherein is also adduced what is contained in the Arcana Coelestia concerning it, it is therefore unnecessary here to add anything further.

XIX. THE CHURCH. That which constitutes heaven with man, also constitutes the church; for as love and faith constitute heaven, so they also constitute the church; thus, from what has been already said concerning heaven, it is evident what the church is.

The church is said to be where the Lord is acknowledged and where the Word is, for the essentials of the church are love and faith in the Lord from the Lord; and the Word teaches how man must live that he may receive love and faith from the Lord.

That there may be a church, there must be doctrine from the Word, since without doctrine the Word is not understood. Doctrine alone, however, does not constitute the church with man, but a life according to it. Hence it follows that faith alone does not constitute the church with man, but the life of faith, which is charity. Genuine doctrine is the doctrine of charity and faith together, and not the doctrine of faith separate from charity; for the doctrine of charity and faith together is the doctrine of life; but not the doctrine of faith without the doctrine of charity.

They who are out of the church and acknowledge one God, and live according to their religious principle, and in some charity towards the neighbor, are in communion with those who are of the church; for no man who believes in God and lives well, is condemned. Hence it is evident, that the church of the Lord is in the whole world, although specifically, where the Lord is acknowledged, and where the Word is.

Everyone with whom the church exists, is saved; but everyone in whom it is not, is condemned.

FROM THE ARCANA COELESTIA. The church exists specifically where the Word is, and where the Lord is thereby known, and thus where Divine truths are revealed (n. 3857, 10761). Still they who are born where the Word is, and where the Lord is thereby known, are not of the church, but they who are regenerated by the Lord by the truths of the Word, that is, they who live the life of charity (n. 6637, 10143, 10153, 10578, 10645, 10829). They who are of the church, or in whom the church is, are in the affection of truth for the sake of truth, that is, they love truth because it is truth; and they examine from the Word whether the doctrinals of the church in which they were born are true (n. 5432, 6047). Otherwise the truth possessed by everyone would be derived from another, and from his native soil (n. 6047). The church of the Lord is with all in the whole world who live in good according to their religious principles (n. 3263, 6637, 10765). All who live in good wherever they are, and acknowledge one God, are accepted by the Lord and come into heaven; since all who are in good acknowledge the Lord, because good is from the Lord, and the Lord is in good (n. 2589-2604, 2861, 2863, 3263, 4190, 4197, 6700, 9256). The universal church on earth before the Lord is as one man (n. 7396, 9276). As heaven is, because the church is heaven or the kingdom of the Lord on earth (n. 2853, 2996, 2998, 3624-3629, 3636-3643, 3741-3745, 4625). But the church, where the Lord is known and where the Word is, is like the heart and lungs in man in respect to the other parts of the body, which live from the heart and lungs as from the fountains of their life (n. 637, 931, 2054, 2853). Hence it is, that unless there were a church where the Word is, and where the Lord is thereby known, the human race could not be saved (n. 468, 637, 931, 4545, 10452). The church is the foundation of heaven (n. 4060). The church is internal and external (n. 1242, 6587, 9375, 9680, 10762). The internal of the church is love to the Lord and charity towards the neighbor. Thence they who are in the affection of good and truth from love to the Lord and from charity towards the neighbor, constitute the internal church; and they who are in external worship from obedience and faith, constitute the external church (n. 1083, 1098, 4288, 6380, 6587, 7840, 8762). To know truth and good, and to act from thence, is the external of the church, but to will and love truth and good, and to act from thence, is the internal of the church (n. 4899, 6775). The internal of the church is in the worship of those who are of the external church, although in obscurity (n. 6775). The internal and external church make one church (n. 409, 10762). Man has an internal and an external, an internal after the image of heaven, and an external after the image of the world; and therefore, in order that the man may be a church, his external must act in unity with his internal (n. 3628, 4523, 4524, 6057, 6314, 9706, 10472). The church is in the internal of man and at the same time in the external, but not in the external without the internal (n. 1795, 6580, 10691). The internal of the church is according to truths and their quality, and according to their implantation in good by life (n. 1238). The church like heaven is in man, and thus the church in general consists of the men in whom the church is (n. 3884). In order that a church may exist, there must be the doctrine of life, that is, the doctrine of charity (n. 3445, 10763, 10764). Charity makes the church, and not faith separated from charity (n. 916). Consequently, not the doctrine of faith separated from charity, but the doctrine of faith conjoined therewith, and a life conformable to it (n. 809, 1798, 1799, 1834, 1844, 4468, 4672, 4689, 4766, 5826, 6637). The church is not with man, unless the truths of doctrine are implanted in the good of charity with him, thus in the life (n. 3310, 3963, 5826). There is no church with man, if he is only in the truths, which are called the truths of faith (n. 5826). How much good would be in the church, if charity were in the first place and faith in the second (n. 6269). And how much evil, if faith is in the first place (n. 6272). In the ancient churches charity was the principal and essential of the church (n. 4680). The church would be like heaven, if all had charity (n. 2385, 2853). If good were the characteristic of the church, and not truth without good, thus if charity were its characteristic, and not faith separate, the church would be one, and differences with respect to the doctrinals of faith, and external worship, would be accounted as nothing (n. 1285, 1316, 2982, 3267, 3445, 3451). Every church begins from charity, but declines therefrom in process of time (n. 494, 501, 1327, 3773, 4689). Thus to falsities from evil, and at length to evils (n. 1834, 1835, 2910, 4683, 4689). A comparison of the church at its beginning and decline with the infancy and old age of man (n. 10134). And also with the rising and the setting of the sun (n. 1837). Concerning the successive states of the Christian Church even to its last state; wherein are explained the particulars which the Lord foretold concerning "the consummation of the age," and His "coming," in Matt. chap. 24 from the beginning to the end (n. 3353-3356, 3486-3489, 3650-3655, 3571-3757, 3897-3901, 4057-4060, 4229-4335, 4422-4424, 4635-4638, 4807-4810, 4954-4959, 5063-5071). The Christian church is at this day in its last states, there being no faith therein because there is no charity (n. 3489, 4689). The Last Judgment is the last time of the church (n. 2118, 3353, 4057, 4333, 4535). Of the vastation

of the church (n. 407-411). The consummation of the age and the coming of the
Lord is the last time of the old church and the beginning of the new (n. 2243,
4535, 10622). When the old church is vastated, interior truths are revealed for
the service of the new church which is then established (n. 3398, 3786).
Concerning the establishment of the church with the Gentiles (n. 1366, 2986,
4747, 9256).

Of the Ancient Churches. The first and Most Ancient Church on this earth,
which is described in the first chapters of Genesis, was a celestial church, and
the chief of all the rest (n. 607, 895, 920, 1121-1124, 2896, 4493, 8891, 9942,
10545). Of the quality of those in heaven who belonged to it (n. 1114-1125).
They are in the highest degree of light (n. 1116, 1117). There were various
churches after the flood, called in one word, the Ancient Church, concerning
which (n. 1125-1127, 1327, 10355). Through how many kingdoms of Asia the
Ancient Church was extended (n. 1238, 2385). The quality of the men of the
Ancient Church (n. 609, 895). The Ancient Church was a representative church,
and its representatives were collected into one by certain men of the Most
Ancient Church (n. 519, 521, 2896). The Ancient Church had a Word, but it was
lost (n. 2897). The quality of the Ancient Church when it began to decline (n.
1128). The difference between the Most Ancient and the Ancient Churches (n.
597, 607, 640, 641, 765, 784, 895, 4493). The Most Ancient Church and the
Ancient were also in the land of Canaan, and hence came the representatives
of the places therein (n. 3686, 4447, 4454). Of the church that began from Eber,
which was called the Hebrew Church (n. 1238, 1241, 1343, 4516, 4517). The
difference between the Ancient and the Hebrew Churches (n. 1343, 4874). Eber
instituted sacrifices which were wholly unknown in the Ancient Churches (n.
1343). The Ancient Churches agreed with the Christian Church as to internals,
but not as to externals (n. 3478, 4489, 4772, 4904, 10149). In the Most Ancient
Church there was immediate revelation; in the Ancient Church, revelation by
correspondences; in the Jewish Church, by a living voice; and in the Christian
Church, by the Word (n. 10355). The Lord was the God of the Most Ancient
Church, and was called Jehovah (n. 1343, 6846). The Lord is heaven, and He is
the church (n. 4766, 10125, 10151, 10157). The Divine of the Lord makes
heaven, see the work on Heaven and Hell (n. 7-12 and 78-86); and thus also the
church, since what constitutes heaven with man, constitutes also the church,
as was shown in the doctrine above.

Of the Jewish Church and of the Jews. The statutes, judgments, and laws,
which were commanded in the Jewish Church, were in part like those in the
Ancient Church (n. 4449, 4835). In what respect the representative rites of the
Jewish Church differed from those of the Ancient Church (n. 4288, 10149). A
representative church was instituted with that nation, but there was no church
in that nation itself (n. 4899, 4912, 6304). Therefore as to that nation itself, it
was the representative of a church, but not a church (n. 4281, 4288, 4311, 4500,
6304, 7048, 9320, 10396, 10526, 10535, 10698). The Israelitish and Jewish
nation was not elected, but only received, in order that it might represent a
church, on account of the obstinacy with which their fathers and Moses insisted
(n. 4290, 4293, 7051, 7439, 10430, 10535, 10632). Their worship was merely
external, without any internal worship (n. 1200, 3147, 3479, 8871). They were
entirely unacquainted with the internals of worship, and were not willing to

know them (n. 301-303, 3479, 4429, 4433, 4680, 4844, 4847, 10396, 10401, 10407, 10694, 10701, 10707). In what manner they consider the internals of worship, of the church, and the Word (n. 4865). Their interiors were filthy, full of the loves of self and of the world, and of avarice (n. 3480, 9962, 10454-10457, 10462-10466, 10575). On this account the internals of the church were not disclosed to them, because they would have profaned them (n. 2520, 3398, 3480, 4289). The Word is wholly shut to them (n. 3769). They see the Word from without and not from within (n. 10549-10551). Therefore their internal, when in worship, was shut (n. 8788, 8806, 9320, 9377, 9380, 9962, 10396, 10401, 10407, 10492, 10498, 10500, 10575, 10629, 10694). That nation was of such a quality, that they could be in a holy external, when the internal was shut, more than others (n. 4293, 4311, 4903, 9373, 9377, 9380). Their state at that time (n. 4311). They are therefore preserved to this day (n. 3479). Their holy external was miraculously elevated by the Lord into heaven, and the interior things of worship, of the church, and the Word perceived there (n. 3480, 4307, 4311, 6304, 8588, 10492, 10500, 10602). For this purpose they were forced by external means strictly to observe their rites in their external form (n. 3147, 4281, 10149). Because they could be in a holy external without an internal, they could represent the holy things of the church and heaven (n. 3479, 3881, 4208, 6306, 8588, 9377, 10430, 10500, 10570). Still those holy things did not affect them (n. 3479). The quality of the person who represents is of no importance, because the representation regards the thing represented, and not the person (n. 665, 1097, 1361, 3147, 3881, 4208, 4281, 4288, 4292, 4307, 4444, 4500, 6304, 7048, 7439, 8588, 8788, 8806). That nation was worse than other nations, their quality also described from the Word of both Testaments (n. 4314, 4316, 4317, 4444, 4503, 4750, 4751, 4815, 4820, 4832, 5057, 5998, 7248, 8819, 9320, 10454-10547, 10462-10466). The tribe of Judah departed into worse things than the other tribes (n. 4815). How cruelly they treated the Gentiles, from delight (n. 5057, 7248, 9320). That nation was idolatrous in heart; and more than other nations worshiped other gods (n. 3732, 4208, 4444, 4825, 5998, 6877, 7401, 8301, 8871, 8882). Even their worship was idolatrous when considered as to that nation itself, because it was external without internal (n. 4281, 4825, 8871, 8882). They worshiped Jehovah only in name (n. 6877, 10559-10561, 10566). And only on account of miracles (n. 4299). They who believe that the Jews will be converted at the end of the church, and brought again into the land of Canaan, think erroneously (n. 4847, 7051, 8301). Many passages adduced from the Word concerning this matter, but which are to be understood according to the internal sense, and differently from the sense of the letter (n. 7051). The Word was changed on account of that nation, as to its external sense, but not as to its internal sense (n. 10453, 10461, 10603, 10604). Jehovah appeared to them on Mount Sinai, according to their quality, in a consuming fire, a thick cloud, and smoke as of a furnace (n. 1861, 6832, 8814, 8819, 9434). The Lord appears to everyone according to his quality, as a vivifying and recreating fire to those who are in good, and as a consuming fire to those who are in evil (n. 934, 1861, 6832, 8814, 8819, 9434, 10551). One origin of that nation was from a Canaanitess and the two others from whoredom with a daughter-in-law (n. 1167, 4818, 4820, 4874, 4899, 4913). These origins signify the nature of their conjunction with the church, as being like conjunction with the Canaanitess, and whoredom with a

The Teachings of Emanuel Swedenborg Vol. II 187

daughter-in-law (n. 4868, 4874, 4899, 4911, 4913). Of the state of the Jews in the other life (n. 939, 940, 5057). Since this nation, although of such a quality, represented the church; and since the Word was written among them and concerning them; therefore Divine celestial things were signified by their names, as by "Reuben," "Simeon," "Levi," "Judah," "Ephraim," "Joseph," and the rest. That "Judah," in the internal sense, signifies the Lord as to celestial love, and His celestial kingdom (n. 3654, 3881, 5583, 5603, 5782, 6363). The prophecy of Israel concerning Judah, in which the Lord is treated of, explained, Gen. 49:8-12 (n. 6362-6381). "The tribe of Judah" and "Judea" signify the celestial church (n. 3654, 6364). The twelve tribes represented, and thence signified all things of love and faith in the complex (n. 3858, 3926, 4060, 6335); thus also heaven and the church (n. 6337, 6637, 7836, 7891). They signify according to the order in which they are named (n. 3862, 3926, 3939, 4603, seq., 6337, 6640). The twelve tribes were divided into two kingdoms, in order that the Jews might represent the celestial kingdom, and the Israelites the spiritual kingdom (n. 8770, 9320). "The seed of Abraham," of "Isaac," and of "Jacob," signifies the goods and truths of the church (n. 3373, 10445).

XX. THE SACRED SCRIPTURE, OR THE WORD. Without a revelation from the Divine, man cannot know anything concerning eternal life, nor even anything concerning God, and still less concerning love to, and faith in Him; for man is born into mere ignorance, and must therefore learn everything from worldly things, from which he must form his understanding. He is also born hereditarily into every evil which is from the love of self and of the world; the delights from thence reign continually, and suggest such things as are diametrically contrary to the Divine. Hence it is that man knows nothing concerning eternal life; wherefore there must necessarily be a revelation from which he may know.

That the evils of the love of self and of the world induce such ignorance concerning those things which are of eternal life, appears manifestly from those within the church; who, although they know from revelation that there is a God, that there is a heaven and a hell, that there is eternal life, and that eternal life is to be acquired by the good of love and faith, still lapse into denial concerning those things, both the learned and the unlearned. Hence it is further evident how great ignorance there would be, if there were no revelation.

Footnotes
201-1 The translator omits the phrase "beyond all others." But the Latin, "prae omnibus" requires it.

Section 5

Since therefore man lives after death, and then lives to eternity, and a life awaits him according to his love and faith, it follows that the Divine, out of love towards the human race, has revealed such things as may lead to that life, and conduce to man's salvation. What the Divine has revealed, is with us the Word.

The Word, because it is a revelation from the Divine, is Divine in each and all things; for what is from the Divine cannot be otherwise. What is from the Divine descends through the heavens even to man; wherefore in the heavens it is accommodated to the wisdom of the angels who are there, and on earth it is accommodated to the apprehension of the men who are there. Wherefore in the Word there is an internal sense, which is spiritual, for the angels, and an external sense, which is natural, for men. Hence it is that the conjunction of heaven with man is effected through the Word.

No others understand the genuine sense of the Word but they who are enlightened; and they only are enlightened who are in love to, and have faith in, the Lord; for their interiors are elevated by the Lord into the light of heaven.

The Word in the letter cannot be understood, but by doctrine from the Word drawn by one who is enlightened. The sense of its letter is accommodated to the apprehension even of simple men, wherefore doctrine from the Word must serve them for a lamp.

FROM THE ARCANA COELESTIA. Of the necessity and Excellence of the Word. From the light of nature, nothing is known concerning the Lord, concerning heaven and hell, concerning the life of man after death, and concerning the Divine truths by which man has spiritual and eternal life (n. 8944, 10318-10320). This may be manifest from this, that many, and among them the learned, do not believe them, although they were born where the Word is, and are thereby instructed concerning them (n. 10319). It was therefore necessary that there should be some revelation from heaven, because man was born for heaven (n. 1775). Therefore in all time there has been a revelation (n. 2895). Concerning the various kinds of revelation which have been successively made on this earth (n. 10355, 10632). The most ancient people who lived before the flood, and whose age was called the golden age, had immediate revelation, and hence Divine truth was inscribed on their hearts (n. 2896). In the ancient churches which were after the flood, there was a Word, both historical and prophetical (n. 2686, 2897); concerning which churches see above (n. 247). Its historical parts were called the Wars of Jehovah, and its prophetical parts, Enunciations (n. 2897). That Word was like our Word as to inspiration (n. 2897). It is mentioned by Moses (n. 2686, 2897). But that Word is lost (n. 2897). There were also prophetic revelations with others, as appears from the prophecies of Balaam (n. 2898). The Word is Divine in each and every particular (n. 639, 680, 10321, 10637). The Word is Divine and holy as to every jot and tittle, from experience (n. 9349). How it is explained at this day, that the Word is inspired as to every jot (n. 1886). The church exists specifically where the Word is, and where the Lord is thereby known and Divine truths are revealed (n. 3857, 10761). But it does not follow from hence, that they are of the church who are born where the Word is, and where the Lord is thereby known, but they who by means of truths from the Word are regenerated by the Lord, that is, who live according to the truths therein, thus who lead a life of love and of faith (n. 6637, 10143, 10153, 10578, 10645, 10829).

The Word is not understood except by those who are enlightened. The human rational cannot apprehend Divine things, nor even spiritual things, unless it is enlightened by the Lord (n. 2196, 2203, 2209, 2654). Thus only they who are enlightened apprehend the Word (n. 10323). The Lord enables those who are enlightened to understand truth, and to see how to reconcile those things in the Word which may appear to contradict each other (n. 9382, 10659). The Word in the sense of the letter is not consistent with itself, and sometimes it appears contradictory (n. 9025). And therefore it may be explained and strained by those who are not enlightened, to confirm any opinion or heresy whatever, and to patronize any worldly and corporeal love (n. 4783, 10399, 10400). They who read the Word from the love of truth and good, are enlightened from it, but not they who read it from the love of fame, gain, or honor, thus from the love of self (n. 9382, 10548-10550). They who are in the good of life, and thereby in the affection of truth, are enlightened (n. 8694). They whose internal is open, and who thus as to their internal man are capable of being elevated into the light of heaven, are enlightened (n. 10400, 10402, 10691, 10694). Enlightenment is an actual opening of the interiors of the mind, and elevation of them into the light of heaven (n. 10330). Holiness from the internal, that is, through the internal from the Lord, inflows with those who esteem the Word to be holy, though they themselves do not know it (n. 6789). They who are led by the Lord are enlightened, and see truths in the Word, but not they who are led by self (n. 10638). They who love truth because it is truth, that is, who love to live according to Divine truths, are led by the Lord (n. 10578, 10645, 10829). The Word is vivified with man, according to his life of love and faith (n. 1776). Those things which are from one's own intelligence have no life in them, since nothing good proceeds from man's proprium (n. 8491, 8944). They who have much confirmed themselves in false doctrine cannot be enlightened (n. 10640). It is the understanding that is enlightened (n. 6608, 9300). Because the understanding is recipient of truth (n. 6222, 6608, 10659). There are ideas concerning every doctrinal of the church, according to which is the understanding of the subject (n. 3310, 3825). A man's ideas, so long as he lives in the world, are natural, because he then thinks in the natural, but nevertheless spiritual ideas lie concealed therein with those who are in the affection of truth for the sake of truth (n. 10237, 10240, 10551). There is no perception of any subject without ideas (n. 3825). The ideas concerning the things of faith are opened in the other life, and their quality is then seen by the angels (n. 1869, 3310, 5510, 6200, 8885). Therefore the Word is not understood except by a rational man; for to believe anything without having an idea of the subject, and without a rational view of it, is only to retain words in the memory, destitute of all the life of perception and affection, which is not believing (n. 2553). The literal sense of the Word is what is enlightened (n. 34, 36, 9824, 9905, 10548).

The Word cannot be understood but by means of doctrine from the Word. The doctrine of the church must be from the Word (n. 3464, 5402, 6832, 10763, 10765). The Word without doctrine is not understood (n. 9025, 9409, 9424, 9430, 10324, 10431, 10582). True doctrine is a lamp to those who read the Word (n. 10400). Genuine doctrine must be formed by those who are in enlightenment from the Lord (n. 2510, 2516, 2519, 9424, 10105). The Word is understood by means of doctrine formed by one who is enlightened (n. 10324). They who are in enlightenment form doctrine for themselves from the Word (n. 9382, 10659). The difference between those who teach and learn from the doctrine of the church, and those who teach and learn only from the sense of the letter, their quality (n. 9025). They who are in the sense of the letter without doctrine, come into no understanding of Divine truths (n. 9409, 9410, 10582). They fall into many errors (n. 10431). They who are in the affection of truth for the sake of truth, when they arrive at adult age, and can see from their own understanding, do not simply abide in the doctrinals of their own church, but examine from the Word whether they are truths (n. 5402, 5432, 6047). Otherwise every man's truth would be derived from others, and from his native soil, whether he was born a Jew or a Greek (n. 6047). Nevertheless such things as are become of faith from the literal sense of the Word, ought not to be extinguished till after a full view (n. 9039). The true doctrine of the church is the doctrine of charity and faith (n. 2417, 4766, 10763, 10764). The doctrine of faith does not make the church, but the life of faith, which is charity (n. 809, 1798, 1799, 1834, 4468, 4672, 4766, 5826, 6637). Doctrinals are nothing unless one lives according to them (n. 1515, 2049, 2116). In the churches at this day the doctrine of faith is taught, and not the doctrine of charity, the latter being degraded into a science which is called moral theology (n. 2417). The church would be one, if men were acknowledged as members of the church from life, thus from charity (n. 1285, 1316, 2982, 3267, 3445, 3451, 3452). How much superior the doctrine of charity is to that of faith separate from charity (n. 4844). They who do not know anything concerning charity, are in ignorance concerning heavenly things (n. 2435). Into how many errors they fall who only hold the doctrine of faith, and not that of charity at the same time (n. 2338, 2417, 3146, 3325, 3412, 3413, 3416, 3773, 4672, 4730, 4783, 4925, 5351, 7623-7627, 7752-7762, 7790, 8094, 8313, 8530, 8765, 9186, 9224, 10555). They who are only in the doctrine of faith, and not in the life of faith, which is charity, were formerly called uncircumcised, or Philistines (n. 3412, 3413, 8093). The ancients held the doctrine of love to the Lord, and of charity towards the neighbor, and made the doctrine of faith subservient thereto (n. 2417, 3419, 4844, 4955). Doctrine made by one enlightened may be afterwards confirmed by means of rational things, and thus it is more fully understood, and is corroborated (n. 2553, 2719, 2720, 3052, 3310, 6047). See more on this subject (at n. 51 above). They who are in faith separate from charity would have the doctrinals of the church implicitly believed without any rational intuition (n. 3394). It is not the part of a wise man to confirm a dogma, but to see whether it is true before he confirms it, as is the case with those who are in enlightenment (n. 1017, 4741, 7012, 7680, 7950). The light of confirmation is natural light, and not spiritual, and may exist even with the evil (n. 8780). All things, even falsities, can be confirmed so as to appear like truths (n. 2480,

2490, 5033, 6865, 8521).

In the Word there is a spiritual sense, which is called the internal sense. No one can know what the internal sense of the Word is, unless he knows what correspondence is (n. 2895, 4322). The whole and every part, even to the most minute, of the natural world, corresponds to spiritual things, and thence is significative of them (n. 1886-1889, 2987-3003, 3213-3227). The spiritual things to which natural things correspond assume another appearance in the natural, so that they are not distinguished (n. 1887, 2395, 8920). Scarcely anyone knows at this day, where, or in what part is the Divine of the Word, when nevertheless it is in its internal or spiritual sense, which at this day is not known (n. 2899, 4989). The mystic things of the Word are nothing else than what its internal or spiritual sense contains, which treats of the Lord, of His kingdom, and of the church, and not of the natural things which are in the world (n. 4923). The prophetic parts of the Word are in many places unintelligible, and therefore of no use without the internal sense; illustrated by examples (n. 2608, 8020, 8398). As what is signified by "the white horse," mentioned in Revelation (n. 2760 seq.). By "the keys of the kingdom of the heavens" that were given to Peter, see the Preface to the 22nd chapter of Genesis (n. 9410). By "the flesh," "blood," "bread," and "wine," in the Holy Supper, and thus why it was instituted by the Lord (n. 8682). By the prophecies of Jacob concerning his sons in the 49th chapter of Genesis (n. 6306, 6333-6465). By many prophecies concerning Judah and Israel, which by no means tally with that people, nor in the literal sense have any coincidence with their history (n. 6333, 6361, 6415, 6438, 6444). Besides innumerable other instances (n. 2608). Of the spiritual or internal sense of the Word in a summary (n. 1767-1777, 1869-1879). There is an internal sense in the whole and in every particular part of the Word (n. 1143, 1984, 2135, 2333, 2395, 2495, 2619). Such things do not appear in the sense of the letter, but nevertheless they are contained within it (n. 4442).

The internal sense of the Word is principally for the use of angels, and it is also for the use of men. In order that it may be known what the internal sense is, of what quality it is, and whence it is, it may here be observed in general, that they speak and think in heaven differently from the way they do in the world; in heaven spiritually, but in the world naturally; therefore when man reads the Word, the angels who are with him perceive it spiritually, whilst he perceives it naturally; consequently, the angels are in the internal sense, whilst men are in the external sense; nevertheless these two senses make one by correspondence. The Word is understood differently by the angels in the heavens and by men on earth, the angels perceiving the internal or spiritual sense, but men the external or natural sense (n. 1887, 2395). The angels perceive the Word in its internal sense, and not in its external sense, proved from the experience of those who spoke with me from heaven, whilst I was reading the Word (n. 1769-1772). The ideas and speech of the angels are spiritual, but the ideas and speech of men are natural; therefore there is an internal sense, which is spiritual, for the use of the angels, illustrated by experience (n. 2333). Nevertheless the sense of the letter of the Word serves the spiritual ideas of the angels as a means of conveyance, just as the words of speech serve men to convey the sense of the subject (n. 2143). The things relating to the internal sense of the Word, fall into such things as belong to the light of heaven, thus into the perception of angels (n. 2618, 2619, 2629, 3086). The things which the angels perceive from the Word are on this account precious to them (n. 2540, 2541, 2545, 2551). The angels do not understand a single syllable of the sense of the letter of the Word (n. 64, 65, 1434, 1929). They do not know the names of persons and places mentioned in the Word (n. 1434, 1888, 4442, 4480). Names cannot enter heaven, nor be pronounced there (n. 1876, 1888). All names mentioned in the Word signify things, and in heaven are changed into the ideas of the thing (n. 768, 1888, 4310, 4442, 5225, 5287, 10329). The angels think abstractly from persons (n. 6613, 8343, 8985, 9007). How elegant the internal sense of the Word is, even where nothing but mere names occur, shown by examples from the Word (n. 1224, 1888, 2395). Many names in a series express one thing in the internal sense (n. 5095). All numbers in the Word signify things (n. 482, 487, 647, 648, 755, 813, 1963, 1988, 2075, 2252, 3252, 4264, 6175, 9488, 9659, 10217, 10253). Spirits also perceive the Word in its internal sense, so far as their interiors are open into heaven (n. 1771). The sense of the letter of the Word, which is natural, is changed instantly with the angels into the spiritual sense, because there is a correspondence (n. 5648). And this is effected without their hearing or knowing what is contained in the literal or external sense (n. 10215). Thus the literal or external sense is only with man, and proceeds no further (n. 2015). There is an internal sense of the Word, and likewise an inmost or supreme sense, concerning which see (n. 9407, 10604, 10614, 10627). The spiritual angels, that is, those who belong to the spiritual kingdom of the Lord, perceive the Word in its internal sense, and the celestial angels, that is, those who belong to the celestial kingdom of the Lord, perceive the Word in its inmost sense (n. 2157, 2275). The Word is for men, and also for angels, being accommodated to each (n. 7381, 8862, 10322). The Word is the means of uniting heaven and earth (n. 2310, 2495, 9212, 9216, 9357). The conjunction of heaven with man is effected by means of the Word (n. 9396, 9400, 9401, 10452). Therefore the Word is called "a covenant" (n. 9396). Because "covenant" signifies conjunction (n. 665, 666, 1023, 1038, 1864, 1996, 2003, 2021, 6804, 8767, 8778, 9396, 10632). There is an internal sense in the Word, because the Word has descended from the Lord through the three heavens to man (n. 2310, 6597). And thereby it is accommodated to the angels of the three heavens, and also to men (n. 7381, 8862). Hence it is that the Word is Divine (n. 2989, 4989); and is holy (n. 10276); and is spiritual (n. 4480); and is divinely inspired (n. 9094). This is the meaning of inspiration (n. 9094). The regenerate man also, is actually in the internal sense of the Word, although he knows it not, since his internal man, which is endowed with spiritual perception, is open (n. 10400). But in this case the spiritual of the Word flows into natural ideas, and thus is presented naturally, because, while man lives in the world, he thinks in the natural (n. 5614). Hence the light of truth, with the enlightened, is from their internal, that is, through their internal from the Lord (n. 10691, 10694). By the same way holiness flows in with those who esteem the Word holy (n. 6789). As the regenerate man is actually in the internal sense of the Word, and in the sanctity of that sense, although he does not know it, therefore after death he comes into it, and is no longer in the sense of the letter (n. 3226, 3342, 3343).

The internal or spiritual sense of the Word contains innumerable arcana.

The Word in its internal sense contains innumerable things, which exceed human comprehension (n. 3085, 3086). It also contains inexplicable things (n. 1965). Which are represented only to angels, and understood by them (n. 167). The internal sense of the Word contains arcana of heaven, which relate to the Lord and His kingdom in the heavens and on earth (n. 1-4, 937). Those arcana do not appear in the sense of the letter (n. 937, 1502, 2161). Many things in the prophets appear to be disconnected, when yet in their internal sense they cohere in a regular and beautiful series (n. 7153, 9022). Not a single word, nor even a single iota can be omitted in the sense of the letter of the Word, without an interruption in the internal sense, and therefore, by the Divine Providence of the Lord, the Word has been preserved so entire as to every word and every point (n. 7933). Innumerable things are contained in every particular of the Word (n. 6617, 6620, 8920); and in every expression (n. 1689). There are innumerable things contained in the Lord's prayer, and in every part thereof (n. 6619). And in the precepts of the Decalogue; in the external sense of which, notwithstanding, some things are such as are known to every nation without revelation (n. 8867, 8900). In the Word, and particularly in the prophetical parts of it, two expressions are used that seem to signify the same thing, but one expression has relation to good, and the other to truth; thus one relates to what is spiritual, the other to what is celestial (n. 683, 707, 2516, 8339). Goods and truths are conjoined in a wonderful manner in the Word, and that conjunction is apparent only to him who knows the internal sense (n. 10554). And thus there is a Divine marriage and a heavenly marriage in the Word, and in every part thereof (n. 683, 793, 801, 2173, 2516, 2712, 5138, 7022). The Divine marriage is the marriage of Divine good and Divine truth, thus it is the Lord, in whom alone that marriage exists (n. 3004, 3005, 3009, 5138, 5194, 5502, 6343, 7945, 8339, 9263, 9314). "Jesus" signifies the Divine good, and "Christ" the Divine truth; and both the Divine marriage in heaven, which is the marriage of the Divine good and the Divine truth (n. 3004, 3005, 3009). This marriage is in every part of the Word, in its internal sense; thus the Lord, as to the Divine good and the Divine truth, is in every part of the Word (n. 5502). The marriage of good and truth from the Lord in heaven and the church, is called the heavenly marriage (n. 2508, 2618, 2803, 3004, 3211, 3952, 6179). Therefore in this respect the Word is a kind of heaven (n. 2173, 10126). Heaven is compared in the Word to a marriage, on account of the marriage of good and truth therein (n. 2758, 3132, 4434, 4835). The internal sense is the very doctrine of the church (n. 9025, 9430, 10400). They who understand the Word according to the internal sense, know the essential true doctrine of the church, inasmuch as the internal sense contains it (n. 9025; 9430, 10400). The internal of the Word is also the internal of the church, and likewise the internal of worship (n. 10460). The Word is the doctrine of love to the Lord, and of charity towards the neighbor (n. 3419, 3420). The Word in the letter is as a cloud, and in the internal sense it is glory, see the Preface to the 18th chapter of Genesis (n. 5922, 6343), where the words, "The Lord shall come in the clouds of heaven with glory," are explained. "A cloud" in the Word signifies the Word in the sense of the letter, and "glory" signifies the Word in the internal sense, see the Preface to the 18th chapter of Genesis (n. 4060, 4391, 5922, 6343, 6752, 8106, 8781, 9430, 10551, 10574). Those things which are in the sense of the letter, respectively to those which are in the internal sense, are like rude projections round a polished optical cylinder, by which nevertheless is exhibited in the cylinder a beautiful image of a man (n. 1871). In the other life, they who only allow and acknowledge the sense of the letter of the Word, are represented by a deformed old woman; but they who allow and acknowledge the internal sense, together with the literal sense, are represented by a virgin beautifully clothed (n. 1774). The Word in its whole complex is an image of heaven, since the Word is the Divine truth, and the Divine truth makes heaven; and as heaven relates to one man, therefore the Word is in that respect as an image of man (n. 1871). Heaven in one complex relates to one man, may be seen in the work on Heaven and Hell (n. 59-67). And the Divine truth proceeding from the Lord makes heaven (n. 126-140, 200-212). The Word is beautifully and agreeably exhibited before the angels (n. 1767, 1768). The sense of the letter is as the body, and the internal sense, as the soul of that body (n. 8943). Thence the life of the Word is from its internal sense (n. 1405, 4857). The Word is pure in the internal sense, and does not appear so in the literal sense (n. 2362, 2395). The things which are in the sense of the letter of the Word are holy from the internal (n. 10126, 10728). In the historical parts of the Word there is also an internal sense, but within them (n. 4989). Thus the historical as well as the prophetic parts of the Word contain arcana of heaven (n. 755, 1659, 1709, 2310, 2333). The angels do not perceive those historical things, but spiritually (n. 6884). The reason why the interior arcana which are in the historicals, are less evident to man than those that are in the propheticals (n. 2176, 6597). The quality of the internal sense of the Word further shown (n. 1756, 1984, 2004, 2663, 3035, 7089, 10604, 10614). And illustrated by comparisons (n. 1873).

The Word is written by correspondences, and thus by representatives. The Word, as to its literal sense, is written by mere correspondences, thus by such things as represent and signify spiritual things which relate to heaven and the church (n. 1404, 1408, 1409, 1540, 1619, 1659, 1709, 1783, 2179, 2763, 2899). This was done for the sake of the internal sense, which is contained in every part (n. 2899). For the sake of heaven, since those who are in heaven do not understand the Word according to the sense of the letter, which is natural, but according to its internal sense, which is spiritual (n. 2899). The Lord spoke by correspondences, representatives, and significatives, because He spoke from the Divine (n. 9048, 9063, 9086, 10126, 10728). Thus the Lord spoke at the same time before the world and before heaven (n. 2533, 4807, 9048, 9063, 9086). The things which the Lord spoke filled the entire heaven (n. 4637). The historicals of the Word are representative, and the words significative (n. 1540, 1659, 1709, 1783, 2686). The Word could not be written in any other style, that by it there might be a communication and conjunction with the heavens (n. 2899, 6943, 9481). They who despise the Word on account of the apparent simplicity and rudeness of its style, and who fancy that they would receive the Word, if it were written in a different style, are in a great error (n. 8783). The mode and style of writing, which prevailed amongst the most ancient people, was by representatives and significatives (n. 605, 1756, 9942). The ancient wise men were delighted with the Word, because of the representatives and significatives therein, from experience (n. 2592, 2593). If a man of the Most Ancient Church had read the Word, he would have seen the things which are in the internal sense clearly, and those which are in the external sense obscurely (n. 4493). The sons of Jacob were brought into the land of Canaan, because all the places in that land, from the most ancient times, were made representative (n. 1585, 3686, 4447, 5136, 6516). And thus that the Word might there be written, in which Word those places were to be mentioned for the sake of the internal sense (n. 3686, 4447, 5136, 6516). But nevertheless the Word was changed, for the sake of that nation, as to the external sense, but not as to the internal sense (n. 10453, 10461, 10603, 10604). In order that it may be known what the correspondences and representatives in the Word are, and what is their quality, something shall also be said concerning them. All things which correspond are likewise representative, and thereby significative, thus that correspondences and representatives are one (n. 2896, 2897, 2973, 2987, 2989, 2990, 3002, 3225). What correspondences and representations are, from experience and examples (n. 2763, 2987-3002, 3213-3226, 3337-3352, 3472-3485, 4218-4228, 9280). The knowledge of correspondences and representations was the chief science amongst the ancients (n. 3021, 3419, 4280, 4748, 4844, 4964, 4966, 6004, 7729, 10252). Especially with the Orientals (n. 5702, 6692, 7097, 7779, 9391, 10252, 10407); and in Egypt more than in other countries (n. 5702, 6692, 7097, 7779, 9391, 10407). Also among the Gentiles, as in Greece and other places (n. 2762, 7729). But at this day it is among the sciences which are lost, particularly in Europe (n. 2894, 2895, 2994, 3630, 3632, 3747-3749, 4581, 4966, 10252). Nevertheless this science is more excellent than all other sciences, since without it the Word is not understood, nor the signification of the rites of the Jewish church, which are recorded in the Word; neither is it known what heaven is, nor what the spiritual is, nor in what manner spiritual influx takes place into what is natural, with many other things (n. 4280, and in the places above cited). All the things which appear before angels and spirits, are representatives, according to correspondences of such things as relate to love and faith (n. 1971, 3213-3226, 3449, 3475, 3485, 9481, 9574, 9576, 9577). The heavens are full of representatives (n. 1521, 1532, 1619). Representatives are more beautiful, and more perfect, in proportion as they are more interiorly in the heavens (n. 3475). Representatives there are real appearances, being derived from the light of heaven, which is Divine truth, and which is the very essential of the existence of all things (n. 3485). The reason why each and all things in the spiritual world are represented in the natural world, is because what is internal assumes a suitable clothing in what is external, whereby it makes itself visible and apparent (n. 6275, 6284, 6299). Thus the end assumes a suitable clothing, that it may exist as the cause in a lower sphere, and afterwards that it may exist as the effect in a sphere lower still; and when the end, by means of the cause, becomes the effect, it then becomes visible, or appears before the eyes (n. 5711). This may be illustrated by the influx of the soul into the body, whereby the soul assumes a clothing of such things in the body, as enable all the things which it thinks and wills, to appear and become visible; wherefore the thought, when it flows down into the body, is represented by gestures and actions which correspond thereto (n. 2988). The affections, which are of the mind, are manifestly represented in the face, by the variations of the countenance, so that they may be seen therein (n. 4791-4805, 5695). Hence it is evident, that each and all things in nature have in them a latent cause and end from the spiritual world (n. 3562, 5711). Since the things in nature are ultimate effects, which contain prior things (n. 4240, 4939, 5051, 6275, 6284, 6299, 9216). Internal things are represented, and external things represent (n. 4292). Since all things in nature are representative of spiritual and celestial things, therefore, in ancient times, there were churches, wherein all the externals, which are rituals, were representative; wherefore those churches were called representative churches (n. 519, 521, 2896). The church founded with the sons of Israel was a representative church (n. 1003, 2179, 10149). All its rituals were external things, which represented the internal things of heaven and the church (n. 4288, 4874). Representatives of the church and of worship ceased when the Lord came into the world, because the Lord opened the internal things of the church, and because all the externals of the church in the highest sense regarded Him (n. 4832).

Of the literal or external sense of the Word. The sense of the letter of the Word is according to appearances in the world (n. 589, 926, 1408, 2719, 2720, 1832, 1874, 2242, 2520, 2533). And is adapted to the capacity of the simple (n. 2533, 9048, 9063, 9086). The Word in its literal sense is natural (n. 8783). Because what is natural is the ultimate wherein spiritual and celestial things terminate, and upon which they rest like a house upon its foundation; and otherwise the internal sense of the Word without the external, would be like a house without a foundation (n. 9360, 9430, 9433, 9824, 10044, 10436). The Word is the containant of a spiritual and celestial sense, because it is of such a quality (n. 9407). And that it is holy and Divine in the sense of the letter as to each and all things therein, even to every iota, because it is of such a quality (n. 639, 680, 1869, 1870, 9198, 10321, 10637). The laws enacted for the sons of Israel, are yet the Holy Word, notwithstanding their abrogation, on account of the internal sense which they contain (n. 9211, 9259, 9349). Of the laws, judgments and statutes, for the Israelitish and Jewish church, which was a representative church, there are some which are still in force, both in their external and internal sense; some which ought to be strictly observed in their external sense; some which may be of use, if people are disposed to observe them, and some which are altogether abrogated (n. 9349). The Word is Divine, even as to those which are abrogated (n. 10637). The quality of the Word as to the sense of the letter, if not understood at the same time as to the internal sense, or what is the same thing, according to true doctrine from the Word (n. 10402). Innumerable heresies arise from the sense of the letter without the internal sense, or without true doctrine from the Word (n. 10400). They who are in an external without an internal cannot endure the interior things of the Word (n. 10694). The Jews were of such a quality, and they are also such at this day (n. 301-303, 3479, 4429, 4433, 4680, 4844, 4847, 10396, 10401, 10407, 10694, 10701, 10707).

The Lord is the Word. The Word in its inmost sense treats only of the Lord, and describes all the states of the glorification of His Human, that is, of its union with the Divine itself; and likewise all the states of the subjugation of the hells, and of the ordination of all things therein and in the heavens (n. 2249, 7014). Thus the Lord's whole life in the world is described in that sense, and thereby the Lord is continually present with the angels (n. 2523). Consequently the Lord alone is in the inmost of the Word, and the Divinity and sanctity of the Word is from thence (n. 1873, 9357). The Lord's saying that all the Scripture

concerning Him was fulfilled, signifies that all things which are contained in the
inmost sense were fulfilled (n. 7933). The Word signifies the Divine truth (n.
4692, 5075, 9987). The Lord is the Word because He is the Divine truth (n.
2533). The Lord is the Word also because the Word is from Him, and treats of
Him (n. 2859). And because it treats of the Lord alone in its inmost sense, thus
because the Lord Himself is therein (n. 1873, 9357). And because in each and
all things of the Word there is a marriage of Divine good and Divine truth (n.
3004, 5502). "Jesus" is the Divine good, and "Christ" the Divine truth (n. 3004,
3005, 3009). The Divine truth is alone real, and that in which Divine truth is,
which is from the Divine, is alone substantial (n. 5272, 6880, 7004, 8200). And
as the Divine truth proceeding from the Lord is light in heaven, and the Divine
good is heat in heaven; and as all things in heaven derive their existence from
the Divine good and the Divine truth; and as the natural world has its existence
through heaven, or the spiritual world; it is plain that all things which were
created, were created from the Divine truth, or from the Word, according to
these words in John: In the beginning was the Word, and the Word was with
God, and God was the Word, and by it were all things made which were made;
and the Word was made flesh (John 1:1, 3, 14; n. 2803, 2894, 5272, 6880).
Further particulars concerning the creation of all things by the Divine truth,
consequently by the Lord, may be seen in the work on Heaven and Hell (n. 137).
And more fully in the two articles therein (n. 116-125, and n. 126-140). The
conjunction of the Lord with man is effected through the Word, by means of the
internal sense (n. 10375). Conjunction is effected by each and all things of the
Word, and the Word is therefore more wonderful than all other writings (n.
10632-10634). Since the Word has been written, the Lord thereby speaks with
men (n. 10290).

Of those who are against the Word. Of those who despise, mock at,
blaspheme, and profane the Word (n. 1878). Their quality in the other life (n.
1761, 9322). They may be compared to the viscous parts of the blood (n. 5719).
The danger of profaning the Word (n. 571-582). How hurtful it is if principles
of falsity, particularly those which favor the loves of self and of the world, are
confirmed by the Word (n. 589). They who are in no affection of truth for the
sake of truth, utterly reject the internal sense of the Word, and nauseate it,
from experience (n. 5702). Some in the other life who have rejected the interior
things of the Word, are deprived of rationality (n. 1879).

Further particulars concerning the Word. The term "Word" in the Hebrew
tongue signifies various things, as speech, thought of the mind, everything that
has a real existence, and also anything (n. 9987). "Word" signifies the Divine
truth and the Lord (n. 4692, 5075, 9987). "Words" signify truths (n. 4692, 5075).
They signify doctrinals (n. 1288). The "ten words" signify all Divine truths (n.
10688). They signify things which really exist (n. 1785, 5075, 5272). In the
Word, particularly in the propheticals, there are two expressions to signify one
thing, and the one has relation to good and the other to truth, which are thus
conjoined (n. 683, 707, 2516, 8339). It cannot be known what expression has
relation to good, and what to truth, but from the internal sense of the Word; for
there are appropriate words by which the things relating to good are expressed,
and appropriate words by which the things relating to truth are expressed (n.
793, 801). And this so that it may be known merely from the words predicated,

whether the subject treated of is good, or whether it is truth (n. 2722). Frequently one expression implies a general, and the other expression implies a certain specific particular of that general (n. 2212). There is a species of reciprocation in the Word, concerning which see n. 2240. Most things in the Word have also an opposite sense (n. 4816). The internal sense proceeds regularly according to the subject predicated (n. 4502). They who have been delighted with the Word, in the other life receive the heat of heaven, wherein is celestial love, according to the quality and quantity of their delight from love (n. 1773).

What are the Books of the Word. The books of the Word are all those which have the internal sense; but those books which have not the internal sense, are not the Word. The books of the Word, in the Old Testament, are the five Books of Moses, the Book of Joshua, the Book of Judges, the two Books of Samuel, the two Books of Kings, the Psalms of David, the Prophets Isaiah, Jeremiah, Lamentations, Ezekiel, Daniel, Hosea, Joel, Amos, Obadiah, Jonah, Micah, Nahum, Habakkuk, Zephaniah, Haggai, Zechariah, Malachi: and in the New Testament, the four Evangelists, Matthew, Mark, Luke, John; and the Apocalypse. The rest have not the internal sense (10325).

XXI. PROVIDENCE. The government of the Lord in the heavens and in the earths is called Providence; and because all the good of love and all the truth of faith, from which is salvation, are from Him, and nothing at all from man, it is evident therefrom that the Divine Providence of the Lord is in each and all the things which conduce to the salvation of the human race. This the Lord thus teaches in John: I am the way, the truth, and the life (John 14:6); and in another place: As the branch cannot bear fruit of itself, unless it shall abide in the vine, so neither can ye, unless ye shall abide in Me; without Me ye cannot do anything (John 15:4, 5).

The Divine Providence of the Lord extends to the most minute things of a man's life; for there is only one fountain of life, which is the Lord, from whom we are, we live, and we act.

They who think from worldly things concerning the Divine Providence, conclude from them that it is only universal, and that the particulars appertain to man. But they do not know the arcana of heaven, for they form their conclusions only from the loves of self and of the world, and their pleasures; wherefore, when they see the evil exalted to honors, and acquire wealth more than the good, and also succeed in evils according to their arts, they say in their heart, that it would not be so if the Divine Providence were in each and all things; but they do not consider that the Divine Providence does not regard that which soon passes away, and ends with the life of man in the world, but that it regards that which remains to eternity, thus which has no end. What has no end, that is; but what has an end, that respectively is not. Let him who can, think whether a hundred thousand years are anything compared to eternity, and he will perceive that they are not; what then are some years of life in the world?

Everyone who rightly considers, may know that eminence and opulence in the world are not real divine blessings, notwithstanding man, from his pleasure in them, calls them so; for they pass away, and also seduce many, and turn them away from heaven; but that eternal life, and its happiness, are real blessings, which are from the Divine: this the Lord also teaches in Luke: Make to yourselves a treasure in the heavens that faileth not, where the thief approacheth not, neither the moth corrupteth; for where your treasure is, there will your heart be also (Luke 12:33, 34).

The reason why the evil succeed in evils according to their arts is, because it is according to Divine order that everyone should act what he acts from reason, and also from freedom; wherefore, unless man were left to act from freedom according to his reason, and thus unless the arts which are thence derived were to succeed, man could by no means be disposed to receive eternal life, for this is insinuated when man is in freedom, and his reason is enlightened. For no one can be compelled to good because nothing that is compelled inheres with him, for it is not his own: that becomes a man's own, which is done from freedom according to his reason, and that is done from freedom which is done from the will or love, and the will or love is the man himself. If a man were compelled to that which he does not will, his mind would continually incline to that which he wills; and besides, everyone strives after what is forbidden, and this from a latent cause, because he strives for freedom. Whence it is evident that unless man were kept in freedom, good could not be provided for him.

To leave man from his own freedom also to think, to will, and, so far as the laws do not restrain him, to do evil, is called permitting.

To be led to felicities in the world by arts, appears to man as if it were from his own prudence, but still the Divine providence continually accompanies by permitting and continually leading away from evil. But to be led to felicities in heaven is known and perceived to be not from man's own prudence, because it is from the Lord, and is effected of His Divine providence by disposing and continually leading to good.

That this is so, man cannot comprehend from the light of nature, for from that light he does not know the laws of Divine order.

It is to be known that there is providence, and there is foresight; good is what is provided by the Lord, but evil is what is foreseen by the Lord. The one must accompany the other, for what comes from man is nothing but evil, but what comes from the Lord is nothing but good. FROM THE ARCANA COELESTIA Since all the good which is provided for man by the Lord flows in, we will therefore adduce from the Arcana Coelestia the particulars there concerning Influx: and since the Lord provides all things according to Divine order, we will also adduce from that work the particulars concerning Order.

Of Providence. Providence is the government of the Lord in the heavens and on the earth (n. 10773). The Lord, from providence, rules all things according to order, and thus providence is government according to order (n. 1755, 2447). And He rules all things either from will or from leave, or from permission; thus in various respects according to man's quality (n. 1755, 2447, 3704, 9940). Providence acts invisibly (n. 5508). Most things which are done from providence appeal to man as contingencies (n. 5508). Providence acts invisibly, in order that man may not be compelled to believe from visible things, and thus that his free-will may not be injured; for unless man has freedom he cannot be reformed, thus he cannot be saved (n. 1937, 1947, 2876, 2881, 3854, 5508, 5982, 6477, 8209, 8987, 9588, 10409, 10777). The Divine providence does not regard temporary things which soon pass away, but eternal things (n. 5264, 8717, 10776; illustrated n. 6491). They who do not comprehend this, believe that opulence and eminence in the world are the only things to be provided, and call such things blessings from the Divine, when nevertheless they are not regarded as blessings by the Lord, but only as means conducive to the life of man in the world; but that those things are regarded by the Lord which conduce to man's eternal happiness (n. 10409, 10776). They who are in the Divine providence of the Lord, are led in each and all things to eternal happiness (n. 8478, 8480). They who ascribe all things to nature and man's own prudence, and nothing to the Divine, do not think or comprehend this (n. 6481, 10409, 10775). The Divine providence of the Lord is not, as believed in the world, universal only, and the particulars and single thing dependent on man's prudence (n. 8717, 10775). No universal exists but from and with single things, because single things taken together are called a universal, as particulars taken together are called a general (n. 1919, 6159, 6338, 6482-6484). Every universal is such as the single things of which it is formed, and with which it is (n. 917, 1040, 6483, 8857). The providence of the Lord is universal, because existing in the most single things (n. 1919, 2694, 4329, 5122, 5904, 6058, 6481-6486, 6490, 7004, 7007, 8717, 10774); confirmed from heaven (n. 6486). Unless the Divine providence of the Lord were universal, from and in the most single things, nothing could subsist (n. 6338). All things are disposed by it into order, and kept in order both in general and in particular (n. 6338). How the case herein is comparatively with that of a king on earth (n. 6482, 10800). Man's own proper prudence is like a small speck of dirt in the universe, whilst the Divine providence is respectively as the universe itself (n. 6485). This can hardly be comprehended by men in the world (n. 8717, 10775, 10780). Because many fallacies assail them, and induce blindness (n. 6481). Of a certain person in the other life, who believed from confirmation in the world, that all things were dependent on man's own prudence, and nothing on the Divine providence; the things belonging to him appeared infernal (n. 6484). The quality of the Lord's providence with respect to evils (n. 6481, 6495, 6574, 10777, 10779). Evils are ruled by the Lord by the laws of permission, and they are permitted for the sake of order (n. 8700, 10778). The permission of evil by the Lord is not that of one who wills, but of one who does not will, but who cannot bring aid on account of the urgency of the end, which is salvation (n. 7887). To leave man from his own freedom to think and will evil, and so far as the laws do not forbid, to do evil, is to permit (n. 10778). Without freedom, thus without this permission, man could not be reformed, thus could not be saved, may be seen above in the doctrine of Freedom (n. 141-149). The Lord has providence and foresight, and the one does not exist without the other (n. 5195, 6489). Good is provided by the Lord, and evil foreseen (n. 5155, 5195, 6489, 10781). There is no such thing as predestination or fate (n. 6487). All are predestined to heaven, and none to hell (n. 6488). Man is under no absolute necessity from providence but has full liberty, illustrated by comparison (n. 6487). The "elect" in the Word are they who are in the life of good, and thence of truth (n. 3755, 3900, 5057, 5058). How it is to be understood that "God would deliver one man into another's hand" (Exod. 21:13) (n. 9010). Fortune, which appears in the world wonderful in many circumstances, is an operation of the Divine providence in the ultimate of order, according to the quality of man's state; and this may afford proof, that the Divine providence is in the most single of all things (n. 5049, 5179, 6493, 6494). This operation and its variations are from the spiritual world, proved from experience (n. 5179, 6493, 6494).

Of Influx. Of the influx of heaven into the world, and of the influx of the soul into all things of the body, from experience (n. 6053-6058, 6189-6215, 6307-6327, 6466-6495, 6598- 6626). Nothing exists of or from itself, but from what is prior to itself, thus all things from the First (n. 4523, 4524, 6040, 6056). As all things existed, they also subsist, because subsistence is perpetual existence (n. 2886, 2888, 3627, 3628, 3648, 4523, 4524, 6040, 6056). Influx takes place according to that order (n. 7270). Hence it is plain that all things subsist perpetually from the first esse, because they exist from it (n. 4523, 4524, 6040, 6056). The all of life flows in from the First, because it is thence derived, thus from the Lord (n. 3001, 3318, 3337, 3338, 3344, 3484, 3628, 3629, 3741-3743, 4318-4320, 4417, 4524, 4882, 5847, 5986, 6325, 6468-6470, 6479, 9279, 10196). Every existere is from an esse, and nothing can exist unless its esse be in it (n. 4523, 4524, 6040, 6056). All things which a man thinks and wills flow into him, from experience (n. 904, 2886-2888, 4151, 4319, 4320, 5846, 5848, 6189, 6191, 6194, 6197-6199, 6213, 7147, 10219). Man's ability of examining things, and of thinking and forming analytic conclusions, is from influx (n. 2888, 4319, 4320). Man could not live a moment if the influx from the spiritual world were taken away from him; but still man is in freedom, from experience (n. 2887, 5849, 5854, 6321). The life which flows in from the Lord is varied according to man's state and according to reception (n. 2069, 5986, 6472, 7343). With the evil, the good which flows from the Lord is turned into evil, and the truth into falsity, from experience (n. 3643, 4632). The good and truth, which continually flow from the Lord, are so far received, as evil and falsity do not oppose their reception (n. 2411, 3142, 3147, 5828). All good flows in from the Lord, and all evil from hell (n. 904, 4151). At this day man believes all things to be in himself and from himself, when nevertheless they inflow, as he might know from the doctrinal of the church, that all good is from heaven, and all evil from hell (n. 4249, 6193, 6206). But if he would believe as the thing is, he would not appropriate evil to himself, but cast it back from himself into hell, neither would he make good his own, and thus would not claim any merit from it (n. 6206, 6324, 6325). How happy the state of man would then be, as he would view both good and evil from within, from the Lord (n. 6325). They who deny heaven, or know nothing about it, do not know there is any influx thence (n. 4322, 5649, 6193, 6479). What influx is, illustrated by comparisons (n. 6128, 6190, 9407). Influx is spiritual, and not physical, thus it is from the spiritual world into the natural, and not from the natural world into the spiritual (n. 3219, 5119, 5259, 5427, 5428, 5477, 6322, 9109, 9110). Influx is through the internal man, into the external, and not contrariwise (n. 1702, 1707, 1940, 1954, 5119, 5259, 5779, 6322, 9380). Because the internal man is in the spiritual world, and the external in the natural world (n. 978, 1015, 3628, 4459, 4523, 4524, 6057, 6309, 9701-9709, 10156, 10472). It appears as if influx is from externals into internals; this is a fallacy (n. 3721). Influx is into man's rational and through this into things scientific, and not contrariwise (n. 1495, 1707, 1940). The order of influx (n. 775, 880, 1096, 1495, 7270). There is immediate influx from the

Lord, and also mediate influx through the spiritual world or heaven (n. 6063, 6307, 6472, 9682, 9683). The immediate influx from the Lord enters into the most single of all things (n. 6058, 6474-6478, 8717, 8728). Of the mediate influx of the Lord through heaven (n. 4067, 6982, 6985, 6996). It is effected through the spirits and angels who are adjoined to man (n. 697, 5846-5866). The Lord, by means of angels, flows into the ends from which, and for the sake of which, a man so thinks, wills, and acts (n. 1317, 1645, 5846, 5854). And thus into those things which are of conscience with man (n. 6207, 6213). But by means of spirits into the thoughts, and thence into the things of the memory (n. 4186, 5854, 5858, 6192, 6193, 6198, 6199, 6319). This can with difficulty be believed by man (n. 6214). The Lord inflows into firsts and at the same time into ultimates, or into inmosts and at the same time into outmosts, how (n. 5147, 5150, 6473, 7004, 7007, 7270). The influx of the Lord is into good with man, and through good into truth, and not contrariwise (n. 5482, 5649, 6027, 8685, 8701, 10153). Good gives the faculty of receiving influx from the Lord, but not truth without good (n. 8321). It is not what enters the thought, but what enters the will, that is hurtful, because this is appropriated to the man (n. 6308). The Divine in the highest is tacit and pacific, but as it descends towards lower things in man, it becomes unpacific and tumultuous, on account of the things therein being in disorder (n. 8823). The quality of the Lord's influx with the prophets (n. 6212). There is a general influx, its quality (n. 5850). It is a continual effort of acting according to order (n. 6211). This influx takes place into the lives of animals (n. 5850). And also into the subjects of the vegetable kingdom (n. 3648). That thought is formed into speech and will into gestures with man, according to this general influx (n. 5862, 5990, 6192, 6211).

Of the influx of life with man in particular. There is one only fountain of life, from which all live both in heaven and in the world (n. 1954, 2021, 2536, 2658, 2886-2889, 3001, 3484, 3742, 5847, 6467). This life is from the Lord alone, illustrated by various things (n. 2886-2889, 3344, 3484, 4319, 4320, 4524, 4882, 5986, 6325, 6468-6470, 9276, 10196). The Lord is life itself, may be seen (John 1:1, 4; 5:26; 14:6). Life from the Lord flows in with angels, spirits, and men, in a wonderful manner (n. 2886-2889, 3337, 3338, 3484, 3742). The Lord flows in from His Divine love, which is of such that it wills that what is its own should be another's (n. 3742, 4320). All love is such; thus the Divine love is infinitely more so (n. 1820, 1865, 2253, 6872). Hence life appears as if it were in man, and not as inflowing (n. 3742, 4320). Life appears as if it were in man, because the principal cause, which is life from the Lord, and the instrumental cause, which is the recipient form, act as one cause, which is felt in the instrumental (n. 6325). The chief of the wisdom and intelligence of the angels consists in perceiving and knowing that the all of life is from the Lord (n. 4318). Concerning the joy of angels perceived and shown by their discourse to me, from this that they do not live from themselves, but from the Lord (n. 6469). The evil are not willing to be convinced that life inflows (n. 3743). Doubts concerning the influx of life from the Lord cannot be removed, so long as fallacies, ignorance, and the negative reign (n. 6479). All in the church know that all good and truth is from heaven, that is, through heaven from the Lord, and that all evil and falsity is from hell; and yet the all of life has relation to good and truth, and to evil and falsity, there being nothing of life without them (n. 2893, 4151). The doctrinal of the church derived from the Word teaches the same thing (n. 4249). Nevertheless man does not believe that life inflows (n. 4249). If communication and connection with spirits and angels were taken away, man would instantly die (n. 2887). It is evident from hence, that the all of life flows in from the first esse of life, because nothing exists from itself, but from things prior to itself, thus each and all things exist from the First; and because everything must subsist from the same source from which it first existed, since subsistence is perpetual existence (n. 4523, 4524). Angels, spirits, and men, were created to receive life, thus they are only forms recipient of life (n. 2021, 3001, 3318, 3344, 3484, 3742, 4151, 5114, 5986). Their forms are such as the quality of their reception (n. 2888, 3001, 3484, 5847, 5986, 6467, 6472). Men, spirits, and angels, are therefore such as are their forms recipient of life from the Lord (n. 2888, 5847, 5986, 6467, 6472). Man is so created, that in his inmost, and hence in those which follow in order, he can receive the Divine, and be elevated to the Divine, and be conjoined with the Divine by the good of love and the truths of faith, and on this account he lives to eternity, otherwise than beasts (n. 5114). Life from the Lord flows in also with the evil, thus also with those who are in hell (n. 2706, 3743, 4417, 10196). But they turn good into evil and truth into falsity, and thus life into spiritual death, for such as the man is, such is his reception of life (n. 4319, 4320, 4417). Goods and truths from the Lord also continually inflow with them, but they either reject, suffocate, or pervert them (n. 3743). They who are in evils, and thence in falsities, have no real life; the quality of their life (n. 726, 4623, 4747, 10284, 10286).

Of Order. The Divine truth proceeding from the Lord is the source of order, and the Divine good is the essential of order (n. 1728, 2258, 8700, 8988). The Lord is order, since the Divine good and the Divine truth are from the Lord, yea, are the Lord, in the heavens and on earth (n. 1919, 2011, 5110, 5703, 10336, 10619). Divine truths are the laws of order (n. 2447, 7995). Where order is, the Lord is present, but where order is not, the Lord is not present (n. 5703). As the Divine truth is order, and the Divine good the essential of order, therefore each and all things in the universe have relation to good and truth, that they may be anything, because they have relation to order (n. 2452, 3166, 4390, 4409, 5232, 7256, 10122, 10555). Good, because it is the essential of order, disposes truths into order, and not vice versa (n. 3316, 3470, 4302, 5704, 5709, 6028, 6690). The entire heaven, as to all the angelic societies, is arranged by the Lord according to His Divine order, because the Divine of the Lord with the angels makes heaven (n. 3038, 7211, 9128, 9338, 10125, 10151, 10157). Hence the form of heaven is a form according to Divine order (n. 4040-4043, 6607, 9877). So far as man lives according to order, thus so far as he lives in good according to Divine truths, which are the laws of order, so far is he a man (n. 4839). Yea, as far as a man thus lives, so far he appears in the other life as a perfect and beautiful man, but so far as he does not thus live, so far he appears as a monster (n. 4839, 6605, 6626). Hence it appears that all things of Divine order are collected together in man, and that from creation he is Divine order in form (n. 4219, 4220, 4223, 4523, 4524, 5114, 5368, 6013, 6057, 6605, 6626, 9706, 10156, 10742). Every angel is in the human form because he is a recipient of Divine order from the Lord, perfect and beautiful according to reception (n. 322, 1880, 1881, 3633, 3804, 4622, 4735, 4797, 4985, 5199, 5530, 6054, 9879, 10177, 10594). The

angelic heaven also in its whole complex is in the human form, because the
whole heaven as to all its angelic societies, is disposed by the Lord according to
Divine order (n. 2996, 2998, 3624-3629, 3636-3643, 3741-3745, 4625). Hence it
is evident, that the Divine Human is the source from which all these things are
derived (n. 2996-2998, 3624-3649, 3741-3745). Hence also it follows that the
Lord is the only Man, and that they are men who receive the Divine from Him
(n. 1894). So far as they receive it, so far they are images of the Lord (n. 8547).
Man is not born into good and truth, but into evil and falsity, thus not into
Divine order, but into what is contrary to order, and on this account into mere
ignorance, and he ought therefore necessarily to be born anew, that is
regenerated, which is done by Divine truths from the Lord, and by a life
according to them, to the intent that he may be inaugurated into order, and
thus become a man (n. 1047, 2307, 2308, 3518, 3812, 8480, 8550, 10283, 10284,
10286, 10731). When the Lord regenerates man, He disposes all things with
him according to order, that is, according to the form of heaven (n. 5700, 6690,
9931, 10303). The man who is led by the Lord, is led according to Divine order
(n. 8512). The interiors which are of the mind are open into heaven, even to the
Lord, with the man who is in Divine order, but shut with him who is not in
Divine order (n. 8513). So far as man lives according to order, so far he has
intelligence and wisdom (n. 2592). The Lord rules the firsts and the ultimates
of order, and the firsts from the ultimates and the ultimates from the firsts; and
thus keeps all things in connection and order (n. 3702, 3739, 6040, 6056, 9828).
Of successive order; and of the ultimate of order, in which things successive are
together in their order (n. 634, 3691, 4145, 5114, 5897, 6239, 6326, 6465, 8603,
9215, 9216, 9828, 9836, 10044, 10099, 10329, 10335). Evils and falsities are
contrary to order, and still they are ruled by the Lord, not according to order,
but from order (n. 4839, 7877, 10778). Evils and falsities are ruled by the laws
of permission, and this is for the sake of order (n. 7877, 8700, 10778). What is
contrary to Divine order is impossible, as that a man who lives in evil can be
saved from mercy alone, as likewise that the evil can be consociated with the
good in the other life, and many other things (n. 8700).

XXII. THE LORD. There is One God, who is the Creator and Conservator
of the universe; thus who is the God of heaven and the God of the earth.

There are two things which make the life of heaven with man, the good of
love and the truth of faith. Man has this life from God, and nothing at all of it
is from man. Therefore the primary principle of the church is, to acknowledge
God, to believe in God, and to love Him.

They who are born within the church ought to acknowledge the Lord, His
Divine and His Human, and to believe in Him and love Him; for all salvation
is from the Lord. This the Lord teaches in John: He that believeth on the Son
hath eternal life; and he that believeth not the Son shall not see life; but the
anger of God abideth on him (3:36). Again: This is the will of Him that sent Me,
that every one which seeth the Son, and believeth on Him, may have eternal
life; and I will raise him up at the last day (6:40). In the same: Jesus said, I am
the resurrection and the life; he that believeth in Me though he die, shall live;
but whosoever liveth and believeth in Me shall not die to eternity (11:25, 26).

Therefore, they within the church who do not acknowledge the Lord and His
Divine, cannot be conjoined to God, and thus cannot have any lot with the

angels in heaven; for no one can be conjoined to God but from the Lord, and in the Lord. That no one can be conjoined to God but from the Lord, the Lord teaches in John: No one hath seen God at any time; the Only-begotten Son, who is in the bosom of the Father, He hath manifested Him (1:20). In the same: Ye have never head the voice of the Father, nor seen His shape (5:37). In Matthew: No one knoweth the Father but the Son, and he to whom the Son will reveal Him (11:27). And in John: I am the way, the truth, and the life; no one cometh to the Father but by Me (14:6). The reason why no one can be conjoined to God but in the Lord, is because the Father is in Him, and they are one, as He also teaches in John: If ye know Me, ye know My Father also; He who seeth Me seeth the Father; Philip, believest thou not that I am in the Father and the Father in Me? believe Me that I am in the Father and the Father in Me (John 14:7-11). And in the same: The Father and I are One; that ye may know and believe that I am in the Father and the Father in Me (John 10:30, 38).

Because the Father is in the Lord, and the Father and the Lord are one; and because we must believe in Him, and he that believes in Him has eternal life, it is evident that the Lord is God. That the Lord is God, the Word teaches, as in John: In the beginning was the Word. and the Word was with God, and God was the Word; all things were made by Him, and without Him was not any thing made which was made; and the Word was made flesh, and dwelt among us, and we saw His glory, the glory as of the Only-begotten of the Father (John 1:1, 3, 14). In Isaiah: A Boy is born to us, a Son is given to us, on whose shoulder is the government, and His name shall be called God, Hero, the Father of Eternity, the Prince of Peace (Isa. 9:6). In the same: A virgin shall conceive and bring forth, and His name shall be called God with us (Isa. 7:14; Matt. 1:23). And in Jeremiah: Behold the days shall come when I will raise up to David a just Branch, who shall reign King, and shall prosper; and this is His name which they shall call Him, Jehovah our Justice (Jer. 23:5, 6; 33:15, 16).

All they who are of the church, and in light from heaven, see the Divine in the Lord; but they who are not in light from heaven, see nothing but the Human in the Lord; when yet the Divine and the Human are in Him so united, that they are one; as the Lord also taught in another place in John: Father, all Mine are Thine, and all Thine Mine (17:10).

That the Lord was conceived from Jehovah the Father, and thus was God from conception, is known in the church; and also that He rose again with the whole body, for He left nothing in the sepulchre; of which He also afterwards confirmed the disciples, saying: See My hands and My feet, that it is I Myself; feel Me and see; for a spirit hath not flesh and bones as ye see Me have (Luke 24:39). And although He was Man as to flesh and bones, still He entered through the closed doors, and, after He had manifested Himself, became invisible (John 20:19, 26; Luke 24:31). The case is otherwise with every man, for man only rises again, as to the spirit, and not as to the body, wherefore when He said, that He is not as a spirit, He said that He is not as another man. Hence it is evident that the Human in the Lord is also Divine.

Every man has his esse of life, which is called his soul, from the father; the existere of life thence derived is what is called the body; hence the body is the effigy of its soul, for the soul, by means of the body, exercises its life at will. Hence it is that men are born into the likeness of their parents, and that families are distinguished from each other. From this it is evident what was the quality of the body or Human of the Lord, namely, that it was as the Divine itself, which was the esse of His life, or the soul from the Father, wherefore He said: He that seeth Me, seeth the Father (John 14:9).

That the Divine and Human of the Lord is one Person, is from the faith received in the whole Christian world, which is to this effect: Although Christ is God and Man, still He is not two, but one Christ; yea, He is altogether one and a single Person; because as the body and the soul are one man, so also God and Man are one Christ. This is from the Athanasian creed.

They who, concerning the Divinity, have the idea of three Persons, cannot have the idea of one God; if with the mouth they say one, still they think three; but they who, concerning the Divinity, have the idea of three in one Person, can have the idea of one God, and can say one God, and also think one God.

The idea of three in one Person is had, when it is thought that the Father is in the Lord, and that the Holy Spirit proceeds from Him; the Trinity is then in the Lord, the Divine itself which is called the Father, and the Divine Human which is called the Son, and the Divine proceeding which is called the Holy Spirit.

Because all the Divine is in the Lord, therefore He has all power in the heavens and in the earths; which he also says in John: The Father hath given all things into the hand of the Son (3:35). In the same: The Father hath given to the Son power over all flesh (17:2). In Matthew: All things are delivered to Me by the Father (11:27). In the same All power is given to Me in heaven and m earth (28:18). Such power is Divine.

They who make the Human of the Lord like the human of another man, do not think of His conception from the Divine itself, nor do they consider that the body of everyone is an effigy of his soul. Neither do they think of His resurrection with the whole body; nor of His appearance when He was transformed, that His face shone as the sun. Neither do they think, respecting those things which the Lord said concerning faith in Him, concerning His unity with the Father, concerning His glorification, and concerning His power over heaven and earth, that these are Divine, and were said of His Human. Neither do they remember that the Lord is omnipresent also as to His Human (Matt. 23:20); when yet the faith of His omnipresence in the Holy Supper is thence derived; omnipresence is Divine. Yea, perhaps they do not think that the Divine, which is called the Holy Spirit, proceeds from His Human; when yet it proceeds from His glorified Human, for it is said: The Holy Spirit was not yet, because Jesus was not yet glorified (John 7:39).

The Lord came into the world that He might save the human race, which otherwise would have perished in eternal death; and He saved them by this, that He subjugated the hells, which infested every man coming into the world and going out of the world; and at the same time by this, that He glorified His Human: for thus He can keep the hells in subjugation to eternity. The subjugation of the hells, and the glorification of His Human at the same time, were effected by means of temptations admitted into the human which He had from the mother, and by continual victories therein. His passion on the cross was the last temptation and full victory.

That the Lord subjugated the hells, He Himself teaches in John: when the passion of the cross was at hand, then Jesus said: Now is the judgment of this world; now the prince of this world shall be cast out (12:27, 28, 31). In the same: Have confidence, I have overcome the world (16:33). And in Isaiah: Who is this that cometh from Edom, going on in the multitude of His strength, great to save? My own arm brought salvation to Me; so He became to them for a Saviour (63:1-19; 59:16-21). That He glorified His Human, and that the passion of the cross was the last temptation and full victory, by which He glorified it, He teaches also in John: After Judas went out, Jesus said, Now is the Son of man glorified, and God will glorify Him in Himself, and will immediately glorify Him (13:31, 32). In the same: Father, the hour has come; glorify Thy Son, that Thy Son also may glorify Thee (17:1, 5). In the same: Now is my soul troubled; Father, glorify Thy name; and a voice came out from heaven, saying, I have both glorified it, and will glorify it again (12:27, 28). And in Luke: Ought not Christ to suffer this, and to enter into His glory? (24:26.) These words were said in relation to His passion: "to glorify" is to make Divine. Hence, now, it is manifest, that, unless the Lord had come into the world, and been made Man, and in this manner had liberated from hell all those who believe in Him and love Him, no mortal could be saved; this is understood by the saying, that without the Lord there is no salvation.

When the Lord fully glorified His Human, He then put off the human from the mother, and put on the Human from the Father, which is the Divine Human, wherefore He was then no longer the son of Mary.

The first and primary principle of the church is, to know and acknowledge its God; for without that knowledge and acknowledgment there is no conjunction; thus, in the church, without the acknowledgment of the Lord. This the Lord teaches in John: He who believeth in the Son hath eternal life, but he who believeth not the Son shall not see life, but the anger of God abideth with him (3:36). And in another place: Except ye believe that I am, ye shall die in your sins (8:24).

That there is a Trine in the Lord, namely, the Divine itself, the Divine Human, and the Divine proceeding, is an arcanum from heaven, and is for those who will be in the holy Jerusalem.

FROM THE ARCANA COELESTIA. The Divine was in the Lord from His very conception. The Lord had the Divine from the Father (n. 4641, 4963, 5041, 5157, 6716, 10125). The Lord alone had Divine seed (n. 1438). His soul was Jehovah (n. 1999, 2004, 2005, 2018, 2025). Thus the inmost of the Lord was the Divine itself, the covering 298-1 was from the mother (n. 5041). The Divine itself was the Lord's esse of life from which the human afterwards went forth, and became an existere from that esse (n. 3194, 3210, 10270, 10372).

The Divine of the Lord is to be acknowledged. Within the church where the Word is, and where the Lord is thereby known, the Divine of the Lord ought not to be denied, nor the holy proceeding from Him (n. 2359). They within the church who do not acknowledge the Lord, have no conjunction with the Divine, which is not the case with those who are out of the church (n. 10205). It is an essential of the church to acknowledge the Divine of the Lord, and His unition with the Father (n. 10083, 10112, 10370, 10730, 10738, 10816-10818, 10820).

The Lord glorified His Human in the world. The glorification of the Lord is treated of in many places in the Word (n. 10828); and everywhere in the internal sense (n. 2249, 2523, 3245). The Lord glorified His Human, but not His Divine, as this was glorified in itself (n. 10057). The Lord came into the world to glorify His Human (n. 3637, 4287, 9315). The Lord glorified His Human by the Divine which was in Him from conception (n. 4727). The idea of the regeneration of man may give an idea of the glorification of the Lord's Human, since the Lord regenerates man in the same manner as He glorified His Human (n. 3043, 3138, 3212, 3296, 3490, 4402, 5688). Some of the arcana respecting the glorification of the Lord's Human (n. 10057). The Lord saved the human race by glorifying His Human (n. 1676, 4180). Concerning the Lord's state of glorification and humiliation (n. 1785, 1999, 2159, 6866). Glorification, when predicated of the Lord, is the unition of His Human with the Divine, and to glorify is to make Divine (n. 1603, 10053, 10828).

Footnotes
298-1 The original Latin has "inductis" for"induitio."

Section 6

The Lord from His Human subjugated the hells when He was in the world. The Lord, when He was in the world, subjugated all the hells, and He then reduced all things to order both in the heavens and in the hells (n. 4075, 4287, 9937). The Lord then delivered the spiritual world from the antediluvians (n. 1266). What quality they were of (n. 310, 311, 560, 562, 563, 570, 581, 607, 660, 805, 808, 1034, 1120, 1265-1272). By the subjugation of the hells, and the glorification of His Human at the same time, the Lord saved mankind (n. 4180, 10019, 10152, 10655, 10659, 10828).

The glorification of the Lord's Human, and the subjugation of the hells, were effected by temptations. The Lord more than all endured the most grievous temptations (n. 1663, 1668, 1787, 2776, 2786, 2795, 2816, 4295, 9528). The Lord fought from His Divine love toward the human race (n. 1690, 1691, 1812, 1813, 1820). The Lord's love was the salvation of the human race (n. 1820). The hells fought against the Lord's love (n. 1820). The Lord alone, from His own proper power, fought against the hells, and overcame them (n. 1692, 1813, 2816, 4295, 8273, 9937). Thence the Lord alone became justice and merit (n. 1813, 2025-2027, 9715, 9809, 10019). The last temptation of the Lord was in Gethsemane and on the cross, at which time He gained a full victory, by which He subjugated the hells, and at the same time glorified His Human (n. 2776, 2803, 2813, 2814, 10655, 10659, 10828). The Lord could not be tempted as to the Divine itself (n. 2795, 2803, 2813, 2814). Therefore He assumed an infirm human from the mother, into which He admitted temptations (n. 1414, 1444, 1573, 5041, 5157, 7193, 9315). By means of temptations and victories He expelled all that was hereditary from the mother, and put off the human which He had from her, till at length He was no longer her son (n. 2159, 2574, 2649, 3036, 10830). Jehovah, who was in Him, appeared in temptations as if absent, and this so far as He was in the human from the mother (n. 1815). This state was the Lord's state of humiliation (n. 1785, 1999, 2159, 6866). The Lord by temptations and victories arranged all things in the heavens into order (n. 4287, 4295, 9528, 9937). By the same means He also united His Human with His Divine, that is, He glorified His Human (n. 1725, 1729, 1733, 1737, 3318, 3381, 3382, 4286, 4287, 4295, 9528, 9937).

The Lord's Human, when He was in the world, was Divine truth. The Lord, when He was in the world, made His Human Divine truth from the Divine good which was in Him (n. 2803, 3194, 3195, 3210, 6716, 6864, 7014, 7499, 8127, 8724, 9199). The Lord then arranged all things in Himself into a heavenly form, which is according to the Divine truth (n. 1928, 3633). Consequently, that heaven was then in the Lord, and the Lord was as heaven (n. 911, 1900, 1928, 3624-3631, 3634, 3884, 4041, 4279, 4523-4525, 6013, 6057, 6690, 9279, 9632, 9931, 10303). The Lord spoke from the Divine truth itself (n. 8127). Therefore the Lord spoke in the Word by correspondences (n. 3131, 3472-3485, 8615, 10687). Hence the Lord is the Word, and is called the Word, which is the Divine truth (n. 2533, 2813, 2859, 2894, 3393, 3712). In the Word "the Son of man" signifies the Divine truth, and "the Father" the Divine good (n. 2803, 3704, 7499, 8724, 9194). Because the Lord was the Divine truth, He was the Divine wisdom (n. 2500, 2572). The Lord alone had perception and thought from Himself, above all angelic perception and thought (n. 1904, 1914, 1919). The Divine truth could be tempted, but not the Divine good (n. 2814).

The Lord united the Divine truth to the Divine good, thus His Human to the Divine itself The Lord was instructed as another man (n. 1457, 1461, 2523, 3030). The Lord successively advanced to union with the Father (n. 1864, 2033, 2632, 3141, 4585, 7014, 10076). So far as the Lord was united with the Father, so far He spoke as with himself; but at other times as with another (n. 1745, 1999, 7058). The Lord united His Human with the Divine from His own power (n. 1616, 1749, 1752, 1813, 1921, 2025, 2026, 2523, 3141, 5005, 5045, 6716). The Lord united the Divine truth, which was Himself, with the Divine good which was in Himself (n. 10047, 10052, 10076). The unition was reciprocal (n. 2004, 10067). The Lord, when He went out of the world, made His Human the Divine good (n. 3194, 3210, 6864, 7499, 8724, 9199, 10076). Thus He came forth from the Father, and returned to the Father (n. 3194, 3210). Thus He became one with the Father (n. 2751, 3704, 4766). The Lord, in His unition with the Divine itself which was in Him, regarded the conjunction of Himself with the human race (n. 2034). After the unition, the Divine truth proceeds from the Lord (n. 3704, 3712, 3969, 4577, 5704, 7499, 8127, 8241, 9199, 9398). How the Divine truth proceeds, illustrated (n. 7270, 9407). Unless the Divine had been in the Lord's Human from conception, the Human could not have been united with the Divine itself, on account of the ardor of the infinite love in which the Divine itself is (n. 6849). Therefore no angel can ever be united with the Divine itself except at a distance, and by means of a veiling; for otherwise he would be consumed (n. 6849). The Divine love is of such a quality (n. 8644). Hence it may appear that the Human of the Lord was not like the human of another man (n. 10125, 10826). His union with the Father, from whom was His soul, was not like a union between two, but like that between soul and body (n. 3737, 10824). Union is said of the Lord's Human and the Divine, but conjunction between man and the Divine (n. 2021).

Thus the Lord made His Human Divine. The Human of the Lord is Divine, because it was from the esse of the Father, which was His soul, illustrated by the likeness of a father and children (n. 10269, 10372, 10823). And because it was from the Divine love which was in Him (n. 6872). Every man is such as his love is, and he is his own love (n. 6872, 10177, 10284). The Lord was the Divine love (n. 2077, 2253). The Lord made all His Human, both the internal and the external, Divine (n. 1603, 1815, 1902, 1926, 2093, 2803). Therefore He rose again as to the whole body, differently from any man (n. 1729, 2083, 5078, 10825). That the Lord's Human is Divine, is acknowledged from the omnipresence of His Human in the Holy Supper (n. 2343, 2359). And it is evident from His transfiguration before the three disciples (n. 3212). And likewise from the Word (n. 10154). And He was there called Jehovah (n. 1603, 1736, 1815, 1902, 2921, 3035, 5110, 6281, 6303, 8864, 9194, 9315). In the sense of the letter there is a distinction made between the Father and the Son, or Jehovah and the Lord, but not in the internal sense, in which the angels are (n.

3035). The Christian world does not acknowledge the Human of the Lord to be Divine, in consequence of a decree passed by a council in favor of the Pope, that he might be acknowledged as the Lord's vicar; from conversation with them in another life (n. 4738). The Divine Human from eternity was the Divine truth in heaven, thus the Divine existere, which was afterwards made in the Lord the Divine esse, from which is the Divine existere in heaven (n. 3061, 6280, 6880, 10579). The previous state of heaven described (n. 6371-6373). The Divine was not perceptible, and therefore not capable of being received, until it passed through heaven (n. 6982, 6996, 7004). The Lord from eternity was the Divine truth in heaven (n. 2803, 3195, 3704). This is the Son of God born from eternity (n. 2628, 2798). In heaven no other Divine is perceived but the Divine Human (n. 6475, 9303, 9356, 9571, 10067). The most ancient people could not adore the infinite esse, but the infinite existere, which is the Divine Human (n. 4687, 5321). The ancients acknowledged the Divine, because it appeared in a human form, and this was the Divine Human (n. 5110, 5663, 6846, 10737). The inhabitants of all the earths adore the Divine under a human form, and they rejoice when they hear that God actually became Man (n. 6700, 8541-8547, 9361, 10736-10738). See also Earths in Our Solar System, and in the Starry Heaven. God cannot be thought of, but in a human form, and that which is incomprehensible cannot fall into any idea (n. 9359, 9972). Man can worship what he has some idea of, but not what he has no idea of (n. 4733, 5110, 5663, 7211, 9356, 10067). Therefore the Divine is worshiped under a human form by most in the whole globe, and this is through an influx from heaven (n. 10159). All who are in good as to life, when they think of the Lord, think of a Divine Human, but not of the Human separated from the Divine (n. 2326, 4724, 4731, 4766, 8878, 9193, 9198). They in the church at this day who are in evil as to life, and they who are in faith separate from charity, think of the Human of the Lord without the Divine, and do not comprehend what the Divine Human is, the causes thereof (n. 3212, 3241, 4689, 4692, 4724, 4731, 5321, 6371, 8878, 9193, 9198).

The trinity is in the Lord. Christians were examined in the other life concerning the idea they had of one God, and it was found that they had an idea of three Gods (n. 2329, 5256, 10736-10738, 10821). The Divine Trinity may be conceived of in one Person, and thus as one God, but not in three Persons (n. 10738, 10821, 10822). The Trinity in one Person, thus in the Lord, is the Divine itself, which is called the Father; the Divine Human, which is called the Son; and the Divine proceeding, which is called the Holy Spirit; thus the Trinity is one (n. 2149, 2156, 2288, 2321, 2329, 2447, 3704, 6993, 7182, 10738, 10822, 10823). The Divine Trinity in the Lord is acknowledged in heaven (n. 14, 15, 1729, 2005, 5256, 9303). The Lord is one with the Father, thus He is the Divine itself, and the Divine Human (n. 1729, 2004, 2005, 2018, 2025, 2751, 3704, 3736, 4766). His Divine proceeding is also His Divine in heaven, which is called the Holy Spirit (n. 3969, 4673, 6788, 6993, 7499, 8127, 8302, 9199, 9228, 9229, 9278, 9407, 9818, 9820, 10330). Thus the Lord is the one and only God (n. 1607, 2149, 2156, 2329, 2447, 2751, 3194, 3704, 3712, 3938, 4577, 4687, 5321, 6280, 6371, 6849, 6993, 7014, 7091, 7182, 7209, 8241, 8724, 8760, 8864, 8865, 9194, 9303).

Of the Lord in heaven. The Lord appears in heaven both as a sun and a moon; as a sun to those who are in the celestial kingdom, and as a moon to those who are in the spiritual kingdom (n. 1053, 1521, 1529-1531, 3636, 3641, 4321, 5097, 7078, 7083, 7173, 7270, 8812, 10809). The light which proceeds from the Lord as a sun is the Divine truth, from which the angels derive all their wisdom and intelligence (n. 1053, 1521-1533, 2776, 3138, 3195, 3222, 3223, 3225, 3339, 3341, 3636, 3643, 3993, 4180, 4302, 4415, 5400, 9399, 9407, 9548, 9571, 9684). And the heat which proceeds from the Lord as a sun is the Divine good, from which the angels derive their love (n. 3338, 3636, 3643, 5215). The Lord's Divine itself is far above His Divine in heaven (n. 7270, 8760). The Divine truth is not in the Lord, but proceeds from the Lord, as light is not in the sun, but proceeds from the sun (n. 3969). Esse is in the Lord, and existere from the Lord (n. 3938). The Lord is the common center to which all the angels in heaven turn (n. 3633, 9828, 10130, 10189). Nevertheless the angels do not turn themselves to the Lord, but the Lord turns them to Himself (n. 10189); because the angels are not present with the Lord, but the Lord is present with the angels (n. 9415). The Lord's presence with the angels is according to their reception of the good of love and charity from Him (n. 904, 4198, 4206, 4211, 4320, 6280, 6832, 7042, 8819, 9680, 9682, 9683, 10106, 10810). The Lord is present with all in heaven, and also in hell (n. 2776, 3642, 3644). The Lord from His Divine love wishes to draw all men to Himself into heaven (n. 6645). The Lord is in a continual endeavor of conjunction with man, but the influx and conjunction are impeded by the loves of man's proprium (n. 2041, 2053, 2411, 5696). The Divine Human of the Lord flows into heaven, and makes heaven, and there is no conjunction with the Divine itself in heaven, but with the Divine Human (n. 3038, 4211, 4724, 5663). And the Divine Human flows in with men out of heaven and through heaven (n. 1925). The Lord is the all of heaven, and the life of heaven (n. 7211, 9128). The Lord dwells with the angels in what is His own (n. 9338, 10125, 10151, 10157). Hence they who are in heaven are in the Lord (n. 3637, 3638). Heaven corresponds to the Divine Human of the Lord, and man as to each and all things, corresponds to heaven, whence heaven in general is as one man, and is therefore called the Greatest Man (n. 2988, 2996, 3624-3629, 3636-3643, 3741-3745, 4625). The Lord is the only Man, and they only are men who receive the Divine from Him (n. 1894). So far as they receive, so far they become images of the Lord (n. 8547). The angels are forms of love and charity in a human form, and this is from the Lord (n. 3804, 3735, 4797, 4985, 5199, 5530, 9879, 10177).

All good and truth are from the Lord. The Lord is good itself and truth itself (n. 2011, 5110, 10336, 10619). All good and truth, consequently all peace, innocence, love, charity, and faith, are from the Lord (n. 1614, 2016, 2751, 2882, 2883, 2891, 2892, 2904). And all wisdom and intelligence are from Him (n. 109, 112, 121, 124). Nothing but good comes from the Lord, but the evil turn the good which is from the Lord into evil (n. 7643, 7679, 7710, 8632). The angels know that all good and truth are from the Lord, but the evil are not willing to know this (n. 6193, 9128). The angels at the presence of the Lord are more in good, but the infernals at the presence of the Lord are more in evils (n. 7989). The evil cast themselves into hell at the mere presence of the Lord (n. 8137, 8265). The Lord judges all from good (n. 2335). The Lord regards all from mercy (n. 223). The Lord is never angry with anyone, nor does evil to anyone, and does not send anyone to hell (n. 245, 1683, 2335, 8632). In what sense those parts of the Word are to be understood, where it is said that Jehovah or the Lord is angry, that He kills, that He casts into hell, and other things of the like nature (n. 592, 696, 1093, 1874, 1875, 2395, 2447, 3605, 3607, 3614, 6071, 6997).

The Lord has all power in the heavens and on earth. The entire heaven is the Lord's (n. 2751, 7086). And He has all power in the heavens and on earth (n. 1607, 10089, 10827). As the Lord rules the whole heaven, He also rules all things which depend thereon, thus all things in the world (n. 2026, 2027, 4523, 4524). He also rules the hells (n. 3642). The Lord rules all things from the Divine, by the Divine Human (n. 8864, 8865). The Lord rules all things according to Divine order, and the Divine order has relation to those things which are of His will, to those things which are done from leave, and to those things which are done from permission (n. 1755, 2447, 6574, 9940); concerning order, see above (n. 279). The Lord rules ultimates from firsts, and firsts from ultimates, and this is the reason why He is called "the First and the Last" (n. 3702, 6040, 6056). The Lord alone has the power of removing the hells, of withholding from evils, and of keeping in good, thus of saving (n. 10019). Judgment belongs to the Lord (n. 2319-2321, 10810, 10811). What the Lord's priesthood is, and what His royalty is (n. 1728, 2015).

In what manner some expressions in the Word, which relate to the Lord, are to be understood. What is meant by "the seed of the woman," in the prophecy concerning the Lord (n. 256). What "the Son of man" and "the Son of God" signify in the Word (n. 2159, 2813). What the two names "Jesus Christ" signify (n. 3004-3011). What is signified by the Lord's being said to be "sent by the Father" (n. 2397, 6831, 10561). How it is to be understood that the Lord bore the iniquities of all (n. 9937). How it is to be understood that the Lord redeemed man by His blood (n. 10152). How it is to be understood that the Lord fulfilled all things of the law (n. 10239). How it is to be understood that the Lord intercedes for man (n. 2250, 8573, 8705). How it is to be understood, that without the Lord there is no salvation (n. 10828). Salvation is not effected by looking to the Father, or by praying to Him to have mercy for the sake of His Son; for the Lord says, "I am the way, the truth, and life; no one cometh to the Father but by me" (John 14:6; n. 2854). The contradictions which are involved in the received faith, that the Lord reconciled the human race to the Father, by the passion of the cross (n. 10659). The coming of the Lord is His presence in the Word (n. 3900, 4060). The Lord does not desire glory from man for the sake of Himself, but of man's salvation (n. 5957, 10646). Wherever the name "Lord" occurs in the Word, it signifies the Divine good (n. 4973, 9167, 9194). Where the name "Christ" occurs, it signifies the Divine truth (n. 3004-3009). The true acknowledgment and true worship of the Lord is to do His commandments, shown from the Word (n. 10143, 10153, 10578, 10645, 10829).

XXII. ECCLESIASTICAL and CIVIL GOVERNMENT There are two things which ought to be in order with men, namely, the things which are of heaven, and the things which are of the world. The things which are of heaven are called ecclesiastical, and those which are of the world are called civil.

Order cannot be maintained in the world without governors, who are to observe all things which are done according to order, and which are done contrary to order; and who are to reward those who live according to order, and punish those who live contrary to order. If this be not done, the human race will perish; for the will to command others, and to possess the goods of others, from heredity is connate with everyone, whence proceed enmities, envyings, hatreds, revenges, deceits, cruelties, and many other evils. Wherefore, unless they were kept under restraint by the laws, and by rewards suited to their loves, which are honors and gains for those who do goods; and by punishments contrary to those loves, which are the loss of honors, of possessions, and of life, for those who do evils; the human race would perish.

There must therefore be governors to keep the assemblages of men in order, who should be skilled in the law, wise, and who fear God. There must also be order among the governors, lest anyone, from caprice or ignorance, should permit evils which are contrary to order, and thereby destroy it. This is guarded against when there are superior and inferior governors, among whom there is subordination.

Governors over those things with men which relate to heaven, or over ecclesiastical affairs, are called priests, and their office is called the priesthood. But governors over those things with men which relate to the world, or over civil affairs, are called magistrates, and their chief, where such a form of government prevails, is called king.

With respect to the priests, they ought to teach men the way to heaven, and also to lead them; they ought to teach them according to the doctrine of their church from the Word, and to lead them to live according to it. Priests who teach truths, and thereby lead to the good of life, and so to the Lord, are good shepherds of the sheep; but they who teach and do not lead to the good of life, and so to the Lord, are evil shepherds.

Priests ought not to claim to themselves any power over the souls of men, because they do not know in what state the interiors of a man are; still less ought they to claim the power of opening and shutting heaven, since that power belongs to the Lord alone.

Dignity and honor ought to be paid to priests on account of the holy things which they administer; but they who are wise give the honor to the Lord, from whom the holy things are, and not to themselves; but they who are not wise attribute the honor to themselves; these take it away from the Lord. They who attribute honor to themselves, on account of the holy things which they administer, prefer honor and gain to the salvation of souls, which they ought to provide for; but they who give the honor to the Lord, and not to themselves, prefer the salvation of souls to honor and gain. The honor of any employment is not in the person, but is adjoined to him according to the dignity of the thing which he administers; and what is adjoined does not belong to the person himself, and is also separated from him with the employment. All personal honor is the honor of wisdom and the fear of the Lord.

Priests ought to teach the people, and to lead them by truths to the good of life, but still they ought to compel no one, since no one can be compelled to believe contrary to what he thinks from his heart to be true. He who believes otherwise than the priest, and makes no disturbance, ought to be left in peace; but he who makes disturbance, ought to be separated; for this also is of order, for the sake of which the priesthood is established.

As priests are appointed to administer those things which relate to the Divine law and worship, so kings and magistrates are appointed to administer those things which relate to civil law and judgment.

Because the king alone cannot administer all things, therefore there are governors under him, to each of whom a province is given to administer, which the king cannot and is not able to administer alone. These governors, taken together, constitute the royalty, but the king himself is the chief.

Royalty itself is not in the person, but is adjoined to the person. The king who believes that royalty is in his own person, and the governor who believes that the dignity of the government is in his own person, is not wise.

Royalty consists in administering according to the laws of the realm and in judging according to them from justice. The king who regards the laws as above himself is wise, but he who regards himself as above the laws is not wise. The king who regards the laws as above himself places the royalty in the law, and the law has dominion over him, for he knows that the law is justice, and that all justice which is justice is Divine. But he who regards himself as above the laws places the royalty in himself, and either believes himself to be the law, or the law, which is justice, to be from himself; hence he arrogates to himself that which is Divine, under which nevertheless he ought to be.

The law which is justice ought to be enacted in the realm by persons skilled in the law, wise, and who fear God; then both the king and his subjects ought to live according to it. The king who lives according to the enacted law, and in this precedes his subjects by his example, is truly a king.

A king who has absolute power, who believes that his subjects are such slaves that he has a right to their possessions and lives, and if he exercises it, is not a king, but a tyrant.

There ought to be obedience to the king according to the laws of the realm, nor should he be injured by any means either by deeds or words; for on this the public security depends.

www.ingramcontent.com/pod-product-compliance
Lightning Source LLC
Chambersburg PA
CBHW030926090426
42737CB00007B/335